# Economic welfare and the economics of Soviet socialism

*Essays in honor of Abram Bergson*

Abram Bergson

# Economic welfare and the economics of Soviet socialism

*Essays in honor of Abram Bergson*

EDITED BY STEVEN ROSEFIELDE

CAMBRIDGE UNIVERSITY PRESS

CAMBRIDGE
LONDON   NEW YORK   NEW ROCHELLE
MELBOURNE   SYDNEY

Published by the Press Syndicate of the University of Cambridge
The Pitt Building, Trumpington Street, Cambridge CB2 1RP
32 East 57th Street, New York, NY 10022, USA
296 Beaconsfield Parade, Middle Park, Melbourne 3206, Australia

First published 1981

Printed in the United States of America

*Library of Congress Cataloging in Publication Data*

Main entry under title:

Economic welfare and the economics of Soviet socialism.

Bibliography: p.

Includes index.

Contents: Knowledge and socialism / Steven Rosefielde – Economic growth and structural change in czarist Russia and the Soviet Union / Paul R. Gregory – Corruption in a Soviet-type economy / John M. Montias and Susan Rose-Ackerman – [etc.]
1. Soviet Union – Economic conditions – 1918–   – Addresses, essays, lectures.
2. Welfare economics – Addresses, essays, lectures.   3. Bergson, Abram, 1914–
I. Bergson, Abram, 1914–.   II. Rosefielde, Steven.
HC335.E27   330.947′0853       81-6147
ISBN 0 521 23273 2              AACR2

*To*
**Abram Bergson**

# Contents

viii   **Contents**

**Part II: Economic welfare**

# Contributors

**Kenneth J. Arrow,** Joan Kenney Professor of Economics and Professor of Operations Research, Stanford University, awarded John Bates Clark Medal of American Economic Association (1957) and Nobel Memorial Prize in Economic Science (1972). Author of *Social Choice and Individual Values, Essays in the Theory of Risk-Bearing,* and *The Limits of Organization;* coauthor of *Mathematical Studies in Inventory and Production, Studies in Linear and Nonlinear Programming, A Time Series Study of Interindustry Demands, Public Investment, The Rate of Return on Optimal Fiscal Policy,* and *General Competitive Analysis.*

**Joseph S. Berliner,** Professor of Economics, Brandeis University, and Associate, Russian Research Center, Harvard University. Author of *Factory and Manager in the USSR, Soviet Economic Aid, Economy Society and Welfare, The Innovation Decision in Soviet Industry.*

**David Granick,** Professor of Economics, University of Wisconsin-Madison. Author of *Enterprise Guidance in Eastern Europe, Managerial Comparisons of Four Developed Countries: France, Britain, United States and Russia, Soviet Metal-Fabricating and Economic Development, The European Executive, Management of the Industrial Firm in the USSR.*

**Paul Gregory,** Professor of Economics, University of Houston. Author of *Socialist and Nonsocialist Industrialization Patterns;* coauthor of *Soviet Economic Structure and Performance, Comparative Economic Systems.*

**Franklyn D. Holzman,** Professor of Economics, Tufts University; fellow Harvard Russian Research Center. Author of *International Trade Under Communism: Politics and Economics, Financial Checks on Soviet Defense Expenditures, Foreign Trade Under Central Planning, Soviet Taxation.*

**Simon Kuznets,** George F. Baker Professor of Economics, Emeritus, of Harvard University; awarded the Nobel Memorial Prize in Economic Science, 1971, and the Francis A. Walker Medal of the American Eco-

ix

nomic Association, 1977. Author of *Modern Economic Growth, Economic Growth of Nations*.

**John Michael Montias,** Professor of Economics, Institution for Social and Policy Studies, Yale University. Editor of *Journal of Comparative Economics;* author of *Central Planning in Poland, Economic Development in Communist Romania, The Structure of Economic Systems*.

**Gur Ofer,** Associate Professor, Hebrew University, Jerusalem. Author of *The Service Industries in a Developed Economy: Israel as a Case Study, The Service Sector in Soviet Economic Growth: A Comparative Study*.

**Susan Rose-Ackerman,** Associate Professor, Department of Economics and Institution for Social and Policy Studies, Yale University. Author of *Corruption: A Study in Political Economy;* coauthor of *The Uncertain Search for Environmental Policy*.

**Steven Rosefielde,** Associate Professor of Economics, University of North Carolina. Author of *Soviet International Trade in Heckscher-Ohlin Perspective, World Communism at the Crossroads: Military Ascendancy, Political Economy and Human Welfare, False Science: Underestimating the Soviet Arms Buildup*.

**Paul A. Samuelson,** Institute Professor of Economics, Massachusetts Institute of Technology; awarded the John Bates Clark Medal of the AEA (1947) and the Nobel Memorial Prize in Economic Science (1970). Author of *Foundations of Economic Analysis, Collected Scientific Papers of Paul Samuelson (Volumes I–IV), Economics: An Introductory Analysis* (eds. 1–11).

**Martin Spechler,** Lecturer in Economics and in Economic History, Tel-Aviv University. Author of the forthcoming book *Product Quality in Soviet Planning*.

**Jan Tinbergen,** Emeritus Professor of Development Planning, Erasmus University; awarded the Nobel Memorial Prize in Economic Science (1969). Author of *Economic Policy: Principles and Design, Income Distribution: Analysis and Policies*.

**Aaron Vinokur,** Senior Lecturer in Sociology, University of Haifa, and Research Fellow, Hebrew University. Author of *Material Interest of Workers in Labor and Its Results;* coauthor of *Sociological Experiment, Efficiency of Paying Premiums to Workers*.

# Editor's preface

This collection of essays in honor of Abram Bergson pays tribute to a distinguished teacher, scholar, and friend whose intellectual vision has vivified research in the fields of welfare economics and the economics of Soviet socialism. The enormous impact that his works have had on the development of these disciplines during the last four decades is attributable not only to the innovative spirit of his scholarship, but also to its unity. The common thread tying together the disparate strands of his life's work lies in his overriding concern with the phenomenon of human welfare. Soviet economic institutions and working arrangements are of interest not simply because they exist, but because they shed light on the possibility of organizing society in a better way, a way that improves the quality of life. This possibility, however, as Bergson never tires of stressing, should not be confused with its realization. The consequences of social action are often complex and contradictory. Their appraisal depends not only on scrupulous quantification but on a lucid understanding of the factors determining economic welfare. It was one of Bergson's greatest achievements to clearly recognize at the outset that the comparative economic merit of Soviet socialism could not be assessed without the aid of a rigorously elaborated, pure theory of economic welfare. His seminal research on social welfare functions should be seen in this light, attesting to his enduring commitment to advance our scientific understanding of the determinants of human welfare. For this and his many other distinguished accomplishments, we, his students, colleagues, and friends, have compiled this Festschrift as a gesture of our great esteem.

The editor wishes to thank all those who participated in bringing the Bergson Festschrift to fruition. First and foremost I want to express my gratitude to all the contributors, both for the high quality of their essays and the agreeable way in which they revised their manuscripts when necessary. Ralph W. Pfouts proofread and checked the mathematical portions of the essays written by Professors Arrow, Samuelson, and Tinbergen. Paul Gregory and Martin Spechler edited my essay, "Knowledge and Socialism." J. M. Montias and Paul Marer provided helpful comments on an earlier version of "Comparative Advantage and the Evolving Pattern of Soviet International Commodity Specialization, 1950–1973." To all my coeditors I offer my warmest appreciation.

Gottfried Haberler, Gregory Grossman, Evsei Domar, Tjalling Koopmans, and Quinn Mills also assisted me in diverse ways. Joseph Berliner was instrumental in acquiring the handsome photograph that appears as the frontispiece to this volume. Sarah Mason ably typed portions of the manuscript. To them all, I express my gratitude.

Generous financial support for the Bergson Festschrift was provided by the George F. Baker Foundation, and George F. Baker, Jr., personally gave me the warmest possible encouragement. Since Abram Bergson is George F. Baker Professor of Economics at Harvard, the assistance rendered by Mr. Baker was especially apt and gratifying. I am deeply appreciative.

Finally, I want to thank my wife, Susan Rosefielde, for all her excellent advice and enthusiastic support.

S.R.

# Introduction

In the spirit of Abram Bergson's life's work, the essays contained in this volume are devoted to the theme of economic welfare, assessed both from the standpoint of pure theory and the behavior of the Soviet economic system. The book is divided into two parts. The first deals with the Soviet economy. The chapters in this section are arranged according to their generality, beginning with an overview of the development of Soviet economic studies and concluding with a detailed empirical analysis of the determinants of Soviet international trade. Part II focuses on welfare economics. Abram Bergson's contribution to welfare theory is appraised by Paul Samuelson in the opening essay. Special topics in the field of economic welfare are then explored by Kenneth Arrow, Simon Kuznets, and Jan Tinbergen. The section concludes with Martin Spechler's reappraisal of the economics of socialism, a subject that epitomizes Bergson's intellectual vision. A short biographical sketch and a complete list of Abram Bergson's publications are provided at the back of the volume for those wishing to delve systematically into his oeuvres.

# Part I

# Soviet Socialism

# 1 Knowledge and socialism: deciphering the Soviet experience

*Steven Rosefielde*

## I. Introduction: the problem of Soviet socialism

Few would deny that the Bolshevik Revolution was a "world historical event" in the Hegelian–Marxist sense.[1] November 7, 1917, was "a day that shook the world."[2] Not only did it occasion the fall of the moribund Czarist autocracy, but it appeared to mark the ascendancy of a new social order in which the welfare of the "toiling masses" would supersede the minority interests of the nobility, or property-owning classes. Certainly, the Bolsheviks construed their own actions in these terms, proclaiming without reservation that their triumph would usher in a new era of (Marxist) socialism, followed ineluctably by full communism.[3]

This ecstatic characterization, however, was vehemently contested not just by those who flourished under Czarism – the nobility and the bourgeoisie – but by a large spectrum of socialist dissent. Anarchists, populists, Socialist Revolutionaries, Mensheviks, suppressed, interned in concentration camps (by mid-1918), and not infrequently "exed" (executed by the Revolutionary Tribunal) rejected what seemed to them to be a perversion of the very social ideals that the Bolsheviks so fervidly professed.[4] Leninist socialism, although it may have possessed some attributes of a legitimate socialist order (nationalization of the means of production, a working-class ideology, abolition of market relations, etc.), nonetheless from the dissenters' standpoint was inimical to other higher socialist ideals, the welfare of the masses, democracy, due process, civil liberties, and authentic socialist consciousness. The negative judgment of these domestic dissenters was widely supported by the leaders of the West European Socialist Democratic movement, including Karl Kautsky and Rosa Luxemburg.[5] After a brief period of utopian enthusiasm, their appraisal came to be shared by advocates of diverse schools of non-Marxist socialist thought, most notably the syndicalists.[6] With Stalin's rise to power, the growth of bureaucratic privilege, collectivization, forced in-

5

dustrialization, and Gulag new detractors emerged, among whom Trotsky and his followers were most conspicuous in their assertion that the revolution had been betrayed by an usurping bureaucratic cast.[7]

The Bolshevik Revolution was a "world historical event," but amid all this contumely, what did it signify? The meaning of Soviet socialism was further clouded by three additional factors: the Great Depression, fascism, and the questionable reliability of Soviet economic statistics. Given the difficulties besetting the democratic, market economies of the West, many intellectuals were inclined to see Soviet economic arrangements as a viable alternative to imperfect competition, especially so since the Soviets claimed, then as now, to have achieved unparalleled progress at a time when the West was in decline. But could Soviet statistics be trusted? Did national income and gross industrial output really grow at annual rates of 16.8 and 23.5 percent, respectively, during the First Five Year Plan, 1928–32?[8]

To cut through the morass posed by this question and the broader issues of Soviet socialism, a comparatively dispassionate methodology was needed, one whose legitimacy, although not absolute (in the social sciences no methodology is incontestably superior to all others), was still sufficiently cogent that it could serve either as a standard in itself or as a stepping stone for the construction of a better alternative. Abram Bergson was the first scholar to formulate and implement such a methodology in the pioneering years of Soviet studies.

## II. A dispassionate methodology for appraising the Soviet economy and its socialist content

Bergson's point of departure was the insight that the reliability of Soviet statistics and in turn the evaluation of Soviet socialist economic performance depended not only on whether physical production data were falsified, but on the conventions employed to value output as well.[9] Soviet statistics were assailable on both counts. The selective publication of data, often in the form of growth rates rather than absolute values, encouraged the supposition that Soviet statistics were at least in part freely invented to advance the purposes of the proletarian revolution. Similarly, as Soviet prices were formed according to principles of Marxist labor value theory, reflecting neither consumer demand nor marginal factor cost, it could be argued that valuation was fundamentally arbitrary and hence meaningless.

Bergson acknowledged that there was merit to both criticisms, but argued that neither precluded rational evaluation. The issue of free invention was joined semantically. A fine distinction was made between minor fraud and the incompetence of subordinate reporting agencies and deliberate free invention at the center.[10] Although recognizing that the central authorities were notably tolerant of statistical manipulations that unfailingly cast Soviet economic performance in a favorable light, he contended nonetheless that the internal consistency of the series which were published made it seem highly unlikely that the central authorities resorted to free invention in the sense that they maintained two sets of books, one with true figures, the other enhanced for public consumption.[11] This line of reasoning suggested that although data on the physical volume of output might be somewhat less reliable than similar data published by other countries (the notorious practice of weighing grain wet in the field rather than dry in the barn being a case in point), if a really significant and cumulative bias existed in Soviet statistics, it was to be found in the value series rather than the physical production data.[12]

The objective evaluation of Soviet economic behavior in this way was made to depend on whether putatively meaningless value statistics could somehow be rendered meaningful. To solve this critical problem, Bergson devised and perfected an analytic technique which for conciseness we shall describe as the "theory-normed valuative method." The logical essence of this methodology is the use of "pure neoclassical economic theory" as a "norm" for determining "valuation conventions" that are appropriate for the appraisal of Soviet economic performance.[13] In practice, Bergson's method took two forms: the adjusted factor cost standard and index number relativity analysis.[14] The former established a procedure for transforming labor values in a rough way into quasi-opportunity-cost values which could be meaningfully interpreted from the standpoint of marginalist theory. The latter constituted a technique for verifying that Soviet production data valued in Marxian prices behaved much like conventional value series, legitimating their use for the analysis of a wide range of classical economic issues. Both dimensions of the theory-normed valuative method demonstrated beyond a reasonable doubt that the apprehensions of the skeptics were overdrawn.[15] Soviet value data could be evaluated sensibly and the unparalleled achievements of the Great Leap Forward explained.

The riddle posed by labor cost valuation was disposed of incisively. Careful analysis revealed that although the Soviets did set prices administratively without direct reference to short run supply and demand, Soviet prices were not entirely arbitrary. They were formed in the main by computing average industry-wide production costs, excluding charges for interest and rent. These production costs were governed principally by direct and indirect labor costs where wages, although not negotiated, were nonetheless set to clear the market in the sense that workers were allocated in reasonable proportion to their best use.[16] With the exception of scarcity charges and arbitrary turnover taxes levied in a complex manner on certain commodities, Soviet prices could therefore be construed as average cost approximations to conventional market prices.

Noting this correspondence, Bergson argued that the deficiencies of Soviet valuation could be mitigated sufficiently to facilitate rational evaluation by deducting turnover taxes and imputing interest and rent to the value of output. These adjustments, which were the core elements of his adjusted factor cost method, did not of course transform Soviet accounting prices into true general equilibrium prices. At best the adjusted value of aggregate output might tolerably approximate the magnitude that would have prevailed in an economic regime in which the government first administratively determined the structure of production and then established prices that cleared the market subject to this constraint. Adjusted factor cost prices, however, could not be made to reflect aggregate values in a freely competitive environment.[17]

This was a troublesome lacunae. State regulation of production was not entirely unknown in the West, but nowhere was it practiced as comprehensively as in the Soviet Union. Pushing his theory-normed valuation method one step further, Bergson was, however, able to clarify effectively how adjusted factor cost values might be given a cogent interpretation. He argued that a sharp distinction should be drawn between production potential on the one hand and consumers' or planners' choice on the other.[18] The production potential standard took the structure of production as given and permitted inferences to be drawn concerning productivity and efficiency without reference to demand. If the structure of production were capricious, it is doubtful that the production potential standard would hold much interest. But the structure of Soviet production was hardly random. The product mix was determined by planners' choice, so that the adjusted factor cost standard imparted a definite meaning to Soviet national income statistics. It measured proximately the opportunity costs of producing a bundle of goods that accorded with planners' preferences. This still was not, of course, the same thing as consumer sovereignty,[19] but if the choices made by the planners took into consideration the welfare of the masses, adjusted factor cost would not only make production potential comparisons meaningful, but would contain valid information on the level of socialist welfare.[20] The theory-normed valuative method therefore did obviate, or at least sharply reduce, the cogency of the view that Soviet economic performance defied rational appraisal because Soviet economic statistics were meaningless.

Bergson's hypothesis that the ostensibly unprecedented achievements of the first two Five Year Plans could be largely explained by the conventions used to value production was confirmed by another application of the theory-normed valuative method. Published Soviet growth statistics were valued in prices of 1926–7, which were in force on the eve of the

First Five Year Plan. The use of base-year prices was conventional and under ordinary circumstances should not have significantly distorted the real rate of growth. But were these ordinary circumstances?

On the one hand, they were. Prices in 1926 and 1927 were determined to a considerable extent in the marketplace and therefore did not depart from ordinary practice on that score.[21] On the other hand, the Bolsheviks employed sundry, and often inconsistent price control policies during the 1920s, which on balance may well have imparted a significant upward bias to the production of those goods that the NEP industrial cartels intended to expand most rapidly.[22] Industrial prices that normally should have been high in a predominantly agrarian society may have been inordinately high as the consequence of chaotic state price policies.

Circumstances were extraordinary in another sense as well. The Bolsheviks claimed that in the span of nine short years a revolutionary transformation had occurred in the structure of Soviet production. Not only did the industrial sector grow prodigiously, but heavy industry replaced light industry as the dominant subsector.[23] If this characterization were accurate, it implied that the prices prevailing in 1937 differed substantially from those in force in 1926–7.

In view of these qualifications, particularly the latter point regarding structural change, Bergson recalculated Soviet national income in 1926–7 and 1937 prices.[24] This was a monumental undertaking because the Soviets did not publish the sectoral price indices that were needed for an independent calculation of real gross national product. The requisite price series had to be laboriously calculated from primary price data instead.[25] The effort, however, was rewarded in several ways. First, it was discovered that when Western national income conventions were employed, GNP grew at 11.5 percent, valued in prevailing 1926–7 rubles compared to the officially reported NMP (net material product) rate of 16.8 percent.[26] Even without making any adjustment for what may have been an artificially high level of industrial prices in 1926–7, it turned out that a significant proportion of the officially claimed rate of growth was attributable to the measure of national product used by the Soviets (NMP), which excluded the service sector, and by the aggregation weights the Soviets implicitly employed in computing their net material product. Second, Bergson found that the putative rate of growth was further drastically reduced to 4.9 percent when 1937 prices were employed to value production.[27]

These were astounding findings, but how should they be interpreted? Applying the theory-normed valuative method, Bergson first demonstrated that his results were not artifacts of Marxian prices by computing analogous rates of growth in adjusted factor cost prices. The difference between these rates and those in prevailing prices was negligible.[28] It followed, therefore, that turnover taxes and the exclusion of scarcity charges for capital and land did not explain the sensitivity of Soviet GNP growth to the choice of alternative price weights.

Building on this correspondence, he demonstrated next that under conditions of rapid structural change, base-year prices will normally overstate growth whereas final-year prices understate it. This phenomenon, known as index number relativity, not only enabled Western analysts to establish the parameters of the real Soviet achievement, but equally important, served to strongly confirm that Soviet statistics could be employed to evaluate economic performance, because observed behavior measured in prevailing rubles diverged little from observed behavior valued with adjusted factor cost prices.

The theory-normed valuative method had therefore proven its worth. It enabled Bergson to verify that the unparalleled achievements claimed by the Soviets were largely (although not entirely) explicable in terms of price phenomena and to infer that Soviet statistics were sufficiently reliable to support scholarly assessments of Soviet economic behavior. The riddle of Soviet statistics had been solved. Bergson had shown that Soviet economics need not merely be an arena for sterile ideological confrontation, but was amenable to rational discourse and legitimate scientific inquiry.

### III. The theory-normed valuative method

The merit of the theory-normed valuative method as a technique for assessing the feasibility of scientific research on the Soviet economy and for analyzing the behavioral properties of Soviet economic statistics has been established beyond reasonable doubt. This accomplishment, however, does not necessarily imply that the theory-normed valuative method itself provides a complete and accurate description of Soviet economic performance. At stake here is the fundamental epistemology issue of knowledge. How should the information derived from the theory-normed valuative method be interpreted from the standpoint of the philosophy of science? What are its strengths, and what are its limitations?

The theory-normed valuative method is a technique that employs neoclassical economic theory to evaluate the meaning of economic data,[29] to establish theoretical criteria of correct valuation[30] and to appraise whether the behavioral patterns exhibited by diversely valued statistical series are logically consistent.[31] Although the method both facilitates proper empirical quantification and serves as a standard of empirical appraisal in most applications, it is not an experimental method in the sense that observed behavior functions as a norm for judging the goodness of the theory.[32] Rather, the inferential process runs in precisely the reverse direction.

Theory acts as the norm for assessing the meaning of observed economic behavior. The truth of the theory is presupposed, not tested. As a consequence, the theory-normed valuative method is *not* an *empirical method* in the classical meaning of that concept. It is an interpretative technique, a hypotheticodeductive device for drawing inferences from a priori theory rather than a method of empirically verifying causal relationships.

From the perspective of the philosophy of science it should be classified neither as a positivist nor as a realist methodology.[33] Its filial connections lie elsewhere, with the Cartesian tradition, with a priori rationalism.

Once the rationalist foundations of the theory-normed valuative method are recognized, an assessment of its strengths and weaknesses follows directly. Like all a priori theoretical techniques, the theory-normed valuative method has as its chief virtues conceptual clarity and logical consistency. It requires that all the elements of a hypothetical construct be articulated and arranged so that their intended meanings can be sustained by an underlying body of theory that is both necessary and sufficient for the phenomenon to exhibit the behavioral properties ascribed to it. The process of testing the logical assumptions of rational, a priori theories is a very powerful device for evaluating the comparative merit of competing hypotheses displaying different degrees of logical cohesiveness. A great deal of unnecessary confusion can be eliminated by rejecting theories whose conclusions are predicated on a weakly consistent logical foundation.

As is widely understood, however, logical consistency alone, even when theories are necessary and sufficient in their own terms, does not settle the question of causality. Many theories of equal plausibility and equal consistency may coexist. Their comparative merit is an empirical matter to be settled by traditional quantitative and/or statistical methods, assuming, of course, that the data have been properly formulated and are accurate.

The truth value of the theory-normed valuative method is therefore necessarily circumscribed. It can be asserted on the basis of the method that adjusted factor cost valuation could be construed as an average factor cost approximation to market values given planners' preferences, but it cannot be maintained that this correspondence has existential import. Whether adjusted factor cost values really reflect planners' preferences or by extension proletarian welfare can only be settled empirically through econometric analysis of the implied behavioral relationships. Similarly, the contention that the parameters of Soviet economic performance can be adequately measured by valuing production in diverse "theory-normed" prices has only restricted validity. It is entirely possible that if "true" marginal cost prices were employed for 1928 and 1937, the results would diverge substantially from Bergson's findings.

The point to grasp from these examples is not, of course, that Bergson's conclusions regarding the interpretation of adjusted factor cost, or the reliability of Soviet statistics, are false. Only a comprehensive econometric assessment could (might) settle these questions. The issue at stake here is more universal. The theory-normed valuative method as a method cannot in and of itself sustain assertions about the true state of reality. It can validly interpret economic behavior given certain assumptions, but it contains no mechanisms to assure that those assumptions are met. It follows directly that our understanding of Soviet economic behavior, both in the present and the past, is a good deal less certain than is usually supposed, and that a considerable amount of econometric research will be required before our interpretations of Soviet economic behavior can begin to attain the status of *knowledge* in an authentic epistemological sense.

### IV. Analytic clarity versus ambiguous econometric empiricism

Although the epistemological limitations of the theory-normed valuative method described above are both real and palpable, they are not fatal and should not be construed as a judgment on the comparative merit of the methodology. Empiricism is epistemologically flawed as well. The shortcomings of empirical research, especially in the social sciences, have been widely analyzed in the philosophy of science.[34] They include the unreliability of the data, the mutability of the underlying phenomena, and most important of all, specificational indeterminism. "Fitting the data" has proven to be far easier than discriminating among the comparative merits of alternative specifications, all exhibiting more or less the same degree of statistical goodness.[35]

As a consequence of these ambiguities, the successes of econometric empiricism in the field of Soviet economics have not been commensurate with our expectations. In some areas, such as production function analysis, the best work has been suggestive but inconclusive. In other branches of the discipline, mindless positivism seems to prevail. Inappropriate data, often obtained from inconsistent sources, are employed together with various specifications adopted largely for reasons of expediency to ascertain empirically how the Soviet system functions. The results are hardly edifying and raise the important issue of comparative methodological merit.

Of course, the first best alternative would be one in which the specification of causal processes and the valuation of relevant variables were determined by the theory-normed valuative method and then comprehensively tested with the most advanced econometric procedures available. Instances of this sort are rare.[36] A production function, for example, may take many forms, none of which are superior on a priori grounds alone.

If they all provide good fits, the first best method may be of little avail.[37]

As a practical matter, therefore, the analysis of Soviet economic behavior will depend on the comparative merit of methodologies that by themselves are necessarily epistemologically inconclusive. How does the theory-normed valuative method fare under these conditions? The answer here seems to be contingent on the particular problem at issue.

Consider once more the question of the meaning and reliability of Soviet economic statistics. Aside from the possibility that empiricists might prove that there was more "free invention" in the 1930s than had been previously suspected, with the data at hand econometrics can shed very little light on the validity of behavioral assumptions on which Bergson's calculations are predicated, nor can it be employed to reliably calculate true opportunity costs as opposed to the average cost approximations used to derive adjusted factor cost estimates of real Soviet national income. The theory-normed valuative method therefore may be vulnerable on epistemological grounds, but it is better than the alternatives for evaluating aggregate Soviet economic performance during the first three Five Year Plans.

A similar but less compelling argument can be made for the efficacy of the method in the postwar period. The Soviets now publish an incomplete, but nonetheless voluminous amount of statistical data. Although the reliability and meaning of these data remain an issue, attention has shifted from these narrow concerns to broader behavioral questions, including productivity, efficiency, growth, and the comparative merit of Soviet socialism.

Bergson, for example, has extended his research on the level and growth of Soviet GNP to an evaluation of their determinants.[38] He has calculated factor productivity ratios using diverse theory-normed weights[39] and assessed dynamic productivity growth with the theory-normed Solow–Abramovich residual technique.[40] These deterministic computations were performed not just for the Soviet Union but for the economies of Eastern Europe and the OECD. Like his earlier work, Bergson's research on productivity has been directed toward evaluating the performance of the Soviet economy in a broad historical and trans-systemic perspective. Applying the theory-normed valuative method, he has succeeded in devising common standards of accounting and valuation that have made it possible to measure performance on the basis of uniform theoretical norms. Also as in the past, his findings indicate that Soviet achievements both in terms of aggregate static and dynamic productivity are much less impressive than officially claimed, lying toward the middle of the international spectrum and toward the bottom if consumer welfare is taken as the ultimate desideratum.[41]

Building on this foundation, Bergson has attempted to extend his analysis further, drawing inferences on the comparative efficiency and merit of socialism.[42] He has rigorously elaborated a set of conditions under which productivity measures may serve as proxies for efficiency and has argued that the economies of the Soviet Union and with some exceptions of Eastern Europe as well can be treated as exemplars of socialism because they are centrally planned with state ownership of the means of production.[43]

These extensions, however, which go to the heart of the issue raised long ago by the Bolshevik Revolution, place a crushing burden on the theory-normed valuative method. The productivity measures computed by Bergson are simple arithmetic ratios. Output elasticities are not estimated econometrically and cannot be appraised statistically. Their merit therefore depends on the a priori validity of the theoretical assumptions upon which his computations are based. As was pointed out earlier, however, testing assumptions is an inadequate technique for assessing whether any particular theory (in this case the form of the relevant production function) is true. As the measurement of comparative international productivity is extremely sensitive to the form of the production function specified, any evaluation of the comparative merit of Soviet economic performance must necessarily be controversial.[44] Similarly, analyzing the conditions under which productivity and efficiency measures become close substitutes does not assure us that these assumptions are correct.[45] Nor can arithmetic examples designed to show the robustness of productivity measures to notional variations in the abstract parameter of production overcome the ambiguities of specificational indeterminism, because the effect of these variations on the underlying statistical fit go entirely unobserved.[46]

It appears, therefore, that the power of the theory-normed valuative method is directly correlated with the ability of a priori reason to identify necessary functional forms. As the number of plausible specifications proliferate, the net advantage of the theory-normed valuative method over conventional econometrics diminishes. This implies that if the important class of economic problems under discussion is to be resolved in a remotely satisfactory manner, the theory-normed valuative method cannot be restricted to deterministic (largely arithmetic) analysis. The theoretical canons pioneered by Bergson and embodied in his empirical work must be extended to the econometric evaluation of a broad range of equally plausible a priori functional specifications. Ideally, this procedure might lead to the discovery of uniquely first best explanations of causal processes, but even if it did not (as seems likely), knowledge of the behavior of the Soviet economy could be advanced if the same standards of analytic clarity exhibited in Bergson's numerical calculations were applied in interpreting the theoretical implications of analogous econometric studies. Thus, it appears that after four decades of successful application, the theory-normed valuative method remains a sine qua non for the scientific analysis of Soviet socialism.

## V. Knowledge and socialism

Sixty-four years have elapsed since the Bolsheviks stormed the Winter Palace, replacing Czarism with the chimera of a socialist commonwealth. What was accomplished? What do we really know about the behavior of the Soviet economy and its socialist content? A full appraisal of this important theme would require many volumes and cannot be undertaken within the scope of this essay. A more limited evaluation, however, can be hazarded on the basis of our epistemological inquiry.

First and foremost, it has been shown that we know with considerable confidence that the Soviets were successful in carrying out a program of rapid industrialization during the 1930s. The official Soviet position in this regard is broadly confirmed by the technical behavior of Soviet production indices (index number relativity), which indicates significant structural change whether valuation is in prevailing rubles or in adjusted factor cost prices.

On a similar basis it has also been convincingly demonstrated that despite rapid industrialization, the real rate of aggregate growth during the first three Five Year Plans was substantially lower than officially claimed, whether 1926–7 or 1937 prices are taken as the valuation standard. The poorest-performing component of the Soviet economy during this period undoubtedly was the consumer sector. It is highly probable that consumer welfare declined, perhaps significantly, as a consequence of the industrialization drive. These conclusions follow even if no allowance at all is made for the possible overvaluation of industrial prices in 1926–7. They are confirmed by adjusted factor cost valuation but can also be deduced from data valued in official prevailing prices.

The exact magnitude of Soviet industrial growth and the extent of the decline in consumer welfare, however, is still obscured by the issue of free invention. A considerable volume of information has surfaced in recent years, much of it emanating from the Gulag literature, which suggests that free invention may have been much more significant than Bergson originally supposed.[47]

Knowledge of Soviet economic behavior in the postwar period has benefited from an increased flow of official statistical data. This fact has greatly reduced the need for laboriously piecing together information from diverse sources to fill in critical gaps in the statistical record. On the basis of these data we are reasonably certain that postwar Soviet growth has undergone a gradual, but persistent secular deceleration, that Soviet economic performance is probably not exceptional by historical world standards, and that consumer welfare continues to lag.

The broader issues of comparative systems merit and, above all, causation, however, remain intensely controversial. Neither econometrics nor the theory-normed valuative method[48] has been notably successful in discriminating best explanations from among the large set of competing, equally plausible hypotheses, which warrant impartial consideration. In this regard our knowledge of Soviet economic processes is far from satisfactory.

The gaps in our understanding of the basic mechanics of the Soviet economy are miniscule, though, compared with the obscurity that still surrounds the ultimate question of Soviet socialism. Should the Soviet Union be considered a socialist society because its constitution affirms it to be so? Should it be deemed socialist because it professes a proletarian ideology, because state ownership of the means of production prevails, or because the economy is regulated by an administrative plan? As late as the 1960s, most observers influenced by the authority of the Marx–Engels–Leninist tradition would have answered these rhetorical questions in the affirmative. The rise of Eurocommunism, Maoism, alternative non-Marxist schools of socialist thought, and the Gulag revelations have rendered this standard of judgment obsolete.[49] As the socialist opposition long ago made clear, the superficial correspondence of some aspects of the Bolshevik system with the tenents of socialism cannot offset the fact that the real content of social, political, and economic life in the Soviet Union is fundamentally inimical to the values most socialists claim to affirm. From an epistemological standpoint our grasp of the real content of the Soviet system is woefully rudimentary. A greal deal of suggestive material exists, but the groundwork required for a comprehensive, scientific, appraisal of the effect the Soviet system has had on the human welfare of its citizens has hardly begun.

The lack of success in this regard, of course, bears on the issue of socialism in general. At the present juncture, owing in large part to the scholarship of Abram Bergson, it is possible to make some intelligent judgments about the comparative merit of market and Soviet-type economies, but until a new consensus about the operative characteristics of authentic socialist economic systems emerges, any grand appraisal of those illusive abstractions "capitalism" and "socialism" will remain more a matter of metaphysical speculation than of analytic science.[50] Thus, although it is true that the discipline has made enormous strides since Abram Bergson first discovered how Soviet data could be scientifically evaluated, many of the "earthshaking" questions posed by the triumph of Bolshevism still await definitive resolution.

## Notes

1 G. W. F. Hegel, *The Phenomenology of Mind*, Harper & Row, New York, 1967.
2 John Reed, *Ten Days That Shook the World*, Vintage Books, New York, 1960.
3 Nikolai Bukharin and Evgeny Preobrazhenky, *The ABC's of Communism*, Penguin Books, Baltimore, Md., 1969.
4 Emma Goldman, *My Disillusionment in Russia*, Apollo Editions, New York, 1970; Alexandra Kollontai, *The Workers' Opposition*, Solidarity Pamphlet No. 7, Bromley, Kent; David Dallin, *The Real Soviet Russia*, Yale University Press, New Haven, Conn., 1948; Alexander Solzhenitsyn, *The Gulag Archipelago*, Vol. II, Harper & Row, New York, 1975.
5 Karl Kautsky, *Terrorism and Communism*, National Labor Press, London, 1920; Rosa Luxemburg, *The Russian Revolution*, University of Michigan Press, Ann Arbor, Mich., 1961.
6 F. F. Ridley, *Revolutionary Syndicalism in France*, Cambridge University Press, Cambridge, 1970.
7 Leon Trotsky, *The Third International after Lenin*, Pioneer Publishers, New York, 1936; Irving Howe (ed.), *The Basic Writings of Trotsky*, Vintage Books, New York, 1963.
8 V. Ivanchenko, "Leninskie idei o planovom upravelenii ekonomikoi v deistvii," *Voprosy ekonomiki*, April 1979, 7.
9 Abram Bergson, "Reliability and Usability of Soviet Statistics: A Summary Appraisal," *American Statistician*, June–July 1953, 13–16; Abram Bergson, *The Real National Income of Soviet Russia since 1928*, Harvard University Press, Cambridge, Mass., 1961, pp. 25–41; Abram Bergson, "Soviet National Income and Product in 1937, Part I: National Economic Accounts in Current Rubles," *Quarterly Journal of Economics*, May 1950, 208–41, esp. 237–41; Abram Bergson, "Soviet National Income and Product in 1937, Part II: Rubles Prices and the Valuation Problem," *Quarterly Journal of Economics*, August 1950, 408–41.
10 In "Reliability and Usability of Soviet Statistics," Bergson states:

> Contrary to a common supposition, the Russians seem generally not to resort to falsification in the sense of free invention and double book-keeping. I have explained that there is falsification of a local sort. . . . I am now concerned primarily with falsification of a comprehensive character at the center. This latter distinction, I fear, is a fine one. Almost all the deficiencies that have been discovered lead to unduly favorable impressions of the Soviet economy. If the Russians do not wilfully introduce such deficiencies to create such impressions, they are at least notably tolerant of them. [P. 15]

The judgment "the Russians seem generally not to resort to falsification in the sense of free invention" is restated more broadly:

> While it has seemed in order to distinguish in this essay between falsification by lower echelons and falsification at the center, it will be evident that in a number of the grounds for thinking that the latter is not a general practice must apply also to the former. As a result, there is some upper limit to the margin of error introduced by falsification by lower echelons. [P. 16*u*]

11 Ibid.

12 Ibid. These judgments perhaps should be read in the context of the times. Bergson's endorsement of the broad reliability and usability of Soviet statistics may have provided the psychological impetus needed to persevere with research that was by its very nature clouded with extraordinary statistical ambiguities. A brief quote from Alec Nove may suffice to strengthen the point that Soviet statisticians were not shielded from political pressure to "objectively" compute "accurate" statistical series: "In the general atmosphere of terror, it could well be that statisticians concealed (or were ordered to conceal) the truth about deaths in the early Thirties and when it did emerge in a 1937 census, the reaction was to shoot the statisticians and suppress the census" ("Robert Conquest, The Great Terror," *Soviet Studies,* 20, April 1969, 538). The statisticians were literally shot. See also Steven Rosefielde, "An Assessment of the Sources and Uses of Gulag Forced Labour 1929–56," *Soviet Studies,* January 1981; and Steven Rosefielde, "The First Great Leap Forward Reconsidered: The Lessons of Solzhenitsyn's Gulag Archipelago," *Slavic Review,* December 1980.

13 I have coined the phrase "theory-normed valuative method" to describe Bergson's approach to empirical analysis, which consists of using the implications of neoclassical economic theory to determine proper standards for valuing economic data, and appropriate norms for interpreting these data once they have been correctly valued. The method is apriorist. Its epistemological significance is discussed in the next section.

14 Good discussions of both concepts are found in Bergson, "Soviet National Income and Product in 1937, Part II"; Abram Bergson, *Soviet National Income and Product in 1937,* Columbia University Press, New York, 1953; Abram Bergson and Hans Heymann, Jr., *Soviet National Income and Product, 1940–1948,* Columbia University Press, New York, 1954; and Bergson, *Real National Income,* pp. 24–41.

15 Bergson, *Real National Income,* pp. 24–41.

16 Abram Bergson, *The Structure of Soviet Wages,* Harvard University Press, Cambridge, Mass., 1954. Although this statement is substantially valid, it should not be inferred that the Soviet labor market is efficient in either a technical or a welfare sense. Wages are not negotiated, differentials are bureaucratically determined, low wages may affect effort, internal mobility is constrained by a passport system, and forced concentration camp labor is extensive, constituting roughly 20 percent of the nonagricultural work force from the mid-1930s until Stalin's death. See Rosefielde, "How Reliable Are Available Estimates of Forced Concentration Camp Labor in the Soviet Union?" Table 6, p. 38.

17 This point has tended to be lost in the discussion of the "open labor market" in the Soviet Union. By suggesting that money wages are at equilibrium clearing levels for diverse job categories, the fact that the structure of labor demand is inconsistent with consumers' preferences for final goods and services is often overlooked. See Bergson, "Soviet National Income and Product in 1937, Part II," p. 420. The distinction between the production mix and, derivatively, labor demand under conditions of consumer choice and consumer sovereignty is implicit in Abram Bergson, "Socialist Economics," in Bergson, *Essays in Normative Economics,* Harvard University Press, Belknap Press, Cambridge, Mass., 1966, pp. 193–236. For a further discussion of these matters, see Steven Rosefielde, *The Transformation of the 1966 Soviet Input–Output Table from Producers to Adjusted Factor Cost Values,* General

Electric Tempo, Washington, D.C., 1975, pp. 34–41. See also Abram
Bergson, "Principles of Socialist Wages," in Bergson, *Essays in Normative
Economics,* pp. 175–192; and Abram Bergson, "Market Socialism Revisited," *Journal of Political Economy,* October 1967.
18 Bergson, "Socialist Economics"; Bergson, *Real National Income,* pp. 25–41.
For an analysis of these concepts, see Steven Rosefielde, "Sovietology and
Index Number Theory," *Economia Internazionale,* February 1975, 1–15.
19 Bergson, "Socialist Economics."
20 Bergson has rigorously formulated the concept of social welfare. See
Bergson, "A Reformulation of Certain Aspects of Welfare Economics,"
"Collective Decision-Making and Social Welfare," and "On Social Welfare
Once More," in *Essays in Normative Economics,* pp. 3–26, 27–50, 51–92. The
problem of applying adjusted factor cost norms to the formal quantitative
analysis of socialist welfare is discussed in Rosefielde, "Sovietology and
Index Number Theory." See also Steven Rosefielde, "Some Observations on
the Concept of 'Socialism' in Contemporary Economic Theory," *Soviet Studies,* 25, October 1973, 229–43.
21 Bergson, *Real National Income,* pp. 124–6.
22 The tangled subject of 1926–7 prices has yet to be satisfactorily sorted out. In
the mid-1920s the Bolsheviks were following an expansionary monetary policy (despite the runaway inflation just a few years earlier); at the same time,
they sought to *reduce* industrial and agricultural prices by fiat. Maintaining
industrial–agrarian purchasing power price parity at something near the 1913
values was also a goal, but this objective conflicted with the cartels' desire
for high net income and the state's ability to derivatively finance industrialization. It is easily envisaged under these circumstances that the cartels
could have complied with the government's orders to cut prices on some
items while raising them on others in such a way that the nominal industrial
price level declined while the real price level rose together with the cartel income needed to support industrial expansion. This hypothetical mechanism
suggests how the real terms of trade may have been tilting more favorably
toward industry than is usually thought (this indeed was precisely the policy
advocated by Trotsky and Preobrazhensky), imparting an upward bias to
subsequent measures of Soviet growth. A phenomenon of this sort may perhaps explain Davis's finding that industrial production, contrary to expectation, grew more rapidly in 1926–7 and end-period prices than in 1913 prices
during the 1920s. See R. W. Davis, "Soviet Industrial Production, 1928–1937:
The Rival Estimates," CREES Discussion Paper No. 18, Center for Russian
and East European Studies, University of Birmingham, Birmingham, England, 1978, p. 20.
  Paul Gregory has been kind enough to call another explanation of the Davis
index number reversal phenomenon to my attention. Based on new figures he
has developed, Gregory finds that the investment rate in constant 1913 prices
rose from 11 percent to 15 percent between 1913 and 1928. He infers from
this that "there was a shift towards capital goods, essentially along a static
PPS," which "caused an increase in the relative price of capital." And further that "as the PPS expanded in the 30s, the relative price of capital then
fell" (personal correspondence, October 17, 1979). The phenomenon he describes is entirely possible. However, it raises the further question of why increased investment "expanded" the PPS in the 1930s but not in the 1920s.
The usual presumption is that the price of capital falls as the rate of invest-

ment rises in developing countries because the accompanying productivity gains in the capital goods sector is so substantial. But NEP Russia was a queer phenomenon. The possibility that technical progress failed to offset increased short-run marginal costs cannot be dismissed.

On Soviet price policy, see Alec Nove, *An Economic History of the USSR,* Allen Lane, London, 1969, pp. 139–41.

Abram Bergson has always been extremely cautious about 1926–7 prices. In his early writings he expressed the belief that "the official series is subject to a substantial upward bias" ("Soviet National Income and Product in 1937, Part I," p. 238). In his later work Bergson has softened this argument: "In 1937, the base year on which I focus especially, ruble prices appear to have more economic content than in many other years under the five year plans. This probably was true also of 1928. . ." (*Real National Income,* p. 40). See also the detailed discussion in ibid., pp. 124–6. The shift here is particularly notable because in view of the Moorsteen effect (ibid., pp. 31–4), a good case could have been made for the preferability of 1926–7 prices as an indicator of Stalin's preferences. Bergson's reticence here probably reflects his correct judgment that in the final analysis, 1937 prices were less distorted than were 1926–7 prices. Even this surmise, however, is clouded by the stark contrast between Bergson's description of economic conditions in 1937 – "1937 was for the Soviet consumer a year of unexampled prosperity" ("Soviet National Income and Product in 1937, Part II," p. 423) – and the picture of Soviet reality painted in the Gulag literature. It seems difficult, for example, to believe that real rural per capita income in 1937 was higher than in 1928. See Bergson, *Real National Income,* p. 126; Rosefielde, "The First Great Leap Forward Reconsidered"; and Betty Laird and Roy Laird, *To Live Long Enough: The Memoirs of Naum Jasny, Scientific Analyst,* University Press of Kansas, Lawrence, Kans., 1976, pp. 118–20.

23 Paul Gregory, *Socialist and Nonsocialist Industrialization Patterns,* Praeger, New York, 1970, pp. 28–9.

24 Bergson, *Real National Income.*

25 Abram Bergson, Roman Bernaut, and Lynn Turgeon, "Prices of Basic Industrial Products in the U.S.S.R., 1928–50," *Journal of Political Economy,* August 1956, 303–28.

26 Abram Bergson and Simon Kuznets (eds.), *Economic Trends in the Soviet Union,* Harvard University Press, Cambridge, Mass., 1963, p. 336.

27 Ibid.

28 Ibid. Bergson was aware that adjusted factor cost values could be used to test the "meaningfulness" of the proposition that index number relatively confirmed the reliability of Soviet statistics. As early as 1956, long before his adjusted factor cost research was complete, he wrote:

> Although the interpretation is not obvious, we may mention that, like Western market prices, the ruble prices pass the "index number test"; that is, index numbers based on 1928 quantity weights tend to show a greater price inflation than those based on 1937 weights.
>
> However, we do not wish to replace one presupposition on "meaningfulness" by another. Clearly, a sweeping rejection of ruble prices is no more in order than before, and, with this, further speculation along the foregoing lines may best be left to the reader. The ruble prices certainly have some economic content, but the reader will probably feel, as we do, that more information is needed before one can hope to come to

any definite conclusions on this complex question. [Bergson et al., "Prices of Basic Industrial Products," p. 306]

29 Neoclassical economic theory is taken to be the proper standard for interpreting the conceptual implications of economic data formed according to various accounting conventions.

30 Proper valuation is understood to mean that the accounting conceptions utilized to compile economic data series correspond to the definitions established by neoclassical economic theory.

31 Logical consistency in this context means that observed behavior is directly explicable in terms of neoclassical economic theory. The truth value of particular hypotheses is reckoned by testing assumptions. If the data are properly valued, and observed behavior conforms with expectations deduced from pure theory, a hypothesis will be deemed cogent. This is the classical distinction between positivism and rationalism.

32 The theory-normed valuative method cannot be falsified. If the behavior implied by observation is inconsistent with the theory, the behavior is construed as being irrational. The standpoint of the empiricist is just the reverse. Theory cannot be confirmed unless observed behavior corresponds with its predictions. Both methods provide consistent conclusions only in the cases where the data perfectly confirm one and only one hypothesis. For a more detailed discussion of this issue, see Steven Rosefielde, "Economic Theory in the Excluded Middle between Positivism and Rationalism," *Atlantic Economic Journal*, 4, Spring 1979, 1–9; Steven Rosefielde, "Post Positivist Scientific Method and the Appraisal of Nonmarket Economic Behavior," *Quarterly Journal of Ideology*, Fall 1979; Romano Harré, *The Philosophy of Science*, Oxford University Press, London, 1972; Romano Harré and P. F. Secord, *The Explanation of Social Behavior*, Humanities Press, New York, 1975.

33 Harré and Secord, *Explanation of Social Behavior*.

34 Ibid.; Martin Hollis and Edward Nell, *Rational Economic Man: A Philosophical Critique of Neo-Classical Economics*, Cambridge University Press, New York, 1975.

35 Some empiricists cling to the determinist fallacy that because everything is somehow related to everything else, if specifications were sufficiently comprehensive, a uniquely best fit could be found. The problem with this argument is that as specifications become more complex, theory lapses into incoherence long before unequivocally best fits can be obtained, even assuming that complexity improves rather than diminishes explanatory power.

36 One potentially useful approach might be to limit empirical estimation to those alternative specifications of the same behavioral phenomenon that satisfy necessary and sufficient conditions derived from a consistent body of pure theory. For an econometric test of a theory-normed valuative hypothesis, see Steven Rosefielde and Knox Lovell, "The Impact of Adjusted Factor Cost Valuation on the CES Interpretation of Postwar Soviet Economic Growth," *Economica*, 44, 381–92. Nonstochastic applications can be found in Steven Rosefielde, "Factor Proportions and Economic Rationality in Soviet International Trade 1955–1968," *American Economic Review*, 64, September 1974, 670–81; and Steven Rosefielde, "Is the Embodied Factor Content of Soviet Foreign Trade Hyper-irrational? Problems of Theory and Measurement," *Association for Comparative Economics Bulletin*, 21, Summer 1979, 19–51.

37 Steven Rosefielde, "Index Numbers and the Computation of Factor Productivity: A Further Appraisal," *Review of Income and Wealth,* Fall 1979, 223–6.
38 Bergson, "National Income," in Bergson and Kuznets, *Economic Trends,* pp. 1–37; Abram Bergson, "The Great Economic Race," *Challenge Magazine,* March 1963, 4–6; Abram Bergson, *The Economics of Soviet Planning,* Yale University Press, New Haven, Conn., 1964; Abram Bergson, *Planning and Productivity under Soviet Socialism,* Columbia University Press, New York, 1968; Abram Bergson, "Development under Two Systems: Comparative Productivity Growth since 1950," *World Politics,* July 1971, 579–617; Abram Bergson, "Comparative National Income in the USSR and the United States," in J. D. Daly, ed., *International Comparisons of Prices and Output, Studies in Income and Wealth,* Vol. 36, National Bureau of Economic Research, New York, 1972, pp. 145–224; Abram Bergson, "Productivity under Two Systems: USSR versus the West," in Jan Tinbergen, Abram Bergson, Fritz Machlup, and Oskar Morgenstern, *Optimal Social Welfare and Productivity: A Comparative View,* Barnes & Noble, New York, 1972; Abram Bergson, "Soviet Economic Perspectives: Toward a New Growth Model," *Problems of Communism,* March–April 1973, 1–8; Abram Bergson, "Index Numbers and the Computation of Factor Productivity," *Review of Income and Wealth,* September 1975, 259–77; Abram Bergson, *Productivity and the Social System – The USSR and the West,* Harvard University Press, Cambridge, Mass., 1978; Abram Bergson, "Notes on the Production Function in Soviet Postwar Industrial Growth," *Journal of Comparative Economics,* June 1979, 116–26.
39 Bergson, *Productivity and the Social System.*
40 Ibid., esp. pp. 147–92.
41 Ibid.
42 Ibid., esp. pp. 147–92.
43 Ibid.
44 Abram Bergson, "Comparative Soviet and American Productivity and Efficiency," in Bergson, *Productivity and the Social System,* pp. 68–90; Bergson, "Index Numbers and Computation of Factor Productivity"; Abram Bergson, "East–West Comparisons and Comparative Economic Systems: A Reply," *Soviet Studies,* October 1971, 282–95.
45 Rosefielde, "Index Numbers and Computation of Factor Productivity."
46 Ibid. See also Steven Rosefielde, Knox Lovell, Slava Danilin, and Ivan Materov, "Normativnye i stokhasticheskie metody izmereniia i kontrolia effektivnosti raboty firmy i predpriiatiia," *Ekonomika matematicheskie metody,* forthcoming, 1981.
47 Bergson, "Notes on the Production Function," p. 124. Bergson has indicated in a private communication that our viewpoints on this question are not far apart.
48 Rosefielde, "The First Great Leap Forward Reconsidered." This problem persists even in the contemporary period. According to information obtained by the CIA from a knowledgeable source, Soviet defense expenditures in 1975 were 40 billion rubles higher than officially acknowledged in the published state budget, a sum that is equivalent to almost 10 percent of Soviet national income (NMP). The budgetary figure was not literally freely invented, but it bears no rational relationship to the concept it is supposed to designate. The declining trend in this nominal figure is even used by the Soviets to prove that they are in compliance with UN Resolution 3093A call-

ing for the developed nations gradually to reduce their defense expenditures by 10 percent. See Robert Leggett and Sheldon Rabin, ''A Note on the Meaning of the Soviet Defense Budget,'' *Soviet Studies*, 30, October 1978, 558, and *Estimated Soviet Defense Spending in Rubles, 1970–75*, CIA, Washington, D.C., May 1976, SR 76-10121U, p. 1. Bergson has noted the problem; see Bergson, *Productivity and the Social System*, p. 24.

49 See Steven Rosefielde, ''Decentralized Economic Control in the Soviet Union and Maoist China: One-Man-Rule Versus Collective Self-management,'' in Rosefielde (ed.), *World Communism at the Crossroads*, Martinus Nijhoff, Boston, 1980. This essay contains a useful bibliography on the subject of Soviet socialism. See also Ernst Mandel, ''Why the Soviet Bureaucracy Is Not a Ruling Class,'' *Monthly Review*, July–August 1979, 63–76; and Paul Sweezy, ''Paul Sweezy Replies to Ernst Mandel,'' *Monthly Review*, July–August 1979, 76–88.

50 For a revealing exchange on this subject, see Philip Hanson, ''East–West Comparisons and Comparative Economic Systems,'' *Soviet Studies*, 22, January 1971; and Bergson's reply, ''East–West Comparisons,'' *Soviet Studies*, 23, October 1971, 282–95.

# 2 Economic growth and structural change in czarist Russia and the Soviet Union: a long-term comparison

*Paul R. Gregory*

## Czarist growth: Soviet growth in historical perspective

Western empirical research on the planned socialist economies was initiated, in large part, by the pioneering work of Abram Bergson and his associates.[1] Bergson's own recalculations of Soviet national income have served as the model for other researchers, who have extended this line of inquiry to Eastern Europe and to China.[2] This empirical work has allowed economists to deal with the issue of the relative efficiency of planned socialism and to define the characteristics of the socialist model of economic development.[3]

To this point it has been difficult, if not impossible, to evaluate Soviet economic development in proper historical perspective, for relatively little is known of the economy that the Bolsheviks inherited from their czarist predecessors in 1917. The extant evaluations of Soviet economic growth and structural change are usually cast in terms of comparisons with the early (pre-Five-Year-Plan) Soviet period or with the historical or cross-sectional growth experiences of capitalist countries. Bergson's own calculations, for example, begin in 1928 on the eve of the First Five Year Plan; Kuznets's evaluation of Soviet growth rests upon comparisons with the industrialized West.[4]

Lacking are comparisons of economic growth and structural change

The author would like to thank the National Science Foundation and the Humboldt Foundation for their support of this research. Much of this research was undertaken at the Institut für osteuropäische Geschichte der Universität Tübingen, Professor Dietrich Geyer, Director. The author is indebted to Simon Kuznets, R. W. Davies, Thomas Mayor, Erich Klinkmüller, Victor Kamendrowsky, and the editor of this volume for their valuable comments.

25

during the Soviet era with the late czarist era. Such comparisons are important for two reasons: The first is the need to determine the long-term growth rate during the late czarist era, in order to establish whether growth accelerated following the initiation of centralized planning. Such an acceleration is critical to the success of the Soviet experiment because an overriding objective of the Soviet leadership has been to speed up economic growth, despite the ensuing costs. A comparison of Soviet and czarist growth rates would be especially useful if it could be demonstrated that czarist Russia had indeed experienced modern economic growth (or the beginnings thereof), let us say at least in the last three decades before World War I. If so, its growth rate could be taken – despite the obvious problems – as a hypothetical indicator of its long-term growth potential if the capitalist system had survived after 1917.

The second issue relates to the evaluation of structural change during the Five Year Plan era. The impact of the imposition of planners' preferences upon resource allocation in the USSR has had to be judged largely in terms of the economic structure that prevailed in 1928 on the eve of the First Five Year Plan. The economic structure of 1928 must therefore be assumed to be representative of resource allocations prevailing during the late capitalist era, yet this is a questionable assumption. By 1928, the Bolsheviks had been in power for more than a decade; cataclysmic political and social upheavals had taken place (the revolution, the redistribution of wealth, the civil war, the experiments of NEP and War Communism). It is therefore risky to assume a close relationship between 1928 and czarist resource allocations. Moreover, several scholars have detected similarities between the resource-allocation policies of czarist authorities after 1880 and those of the Soviet leadership during the plan era[5] – in particular, the depression of peasant living standards, the emphasis on large-scale production units, draconic indirect taxation, and heavy industry biases. Accordingly, the dramatic shifts in economic structure between 1928 and 1940,[6] which so impressed students of this period, may ultimately be judged as a return to earlier resource-allocation practices once more is known about the late czarist era.

*Available evidence*

The evidence that has been available for evaluating the economic growth and structural change of the czarist economy is not particularly well suited for dealing with these issues. The one major study of economic growth is that by Raymond Goldsmith for the period 1860–1913[7] (published 20 years ago), and most contemporary judgments concerning czarist growth rest upon Goldsmith's estimates. An examination of Goldsmith's figures reveals that they consist principally of two indexes – crop production and factory industrial production – sectors that together accounted for less than 50 percent of national income in 1913.[8] To expand these series into a national income index, Goldsmith introduced more casual estimates of the growth (and weights) of several omitted sectors (handicraft, trade, livestock, and transportation), raising his coverage to some 80% of 1913 national income. From this aggregate index, Goldsmith concluded that the volume of total output grew at an annual real rate of about 2.5 percent between 1860 and 1913, which, with an annual rate of growth of population of about 1.6 percent, yields a per capita annual growth rate of below 1 percent. According to Goldsmith's calculations, growth after 1883 was more rapid, with total output increasing at 2.75 percent per year, a per capita rate of 1.25 percent. To these cited figures, Goldsmith adds possible margins of error of some ±0.25 percent.

The only other set of national income estimates, by the Russian emigré S. N. Prokopovich (for the 50 European provinces only),[9] yields even slower growth rates (for the period 1900–13) than those of Goldsmith. Analysts (including this author) who have used the Goldsmith and Prokopovich data have thus concluded that Russian per capita income growth was slow by contemporaneous standards (even after 1880), although total output growth was respectable, and that czarist Russia thus failed to sustain growth of per capita product high enough to initiate modern economic growth.[10]

This judgment appeared to be confirmed by the slow pace of structural change, with only minimal declines (rises) in the agricultural (industrial) labor force and product shares between 1860 and 1913. It should be noted, for the record, however, that these findings are based upon quite crude and often unreliable data – on the sparse data on labor force distributions and on imputed value-added weights of major economic sectors. On the end-use side, virtually no information was available until recently for the evaluation of investment and consumption proportions.[11]

In any case, this rather pessimistic picture of czarist growth and development was supportive of the conventional view of Russian economic history, promulgated in large part by Alexander Gerschenkron.[12] Despite the rapid growth of factory industry (after 1885) and railroad construction, both promoted by the efforts of the state, overall Russian economic development was unsatisfactory. Failure at the aggregate level was largely the consequence of restrictive agrarian policies, in particular the decisions to retain communal agriculture and to retard the free flow of labor from the countryside to the city. These factors exhausted the tax-paying power of the peasantry, slowed the growth of industry, and resulted in the political unrest of 1905.

*A reevaluation of czarist growth*

Since the Goldsmith study, sufficient new information has become available for a reevaluation of economic growth and structural change during the late czarist era. I have been working for the past few years on a study of Russian national income from the mid-1880s to 1913. The choice of the mid-1880s as a starting point was dictated by two considerations: first, data limitations make it virtually impossible to extend national income estimates back beyond 1883, the approximate date of the upsurge in the rate of growth of factory industrial production; and second, the Russian rail network would not have been adequate prior to the 1880s to support modern economic growth.

I thus observe Russian growth during that time span most likely to yield modern economic growth in Russia. If I were to deal, like Goldsmith, with the entire postemancipation era (after 1861), I believe the outcome would be much the same as that found by Goldsmith – relatively slow growth of output per capita by international and Soviet standards.

Several factors have encouraged me to reopen this issue. The first is that a great deal of research, by both Western and Soviet scholars, has been completed since the Goldsmith study, covering various aspects of the Russian national accounts. Malcolm Falkus has reestimated Prokopovich's 1913 sector-of-origin figures to yield more reliable 1913 value-added weights for Russian national income.[13] A. L. Vainshtein published a major (and outstanding scholarly) work on Russian capital stock for the years 1911–13;[14] Arcadius Kahan has recently published estimates of Russian capital stock for the period 1890–1914,[15] and much valuable research on agricultural marketings has been done by Steve Wheatcroft and R. W. Davies.[16]

Moreover, contrary to the widespread conception of the limited quality and quantity of czarist statistics, I have come to the conclusion that the primary statistical series published by the czarist statistical authorities provide a wealth of raw data, often in need of correction and adjustment, to support a major reevaluation of the Russian national accounts. Probably the best official data are those on government spending, exports and imports, and transportation, but valuable data can be obtained on retail sales, medical expenditures, domestic servants, industrial inventories, and livestock. Furthermore, massive information on prices is available, especially prices of agricultural products and of basic industrial materials, and various organizations and individuals compiled indexes of retail and wholesale prices for the late czarist period. Intertemporal wage series are also available in surprising variety, with detailed reportings of the earnings of railroad workers, farm laborers, and workers subject to factory inspection. Statistical authorities paid considerable attention to agricultural output and peasant consumption patterns.

In sum, I would like to emphasize my view that the Russian statistical raw material is of sufficient quantity and quality to permit a reopening of the whole issue of czarist growth. I suggest that the appropriate yardstick for evaluating this conclusion is the relative reliability of other historical national income series. Although I cannot definitively establish this contention, I believe that the resulting historical series for czarist Russia is generally as reliable as those of the major European countries.

*Estimates of Russian national income: industrial origin*

Given the space limitations set for this essay, I cannot provide a detailed description of my estimates of Russian national income. At best, I can focus on some of the highlights and the important assumptions underlying these estimates. First, I should note that I proceed, for the sake of caution, with two independent estimates of national income, one by sector of origin, the other by end use. Thus, one series can serve as a check on the other. The first set of estimates is a sector-of-origin series, which uses Falkus's 1913 value added weights, extended to incorporate sectors (government, personal services, housing, utilities) omitted by Falkus's (and Prokopovich's) restrictive "material product" definition of national income. The addition of these service categories raises Falkus's 1913 national income estimate by 10 percent, from about 18,500 million rubles to 20,175 million rubles.

The derivation of these new national income estimates by sector of origin is described in the notes to Table 1. The most important finding is a higher growth rate than that of Goldsmith for the same period. I find the 1883–7 to 1909–13 growth rate to be 3.3 percent per annum as compared to Goldsmith's 2.75 percent. This rate is 20 percent higher than Goldsmith's and falls outside the ±0.25 percent error range suggested by Goldsmith.

A few words are called for to explain why this calculated growth rate is higher than that of Goldsmith. There are three reasons. The first is that the growth rates of omitted service sectors (including a slightly different estimate for trade), which accounted for about 20 percent of 1913 national income, are much higher than Goldsmith's. Second, my calculated growth rate of livestock production is substantially higher than Goldsmith's figure.[17] Third, and most important, I calculate the growth rate of grain production at 3.3 percent annually, as compared with Goldsmith's rate of 2.5 percent. As grain production accounted for some one-third of 1913 national income, this difference alone will yield an annual growth rate $\frac{1}{3}$ of 1 percent higher than Goldsmith's. Although Goldsmith is not too specific about his method of calculating grain production, it appears that he em-

**Table 1.** *Russian national income by sector of origin, 1883–7 to 1909–13 (1913 value-added weights)*

| | 1883–7 | 1898–1902 | 1909–13 | 1913 value added (1913 rubles) Million rubles | Per-cent |
|---|---|---|---|---|---|
| **Panel A: Indexes of sector growth** | | | | | |
| 1. Agriculture (including forestry and fishing) | 49 | 73 | 100 | 10,294 | 50.7 |
| 2. Industry, factory | 28 | 69 | 100 | 3,023 | 14.9 |
| 3. Industry, handicraft | 42 | 78 | 100 | 1,311 | 6.5 |
| 4. Transport, communication | 17 | 54 | 100 | 1,173 | 5.8 |
| 5. Construction | 43 | 71 | 100 | 1,035 | 5.1 |
| 6. Trade | 53 | 81 | 100 | 1,640 | 8.1 |
| 7. Net government product | 33 | 58 | 100 | 565 | 2.8 |
| 8. Net housing product | 52 | 71 | 100 | 743 | 3.7 |
| 9. Personal medical services | 37 | 69 | 100 | 126 | 0.6 |
| 10. Domestic service | 78 | 81 | 100 | 264 | 1.3 |
| 11. Utilities | 60 | 69 | 100 | 118 | 0.6 |
| National Income | 43.2 | 71.3 | 100 | 20,292 | 100 |
| **Panel B: Structure of national income, 1913 prices** | | | | | |
| 1. Agriculture | 57.4 | 51.7 | 50.7 | | |
| 2. Industry, construction, transportation, and communication | 23.4 | 30.8 | 32.3 | | |
| 3. Trade | 10.0 ⎫ 19.2 | 9.2 ⎫ 17.5 | 8.1 ⎫ 17.1 | | |
| 4. Service | 9.2 ⎭ | 8.3 ⎭ | 9.0 ⎭ | | |

**Panel C: Annual growth rates, national income, 1913 prices**

1883–7 to 1909–13    3.3
1883–7 to 1898–1902    3.4
1898–1902 to 1909–13    3.1

*Sources: 1913 value-added weights:* Rows 1–6: M. E. Falkus, "Russia's National Income, 1913: A Revaluation," *Economica*, NS 35, 137 (February 1968), 55. Rows 7, 8, 10, 11: Paul Gregory, statistical appendix to the articles: "1913 Russian National Income – Some Insights into Russian Economic Development," *Quarterly Journal of Economics*, 90, 3 (August 1976), 445–60. Row 9 is the estimated annual 1913 earnings of physicians and paramedical personnel from my unpublished study "*Russian National Income, 1885 to 1913*" (mimeographed, 1979). This figure is calculated from the number of physicians, nurses, and feldshers multiplied by their estimated 1913 average earnings.

*Sectoral growth indexes: Agriculture:* Individual indexes of technical crop production, livestock production, and grain production are aggregated using the value-added weights of Falkus, "Russia's National Income, 1913," p. 64. For grains, I include major grains (wheat, rye, barley, oats, and potatoes), which accounted for 88 percent of nontechnical crop production in 1913. Omitted minor grains and vegetables are assumed to grow at the same rate as major grains. The technical crop index is that used by Raymond Goldsmith in his article, "The Economic Growth of Tsarist Russia, 1860–1913," *Economic Development and Cultural Change*, 9, 3 (April 1961), 448–50. Prior to 1895, an index for the 50 European provinces is used. The net grain production data are taken from the following sources: *Bulletin russe de statistique financière et de législation*, 5th ed., 1898, pp. 222–31 (which cites estimates by M. E. Kuhn). The remaining figures are from *Ezhegodnik ministerstva finansov*, 1905 ed., pp. 494–97 and from *Statisticheskii ezhegodnik Rossii*, annual editions 1904 to 1913. Appropriate territorial adjustments are made in the pre-1897 figures, which cover the 50 European provinces and the Polish provinces. 1913 prices are used to weight the individual crop figures. A complete description of the grain series can be found in my paper, "Grain Marketings and Peasant Consumption, Russia, 1885 to 1913," *Explorations in Economic History*, 17, 1980, 135–64.

ployed *gross* output figures weighted by average grain prices near the turn of the century. For lack of better data, he used a series for the 50 provinces alone (which accounted for 78 percent of empire wheat production, 90 percent of rye production, and 82 percent of barley production in 1895) to calculate the growth of grain production prior to 1895. Empire grain production grew at a slightly more rapid rate than production in the 50 provinces throughout the period.

Moreover, my grain production figures are based (prior to 1898) on net

### Notes to Table 1 (*cont.*)

*Industry, factory:* Goldsmith, "Economic Growth," pp. 463–7 (1908 base, imputed weights).

*Industry, handicraft:* I use here the same assumption as Goldsmith, based upon earlier studies by S. G. Strumilin, that handicraft production grew at two-thirds the rate of factory production.

*Transportation and communication:* This is a physical index of freight and passenger rail hauls (tons/km and passengers/km, where the cost of transporting 1 ton/km of freight is roughly equivalent to 1 passenger/km). The series is cited in S. G. Strumilin, *Statistika i ekonomika* (Moscow: Nauka, 1963), p. 409, and is drawn from the *Statisticheskii sbornik Ministerstva putei soobshcheniia* series. A separate series for communications is not derived (weight 0.6 percent of national income), but series on numbers of letters, packages, and telegrams from various official publications suggest similar but slightly slower rates of growth of communications.

*Construction:* No information is available on the output of the construction sector. After consulting the long-term statistics of other countries on national income shares of construction, primarily Simon Kuznets, *Economic Growth of Nations* (Cambridge, Mass.: Harvard University Press, 1971), pp. 144–62, I concluded that the assumption of no change in the national income share of construction would be reasonable. Thus, the growth rate of construction is computed so as to maintain a constant construction share.

*Trade:* The value-added series of the trade sector is a weighted index of employment in wholesale and retail trade from Strumilin, *Statistika i ekonomica*, p. 436, and a deflated index of capital stock in trade establishments (also from Strumilin, p. 441). The price deflator is Podtiagin's index of retail prices cited in Strumilin's *Ocherki ekonomicheskoi istorii Rossii i SSSR* (Moscow: Nauka, 1966), p. 89. The labor weight is calculated to be 85 percent of the total by multiplying 1913 trade employment by the 1913 average industrial wage of 250 rubles.

*Net government product:* This is a constant price series of government expenditures for final goods and services at the imperial and local level. A lengthy discussion would be required to describe the derivation of this series, which is drawn from official budgetary data and wage and price deflators. The reader is referred to the author's unpublished study "Russian National Income, 1885 to 1913," apps. 5 and 6.

*Net housing product:* This series is based upon Arcadius Kahan's series on residential capital stock in constant prices cited in Arcadius Kahan, "The Growth of Capital during the Early Period of Industrialization in Russia," *Cambridge Economic History of Europe* (Cambridge: Cambridge University Press, 1978), statistical appendix.

*Personal medical services:* The index is based upon the number of physicians, nurses, and feldshers in the Russian Empire, where rough earnings weights are used to aggregate the three series. The raw data are drawn from *Statisticheskii ezhegodnik Rossii*, annual series 1904–14, and from *Sbornik svedenii po Rossii*, 1884–5, 1890, and 1896 eds., section heading: *Organizatsiia vrachebnoi pomoshchi*.

*Domestic service:* Domestic service employment is calculated by applying the combined Moscow–Petersburg ratios of domestic servants to population to the urban population of the 50 European provinces to obtain an index of service employment. Annual service employment is calculated by applying this index to Rashin's figure on service employment in 1913 (1.55 million), cited in Gregory, "1913 Russian National Income," statistical appendix. The figures on Moscow–Petersburg service employment are from A. G. Rashin, *Naselenie Rossii za 100 let* (Moscow: Gosstatizdat, 1956), pp. 114, 115, 323–5. The urban population series is from V. Zaitsev and V. G. Groman (eds.), *Vliianie neurozhaev na narodnoe khoziaistvo Rossii,* Part II, 1927, p. 65. The approximate ratios of domestic servants to urban population are: 1885–90, 11%; 1894 and 1896, 10%; 1900, 8.5%; 1903, 8.3%; 1907, 8%; 1910, 7.9%; 1913, 7.7%. These ratios are rough and involve interpolations between benchmarks, but one would imagine that changes in the ratios would be relatively slow and orderly.

*Utility expenditures:* This series has been derived laboriously from data on utility capital stock and expenditures of municipally owned utilities. Its derivation cannot be described briefly, so the reader is again referred to the author's study of Russian national income, app. 3. This is likely the most unreliable series in Table 1, but its weight is only 0.6 percent.

Table 2. *Average annual net national product by end use, Russia, 1885–9 to 1909–13 (1913 prices)*

|  | Net national product | Personal consumption expenditures | Government expenditures | Net domestic investment | Net foreign investment |
|---|---|---|---|---|---|
| *Panel A: Millions of rubles, 1913 prices* | | | | | |
| 1885–9 | 8,477 | 7,078 | 690 | 686 | 23 |
| 1909–13 | 18,228 | 14,502 | 1,765 | 2,214 | −254 |
| *Panel B: Shares of NNP, 1913 prices* | | | | | |
| 1885–9 | 100 | 83.5 | 8.1 | 8.1 | .3 |
| 1909–13 | 100 | 79.6 | 9.7 | 12.1 | −1.5 |
| *Panel C: Average annual growth rates (%)* | | | | | |
| 1885–9 to 1909–13 | 3.25 | 3.05 | 4.05 | 5.0 | — |

production figures for 63 provinces, prepared within the Ministry of Interior by M. E. Kuhn,[18] a contemporary authority on grain statistics. I then link the Kuhn series to net production figures after 1898 cited in various official statistical publications. The ratios of net to gross grain output increased by some 10 percent between 1885–90 and 1909–13, and my use of net output accounts for much of the growth rate differential.[19]

For other sectors, such as factory production and handicraft, I accept Goldsmith's indexes and assumptions, so differences in growth rates of industrial production cannot explain the divergence between the two calculated national income growth rates. Thus, the most important difference between my series and that of Goldsmith is a much higher growth rate of grain production, which accounts for over 50 percent of the difference in aggregate growth rates. The more favorable performance of agriculture than that admitted by Goldsmith is an important finding, for it suggests a more viable agriculture than that generally assumed.

### Russian national income by end use

I test the finding that Goldsmith's study understates the growth of Russian national income by constructing an alternative series by end use. It is not possible within reasonable space limitations to describe the estimation of consumption expenditures, final government expenditures, net domestic investment, and net foreign investment,[20] but I refer the reader to three specialized papers that describe most of these calculations.[21] The methodology is purposely patterned after that of Bergson's *Real National Income of Soviet Russia* to ensure comparability with his Soviet period estimates.

In Table 2, I provide average annual figures from 1885–9 and 1909–13 for NNP, personal consumption, final government expenditures, and net domestic and net foreign investment. I use 5-year averages to smooth out the considerable fluctuations in the annual series. In panel B, NNP shares are given, and in panel C, annual growth rates are given. The alternate NNP end-use series strongly supports my conclusion that Goldsmith understated the growth of Russian national income. In fact, the end-use growth rate is virtually identical to that calculated in Table 1 (3.25 versus 3.3 percent per annum).

One further piece of corroborating evidence can be added: Falkus has revised the Prokopovich figures for 1900 and 1913 and finds an annual growth rate between the two benchmarks of 3.1 percent.[22] In the end-use series, the 1900–13 NNP growth rate is 3.3 percent, only slightly higher than the Falkus estimate. The available evidence thus suggests an annual growth rate of net output of circa 3.3 percent, which combined with an annual growth rate of population of 1.6 percent yields a per capita growth rate of circa 1.7 percent per annum. I agree with Goldsmith's finding that growth between 1860 and the 1880s was much slower (perhaps $\frac{1}{2}$ of 1 percent per annum per capita), but I would regard this slower rate as more indicative of premodern growth in Russia.[23]

This finding of more rapid growth of total product and of product per capita questions the traditional interpretation of Russian economic development. This analysis suggests a much more viable peasantry, a freer flow of labor from the countryside to the city, and places less emphasis on the institutional constraints retarding development than does that of Gerschenkron.

## A comparative appraisal of Russian growth prior to World War I

In the preceding section, I presented evidence that economic growth during the late czarist period was understated and, further, that the emphasis on the entire 1860–1913 era has caused too pessimistic a picture of czarist growth to emerge. It remains to evaluate czarist growth after 1880 in the perspective of the growth performance of the major industrialized countries from the second half of the nineteenth to the early twentieth century. Summary data on average growth rates are presented in Table 3 together with "high-period" rates (see the notes to Table 3) prior to World War II. These growth figures are typically in "late"-year prices.

An examination of Table 3 indicates that the Russian growth rate of total product compared quite favorably with the *average* long-term rates of the industrialized countries between 1850 and 1914. In fact, Russian growth was equaled or surpassed only by that of the United States, Canada, Australia, and Sweden, and it exceeded the growth of the two most important "follower" countries (Japan, Italy) prior to World War I. With the exception of Sweden, Russian growth of total product was simi-

**Table 3.** *Average and high-period* (*HP*) *growth rates of output, population, labor force, output per capita and per worker, incremental capital–output ratios, late nineteenth and early twentieth centuries, Russia and industrialized countries* (*percent per annum*)

| | (A) Total product | (B) Population | (C) Labor force | (D) Per capita product | (E) Product per worker | (F) Incremental net capital/output ratio |
|---|---|---|---|---|---|---|
| 1. Russia (1883–5 to 1909–13) | 3.3 | 1.6 | 1.65 | 1.7 | 1.65 | 3.1 |
| 2. Great Britain (1855–64 to 1920–4) | 2.1 | 1.0 | 0.8 | 1.1 | 1.3 | 3.3 |
| HP: 1870–4 to 1890–9 | 3.0 | 1.2 | 0.8 | 1.8 | 2.2 | — |
| 3. France (1860–70 to 1891–1900) | 1.5 | 0.2 | 0.7 | 1.3 | 0.8 | — |
| 4. Netherlands (1860–70 to 1900–10) | 2.1 | 1.15 | 0.6 | 0.95 | 1.5 | — |
| 5. Germany (1850–9 to 1910–13) | 2.6 | 1.1 | 1.25 | 1.5 | 1.35 | 4.8 |
| HP: 1886–95 to 1911–13 | 2.9 | 1.1 | 1.7 | 1.8 | 1.2 | — |
| 6. U.S. (1880–9 to 1910–14) | 3.5 | 1.9 | 1.7 | 1.6 | 1.9 | 3.1 |
| HP: 1869–78 to 1884–93 | 5.5 | 2.3 | 2.8 | 3.2 | 2.7 | — |
| 7. Canada (1870–4 to 1920–4) | 3.3 | 1.7 | 1.9 | 1.6 | 1.4 | 3.0 |
| HP: 1891–1900 to 1911–20 | 4.0 | 1.6 | 2.4 | 2.4 | 1.6 | — |
| 8. Australia (1861–9 to 1900–4) | 3.4 | 2.85 | — | 0.55 | — | 2.9 |
| HP: 1861–5 to 1876–85 | 4.0 | — | 3.2 | — | 0.8 | — |
| 9. Japan (1970 to 1913) | 2.7 | 1.0 | — | 1.7 | — | 1.6 |
| HP: 1920–4 to 1938–42 | 5.1 | — | — | — | — | — |
| 10. Belgium (1870 to 1913) | 2.7 | 0.95 | 0.9 | 1.75 | 1.8 | — |
| 11. Norway (1870 to 1913) | 2.8 | 0.8 | 0.5 | 2.0 | 2.3 | 4.0 |
| HP: 1915–24 to 1939 | 3.2 | 0.7 | — | 2.5 | — | — |
| 12. Sweden (1870 to 1913) | 3.75 | 0.7 | 0.7 | 3.05 | 3.05 | 2.6 |
| HP: 1926–35 to 1948–52 | 4.2 | 0.7 | 0.3 | 3.5 | 3.9 | — |
| 13. Italy (1870 to 1913) | 1.45 | 0.65 | 0.35 | 0.8 | 1.1 | — |
| HP: 1920–3 to 1938–40 | 2.4 | 1.1 | 0.1 | 1.3 | 2.3 | — |
| 14. Denmark (1870 to 1913) | 3.2 | 1.1 | 0.9 | 2.1 | 2.3 | 2.4 |
| HP: 1890–9 to 1914 | 3.7 | 1.1 | 1.2 | 2.6 | 2.5 | — |

*Note:* Dash denotes data not available.

*Sources:* Simon Kuznets, *Economic Growth of Nations* (Cambridge, Mass.: Harvard University Press, 1971), pp. 11–19; Angus Madison, *Economic Growth in Japan and the USSR* (New York: Norton, 1969), table B-1, app. c; Kuznets, "A Comparative Appraisal," in Abram Bergson and Simon Kuznets (eds.), *Economic Trends in the Soviet Union* (Cambridge, Mass.: Harvard University Press, 1963), pp. 338–9; *Historical Statistics of the United States, Colonial Times to 1970,* Part I, chapts. A, B.

The HP (high-period) figures are from Kuznets, *Economic Trends.* Kuznets defines the high-period rate as the "one period among several distinguished (usually about 20 years in duration . . .) with the highest rate of growth in total product" (p. 339). Kuznets excludes the generally higher growth rates after World War II from this calculation. The approximate HP population growth rates (corresponding to the HP growth time periods) are from B. R. Mitchell, *European Historical Statistics, 1750–1970* (New York: Columbia University Press, 1976), table B1. Labor force figures not supplied by Kuznets are taken from Mitchell, table C1. Often the periods do not coincide exactly with the product and population data, but resulting errors should be minor. The incremental capital/output ratios are from Kuznets, "A Comparative Appraisal" (p. 354), and are calculated by dividing the average ratio of net investment to NNP by the growth rate of NNP. The Russian figures are calculated from Tables 1 and 2 of this chapter.

lar to that of the European offshoots in North America and Australia, countries that experienced rapid population growth through in-migration and high rates of natural increase. In the Russian case, however, this rapid population growth was entirely the consequence of high rates of natural increase.

Thus, it follows that the high (by international standards) Russian growth of total product was, in part, the consequence of rapid population (and thus labor force) growth. However, on a per capita and per worker basis (columns D and E), Russian growth is still quite respectable by the same international standards, surpassed or equaled only by Belgium, Norway, Japan, Sweden, and Denmark.

One must be cautious about the interpretation of the labor force growth figures (column C) and the resulting output per worker growth rates (column E) because of conceptual and statistical differences in the measurement of labor force among nations, particularly in the treatment of farm employment of females. No adjustment can be made for differences in hours worked per employed person, which probably fell during this time span. The Russian figures are themselves suspect, with agricultural employment assumed to grow at the same rate as agricultural population, and the data on the substantial employment in handicraft are unreliable. Moreover, the part-time employment of agricultural workers in handicraft presents enormous difficulties. Similar weaknesses can be found in the labor force statistics of other countries.

A comparison of the labor force and population growth rates fails to reveal a consistent pattern. In some countries, measured labor force growth exceeded measured population growth, in others it fell below, but only in the Italian and Dutch cases are population and labor force growth rate discrepancies substantial. From this, I conclude (together with Kuznets)[24] that, as a general rule, population and labor force grew at roughly equivalent rates during this period and that the long-term growth rates of product per worker should, on the average, roughly equal those of product per capita. This is what Table 3 suggests when the countries are averaged.

Incremental net capital/output ratios are provided in column F and are calculated by dividing the average ratio of net investment to NNP by the annual growth rate of NNP. International comparisons suggest that capital productivity (measured in marginal terms) in Russia was average as judged by the experiences of the other countries in the sample. The exceptional cases appear to be Japan, with a very low, and Germany, with a very high incremental capital/output ratio.

I shall not go through a detailed comparison of high-period (HP) growth rates (some of which date to the period after 1914), but the surprising finding from the HP comparisons is that Russian growth performance remains about average when compared with the HP rates of the other countries in the sample. Russia still grows as fast or faster than the HP rates in Great Britain, Germany, Norway, and Italy, but notably slower than those countries, such as the United States, Canada, Australia, Japan, Sweden, and Denmark, that experienced short periods of exceptionally rapid growth.

The reader should not think that all the growth rate differences noted in Table 3 are significant in a statistical sense. They are based upon different total product concepts (NNP, national income, GNP, GDP), and the labor force statistics are especially unreliable. Nevertheless, I believe the conclusion is warranted that after 1883 the Russian empire grew at total per capita and per worker rates that were *at least* "average" relative to those of other major industrialized and industrializing countries. Surprisingly, this statement would remain valid for NNP even if the lower Goldsmith figure after 1883 were accepted. From this evidence alone, I would further conclude that Russia had begun to experience modern economic growth after 1883, albeit this experience was cut short after 30 years by World War I.

Another means of establishing whether Russia was indeed experiencing the initial stages of modern economic growth after 1883 is to compare the course of structural change in Russia with that of the now-industrialized countries during the first 30 years of their own modern economic growth. Kuznets has attempted to estimate the approximate dates of the initiation of modern economic growth in these countries as well as per capita income at that date,[25] and these figures (which one must regard as illustrative only) are given in Table 4. From additional data supplied by Kuznets, the approximate share changes of the major sectors (agriculture, industry, and services) during the first 30 years of modern economic growth can be calculated, which I then compare with the Russian share changes between 1885 and 1913. I should emphasize the crude nature of these figures; some are in constant, others in current prices; some are shares of GNP, others of national income; and so on. Moreover, rough adjustments have to be made to achieve comparable sector definitions. General conclusions can, however, be drawn despite these shortcomings.

Russia began modern economic growth with a relatively high (low) share of agriculture (industry), much like Japan. Unlike other countries beginning modern economic growth with high agricultural (low industrial) shares, such as Japan, the United Kingdom, Denmark, Italy, the United States, and Canada, the decline in the A share (the rise in the I share) was more gradual in the Russian case. In this respect, Russia parallels the French experience. Nevertheless, the amount of structural change, as measured by the changes in the Russian A and I shares between 1885 and 1913, was average or slightly below average when compared to that of

Table 4. *Structural change at beginning of modern economic growth, first 30 years, Russia and other countries (shares in national product, %)*

| | Initial date of modern economic growth | National income, 1965 dollars at initial date | Agriculture | | | Industry | | | Services | | |
|---|---|---|---|---|---|---|---|---|---|---|---|
| | | | Initial date | Initial date + 30 years | Change | Initial date | Initial date + 30 years | Change | Initial date | Initial date + 30 years | Change |
| 1. Russia | 1883–5 | 260 | 57 | 51 | −6 | 24 | 32 | +8 | 20 | 17 | −3 |
| 2. U.K. | 1765–85 | 227 | 45 | 32 | −13 | 35 | 40 | +5 | 20 | 28 | +8 |
| 3. France | 1831–40 | 242 | 50 | 45 | −5 | 32 | 35 | +3 | 18 | 20 | +2 |
| 4. Germany | 1850–9 | 302 | 32 | 23 | −9 | 33 | 43 | +10 | 35 | 34 | −1 |
| 5. Netherlands | 1865 | 492 | 25 | 20 | −5 | — | — | — | — | — | — |
| 6. Denmark | 1865–9 | 370 | 47 | 29 | −18 | — | — | — | — | — | — |
| 7. Norway | 1865–9 | 287 | 34 | 27 | −7 | 32 | 35 | +3 | 34 | 37 | +3 |
| 8. Sweden | 1861–9 | 215 | 39 | 36 | −3 | 17 | 33 | +16 | 44 | 31 | −13 |
| 9. Italy | 1895–9 | 271 | 47 | 36 | −11 | 20 | 21 | +1 | 25 | 28 | +3 |
| 10. Japan | 1874–9 | 74 | 63 | 39 | −24 | 16 | 31 | +15 | 21 | 31 | +10 |
| 11. U.S. | 1834–43 | 474 | 45 | 30 | −14 | 24 | 39 | +15 | 31 | 31 | 0 |
| 12. Canada | 1870–4 | 508 | 50 | 36 | −14 | 31 | 36 | +5 | 19 | 28 | +9 |
| 13. Australia | 1861–9 | 760 | 18 | 21 | +3 | 31 | 30 | −1 | 51 | 48 | −3 |

*Notes:* Generally, the time spans covered by the Kuznets data exceed 30 years. In such cases, the percentage changes are apportioned by the factor 30 ÷ number of years covered. —, data not available.

*Sources:* Simon Kuznets, *Modern Economic Growth* (New Haven: Yale University Press, 1966), pp. 88–93, 131–2; *Economic Growth of Nations* (Cambridge, Mass.: Harvard University Press, 1971), pp. 24, 144–51.

other countries. Russia, like the United Kingdom, France, Japan, and Canada, appeared to enter modern economic growth with a low share of services, but it is difficult to establish the reliability of this finding, owing to the varying coverage of services in the cited statistics.

Similar statistics could be cited for changes in the consumption, investment, and government shares of total product, but a casual comparison of the Russian data (Table 2) with that of Kuznets indicates that the Russian 1885–1913 experience was generally similar to that of other countries during the early stages of modern growth. Comparative statistics on labor force shares are not cited due to the unreliability of the Russian data; thus, conclusions concerning the pattern of relative sector productivities cannot be drawn.

In sum, the pattern of structural change in Russia between 1885 and 1913 does not appear to differ substantially from that of other countries during the first phases of modern economic growth. The only possible feature that can be singled out in the Russian case is the relatively slow pace of the decline of the agriculture share of product vis-à-vis those countries that began modern economic growth with relatively high agricultural shares. The one country that does appear to differ substantially from others is Japan, a low-income country that compressed substantial structural change into a short period of time during the early stages of modern economic growth.

### Russian and Soviet growth and structural change: a comparative appraisal

In Table 5, I supply data on economic growth and structural change from the late czarist period to 1975, omitting the turbulent transitional period from World War I to the First Five Year Plan (1914–28) and World War II and its immediate aftermath (1940–50). I should note that I rely on one set of estimates for the Soviet postwar period and that alternate calculations, especially for industry, yield slightly different rates.[26] Nevertheless, these differences are relatively small at the aggregate level, and my overall conclusions would not be altered by the use of different calculations.

Turning first to the growth rate figures in panel B, I find that growth of total product and of product per capita was substantially higher during the half-century after 1928 than during the last 30 years of czarism. The approximate ratio of the 1928–75 annual growth rates of total product and product per capita to the corresponding 1883–7 to 1909–13 figures are 1.55 and 2.25, respectively. Thus, growth of total product after 1928 accelerated to a rate 55 percent higher than that of the late czarist era, while growth of product per capita accelerated to an even more rapid rate because of the marked reduction in population growth after 1928 (the latter

Table 5. *Comparative statistics: economic growth and structural change, Russian and Soviet period*

| A. *Structural comparisons:* | 1883–7 | 1909–13 | 1928 | 1937 | 1955 | 1958 | 1975 |
|---|---|---|---|---|---|---|---|
| | | 1913 Prices | 1937 Prices | | | | |
| **1. Sector shares of NNP(%)** | | | | | | | |
| Agriculture | 57 | 51 | 49 | 31 | | 22 | 19 |
| Industry | 24 | 32 | 28 | 45 | | 58 | 62 |
| Services | 20 | 17 | 23 | 24 | | 20 | 19 |
| | | 1913 Prices | 1937 Prices | | | 1970 Prices | |
| **2. End-use shares of NNP(%)** | | | | | | | |
| Consumption | 83.5 | 79.5 | 82 | 55 | 52 | | 51 |
| Government (including communal consumption) | 8 | 10 | 8 | 22 | 26 | | 22 |
| Net domestic investment | 8 | 12 | 10 | 23 | 22 | | 27 |
| Net foreign investment | 0.3 | −1.5 | 0 | 0 | 0 | | 0 |
| | | Current prices | | | | | |
| **3. Foreign trade proportions, (exports + imports ÷ NNP)** | 17 | 15 | 6.2 | 1 | | 5.2 | — |

| B. *Growth comparisons:* | 1883–5 to 1909–13 | 1928–40 | 1950–75 | 1950–60 | 1960–75 |
|---|---|---|---|---|---|
| | 1913 Prices | 1937 Prices | 1970 Prices | | |
| **1.** Annual growth, total product | 3.3 | 5.1 | 5.2 | 5.9 | 4.6 |
| Annual growth, product per capita | 1.7 | 3.9 | 3.8 | 4.3 | 3.5 |
| Annual growth, product per worker | 1.65 | 1.4 | 3.9 | 4.8 | 3.1 |
| **2.** Incremental capital/output ratios (net) | 3.1 | 2.8 | 4.6 | 3.7 | 5.0 |

*Sources: Panel A:* Tables 2 and 3 for 1885 and 1913. For the Soviet period, sector shares are calculated from data cited by Simon Kuznets, in Abram Bergson and Simon Kuznets (eds.), *Economic Trends in the Soviet Union* (Cambridge, Mass.: Harvard University Press, 1963), table VIII.5 (Bergson approximation, 1937 ruble factor cost) and from the sector growth indexes in Rush Greenslade, "The Real Gross National Product of the USSR, 1950–1975," in Joint Economic Committee, *Soviet Economy in a New Perspective* (Washington, D.C.: U.S. Government Printing Office, 1976), p. 271. In using the Greenslade indexes, I assume that NNP and GNP grew at the same rate. The end-use shares are calculated from Abram Bergson, *The Real National Income of Soviet Russia since 1928* (Cambridge, Mass.: Harvard University Press, 1961), p. 128 (ruble factor cost of 1937) and from Bergson's paper in Bergson and Kuznets, *Economic Trends.* The 1975 shares are approximated from Greenslade, "Real Gross National Product," pp. 275–7 by applying one-half of capital repairs to depreciation and applying Abraham Becker's 1965 share of depreciation to GNP to 1975 GNP from Abraham Becker, *Soviet National Income, 1958–1964* (Berkeley, Calif.: University of California Press, 1969), table 5. The Russian foreign trade proportions are in current prices and are from the author's unpublished study of Russian national income. The other trade proportions are from the Holzman article in Bergson and Kuznets, *Economic Trends,* p. 290 (I assume exports balance imports).

*Panel B:* For the Soviet period, the growth figures are from Bergson, in Bergson and Kuznets, *Economic Trends,* pp. 36–7 and from Greenslade, "Real Gross National Product," p. 275. For the period 1950–75, I assume equivalent rates of growth of NNP and GNP. This assumption probably causes a slight overstatement of NNP growth. The incremental capital/output ratios are calculated by dividing the average ratio of net investment to NNP by the growth rate of NNP.

due to declining rates of natural increase, wartime losses, losses during the 1930s, etc.).

The growth rates of product per worker suggest a slight decline during the early years of centralized planning (although the difference may not be statistically significant) and then an increase after World War II to rates well above the historical czarist standard. The incremental capital/output ratio movements suggest the reverse phenomenon: Capital/output ratios may have declined somewhat during the early years of centralized planning (although this decline may again not be statistically significant) and then rose after 1950 well above the czarist ratio and above the historical and post–World War II ratios of the industrialized countries. The better performance of labor than capital productivity in the Soviet era is a likely consequence of the large differential between capital and labor growth rates which has caused diminishing returns to capital.[27]

An important point should be noted at this juncture, and that is that the choice of price weights has a substantial effect on calculated Soviet growth between 1928 and 1940. If constant prices of 1928 are used, the 1928–37 growth rate is 11 percent per annum; in 1950 prices, the corresponding rate is 4.5 percent.[28] This is the well-documented phenomenon of index number relativity,[29] which is especially prominent in the Soviet case, where dramatic structural transformations in sector shares occurred during the early 1930s. In general, one has come to expect higher rates of growth when "preindustrialization" prices are used, and this makes the comparison of growth rates of countries at different stages of development a difficult undertaking.

The index number phenomenon raises serious questions about the comparability of the czarist growth rate figures (weighted in 1913 prices) with those of the Soviet period weighted in "postindustrialization" prices. Would it not be more suitable to compare the czarist growth rates with the much higher 1928 price-weighted Soviet figures?

This is an especially thorny question, for the magnitude of growth acceleration under Soviet central planning hinges upon the choice of price weights. It could be argued philosophically that both the czarist and Soviet periods should be evaluated in the "late" prices of each period. The late-year index will measure the increasing capacity of the economy to produce the late-year output mix, and the czarist economy was producing an output mix in 1913 dictated by market forces, whereas the Soviet economy in a "late" year was producing the output mix dictated by political authorities. Thus, the use of late prices for each era allows one to evaluate growth performance in terms of the goals set separately by each society and does not require imposing the preferences of one society on the other. It is largely for this reason that I believe it more appropriate to use late-year prices from each period.

One cannot assess fully the impact of this choice without knowing the relative price structures of the "late" czarist era and the "early" and "late" Soviet eras. A stylized version of price history can, however, be drawn. According to most accounts,[30] the NEP period (1921–8) witnessed a substantial increase in the relative price of capital, as the priorities shifted in the direction of heavy industry (without an outward shift in production possibilities) and thus created a "capital replacement crisis." This trend was reversed dramatically during the early Five Year Plan era, when investment and labor were channeled almost exclusively into the capital goods industry. The ensuing economies of mass production caused a substantial decline in the relative cost of capital.

If this stylized version is to be believed, the use of "late" czarist prices to assess Soviet growth would yield an index intermediate between those indexes calculated in "early" and "late" Soviet prices, insofar as the relative price of capital would be intermediate between the "early" and "late" Soviet prices. The exact location of this hypothetical index would depend upon the relative price structures, which are not known.

Structural comparisons of the Russian and Soviet economies reveal marked accelerations of the pace of structural change after 1928, which then slowed down (at least in the end-use shares) after 1937. We established in Tables 2 and 3 that the pace of structural change between 1885 and 1913 was fairly "normal" for the early years of Russian modern economic growth. The same cannot be said of the early years of centralized planning: The USSR began the plan era in 1928 with industrial and end-use structures quite similar to the 1913 distributions, if "late" prices are used. Within 9 years, the consumption share dropped by 50 percent from 82 to 55 percent of NNP, the investment share rose from 10 to 23 percent (more than doubled), and the government share (including communal consumption) increased by a factor of almost 3. After 1937, the end-use shares continued to change in the same direction, but at a much more modest pace. The same is true of the industry and agriculture sector shares, although their share changes continued to proceed at a rapid pace up to the late 1950s. As Kuznets and others have noted, structural changes of these magnitudes required 50 to 150 years in the industrialized capitalist countries,[31] and the hallmark of Soviet development during the early plan era was the speed and magnitude of structural change.

Similar dramatic structural changes are to be observed in foreign trade proportions, which declined from 15 percent of NNP in 1913, to 6 percent in 1928, to 1 percent in 1937, and then back to the 1928 ratios after World War II. Even after recovery to the 1928 levels, Soviet foreign trade proportions have remained quite low for a country of that scale and level of economic development. These low trade proportions relative to trade capacity are convincing indicators of the Soviet policy of trade aversion, which has been pursued consistently since 1928.[32] Also net foreign investment, which accounted for almost 20 percent of domestic investment in 1913, declined to a miniscule portion of NNP after 1928.

### An assessment

The existence of comparable data for the late czarist era, the Soviet era, and for industrialized countries allows us to form some judgments about economic performance during the Soviet plan era. In making such an assessment, I leave considerations of income distribution aside, although there is convincing evidence that income was much more equally distributed relative to the czarist era and to the capitalist West under the Soviet regime.[33] I also leave matters of economic stability outside this discussion and concentrate instead on the growth of output and efficiency.

I begin by noting that the two overriding objectives of the Soviet regime have consistently been rapid economic growth and the achievement of a satisfactory level of military power. To achieve these goals, dictatorial control over resource allocation was established, and resources were reallocated in the dramatic fashion described in Table 5, for the purpose of accelerating the growth of output and military power with minimal reliance on the outside world. It is obvious that this redirection of resource use away from consumption and the channeling of labor resources out of household and part-time agricultural pursuits into the labor market called for immense economic sacrifices from the Soviet population. These costs are difficult to measure, but they were obviously substantial.

Against this background, one must assess the gains in the growth of total product and of military power. In the latter area, one must agree that achievements have been impressive, for the USSR has attained what appears to be military parity with the United States, a nation whose total output is almost twice as large. The more critical matter is the payoff of these growth-oriented policies in the form of growth acceleration. One can measure this acceleration in one of two ways: The first is to make a hypothetical calculation of what Soviet economic growth would have been had capitalism been retained in Russia (assuming the democratization of political institutions that normally accompanies modern economic growth). For such a calculation, the long-term growth rate during the last 30 years of czarist rule serves as a convenient starting point. The second alternative is to make a more general comparison of Soviet growth with the long-term experiences of other countries to establish if growth during the plan era was exceptionally high by the standards of the industrialized capitalist countries.

*Economic growth*

I turn first to the hypothetical Russian growth rate under conditions of market capitalism. The reader need not be told that such a calculation is highly conjectural and is made primarily for the purpose of illustration. Yet Kuznets's own data show that there is no consistent pattern of long-term acceleration or deceleration of historical growth patterns in the course of modern economic growth (the possible exception being the post–World War II era),[34] so it is not unlikely that the 1883–1913 Russian rate of 3.3 percent per annum may be a reasonable indicator of long-term Russian growth in the absence of centralized planning. If we ignore the loss of production during World War II as a historical accident, the long-term Soviet growth rate is slightly over 5 percent. Thus, the introduction of centralized planning may have raised the long-term growth rate in what is now the USSR by as much as 1.8 percent per annum. Over a 48-year period, the 3.3 percent rate yields a multiplication factor of approximately 4.9, whereas a 5.0 percent rate yields a multiplication factor of 10.0. Thus, current Soviet GNP may be roughly twice the value that would have prevailed without growth acceleration.

This difference in multiplication factors is a maximal estimate for several reasons. The most important is that we have a severely limited historical perspective in the Soviet case. It may be that centralized planning can successfully accelerate growth during the initial stages of development through rapid shifts in the structure of output and through increases in participation rates (and hours worked per capita); yet when the economy reaches a stage of some maturity, further shifts of this sort are no longer possible and growth comes to depend upon marginal improvements in the decision-making, innovation, and incentive systems. Thus, the rate of growth of Soviet output over the last 5 years for which a record is available (1970–5) is below 4 percent per annum,[35] and if this trend toward deceleration continues, the long-term Soviet growth rate could conceivably approach that of czarist Russia in the distant future.

The limited historical perspective complicates matters in other areas as well. Western growth rates since 1928 are a combination of low rates during the 1930s and high rates during the postwar period, and the two average to yield, in general, growth rates close to long-period historical rates. For this reason, my hypothetical calculation of multiplication factors does not incorporate an accelerated growth rate after 1945, for a capitalist Russia would most likely have participated in the slow growth of the 1930s. In the Soviet case, however, growth was rapid during the 1930s, and the Soviet Union participated as well in the acceleration of growth rates of the postwar era. By international standards, Soviet growth has not been exceptionally high in the postwar era, but because of the absence of negative growth in the 1930s, it is high by international standards for the entire planned era. In fact, the rate of output growth in the USSR after 1928 exceeds the century growth rates of all the major capitalist countries.[36]

Another factor that must be considered is whether the decade of zero growth from 1917 to 1928 was a necessary concomitant of the restructuring following the socialist revolution,[37] just as Soviet theorists argue that depressions and recessions are inherent parts of capitalism. A case could be made that the old economic order had to be destroyed to prepare for the dramatic shifts in resource allocation practices. If one accepts this thesis, the zero growth during the first decade of Soviet rule should be incorporated into the long-term Soviet growth rate. If one performs this calculation, the Soviet long-term declines from 5 percent to under 4 percent per annum, and most of the growth acceleration would be lost. Of course, if the socialist revolution resulted in a *permanent* increase in economic growth, the weight of this period of zero growth would decline over time, but as already noted, one cannot establish the permanency of Soviet growth acceleration.

A third point must be raised, and that is the opinion of prominent students of the czarist period that serious obstacles to growth (primarily semifeudal restrictions in agriculture) were removed only after the revolution of 1905.[38] If one accepts this proposition, the estimated czarist growth rate understates long-term growth potential. I would personally not place too much emphasis on this argument because, as I have already demonstrated, Russian growth was rapid by international standards even prior to 1905.

These reservations are important, but they should not obscure the fact that the *relative* economic position of the Soviet Union has improved substantially since 1928. In 1928, Soviet GNP (GNP per capita) was roughly one-fourth (one-fifth) of that of the United States. In 1975, the ratio had been raised to one-half (40 percent).[39] Thus, whether or not growth acceleration in the Soviet era proves permanent does not change the fact that the relative economic position of the USSR vis-à-vis its major capitalist competitors has improved over the last half-century. This change in relative position does not necessarily prove that centralized resource allocation in favor of growth is the cause. There are other historical examples, such as the relative rise of the United States in the mid-nineteenth century and the relative rise of Japan in the late nineteenth and early twentieth centuries, which occurred without such drastic institutional change. Nevertheless, as our analysis of input policy suggests (below), the centralized command over inputs in the USSR probably explains most of the relative change, and this enhancement of relative position may be regarded by the Soviet leadership as sufficient justification for Soviet growth policy.

*Productivity*

If one assesses Soviet and czarist growth performance in terms of output per unit of conventional input (where the labor and capital inputs measure the major costs of this growth), a better picture of benefit/cost ratios can be obtained. It is difficult to establish the growth rate of output per unit of factor input during the czarist era because the data on labor and capital inputs are inadequate, but it is probably safe to draw the following conclusions. The stock of reproducible capital, judging from the cited data on investment shares, probably grew at a rate only slightly above that of output,[40] while the labor force probably grew at about one-half the rate of output. If one applies fixed weights of 0.7 and 0.3 to labor and capital,[41] respectively, an approximate growth rate of output per unit of conventional factor input of slightly over 1 percent per annum is obtained. In the late czarist era, input growth thus accounted for approximately two-thirds of output growth, and the remaining one-third was accounted for by increases in output per unit of factor input. These figures are, of course, tentative and approximative, but are unlikely to contain a large measurement error.

These productivity results for czarist Russia are generally similar to those of other industrialized countries, which experienced rapid population growth during this time period and for which historical labor and capital records are available (the United States and Canada).[42] In these countries, output per unit of combined factor input grew between 0.9 and 1.2 percent per annum, and approximately two-thirds of the growth of output was "explained" by factor input growth. In the two other countries for which long historical records are available (the United Kingdom and Norway), population and labor force grew more slowly and the growth of output per unit of factor input was slightly slower, but the share of output growth accounted for by input growth was about 50 percent.

If one makes similar calculations for the Soviet era after 1928, again ignoring the period 1940–50, one finds that output grew on average at an annual rate of 5.15 percent, labor at 2.0 percent, and capital at 8 percent.[43] If the same fixed weights of 0.7 and 0.3 are applied, combined factor inputs grew at approximately 3.8 percent and output per unit of factor input at a rate of 1.4 percent. According to this calculation, the growth of inputs accounted for about three-fourths of output growth, a slightly higher proportion than in Russia, the United States, and Canada during the late nineteenth and early twentieth centuries. However, this calculation shows the Soviet experience with productivity growth to be out of step with that of the industrialized capitalist countries in the twentieth century: Although the Soviet growth rate of output per unit of factor input would be about average for this period, among the industrialized countries the Soviet growth rate of factor inputs was exceptionally high relative to that of the industrialized capitalist countries. Thus, the percentage of output growth "explained" by the growth of conventional inputs in the industrialized capitalist countries was more typically one-third, whereas in the Soviet case it was a far less favorable, three-fourths. The same divergence emerges from comparisons of Soviet and capitalist productivity patterns after World War II.

It may be argued that the use of fixed "synthetic" factor shares to calculate combined input growth results in the understatement of Soviet productivity growth. A lengthy literature on Soviet industrial production functions reveals that the large differential between capital and labor growth has made it increasingly difficult to substitute capital for labor.[44] Accordingly, labor has become an increasingly scarce factor in Soviet industry, and labor's true share of industrial value added has risen substantially. If one applies these findings to the entire Soviet economy, a rising labor share would reduce the long-term growth of combined inputs and would thus raise the growth of productivity. However, my experiments show that adjustment for this phenomenon would not alter my conclusions concerning overall Soviet productivity.[45]

What conclusions can be drawn from this evidence? The first is that the major source of growth throughout the Soviet era has been the rapid increase in conventional factor inputs, and thus, despite more rapid growth of product, the Soviet economy has only succeeded in generating "average" rates of growth of output per unit of conventional factor inputs, and it has not succeeded in narrowing, in any substantial way, its initial productivity gap vis-à-vis the capitalist West. This suggests that if the Soviets had been able to achieve ratios of input to output growth equal to the standard capitalist ratio, the same long-term growth rate could have been attained with inputs growing at one-half their actual growth rate. This example serves to illustrate the high-cost nature of Soviet growth. Second, the Soviet plan era pattern of productivity growth appears to be similar to (but likely less favorable than) that of those capitalist countries (the United States, Canada, Russia) that experienced rapid rates of growth of conventional inputs between 1850 and World War I. The evidence of parallels between the Soviet plan era and the European offshoots prior to World War I is not overwhelming because we only have data for two countries, but the resemblance is nevertheless striking.

This second finding raises an interesting question: Does this observed similarity between Soviet productivity patterns and that of capitalist countries experiencing rapid input growth indicate that this phenomenon (the failure of the Soviet planned economy to generate high ratios of productivity growth to output growth) is a characteristic of rapid input growth rather than of centralized planning? This argument cannot be ruled out, but the two countries that have experienced Soviet-type growth of factor inputs after World War II (Japan and West Germany) have succeeded in generating not only exceptionally rapid growth rates of factor productivity, but also the same low ratios of input growth to output growth (of around one-third) as the other industrialized capitalist countries.[46]

These considerations of factor productivity underscore the imponderables involved in estimating the hypothetical secular growth rate of Russia to the present under conditions of capitalism. It is a fairly safe assumption that input growth would not have been as rapid under a capitalist Russia: Russia was in the early stages of its demographic transition at the outbreak of World War I, and population growth would likely have declined with declining birth rates and with continued migration to more affluent countries. Czarist Russia also entered World War I with a relatively high investment rate for a low-per-capita-income country,[47] and it is unlikely that a democratic czarist regime would have had the authority to force the expansion of labor and capital inputs as did the Soviet leadership after 1928. I would speculate that the Russian experience would have been much like that of the United States, Canada, and Australia, and would have experienced a declining rate of growth of labor inputs following the initial high rates of the early period. One cannot be certain of this, as there are examples of countries that have experienced accelerations in the rate of growth of conventional inputs in the course of modern economic growth (e.g., Germany, Japan, and Italy). Nevertheless, the more likely scenario would have been one of declining rates of growth of conventional factor inputs.

On the other hand, a capitalist Russia integrated into the world economy would likely have participated in the high proportion of output growth accounted for by efficiency improvements and would thus have achieved more growth per unit increase in inputs than did the Soviet economy. If one is able to envision a scenario in which combined input growth would have continued at a relatively rapid pace (say at 2 percent per annum), the long-term growth rate of capitalist Russia could have rivaled that of Soviet Russia. Again, I would emphasize the low probability of this scenario, for, if true, it would require a significant acceleration of secular growth rates, and such accelerations appear to be rare in quantitative economic history. Their rarity suggests that the decrease in the ratio of input to output growth is compensated for by the declining growth rates of conventional inputs. The declining ratio of input to output growth is the probable consequence of the more rapid growth of nonconventional inputs, the most important being the quality of human capital, rather than of conventional quantity-measured inputs.

As a final point, the issue of the growth of nonconventional (intangible) inputs should be considered. This matter is important because one explanation for the high Soviet ratio of conventional factor input growth to output growth could be a relatively slow rate of growth of nonconventional inputs. A definitive answer to this question would require a major research effort, but I believe more casual evidence will suffice to demonstrate that nonconventional input growth was also relatively rapid in the Soviet case. For example, in 1914 the ratio of total population enrolled in all educational institutions (excluding child care facilities) was 6 percent in Imperial Russia. By 1970, the ratio had risen to 25 percent. For the United States during the same period, the ratio rose from 21 to 24 percent.[48] One would obtain the same relative answer using other measures of human capital development (e.g., health services). Thus, if anything, one would have to conclude that nonconventional inputs grew more rapidly than did conventional inputs and therefore should have contributed to a lower ratio of conventional input growth to output growth.

A stronger case could be made in the czarist case. Here the growth of nonconventional inputs (say, as measured by the increase in literacy rates) was slow relative to the growth of conventional inputs. Thus, the high ratio of conventional input growth to output growth may be, partially at least, the consequence of slow growth of intangible inputs.

### Notes

1 The teamwork involved in the estimation of Soviet national income is described in Abram Bergson, *The Real National Income of Soviet Russia since 1928* (Cambridge, Mass.: Harvard University Press, 1961), Introduction.
2 American empirical research on the planned economies of Eastern Europe and China is summarized in various publications of the Joint Economic Committee of Congress, such as *Economic Developments in Countries of Eastern Europe*, Washington, D.C., 1970; *East European Economies Post-Helsinki*, Washington, D.C., 1977; and *China: A Reassessment of the Economy*, Washington, D.C., 1975.
3 Abram Bergson has dealt with the issue of the relative efficiency of Soviet socialism in the following works: *Planning and Productivity under Soviet Socialism* (New York: Columbia University Press, 1968); "Productivity under Two Systems: The USSR versus the West," in Jan Tinbergen, Abram Bergson, Fritz Machlup, and Oskar Morgenstern, *Optimum Social Welfare and Productivity: A Comparative View* (New York: New York University Press, 1972), pp. 55–103; and *Productivity and the Social System* (Cambridge, Mass.: Harvard University Press, 1978). The socialist model of economic development has been analyzed by Gur Ofer, *The Service Sector in Soviet Economic Growth: A Comparative Study* (Cambridge, Mass.: Harvard University Press, 1976), and Paul Gregory, *Socialist and Nonsocialist Industrialization Patterns* (New York: Praeger, 1970).

4 Kuznets's comparative appraisal appears in Abram Bergson and Simon Kuznets (eds.), *Economic Trends in the Soviet Union* (Cambridge, Mass.: Harvard University Press, 1963), pp. 333–82.

5 The most noted proponent of this view is Alexander Gerschenkron. See Gerschenkron, "The Early Phases of Industrialization in Russia: Afterthoughts and Counterthoughts," in W. W. Rostow (ed.), *The Economics of Takeoff into Sustained Growth* (New York: St. Martin's Press, 1963).

6 For an appraisal of these resource shifts in a comparative setting, see Kuznets, in Bergson and Kuznets, *Economic Trends,* pp. 342–67.

7 Raymond Goldsmith, "The Economic Growth of Tsarist Russia, 1860–1913," *Economic Development and Cultural Change,* 9, 3 (April 1961), 441–75.

8 This calculation is made from M. E. Falkus, "Russia's National Income, 1913: A Revaluation," *Economica* NS 35, 137 (February 1968), 55, and Paul Gregory, "1913 Russian National Income – Some Insights into Russian Economic Development," *Quarterly Journal of Economics,* 90, 3 (August 1976), statistical appendix.

9 S. N. Prokopovich, *Opyt ischisleniia narodnogo dokhoda 50 gubernii Evropeiskoi Rossii* (Moscow: Sovet Vserossiskikh Kooperativnykh Sezdov, 1918).

10 The author's own earlier work on this topic is Paul Gregory, "Economic Growth and Structural Change in Tsarist Russia," *Soviet Studies,* 23, 3 (January 1972), 418–34. M. E. Falkus, *The Industrialization of Russia 1700–1914* (London: Macmillan, 1972), comes to similar conclusions concerning the economic development of Russia under the czars.

11 Gregory, "1913 Russian National Income," p. 448.

12 Gerschenkron, "The Early Phases."

13 Falkus, "Russia's National Income, 1913," p. 55.

14 A. L. Vainshtein, *Narodnoe bogatstvo i narodnokhoziaistvennoe nakoplenie predrevoliutsionnoi Rossii* (Moscow: Gosstatizdat, 1960).

15 Arcadius Kahan, "Capital Formation during the Period of Early Industrialization in Europe," *Cambridge Economic History of Europe,* vol. 7, part 2 (Cambridge: Cambridge University Press, 1978), pp. 265–307.

16 S. G. Wheatcroft, "The Reliability of Russian Prewar Grain Output Statistics," *Soviet Studies,* 26, 2 (April 1974), 157–80; R. W. Davies, "A Note on Grain Statistics," *Soviet Studies,* 21, 3 (January 1970), 314–30.

17 Apparently, Goldsmith and I use the same official data on livestock reported by the Ministry of Interior and Veterinary Department. The difference is in my treatment of territorial adjustments.

18 The Kuhn estimates are reported in *Bulletin Russe de statistique financière et de législation,* 5th ed., 1898, pp. 222–31.

19 There was a similar shift in the ratios of gross to net cereal crops in Prussia between 1816 and 1864. On this, see R. H. Tilly, "Capital Formation in Germany in the Nineteenth Century," *Cambridge Economic History of Europe,* vol. 7, part 1, (Cambridge: Cambridge University Press, 1978), p. 390. The difference in grain production figures raises a troublesome conflict which I am unable to resolve because I know little of the details of Goldsmith's calculations and the sources of his data. Part of the difference is explained by his use of gross and my use of net production figures, and another part is explained by my use of the Kuhn figures, which cover much more empire grain production (about 7 percent more for grains and 50 percent more for potatoes) than do Goldsmith's. Moreover, the question of weighting is an important one. It is not clear whether Goldsmith deals with tons of grain and potato equiva-

lents or weights the individual grains by their prices. This is important because of the more rapid growth of high-priced wheat than of grain, barley, and potatoes. It may be true that the official growth rates of grain production should be lowered due to better coverage for later periods, but I have no evidence to this effect, and the adjustments that Goldsmith makes for increasing coverage are very small anyway.

20  In this note, I only have space to relate that the two principal components of the consumption series are deflated retail sales and retained agricultural products, both in constant 1913 prices. The retail sales figures are based upon trade turnover data reported to the finance ministry for tax purposes, and the three available retail price indexes (a Petersburg index, a combined Moscow–Petersburg series, and an all-empire series) fortunately are in general agreement concerning price trends over the entire period, although disagreeing on price trends in the early twentieth century. The farm-income-in-kind series is calculated by subtracting shipments of agricultural products outside the village from net agricultural output, and a separate paper describes this series. The current-price government spending figures, especially for imperial expenditures, appear to be quite reliable; so the principal issue is the accuracy of the deflation process. For the deflation of government spending, I use the available wage series for railroad workers and factory workers as well as various (reasonably reliable) wholesale price indexes; I would be surprised if major errors are involved. I have written a separate paper on the net foreign investment account, which I also believe to be reasonably reliable.

21  Paul Gregory, "Grain Marketings and Peasant Consumption, Russia, 1885–1913," *Explorations in Economic History,* 17, 1980, 135–64; "Russian Living Standards during the Industrialization Era, 1885–1913," *Review of Income and Wealth,* 26, March 1980; "The Russian Balance of Payments, the Gold Standard and Monetary Policy: A Historical Example of Foreign Capital Movement," *Journal of Economic History,* 39, 2 (June 1979), 379–400.

22  Falkus, "Russia's National Income, 1913," p. 58.

23  The 1860–80 growth figure is calculated from Gregory, "Economic Growth and Structural Change," p. 422.

24  On this, see Simon Kuznets, *The Economic Growth of Nations* (Cambridge, Mass.: Harvard University Press, 1971), pp. 52–61.

25  Ibid., p. 24.

26  Padma Desai, "The Production Function and Technical Change in Postwar Soviet Industry," *American Economic Review,* 66, 3 (June 1976); Steven Rosefielde and C. A. Knox Lovell, "The Impact of Adjusted Factor Cost Valuation on the CES Interpretation of Postwar Soviet Economic Growth," *Economica,* November 1977.

27  For a discussion of this proposition, see M. L. Weitzman, "Soviet Postwar Economic Growth and Capital–Labor Substitution," *American Economic Review,* 60, 4 (September 1970), 676–92.

28  Bergson, *Real National Income,* p. 180.

29  Alexander Gerschenkron, *Dollar Index of Soviet Machinery Output, 1927–28 to 1937,* Rand Corporation, R-197, 1951.

30  For discussions of relative prices during the 1920s and 1930s, consult A. L. Vainshtein, *Tseny i tsenoobrazovanie v SSSR v vostanovitel'ny period 1921–1928 gg.* (Moscow: Nauka, 1972); Richard Moorsteen, *Prices and Production of Machinery in the Soviet Union* (Cambridge, Mass.: Harvard University Press, 1962); and Bergson, *Real National Income,* Chap. 11.

31 Kuznets, in Bergson and Kuznets, *Economic Trends,* p. 342–67.
32 To some extent, "trade aversion" was forced upon the Soviet leadership by declining agricultural prices and by the lack of credits.
33 For a summary of information on income distribution during the Soviet period, see Paul Gregory and Robert Stuart, *Soviet Economic Structure and Performance* (New York: Harper & Row, 1974), chap. 10. For the czarist period, the following information is known. According to a Ministry of Finance study published in 1906, 400,000 individuals accounted for 1,725 million rubles of income earned in the Russian empire. The study is titled *Opyt priblizitel'nago ischisleniia narodnago dokhoda po razlichnym ego istochnikam i po razmeron V Rossii,* Petersburg, 1907, p. 91. National income in 1905 was probably about 14,000 million rubles according to my preliminary calculations. Although one cannot calculate exact income distributions by households from this information, it does suggest a highly unequal distribution.
34 Kuznets, "Economic Growth and Structural Change," pp. 37–43.
35 Rush Greenslade, "The Real Gross National Product of the USSR, 1950–1975," in Joint Economic Committee, *Soviet Economy in a New Perspective* (Washington, D.C.: U.S. Government Printing Office, 1976), p. 271.
36 This evidence is presented in Gregory and Stuart, *Soviet Economic Structure,* chap. 10.
37 This point is discussed by Kuznets, in Bergson and Kuznets, *Economic Trends,* p. 334.
38 Alexander Gerschenkron, "Agrarian Policies and Industrialization: Russia, 1861–1917", *Cambridge Economic History of Europe,* vol. 6, Part 2 (Cambridge: Cambridge University Press, 1966).
39 Herbert Block, "Soviet Economic Power Growth – Achievements under Handicaps," in JEC, *Soviet Economy in a New Perspective,* p. 246.
40 Kahan, "Capital Formation," p. 296, estimates that private capital grew at a rate roughly one-half that of output between 1890 and 1913. My own preliminary work on Russian capital stock suggests a much higher rate of growth of capital, especially in agriculture. I believe that the Russian capital/output ratio remained at least constant during the period investigated in this study. Moreover, I believe that the substantial decline in capital/output ratios suggested by Kahan's figures to be unlikely in view of the experiences of other countries.
41 We do not know the factor shares for czarist Russia, so I use average shares for the industrial countries prior to World War I from Kuznets, *Modern Economic Growth: Rate, Structure and Spread* (New Haven: Yale University Press, 1966), pp. 168–9.
42 Kuznets, "Economic Growth and Structural Change," p. 74.
43 These figures are updated estimates of those cited in Gregory and Stuart, *Soviet Economic Structure,* chap. 10.
44 Weitzman, "Soviet Postwar Economic Growth"; Desai, "Production Function"; Rosefielde and Lovell, "Impact of Adjusted Factor Cost Valuation"; Steven Rosefielde, "Index Numbers and the Computation of Factor Productivity: A Further Appraisal," *Review of Income and Wealth,* Fall 1979, 225–8.
45 It would require a major study to fit a CES (or even more general) production function to the aggregate Soviet economy, but one can make some speculative judgments concerning the impact of a less than unitary elasticity of substitution for the aggregate economy. First, for the aggregate economy the differential between $K$ and $L$ growth is smaller than in industry; so the impact of diminishing marginal capital productivity should be less pronounced. Second,

even if one assumes substantial factor share changes (say, from 0.5 to 0.8 for labor), the percentage of Soviet growth explained by productivity growth is still small by Western standards. Third, I should emphasize Rosefielde's point that one should be careful about sweeping judgments, because of the sensitivity of estimated production function parameters to changes in functional forms. Nevertheless, I feel that my basic conclusion will hold regardless of the estimation technique used.

46 Kuznets, "Economic Growth and Structural Change," p. 74.
47 Gregory, "1913 Russian National Income," p. 457.
48 These comparisons are made using the following sources: Ts.S.U., *Narodnoe obrazovanie, Nauka, i kul'tura v SSSR* (Moscow: Statistika, 1977), p. 7, and U.S. Department of Commerce, *Historical Statistics of the United States, Colonial Times to 1970,* part 1, sec. 4, Washington, D.C.

# 3 Corruption in a Soviet-type economy: theoretical considerations

*J. M. Montias and Susan Rose-Ackerman*

## I. The basic framework

### A. *Introduction*

Theoretical work on corruption has so far been grounded in the political–economic environment of Western capitalist societies (e.g., Becker and Stigler, 1974, and Rose-Ackerman, 1978) or underdeveloped countries (e.g., Johnson, 1975; Krueger, 1974; and Scott, 1972). Papers discussing corruption in the Soviet Union and Eastern Europe are mainly descriptive and lack both a well-developed theoretical structure and a comparison with Western experience (see Grossman, 1977; Katsenelinboigen, 1978; Kramer, 1977; and Simis, 1979). This chapter attempts to organize the material available on corruption in Soviet-type economies and to develop theoretical principles capable of explaining the behavior of corrupt agents in these systems.

We first identify a few of the most salient characteristics of Soviet-type economies. This exercise permits us to isolate corrupt incentives that may lead people to break the law or to violate the rules laid down by their organizational superiors. We speculate on the efficiency of corrupt transactions and consider how modifications in the rules might deter such behavior. The evidence we supply is anecdotal and is used merely to illustrate our points.[1] The comparisons we make with corruption in market-oriented economies are meant only to set in relief the particular

This paper was prepared for the Workshop on the Second Economy of the USSR held at the annual meeting of the American Association for the Advancement of Slavic Scholarship, New Haven, Connecticut, October 12, 1979. The authors are grateful for the comments of David Conn, Richard Ericson, Truus Koopmans, Leon Lipson, Steven Rosefielde, and the workshop participants.

modes of behavior we think are more likely to be encountered in centrally administered Soviet-type economies.

In our stylized Soviet-type economy the bulk of economic activity is carried on by individuals, called agents, organized in a complete hierarchy (CH).[2] The economic activities, legal or illegal, that go on outside the CH are ignored except insofar as they help explain the incidence of corruption in the CH.

The head of the CH (the Politbureau) and its deputies issue commands to lower-level agents, telling them what and how much to produce, what inputs to use, and how to allocate the finished output. Certain subhierarchies of the CH, called enterprises, buy and sell goods and services at prices set by central authorities. They must meet their expenses from their sales receipts and planned losses (if any). The CH sets rules that tie the incomes of enterprise managers to their fulfillment or overfulfillment of plan targets. All other agents in the CH receive fixed salaries set by their superiors.[3]

In any country where political and economic power is organized in a CH, the activities of the organizations belonging to the hierarchy are imperfectly coordinated and the incentives facing agents are not fully compatible with the interests of the central authorities. Imperfect coordination occurs for several reasons.

1   Much information is lost and distorted as it travels up the hierarchy.
2   It is costly and time consuming to process the information at higher levels.
3   Subordinates, responding to a variety of moral, career, and material incentives, are only imperfectly controlled by their superiors.
4   Lower-level agents may have several superiors if they must carry out closely related activities organized along different hierarchic lines.[4]
5   The orders, in the form of "plans" specifying the production, consumption, and investment activities of lower-level organizations during a forthcoming period, normally make no allowance for alternative "states of the environment"– circumstances beyond the organizations' control that may affect their ability to fulfill the plan (Powell, 1977, p. 54). Plans issued in the form of "strategies" specifying alternative actions for alternative states of the environment cannot be fully carried out without changing many orders already in the process of being implemented. Making these changes while maintaining coordination would be an organizationally insuperable task.

The following features of a CH are of critical importance to the analysis of corruption and are generally believed to be characteristic of Soviet-type economies (see Koopmans and Montias, 1971, and Powell, 1977). First, there exists a surplus demand for most producer goods as well as for many consumer goods at established prices.[5] This is the result of the imperfect coordination of interdependent decisions, of the central agents' macroeconomic policies, and of the system's rules for setting prices and distributing goods. Second, low-level organizations can fairly easily conceal the illicit activities of their members. Because close monitoring and field inspections are expensive (and frequently wasteful), some lower-level agents are able to use the relative autonomy they enjoy to engage in self-seeking actions that violate system rules. Third, agents capable of managing subhierarchies (ministries, chief administrations, enterprises) and of exercising initiative are scarce. Therefore, they cannot be dismissed or imprisoned without causing some loss to the organization to which they belong. Even if replacements can be found with the same intelligence and human capital as those dismissed, they first have to build up a knowledge of the network of CH relations before they can function effectively in the system. Their scarcity, therefore, gives subordinates some bargaining power vis-à-vis their superiors in the economic hierarchy.

This third characteristic, which is less evident and empirically more controversial than the other two, has implications for the control of low-level illicit activity. Illicit activity is controlled not only by the risk of detection but also by the severity of the punishment meted out to those who are caught. Acts violating codified rules or laws are punished by the criminal justice system – a subhierarchy dominated by the Communist party in the USSR but with only weak links to the economic subhierarchies (Lipson, 1958, 1959, 1961). In contrast, in the USSR, a person who violates the rules of an industrial ministry is generally penalized only by his immediate superiors. If those superiors have difficulty replacing key subordinates, the subordinate who violates a rule may escape with only a minor reprimand.

## B. Corruption in a complete hierarchy

### 1. Individual and organizational corruption

We now define a corrupt transaction between an agent $i$ of the CH and an individual $j$, who may or may not belong to CH, as follows. Agent $i$ accepts a gratuity or a favor from individual $j$ in return for doing something that benefits $j$. The payoff may prompt agent $i$ to do what he was supposed to have done anyway, or it may induce him to violate either his superior's orders or the rules of the organization to which he belongs.[6] The gratuity or favor may benefit $i$ as an individual or the subhierarchy to which he belongs (although not necessarily the large hierarchy in which this subhierarchy is embedded). Similarly, $i$'s decision may be advantageous to $j$ or to $j$'s organization. When agents either pay bribes or violate rules or orders in exchange for gratuities or favors benefiting them personally, they are said to engage in "individual corruption." When the organization to which they belong benefits, they carry out "organizational corruption."[7] If corrupt individuals share in the additional bonuses or other legal payoffs that result from corrupt transactions, the incentive system rewarding enterprises for their achievements provides the link between individual and organizational corruption. (see Grossman, 1977, p. 30). The incentives for organizational corruption will be high (1) if the success of the enterprise depends on the favors corrupters can bestow, (2) if the bonuses shared by agents in the enterprise depend on its success as judged by superiors, and (3) if the share of the bonus accruing to the transgressing agent is large.

Agents who set the level of production or who allocate goods in surplus demand are potential targets of corrupt offers by consumers or by agents of enterprises (or subhierarchies) that use these goods as inputs. If an agent is guilty of individual corruption in supplying such goods, he is liable to prosecution under the criminal laws. If he does the same thing in a way that benefits his enterprise (or the larger subhierarchy of which it generally is a part), he will receive only administrative sanctions from his superiors. For example, a buyer may offer a scarce producer good to an enterprise in return for an extra allotment of inputs produced by the enterprise. The scarce producer good may now permit the enterprise manager to increase output above plan and earn a high bonus. Superiors aware of this organizational corruption may impose negligible sanctions or even reward the initiative of the transgressor. They are more likely to do this if their own promotion possibilites and security of tenure depend on the success of their subordinate enterprises.[8] Moreover, if they choose to impose severe punishments, they will risk losing the services of the transgressors, with their scarce skills and detailed knowledge of enterprise operations.

These illicit barter arrangements benefit both transacting enterprises, but they will frequently impose costs on the rest of the economy. Clearly, transactions that deflect inputs from one enterprise to another have different efficiency properties from those exchanges that, without depriving any users of their "rightful shares," make everyone better off. When two enterprises trade surplus products,[9] the exchange normally enhances efficiency in production. In a broad class of cases, however, organizational corruption is likely to reduce rather than to enhance productive efficiency. Suppose, for instance, that an enterprise with 2,000 tons of product $X$ on hand is slated to deliver 1,000 tons of the product to each of two enterprises producing $Y$ with identical production functions. But the $X$-producer makes a special deal with only one of the $Y$-producers. The second $Y$-producer is too geographically distant or too poorly informed to make a counteroffer. In exchange for supplying 1,500 tons of $X$ to the first $Y$-producer, the $X$-producer receives a larger quantity of $Y$ than its plan called for, at the expense of deliveries of $Y$ to a second, identical $X$-producer. The second producer of $Y$ receives only the quantity of $X$ left over, or 500 tons. If the production functions of both $X$ and $Y$ producers are strictly concave, and if the second producer of $X$ does not make a compensating deal, the total output of $X$ and $Y$ by the four enterprises concerned will be smaller if the special deal goes through.[10] Implicit here is the assumption that identical, or even smaller, enterprises will normally be alloted the same amounts of input by their superiors. In general, illegal deals at the expense of third parties will be more detrimental to efficiency, the closer the initial allocation came to equating the marginal rates of technical substitution of the materials allotted to different enterprises. We conjecture that the "tauter" the output plan imposed from above, the more likely it is that the marginal rates of substitution will differ. As long as the producer with the highest marginal product from using the input is also the one who corrupts the suppliers, special deals of this sort may then promote efficiency. This possibility contrasts with the foregoing example, where the planners' efficient initial allocation was undermined by corruption.[11]

Not all agents who seek extralegal allotments of scarce inputs have control over materials and resources that suppliers need. If a two-way barter is not possible, bribers can try to work out multilateral exchanges by bringing other enterprises into their schemes. However, the high transaction costs of illicit operations (as well as their substantial information costs) complicate multilateral deals and restrict their potential scope. Moreover, industries producing primarily for final consumption may have no producer goods to give in return for favors from *any* suppliers. Such enterprises may bribe supplying agents directly. If they happen to produce finished consumer goods, they can proffer better-quality merchandise or scarce items to obtain the materials they require. Suppliers accepting such quid pro quo deals are, of course, guilty of individual corruption.

Other kinds of corrupt deals, however, may increase bonuses at the same time as they increase an official's illegal income. Thus, bribes are sometimes paid to induce an enterprise official to work harder and produce more than the planned output. The payment provides an individual benefit to the official and also produces an organizational benefit. A ruble of bribe money is usually less valuable to the recipient than a ruble of bonus money, however, because of the risk of detection and punishment.

Nevertheless, it seems plausible to assume that the state will not spend many of its scarce enforcement resources in seeking to prevent corruption that leads to higher levels of output.

Unfortunately, it will usually be difficult to disentangle the ultimate efficiency effects of a particular corrupt arrangement. In general, output will increase *and* planned output will be diverted from one enterprise to another.

### 2. High- and low-level individual corruption

Many opportunities for individual corruption exist in a CH. We wish merely to point out two distinctive varieties: one that involves high-level officials, and a second that is apparently pervasive among low-level officials in the Soviet Union.

First, individuals sometimes resort to individual corruption to obtain positions in the CH that permit them either to amass large illicit incomes or to obtain legal benefits and privileges. Thus, in the Soviet Union, individuals compete for high-status jobs on the *nomenklatura,* a civil service list of all significant positions that must be approved by the Communist Party. This list creates a class of individuals who are not only materially privileged vis-à-vis the rest of the population but who are not subject to the same sanctions when they break the rules. Illicit access to the *nomenklatura* through bribery amounts to supercorruption because it gives the briber access to all sorts of ordinary corruption that would not otherwise be within his power.[12]

Second, even quite low-level agents may have the power to extract bribes. Thus, "gatekeepers" or custodians of scarce products can use their institutional position for private gain. The low remuneration of custodians and the fact that they do not share significantly in their organization's payoff (at least licitly) make them particularly open to individual corruption.[13] In the Soviet Union even a legitimate representative of a state-owned enterprise or collective farm equipped with a properly endorsed distribution order may be unable to obtain a scarce producer good unless the individual in charge of a depot or other supply point is willing to release it.

The distribution of consumer goods in short supply provides special opportunities for low-level individual corruption in a CH. In the USSR, some commodities and services sold to individuals are formally rationed (e.g., state-owned housing, coal, automobiles); others are informally rationed (any goods in "short supply"). In the smaller towns of the Soviet Union and particularly in villages in the country, almost all goods are formally or informally rationed (Kaiser, 1976, pp. 88–92). These nonmarket forms of rationing become the means by which people who hold a very low place in the hierarchy (shopkeepers, stockroom clerks, railroad dispatchers) can nonetheless elicit corrupt payments (see Katsenelinboigen, 1978, p. 188; Simis, 1979, p. 51; and Smith, 1976, chap. 3).

The presence of currency facilitates this low-level corruption. All private consumers buy goods and services from CH and may, within the limits prescribed by laws, buy goods and services from each other. All such transactions, involving individuals *qua* consumers, are carried out in currency, whereas transactions between subhierarchies of the CH are effected by bank transfers, all banks being subordinate to a monopoly organization belonging to the CH. Transactions in currency are "anonymous," in the sense that they cannot be traced to a permit or order or to a recorded transfer between named persons. This "anonymity" makes it possible to conceal payoffs. Custodians or "gatekeepers" do not, however, necessarily accept money for the favors they bestow: instead, they may illegally barter goods or services.[14] This reduces the risk of detection even further, and probably also lowers the penalty when the transaction is detected.

## II. Comparisons with market economies

### A. Introduction

This section compares the corrupt incentives in a Soviet-style complete hierarchy (CH) with those in a capitalist economy containing large business firms and government bureaucracies. The capitalist economy has many individual large organizations, including business firms, government agencies, and private universities, but each one has a certain autonomy and independent power. In a Soviet-type economy, organizations not only are large taken by themselves, but are also much more closely integrated, through the CH, with other parts of the political–economic system. As we shall see, this aspect of a planned economy helps determine the level of corrupt incentives even in areas where payoffs also occur in the West.

There are two important categories of activities: (1) actions by agents that are illegal in both societies (e.g., paying a bribe to obtain a job or to prevent a policeman from reporting a traffic violation), and (2) actions that require illicit behavior in the USSR but that are legal in the West (e.g., opening a private atelier to manufacture sweaters).[15] A third category of actions – those that are illegal in the West but legal in the USSR – is probably very small. Finally, we should recognize that certain kinds of corrupt opportunities open to Westerners simply do not exist in the Soviet Union.[16]

*B. Corrupt acts that are illegal in both systems*

*1. Parallels and contrasts*

Beginning with the first type of corrupt action, there are many striking parallels between the USSR and the United States. Corruption occurs in both societies in law enforcement,[17] in inspections,[18] in the choosing of qualified applicants,[19] in the allocation of scarce state-produced services,[20] and in government contracting.[21] The parallels are easiest to find in situations where *government* bureaucrats in the United States perform tasks similar to those of Soviet officials. Large *private* organizations that delegate tasks to subordinate agents, however, may also face the problem of controlling payoffs (Rose-Ackerman, 1978, chaps. 1, 10).

The costs of corruption in each society may be either broadly diffused or extremely concentrated. Corruption in government – whether in the USSR or the United States – frequently affects the public at large or, at least, a large group of people that receives inferior treatment as a result of corrupt favors. Since there are no obvious "victims," the control of payoffs may be very difficult and corruption may flourish. In contrast, where private enterprises are financially autonomous, as most of them are in the West, and must, at least in the long run, meet their expenses from their receipts, the losses due to corruption may be concentrated on the owners or shareholders. In the USSR, just as corruption for organizational gain may benefit individuals in enterprises enjoying some autonomy, so the losses of corruption can affect its members adversely. In both cases, the affected groups have some incentives to control corrupt payments.

We have already argued that imperfect monitoring and information loss in a bureaucracy give low-level agents monopoly power that can be used to extract bribes. This phenomenon is common to both Western and Soviet bureaucracies and is not our concern here. Instead, we consider how corruption in a complete hierarchy differs from corruption in a system with many independent loci of power. We shall argue that the incidence and impact of corruption will be quite different in the two societies even when the cause of corrupt payments is similar. The basic differences are the restricted number of options available to bribers and bribees and the lack of independent "whistleblowers" in a Soviet-style system.

*2. Options and bribes*

The more alternatives available to a potential briber, the smaller the bribe he is willing to pay to a particular agent. A firm that can sell all it wants in the private sector will pay little to obtain a government contract.[22] A college applicant who is accepted by Princeton will not be tempted to pay a bribe to Yale. A person who fails to obtain a liquor license in New York may be able to open a tavern in Connecticut instead of bribing New York state officials. A vigorous private sector means that there are alternatives to government sales. An independent private educational sector implies that admission criteria vary so that no single "gatekeeper" has the right to deny a person access to higher education. A federal system of government combined with free movement of people and capital implies that no single low-level government has much monopoly power.

In contrast, high levels of bribes can be expected in both the USSR and the West when options are costly or simply unavailable. For example, the incentive to pay a bribe is high if someone is selling a special-purpose product to government, needs a zoning variance for a particular piece of land he owns, or can only qualify for a public program if he does not move to a new location.[23] Furthermore, people who are legally unqualified to receive a benefit or who want to escape the consequences of illegal actions (drug dealing, gambling, prostitution) have a restricted range of options. They can only obtain aid from corrupt officials. If some officials are honest, the monopoly power of a corrupt official will be higher when the briber has also done something illegal.[24] In a complete hierarchy where most people have no options, the person seeking a legal benefit is on almost the same footing as someone seeking an illegal benefit. The monopoly power of each official is much greater and, therefore, the supply of bribes to any individual is likely to be higher if the expected punishments are similar in both societies. Poor communication among the various components of the CH, however, is likely to diminish the monopoly power of individual agents. A dissident whose son has been barred from entering a university in Moscow stands a good chance of registering him in Tashkent, where he is unknown. Lacking a computerized all-Union system of centralized information, blacklisting is sufficiently sloppy and inefficient to allow some people to slip through the interstices of the system without resorting to bribery.

### 3. The probability of detection

In the West an important deterrent to corruption appears to be the permeability of many bureaucratic procedures. Any journalist, scholar, or concerned citizen can try to find out how a particular bureaucracy operates and may in the process stumble across corruption. In contrast, in an idealized CH and in portions of Western society, such as the defense and intelligence establishments[25] and some aspects of private business behavior, outsiders are unable to examine what is going on.

Recognizing that a monolithic political–economic structure will deter "whistleblowers," the Soviet Union has structured its society so that several overlapping hierarchies exist with the potential to check up on each other. In addition to direct monitoring through the economic hierarchy, the USSR can control behavior through both the Communist Party and the police and courts. The party is structured regionally rather than functionally, and the highest government officials are subordinate to the highest party officials. Most government officials are also party members and are subject to "party discipline." They must comply with the directives of properly constituted party authorities.[26] There are also two police forces which fight corruption. The OBKhSS, subordinate to the Ministry of Internal Affairs, is charged with preventing the theft of socialist property. The KGB, or national security police, seeks to control high-level corruption that may involve national security problems. Finally, the state controls the mass media and the educational establishment and can use them to expose scandals and to try to persuade the young to avoid all forms of peculation.

These overlapping organizational structures may be relatively ineffective, however, because none appears to be truly independent of the others. All of them are organized as component subhierarchies of the CH that manages the political and economic life of the country. Therefore, none of these organizations has the juridical or administrative independence that allows it to "muckrake," irrespective of consequences (Kaiser, 1976, pp. 217–24). Journalists, state inspectors, and other potential discoverers of wrongdoing in low and high places generally exercise self-censorship to avoid trouble (Kaiser, 1976, pp. 230–2). The courts take directions from the party and are apparently among the least independent organs.[27] The OBKhSS and the KGB have sufficient autonomy to exercise independent initiative because their reports are made on a confidential basis to higher-ups, who may, nevertheless, refuse to act for "political" reasons (see, e.g., Simis, 1979, pp. 49–50). Thus, although multiple enforcement possibilities exist, they may be less effective checks on corruption than a system with many uncoordinated loci of power.[28] When everyone depends in a complex way on everyone else, no one may be willing to expose others for fear that he will only end up harming himself. This is particularly likely to be true for corrupt behavior where there are no impartial observers, and the only witnesses to the breaking of rules are the briber and the bribee.

Furthermore, if potential wrongdoers face a fairly predictable pattern of official controls and methods of detection, it may be relatively easy for them to structure corrupt deals so that they will not be noticed. Unknown outsiders may be in a better position to check corruption if they are sufficiently numerous and if their methods of operation are unpredictable. Stable, certain behavior by enforcement officials facilitates corruption.

The stability of these patterns may be one reason why successful practitioners of "individual corruption" in the USSR (and sometimes also of "organizational corruption" as well) need and are often able to form, fairly large coalitions to achieve their ends. They must enlist in their conspiracy one or more local party members, perhaps an inspector or an auditor, a KGB man, and even, in certain cases, a journalist or another outsider who could expose the scheme to public scrutiny. The expense of cutting in potential "spoilers" increases the costs and lowers the benefits of corruption. But once the setup costs are paid, these "family circles" of solidary interests may acquire a certain permanence. The authorities often find it hard to expose and break them up. Such circles are particularly easy to form among minority nationals speaking a common language, frequently bound by extended-family ties and resentful of Great Russian domination. Ethnic and family ties usually antedate and are often stronger than the organizational links imposed by the state. These organizational short circuits weaken the ability of the various hierarchies to ferret out corruption at the regional level.[29] It often takes an outsider – a Russian or Ukrainian official working in Soviet Asia or in the Caucasus – to expose the conspiracy.[30]

### 4. Punishment and risk

As in the West, the risk of a corrupt action depends both upon one's institutional position and upon the options available to a person convicted of corruption. Those in high positions with the most to lose from a public trial may, in fact, face the smallest expected costs. In both systems, the very severity of the long-term sanctions may protect a bribe taker from being reported or prosecuted. If the likely sentence is very high, a person may be reluctant to report the corruption of a colleague to the police.[31] Prosecutors may be unwilling to try such cases, and there will be great pressure to settle incidents informally. A party member may be shielded by other party members,[32] and top authorities may be reluctant to punish highly placed party members or government officials openly for fear of undermining the legitimacy of the party or the government itself.

Nevertheless, although high-level officials in both the West and the USSR frequently try to protect corrupt associates, this attempt does not always succeed.[33] When a high official is brought to trial, a corruption conviction probably has a more serious impact on one's future career in the Soviet Union than in the West. A high-level Soviet official is unlikely to be able to reestablish himself anywhere in the CH at a position or earnings level comparable to his previous position. In contrast, in the West it is easier for even high-level white-collar criminals to begin again. Usually, they cannot return to the organization they left, but they can engage in legal entrepreneurial activities such as writing a book, giving lectures, starting a new business, or going to work for the firm that made payoffs. Since these options are generally unavailable in the USSR, high-level corruption could be more effectively deterred in the Soviet Union if only the tradition of protecting high-level offenders could be broken.

Low-status bribe payers are in a different position from high-level corrupt officials. Lacking the protection of the party or their hierarchical superiors, the deterrent effects of a monolithic system may be particularly strong. Two factors, however, work against this conclusion. First, even with internal passports and restrictions on movement, the sheer size of the Soviet economy may lower the risks for low-status people. People convicted of crime in one part of the USSR appear to be able to reestablish themselves in another region, although often in less attractive jobs.[34] In a large, unwieldy society such as the United States or the USSR, corruption and crime in general may be less risky for an individual because an accused person may have a better chance of disappearing in the cracks of the system than in a smaller, more easily managed one (such as, say, Hungary or Czechoslovakia). Second, in the USSR, risk-prone individuals may seek positions that permit them to pay or receive bribes. In the West such individuals are unlikely to be bureaucrats. In the USSR almost everyone becomes a member of the CH irrespective of his attitude toward risk. Many adventurous people may end up as frustrated bureaucrats, who find that corruption is one of the few ways of taking chances. In other societies these people might be successful entrepreneurs; in the USSR they may become corrupt or set up illegal private businesses outside the CH. If the society systematically discourages risk taking, then risk lovers are likely to be people with low status who have little to lose from a black mark on their records.

## C. Acts that are illicit only in the USSR

The preceding section concentrated on the corrupt incentives in those bureaucratic transactions that are similar in the USSR and in the West. We now return to corrupt incentives that depend upon the special characteristics of a planned economy. In the USSR many goods and services that are legally sold to the highest bidder in the West are rationed or sold at prices that are too low.[35] We can then ask whether bribe prices will be close to the free market prices of such goods.[36] Comparisons are, of course, difficult because the underlying supply and demand conditions are very different in the two societies. Nevertheless, several observations are possible.

Suppose that there are two towns, each with one shoe store, and that the people in each town must buy shoes from its single store. In the first town the monopoly seller can order shoes from a supplier and set prices to maximize profits. In the second, the state sets a low price for shoes and allocates a certain number of pairs per month to the store, with the result that demand exceeds supply at the fixed price. Whenever shoes arrive, customers line up to buy them. Suppose, first, that the state gives the store exactly the same number of shoes that would be ordered by a monopolist. Corruption, however, will not produce either the monopolist's profit-maximizing price or the same distribution of shoes to customers. The illegality of paying a bribe will affect the way a corrupt system operates. First, the corrupt shopkeeper may be able to price-discriminate. Since the level of bribes is not published, he or she can charge people different "bribe prices" and be fairly sure that they will not communicate with each other. Second, customers are not only engaged in buying shoes; they are also using up time waiting in line. A person's opportunity cost of time will affect his willingness to bribe, especially if the queue cannot be entirely eliminated without arousing the suspicions of the authorities. Thus, individuals who would have been willing to pay the monopolist's price must waste valuable time waiting in line. Thus, corruption cannot entirely eliminate the wastes of queuing (see Rose-Ackerman, 1978, pp. 93–106). Third, the illegality of bribes affects people's willingness to pay. The distribution of shoes across the two populations, then, will reflect not only the willingness of customers to pay for shoes but also their willingness to break the law. In short, when supplies are identical, a corrupt system will produce different distributional consequences, and unless it can eliminate all queuing, will generally be less efficient than a monopoly seller.

Of course, a monopolistic outlet would not be efficient either because it would sell an inefficiently small number of shoes. A planner might conceivably give the state-run shop *more* shoes than were sold by the monopolist. Yet bribery could still occur in the planned system if the official price continued to be too low. But this corrupt system might now be more efficient than the monopolistic one. This is the result, however, not of corruption per se, which still suffers from the difficulties noted above, but rather of the possible superiority of a planned system over a monopolized one. The advantage would evaporate if we permitted entry in the monopolized town so that several shoe stores were allowed to coexist, each selling at marginal cost.[37]

## III. Possibilities of reform

Taking as given the existence of a socialist, centrally planned economic system, we can ask what might be done to control the corruption that now exists. We distinguish between two types of actions: (1) short-run policies, and (2) more fundamental, long-run changes in the system.

*A. Short-run policies*

### 1. Selective enforcement of the laws

The simplest short-run policy is to ignore "organizational corruption" if it is consistent with "social objectives" (e.g., with plan fulfillment) and punish it in the contrary case (if the plan is not fulfilled). If managers are risk-averse, however, this may deter both kinds of corruption. Managers who risk falling below the plan's target may not pay off suppliers to increase their chance of overfulfillment if the chance of underfulfillment is still substantial. Yet it is just in these borderline cases that corruption is most helpful to top authorities. An enterprise manager who pays a bribe when he is already over the planned target is likely to be diverting supplies from a firm that is struggling to fulfill its goal.[38]

### 2. Reducing market pressures

Bribery is frequently a response to market pressures. Thus, even a planned economy might deal with corruption by modifying the conditions that produce an imbalance between supply and demand. One way to do this is to permit a more flexible price system so that prices can rise when supplies are short. Alternatively, the authorities might develop a distribution system that permits people who are willing to pay for a particular good to obtain it without elaborate negotiations and payoffs. This might be especially effective in the countryside – which suffers acutely from the shortcomings of the distribution system. These reforms would not only reduce corruption but also the time spent standing in line. Reducing both the "tautness" of the Soviet plan and the pressure to overfill an enterprise's target output could help limit organizational corruption. "Taut plans," especially when they give rise to directives that cannot possibly be fulfilled, can lead to illicit responses as managers struggle to obtain scarce supplies and to try to ensure that next year's target output will not be too large. There is some evidence that Soviet planning in recent years has been less taut than in the past (see Granick, 1980), but there is little or no information on the consequences of this shift on the level or the efficiency consequences of corruption. In any event, a decrease in tautness may simply shift corruption to the supply side of the economy. On the one hand, enterprises saddled with surplus production may try to unload it on other organizations by offering kickbacks. On the other, in line with a model developed in Section 4 below, if it is easier for an enterprise to dispose of its above-plan output illegally, there will be more illegal possibilities as decreased tautness makes it feasible to exceed targets.

### 3. Changing agents' incentives

The foregoing proposals, however, are hardly a complete response to the problem of payoffs. Instead of changing the way laws are enforced or plans are designed, top officials might restructure the incentive system. We approach this question by relating recent theoretical work on incentive compatible reward systems to the control of bribery. Past work has sought to define reward systems that induce agents to maximize total surplus or lead them to provide accurate information to the principal,[39] but none of this research has taken account of the possibility that agents might accept or receive bribes.[40]

We first construct a Groves-type incentive-compatible scheme and then analyze bribery in this context. We discuss two kinds of corrupt regimes. In the first, the supplier provides planned inputs to firms without a bribe but will accept a bribe in return for giving a customer a larger share of total production. In the second, "extortionary," system no inputs are released unless a bribe is paid.

Consider a simple hierarchy with only two industries, $S$ and $I$. A single firm in $S$ produces a known output $x$ of the good $X$ used as an input by the $n_I$ firms in $I$. An allotment of $X$ to firm $i$ in $I$ is denoted $x_i (i = 1, \ldots, n_I)$. Firm $i$ produces $y_i$ of good $Y$, and its production function, using this unique variable input, is $y_i(x_i)$. This production function is only known to firm $i$. Suppose that every unit of $Y$ is valued at 1 ruble, so that $y_i(x_i)$ can also represent the value of output. The production function communicated by $i$ to the supervisor in charge of allocating input $X$ is written $\hat{y}_i(x_i)$. The supervisor knows only $x$ and $\hat{y}_i(x_i)$ for $i$ in $I$, and tells each firm that a Groves incentive-compatible scheme will be used to allocate $x$.

The supervisor maximizes $\Sigma_{i=1}^{n_I} \hat{y}_i(x_i)$ over all possible allocations $(x_i, \ldots, x_{n_I})$ satisfying $\Sigma_{i=1}^{n_I} x_i \leq x$. An incentive-compatible bonus scheme is one that will induce each firm's bonus-maximizing manager to report his firm's actual production function [i.e., $\hat{y}_i(x_i) = y_i(x_i)$ for each firm $i$]. It has been proved that a bonus scheme giving each firm $i$ a fraction $\alpha$ of $[y_i(x_i) + \Sigma_{j \neq i} \hat{y}_j(x_j)]$ is incentive-compatible (Conn, 1979; Groves, 1973; Loeb and Magat, 1978). The allocation of $X$ that maximizes the supervisor's objective function, when $i$ reports its actual production function, also maximizes the bonus function for $i$.

Such a bonus scheme would also dissuade any firms in $I$ from bribing the supplier of $X$ to obtain a larger allotment at the expense of the other firms. For as long as the total available amount of input $X$ is given, an allocation that fails to maximize the supervisor's objective function cannot increase the firm's expected bonus. Any resources spent on the bribe will be wasted. It is not in a manager's interest to undermine the system either *ex ante* by providing false data or *ex post* by corrupting suppliers.

Suppose, however, that the supplying enterprise has somewhat more extortionary power than we assumed above. The supplier can refuse to release $X$ to firm $i$ until its manager has paid a bribe $b_i$ per unit of $X$. A unit of $Y$ produced by another firm may now be more valuable to firm $i$ [via

$\Sigma_{i \neq j}\hat{y}_j(x_j)]$ than a unit produced by itself that requires a bribe. Therefore, each enterprise $i$ has an incentive to understate its production possibilities when it reports $\hat{y}_i(x_i)$ to the $I$ ministry. Corruption is now likely to distort the assignment of $X$ to firms.[41]

Even when suppliers do not actively seek bribes, corruption in this stylized system can occur if the output of $X$ is not taken as fixed by enterprises in industry $I$ (i.e., when one of Groves' basic assumptions is violated). It may also be worthwhile in this case for a manager to bribe the supplier. The reward received for an increased output of $Y$ may more than offset the cost of the bribe. Suppose that there is no penalty imposed on a manager whose bribery is discovered. Then, if his bonus is a positive fraction $\alpha$ of the expected output of the industry, or $\alpha[y_i + \Sigma_{i \neq j}\hat{y}_j(x_j)]$, and if a bribe leaves the other allotments, $x_j$, unchanged, the maximum bribe $i$ will pay for an increment of $x_i$ is $\alpha(dy_i/dx_i)$, or $\alpha$ times the marginal value product of $x_i$.

### 4. Detection and punishment

As bonuses tied to industry-wide performance are unlikely to eliminate corruption completely, we should also consider the use of penalties levied on those caught paying or receiving bribes. A stylized deterrence strategy has two parts: the probability of detection and the penalties imposed after detection on bribers and bribees. Standard theoretical treatments of the economics of crime can be usefully applied if we take account of a distinctive feature of the Soviet case.[42] In Soviet practice there appears to be an inverse relationship between the probability of detection and the extent of plan overfulfillment. For obvious reasons, central authorities are likely to be less concerned with corruption if it helps distribute a surplus than when it diverts a planned allocation from one firm to another.

Imagine a simplified situation where the supplying enterprises' officials can increase $X$ above the plan at some personal cost to themselves, and managers earn bonuses if they meet or exceed the target output. There is only one supplier of the input $X$ and one consuming enterprise that wishes to induce the supplier to produce larger amounts of the input.

Given these conditions, let $f(x)$ be the probability of detection if $x$ is produced. The probability of detection is lower the larger is $x$, but we assume that $f'(x)$ is discontinuous at $\bar{x}$, the level of planned output. We seek to capture the central authorities' deterrence strategy by assuming that in the neighborhood of $\bar{x}$, $f'(x)$ falls off more rapidly for $x > \bar{x}$ than for $x < \bar{x}$. Thus, letting $f(x) = f_1(x)$ for $x \leq \bar{x}$ and $f(x) = f_2(x)$ for $x \geq \bar{x}$, we have $|f_1'(\bar{x})| < |f_2'(\bar{x})|$. Enforcement activity declines rapidly once the manager has reached the targeted level of output. For large $x$, $f(x)$ approaches zero.

Let $\gamma(x)$ be the penalty levied per dollar of bribe received and $G(x)$ be the net benefit to the manager of producing $x$ if bribes are zero. Thus, $G(x)$ is the manager's bonus and other income if $x$ is produced minus the dollar value of the manager's reduced leisure and any other psychological disutility that he incurs in producing $x$. As $x$ becomes large, $G(x)$ eventually becomes negative, so that $G'(x) < 0$ and $G''(x) < 0$. Thus, if the supplier is risk-neutral, he will accept a total bribe $B(x)$ in return for producing $x$ if

$$R(x) = [1 - f(x)]B(x) - f(x)\gamma(x)B(x) + G(x) > 0$$

and if he earns more from accepting a bribe than from producing $x$ with no illicit payoff, that is, if $R(x) > G(x)$ or $1 > f(x)[1 + \gamma(x)]$.
Then $R(x) = 0$ if

$$B(x) + G(x) = B(x)f(x)[1 + \gamma(x)]$$

$R$ reaches extreme values in its continuous portion, where

$$dR/dx = B'(x) + G'(x) - (1/x)B(x)f(x)[1 + \gamma(x)][\eta_B + \eta_f + \eta_{(1+\gamma)}] = 0$$

where $\eta_k$ is the elasticity of k with respect to $x$.

Let $\hat{x}$ and $\hat{\hat{x}}$ be the output levels where returns are maximized for $x < \bar{x}$ and $x > \bar{x}$, respectively. Let $x_1^*$, and $x_1^{**}$ be the points where $R = 0$ for $x < \bar{x}$ and $x > \bar{x}$, respectively. Not all of these points need exist in a particular application. For example, $R(x)$ need not equal zero either for $0 < x \leq \bar{x}$ or for $\bar{x} \leq x \leq \hat{x}$. Thus, to derive explicit results, we must make some specific assumptions about the form of $B(x)$, $f(x)$, $G(x)$, and $\gamma(x)$. We do this in the Appendix to this chapter. In the cases we consider, two general types of results occur. On the one hand, the state's deterrence strategy may deter large bribes but not small ones. On the other hand, different assumptions about $R(x)$ can produce cases where bribes that require output to be close to or just under the planned target are turned down, but some lower and higher bribes are accepted. The link between the bonus function, $G(x)$, and the returns to corruption is complex. High legal bonuses may either make bribery not worth the risk or else increase the returns from bribery.

Any official penalty strategy, however, will not be fully effective if prosecutions for bribery and similar illicit behavior are politicized. At present, Soviet officials frequently use the corruption statutes for purposes other than reducing bribery.[43] Even where penalties are high,[44] they may not be effective in reducing corruption if most of the people prosecuted are politically untrustworthy, are members of minority religious or ethnic groups, or are involved in personal feuds with their accusers. Ordinary citizens who are not vulnerable to this discretionary enforcement strategy will believe that they will not be punished severely, whatever the legal penalties.

## B. Changes in the system

### 1. Legalizing private initiatives

Corruption might also be reduced by more fundamental changes in the way the system is organized. Thus goods and services now sold in what Katsenelinboigen (1978, pp. 165–70) calls the "gray" or "brown" markets, especially repair and personal services, could be legally sold by private individuals. The market that currently exists in such goods and services would become more public and more efficient. Entry would be easier, prices would fall, and consumers would be better able to compare the quality of goods and services supplied by different suppliers.[45]

### 2. Decentralization

If we take the basic planned structure as given, however, this first systemic solution can only be applied to activities that require little capital accumulation. The next step in an agenda of reform would be to modify the state's economic organization to reduce corruption. One way to do this would be to alter the balance between centralization and decentralization of decision making in a complete hierarchy. As we pointed out above, excessive centralization with poor information is likely to aggravate the mismatch between supply and demand and create opportunities for both corruption and illicit private production. Decentralization, however, may make custodians more secure and enable them to trade on their gatekeeping powers more easily and with less risk of exposure. A compromise must be struck between these conflicting effects. The state may (1) vary the degree of centralization according to the branch of industry and the opportunities for corruption,[46] and (2) couple decentralization in certain industries with increased material incentives for managers.

It may also be possible to organize parts of the system so that clients are not limited to a single supplier. Several officials could be given independent authority to issue a license or permit. This would work well if it is easy to see if an unqualified person has obtained the benefit. Otherwise, competition among officials for bribes may lower the level of payoffs but also increase the number of unqualified clients obtaining the benefit. This strategy will also be more effective if the overall supply of services is not limited. If it is, some central figure must control the overall level of allocations, and that person is an obvious candidate for a bribe (see Rose-Ackerman, 1978, pp. 137–51).

More dramatically, the central authorities could break up large state enterprises into smaller units and let them compete to supply inputs to other enterprises.[47] This would, of course, be incompatible with the planning system as the Soviet party authorities envisage it at present. One difficulty in embarking on such a scheme is that enterprise managers presently lack incentives to compete with each other for business. Merely creating multiple suppliers will not work if no one has a reason to fill orders promptly. If incentives are not reformed in step with changes in the production and distribution system, kickbacks will continue to be used to give managers inducements to perform well.

Strategies that increase the options open to potential bribers within the CH may not only be politically difficult but also bureaucratically complicated for Soviet authorities to carry out. They would require both giving more authority to low-level officials and creating *more* of them. Thus, this proposed reform increases the task of control as long as planners are not willing to let marketlike discipline substitute for their own directives. Although these proposals have a surface plausibility, they are likely to be unacceptable to the USSR's top officials.

### 3. Raising the costs of coalition formation

Instead of trying to increase options for potential bribers, the state may try to make it more difficult for officials to organize a corrupt coalition. One way in which this is frequently done in the Soviet Union and Eastern Europe is to divide up a given task into many pieces in order to multiply the number of "checkpoints" at which corruption can be detected. This strategy, however, will not necessarily reduce the level or impact of corruption. The anticorruption possibilities of this approach depend upon the model of bureaucratic organization through which controls are exercised: fragmented, sequential, or hierarchical (Rose-Ackerman, 1978, pp. 169–71). In the fragmented model a person must have each of several parts of an "application" approved, but each approval procedure is independent of the others, and the applicant can have the portions approved in any order. For example, officials from three different ministries may have to approve an application to change foreign currency. The sequential model is identical to the fragmented except that applicants must have the portions approved in a particular order. No bureaucrat in the sequence, however, reviews the choices made by those who have already acted. Finally, a hierarchical model is a traditional bureaucracy where the behavior of low-level officials can be reviewed by higher-level ones.

The Soviet Union is organized hierarchically, but an individual favor seeker may need to approach officials in several different ministries who have no formal connection except at the level of the Republic or the Union. Therefore, the fragmented or sequential models may best describe the experience of those who deal with the state or party apparatus. Requiring a person to approach officials in different ministries is likely to make it difficult for bureaucrats to form cliques or "family circles," but these organizational strategies may do little to prevent corruption and are likely to increase delay. In the fragmented case some officials may wait until others act and then try to extort a large portion of the client's surplus. In situations where a holdout can make large corrupt gains, moreover, each official may try to be the last one to give approval. Alternatively, in the sequential case a single corrupt official is all that is needed to produce a situation in which a high proportion of the program's benefits to the applicant can be appropriated by bureaucrats.

Stronger hierarchical control will obviously effectively deter corruption only if the top official is honest and if he can monitor the behavior of subordinates.[48] Therefore, the "height" of the hierarchy has no clear-cut implications for the control of corruption. When the top official is honest, a short hierarchy is likely to be best because it makes monitoring easier. When the top official can be corrupted, a tall hierarchy can deter corruption but only under certain circumstances. If the top official is simply choosing a legally qualified contractor, ordering police officers to give extra care to a construction site, or admitting a qualified applicant to a university, he can ask his inferiors to carry out orders without fear of blackmail. Thus, if the act done in return for a bribe is not itself illegal, a tall hierarchy will do nothing to prevent corruption (Rose-Ackerman, 1978, pp. 178–9), since the briber need only pay off the superior official. Suppose, alternatively, that agents at all levels must be given payoffs in return for performing illegal actions. In that case, the probability of detection may be greater the more people are involved in the conspiracy. Furthermore, the greater the risks faced by officials, the higher the payoff each one requires. Therefore, the more people who are involved, the higher the minimum total payment. The required payoff may then be so large that the potential briber is unwilling to meet the officials' demands. Thus, when these conditions hold, a tall hierarchy deters some payoffs, but when bribery does occur, it involves a large-scale transfer of funds.

### 4. Raising real wages

Finally, because corruption is frequently blamed on the low incomes of those accepting bribes, a strategy of raising the real wages of the population, especially of people in "sensitive" positions, could reduce corruption. In the Soviet case, however, prices are not set at market clearing levels and the distribution system is poor. Therefore, an increase in income may be less effective in raising consumer satisfaction than in the West. Moreover, this strategy may increase the *supply* of bribes at the same time as it may reduce the *demand* for them. With higher incomes, people may demand more of those scarce goods that are now most subject to corruption.[49] It would not be sufficient, however, simply to increase the supply of automobiles and houses. The production of complementary goods (gasoline and furniture) would have to be increased as well.[50] In short, a shift toward higher consumer incomes would have to be accompanied by a general reassessment of planning priorities if corruption is to be reduced by this strategy. Otherwise, corruption may increase as new shortages are created.

## IV. Conclusion

Soviet anticorruption campaigns generally ignore the systemic roots of corruption and illicit private activity. Instead, corruption is viewed in official pronouncements as the most flagrant form of self-seeking activity and as an especially pernicious survival of the capitalist mentality.[51] Nevertheless, the Soviet leaders' attitude toward "organizational corruption" is obviously complicated by the fact that in many instances it helps enterprises fulfill planned targets by overcoming frictions in the official distribution system. This indicates the way in which corruption is bound up with the entire system. The USSR is apparently in a sort of institutional equilibrium, no part of which can be substantially altered without forcing basic changes in other parts. The problem with permitting corruption in beneficial cases, however, is that it may be difficult to control in other situations, where it causes deviations from the plan or leads to a distribution of goods judged undesirable by Communist ideology.[52]

If the supply of bribes falls as the number of options available to bribers increases, a reduction in payoffs may require fundamental changes in the way the Soviet system operates. These changes, however, might have other negative results for the Soviet leaders.[53] An increased range of choices in one area of life might lead to pressures for more choices in other politically sensitive areas. The alternative to increasing options and using marketlike incentives more widely is stricter hierarchical control from the center. This, too, appears to be unacceptable to Soviet leaders because it could lead to a revival of Stalinist repression. The decentralized administration of the Soviet system with its toleration of a certain amount of waste, theft, and corruption is probably one reason Soviet citizens do not appear to be in a revolutionary mood. The leaders maintain some measure of public support or, at least, indifference by not pushing their power to its limits.[54]

## Appendix

In the text we presented a model where $R(x) = 0$ if
$$B(x) + G(x) = B(x)f(x)[1 + \gamma(x)]$$
$R$ reaches extreme values where
$$dR/dx = B'(x) + G'(x) - (1/x)B(x)f(x)[1 + \gamma(x)][\eta_B + \eta_f + \eta_{(1+\gamma)}] = 0$$
where $\eta_k$ is the elasticity of $k$ with respect to $x$.

We make some simple assumptions about the form of $f(x)$, $B(x)$, $G(x)$, and $\gamma(x)$. Thus, suppose that

$$f_1(x) = s, \quad s \text{ a constant } 0 < s < 1, \quad \text{for } 0 < x \leq \bar{x}$$
$$f_2(x) = a/x, \quad a \text{ a constant, } a > 0, \quad \text{for } x \geq \bar{x}$$

Thus, $s\bar{x} = a$. Suppose further that the customer's willingness to bribe is proportional to the level of $x$ he obtains, $B(x) = bx$, that $\gamma(x)$ is a constant, $\gamma^* > 0$, and that $G_1(x) = -(\theta/2)x^2$, $\theta > 0$, $x < \bar{x}$,

$$G_2(x) = g + r(x - \bar{x}) - (\theta/2)x^2, \qquad g > 0, \quad x \geq \bar{x}$$

Thus, the manager receives a single lump-sum bonus when he just fulfills the plan and earns $r$ rubles per extra unit of $x$. Let $g > (\theta/2)\bar{x}^2$ so that if $B(x) = 0$ the manager produces at least $\bar{x}$. When $B(x) = 0$ he will maximize his returns at $\bar{x} = r/\theta$, and returns are zero at

$$x_0 = (r/\theta) + (1/\theta)[r^2 - 2\theta(r\bar{x} - g)]^{1/2}$$

When $B(x) > 0$ and $0 < x \leq \bar{x}$, $R = 0$ at

$$x^* = (2b/\theta)[1 - s(1 + \gamma^*)]$$

and $dR/dx = 0$ at

$$\hat{x} = (b/\theta)[1 - s(1 + \gamma^*)]$$

as long as $1 > s(1 + \gamma^*)$ and $0 < \hat{x} < x^* \leq \bar{x}$. $\hat{x}$ is a maximum since $d^2R/dx^2 = -\theta < 0$. If $x \geq \bar{x}$, $R = 0$ at

$$x_1^{**} = \frac{b + r}{\theta} - \frac{1}{\theta}\{(b + r)^2 - 2\theta[ab(1 + \gamma^*) - g + r\bar{x}]\}^{1/2} < \frac{b + r}{\theta}$$

$$x_2^{**} = \frac{b + r}{\theta} + \frac{1}{\theta}\{(b + r)^2 - 2\theta[ab(1 + \gamma^*) - g + r\bar{x}]\}^{1/2} > \frac{b + r}{\theta}$$

as long as $x_i^{**} \geq \bar{x}$ and $(b + r)^2 + 2\theta g > 2\theta ab(1 + \gamma^*) + 2\theta r\bar{x}$.

Since $\eta_f = -1$ when $x > \bar{x}$, $dR/dx = 0$ at $\hat{\hat{x}} = (b + r)/\theta$ as long as $\hat{\hat{x}} \geq \bar{x}$. This is a maximum because $d^2R/dx^2 < 0$. If $x_2^{**}$ exists, then $R_2(\hat{\hat{x}}) > 0$. Therefore, bribery raises the manager's maximum expected return from $r/\theta$ to $(b + r)/\theta$. Net corrupt returns might be negative at the planned output. Even though $g - (\theta\bar{x}^2/2) > 0$, it is possible for $R(x) = b\bar{x}[1 - s(1 + \gamma^*)] + g - (\theta/2)\bar{x}^2 < 0$ if the expected penalty per dollar $(s\gamma^*)$ is sufficiently large.

The values of $x$ for which $R(x) > 0$ then depend upon the size of $\bar{x}$. The five cases are:

1  $\bar{x} < \hat{x}$.
2  $\hat{x} < \bar{x} < x^*$.
3  $\hat{x} < x^* < \bar{x}$ and $R < 0$ for all $x > \bar{x}$.
4  $\hat{x} < x^* < \bar{x} < x_1^{**} < \hat{\hat{x}} < x_2^{**}$.
5  $\hat{x} < x^* < \bar{x} < \hat{\hat{x}} < x_2^{**}$ and $x_1^{**} < \bar{x}$ with $R(\bar{x}) > 0$ when $G_2(\bar{x})$
   holds, and $R(x) < 0$ when $G_1(x)$ holds and $x \to \bar{x}$.

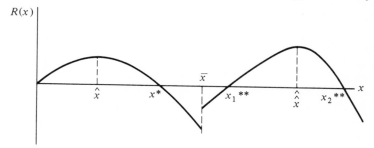

Figure 1. Expected corrupt returns negative in neighborhood of planned output.

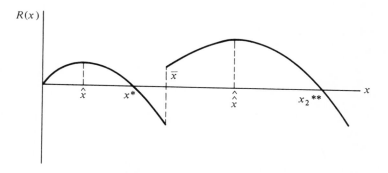

Figure 2. Expected corrupt returns jump discontinuously from negative to positive at planned output.

In the first three cases, if $R(x) > G(\bar{x})$, bribes that require $x$ to be less than some critical $x^*$ or $x^{**}$ will be accepted, and higher bribes will be refused.

The last two cases are the most interesting and are illustrated in Figures 1 and 2. In case 4, as long as $1 > s(1 + \gamma^*)$, bribes that require the manager to produce close to plan are turned down, but small bribes less than $bx^*$, and those between $bx_1^{**}$ and $bx_2^{**}$, are accepted. This case occurs if and only if

$$x^* < \bar{x} < x_1^{**}$$

In our example this condition reduces to $R(\bar{x}) < 0$ or

$$-(\theta/2)\bar{x}^2 + b[1 - s(1 + \gamma^*)]\bar{x} + g < 0$$

Case 5 occurs when $1 > s(1 + \gamma^*)$, $x^* < \bar{x} < \hat{x}$, $x_1^{**} < \bar{x}$, and $R(\bar{x}) > 0$, or

$$-(\theta/2)\bar{x}^2 + b[1 - s(1 + \gamma^*)]\bar{x} + g > 0$$

and

$$(2b/\theta)[1 - s(1 + \gamma^*)] < \bar{x}$$

Bribes that require $x$ to be above plan but less than $x_2^{**}$ are acceptable, as are bribes that generate low levels of output. Bribes are rejected if they require $x$ to be either very large or just short of $\bar{x}$. When bribes are offered conditional on a particular level of $x = x_B$, the manager will compare his net corrupt gains with net returns at $\bar{x} = r/\theta$. The bribe will be accepted if $R(x_B) > G(\bar{x})$. If the supplier can exploit his monopoly power, he seeks a bribe of $b\hat{x}$ and produces $\hat{x} > \bar{x}$.

### Notes

1 There are, of course, no accurate statistics on the level of illicit payments in the USSR or the proportion of the population involved. Grossman (1977, pp. 27–8) believes it is a "commonplace, everyday phenomenon" and cites Soviet journalism, emigré reports, and recent books by two Western correspondents (Kaiser, 1976; Smith, 1976).
2 The concept of a complete hierarchy is developed in Koopmans and Montias (1971). A classic study of the Soviet planning system is Bergson (1964). General descriptions of the entire Soviet system are found in Gregory and Stuart (1974) and Hough (1979). In this chapter the collective farm sector is considered to be part of the CH.
3 We do not consider the more complex case where the rewards of agents in "associations" of enterprises depend upon the performance of their subordinate enterprises.
4 One of the workshop participants, Vladimir Treml, stressed the corrupt incentives inherent in a system that combines decentralization with overlapping authority. He argued that most Soviet managers report to several superiors in different ministries and can use this division of authority to gain room for corrupt maneuvering.
5 A good deal of the discussion in the workshop centered on the question of why the Soviets do not set prices at market clearing levels, thus eliminating one payoff opportunity. Abram Bergson suggested that the Soviets still have a residual hostility to using prices to allocate goods and noted that it may be politically costly to leaders to raise the official prices of important products. Several others suggested that Soviet-style economies set wages first and then use price schedules as a tool for affecting the income distribution. Low-wage people pay for necessities with a combination of time and money prices.
6 The definition is somewhat broader than that in Rose-Ackerman (1978, pp. 6–7).
7 The distinction is similar to Kramer's (1977, p. 214), who contrasts (1) corruption for private gain and (2) corruption for bureaucratic gain. Katsenelinboigen (1978, 165–9) identifies "gray" and "brown" markets. Gray markets are ones that "give the authorities a chance to boost their target functions" (p. 169). "Brown" markets, in contrast, are illegal market responses to scarcity that have "considerable negative consequences" for the authorities (p. 169).
8 In large private Western corporations, managers may also find it in their interest to tacitly encourage the corruption of lower-level officials. For a discussion, see Rose-Ackerman (1978, pp. 191–6).

9  For an analysis of such direct and indirect exchanges in a Soviet-type economy, see Powell (1977).

10 Let $y = f(x)$, where $y$, the output of $Y$, is a strictly concave function of the output $x$ of $X$. Let $f(x)$ be the output function of each $Y$-producer, keeping all other inputs constant. If planned allocations are realized, the output of $Y$ is $2f(1,000)$. If the special deal goes through, $y$ equals $f(500) + f(1,500)$, which is less than $2f(1,000)$ by the assumed concavity of $f$. By the same reasoning, the output of $X$ must also decline (provided that the planned allotments of the two producers of $X$ were equal to begin with).

11 Kramer (1977, p. 217) and Simis (1979, p. 50) both mention the "tautness" of plans as one reason why managers engage in corruption.

12 It is impossible to know if this practice is widespread. Simis (1979, p. 42), however, cites examples from eight of the Soviet Republics.

13 Grossman (1977, p. 30) writes that "in an economy with pervasive goods shortages such as exist in the Soviet Union, physical or administrative control over goods often confers both the power and the opportunity for economic gain to the individual, be he or she ever so humble in the formal hierarchy."

14 For example, government officials purchased meat directly from the collective farm chairman in Tambov province, and in return the farm was not inconvenienced by audits and inspections [*Izvestia,* August 15, 1974, reported in the *Current Digest of the Soviet Press* 26 (September 11, 1974): 33]. In another example the secretary of the extension course division of a university obtained an apartment with the help of a housing inspector. In return, the secretary faked the inspector's university grades (Chalidze, 1977, p. 156).

15 This occurred in Georgia in the USSR (Grossman, 1977, p. 31; Kaiser, 1976, pp. 111–13).

16 For example, given the shortages prevalent in the USSR, firms do not need to pay bribes to obtain sales.

17 Simis (1979, pp. 37, 40) contends that the local militia are frequently given free meals and gifts of food by restaurants and grocery stores. They accept bribes in return for overlooking traffic violations and have been involved in illegal currency speculation. These offenses will sound familiar to any student of police corruption in the United States. See Knapp Commission (1974), Kornblum (1976), and Pennsylvania Crime Commission (1974).

18 According to Simis (1979, p. 40), the militia demand bribes in return for issuing driving licenses and permitting vehicles to pass inspections. Auditors and inspectors of industrial plants are also bribed (Simis, 1979, p. 51). *Pravda* (Nov. 27, 1974) reports the case of an auditor who was bribed not to report the existence of surplus goods [reprinted in *Current Digest of the Soviet Press* 26 (December 25, 1974): 21]. In the United States the bribery of inspectors of buildings, grain, meat, and restaurants has been uncovered in recent scandals. (The cases are cited in Rose-Ackerman, 1978.)

19 *Pravda* (April 11, 1974) reported the case of an inspector in the Social Security Department who forged documents in return for bribes authorizing the payments of pensions or increasing their amounts [reprinted in the *Current Digest of the Soviet Press* 26 (May 8, 1974): 20]. In the USSR the university admissions process is apparently quite corrupt. See Chalidze (1977, p. 156), Kramer (1977, p. 216), and Simis (1979, p. 42). In the United States bribes have been paid by people seeking civil service jobs in some cities and states.

See "6 Top Aides in New Britain Held in Corruption Inquiry," *New York Times,* August 3, 1979, and McNeill (1966) for a discussion of kickbacks in Indiana.

20 In the USSR corruption in obtaining apartments and automobiles is apparently widespread (Grossman, 1977; Kramer, 1977, pp. 214–16). In the United States people have paid bribes to be admitted to public housing (*New Haven Register,* April 1, 1976) and to obtain special protection from policemen (Knapp, 1974; Pennsylvania Crime Commission, 1974).

21 For Soviet examples, see Kramer (1977, pp. 216–17) and Simis (1979, p. 50). See Amick (1976) and Jacoby et al. (1977) for cases involving American business.

22 If the firm is in a competitive industry and if there are no cost advantages in selling to the government, bribes will be zero unless the government will pay more than the prevailing market price. Many government contracts, however, are for special-purpose equipment, permit scale economies to be realized, or are made with firms in oligopolistic industries. In any of these cases corruption is possible. For a discussion of corruption in government contracting, see Rose-Ackerman (1978, pp. 109–35).

23 Cases of corruption in local land-use regulation in the United States are detailed in Gardiner and Lyman (1978).

24 This conclusion must be qualified if law enforcement officials have overlapping authority. No one will pay much to a corrupt policeman if he expects to be arrested by someone else a few hours later. For a discussion, see Rose-Ackerman (1978, pp. 159–63).

25 Wilensky (1967) provides a critical analysis of the costs of secrecy in defense and intelligence.

26 The organization of the Communist Party in the USSR is described in many standard sources (e.g., Hough, 1979). The role of the party at the local level is described in Hough (1969).

27 In a series of articles in *Problems of Communism,* Lipson (1958, 1959, 1961) emphasizes the lack of independence from party control of both the judiciary and the rest of the law enforcement apparatus. Simis (1979, p. 43) writes that "despite the principle of an independent judiciary enshrined in the Constitution, the Soviet courts are an integral part of the state apparatus, which, like any other sector of the state system, is itself, subordinate to the Party apparatus."

28 Kramer (1977, pp. 220–2) reports that the chance of detection and severe punishment are small in spite of harsh laws and a good deal of public high-level official concern.

29 The interdependence of all facets of Soviet society is emphasized by Kramer (1977, p. 222) and Simis (1979, p. 36).

30 Illegal entrepreneurial activity has flourished in Georgia because of such "family circles." An illegal entrepreneur sentenced in 1973 was reported to be in partnership with the wife of the First Secretary of the Communist Party. In the shakeup that followed this scandal, numerous top officials were arrested or dismissed (Kaiser, 1976, pp. 111–12).

31 Chalidze (1977, pp. 148–9) observes that one cannot tell if the harsh Soviet law against bribery "reduces the incidence of bribery or only the number of prosecutions." The severity of punishment may deter potential plaintiffs: "Not everyone wants to see the death penalty or a long term of imprisonment inflicted on someone, who, like many others, accepts a reward for helping individuals to settle their affairs."

32 Simis (1979, pp. 46–50) lists several corruption scandals involving high party officials and notes that, in general, high-level officials were not severely punished.

33 For example, widespread corruption in the Azerbaidjan party and state hierarchy was exposed in 1969 (Simis, 1979, pp. 47–48).

34 Kushev (1975, p. 2) gives several examples of people with no official job or with official jobs that they do not perform.

35 Almost all activities labeled "speculation" by authorities in the USSR are legal in the West. In addition, illicit production of repair services, housing, and consumer goods apparently occurs frequently (Grossman, 1977, p. 31; Kaiser, 1976, pp. 341–3; Kramer, 1977, pp. 214–6).

36 Prices are apparently high on the "gray" and "brown" markets in the USSR (Katsenelinboigen, 1978). For example, a garage built privately cost 65 percent more than if "regular" workers supplied by the hierarchy had been used [*Current Digest* 28 (October 1976): 6].

37 A similar type of illicit activity is the private manufacture of scarce goods or the private sale of services in short supply. Once again, however, the illegality of the activity itself affects its efficiency. First, some inputs may be stolen (see Connor, 1972, pp. 265–6; Grossman, 1977, pp. 26, 29–30; and Kramer, 1977), and work on the illicit products may be carried out during regular working hours. Second, capital accumulation is difficult because fixed investments are hard to keep hidden from the authorities. Third, what would be a fairly routine investment decision in the West involves substantial risks in the USSR. Fifth, illegal entrepreneurs have difficulty "laundering" their earnings. They cannot easily become respectable in their old age and legally pass on a fortune to their children. Nevertheless, some illegal entrepreneurs have apparently been able to transmit some of their gains to their children by purchasing them university admission or jobs in the official hierarchy.

38 Similarly, if we assume that planners care about the welfare of ordinary citizens, they could ignore some kinds of illicit activities without changing the formal legal status of the transactions. All sorts of transactions that are now illicit – such as, say, chauffeurs of official cars picking up paying customers on the way to an assignment (Kaiser, 1976, p. 342; Katsenelinboigen 1978, p. 189) – yield substantial benefits to the transactors and have fairly small ideological costs for the authorities. The authorities could simply signal that certain laws will not be enforced.

39 Bergson (1978), Holmstrom (1979), and Shavell (1979) are concerned with inducing agents to maximize total surplus. Bonin (1976) and Weitzman (1976) design schemes that produce accurate information.

40 Two recent papers have, however, analyzed situations in which a group of agents conspire against the central planner. The authors show that when this happens, incentive compatibility is impossible (Conn and Bennett, 1977; Green and Laffont, 1979).

41 In the following example, there are two firms with actual production functions: $y_1 = \sqrt{x_1}$ and $y_2 = \sqrt{x_2}$. Suppose that the supplier has an asymmetric relationship with the firms that purchase $X$. It requires firm 1 to pay a bribe equal to 0.1 unit of bonus money per unit of $X$, but has no bargaining power vis-à-vis firm 2. Thus, firm 2 pays no bribe. The expected bonus of firm 1 equals $\alpha(\hat{y}_1 + y_2) - 0.1x_1$. Let firm 1 transmit the production function $\hat{y}_1 = 0.9\sqrt{x_1}$, thereby underestimating its potential. There are 8 units of $X$ to be allocated. The allocation that maximizes $(0.9\sqrt{x_1} + \sqrt{x_2})$ is ($x_1 = 3.58$, $x_2 = 4.42$). Firm 1's bonus equals $3.9994\alpha - 0.358$. If firm 1 had transmitted

its actual production function, the optimal allocation would have been $(x_1 = 4, x_2 = 4)$, and the bonus of firm 1 would have been $4\alpha - 0.4$, which is less than $3.994\alpha - 0.358$ for all $0 \le \alpha \le 1$. It is therefore advantageous for the firm to understate its production potential. Note, more generally, that the bonus function of firm 1 net of the bribe is not a member of the class of incentive compatible schemes, which includes all linear transformations $\beta(\sqrt{x_1} + \sqrt{x_2}) + A$, for positive $\beta$, provided that $\beta$ and $A$ are independent of the reported production function $\hat{y}_1(x_1)$ (Conn, 1979, p. 265).

42 In the formal discussion, we ignore the problem of proving guilt and the possibility of a false accusation. The basic framework is drawn from work on the economics of crime (Becker, 1968; Stigler, 1970) and of corruption (Becker and Stigler, 1974; Rose-Ackerman, 1978, pp. 109–36).

43 The case of Mikhail Stern (1977) is apparently an example of the Soviets' use of corruption charges for political purposes. After his sons applied to emigrate to Israel, Stern was accused of accepting gifts or bribes from patients (a common practice in the Soviet Union).

44 Formal legal penalties are high in the USSR; see Chalidze (1977, p. 148).

45 Grossman (1977, p. 40) makes a similar suggestion. This has been done to some extent in Hungary. See "Hungary Tries a Bit of Capitalism to Cure Some Communist Ills," *Wall Street Journal,* June 6, 1979.

46 According to Grossman (1977, pp. 33–4) and Kramer (1977, pp. 214–6), the industries most subject to corruption are farming, housing, transportation (including private cars), the production of vodka, and foreign trade.

47 A recent study has shown that enterprises in Eastern Europe and the USSR are large relative to those in Western Europe (Pryor, 1973).

48 Katsenelinboigen (1978, p. 188) reports that, in retailing, corruption generally involves several hierarchical layers. He states that "even if a young clerk is honest, she is forced to do these things by the department head to whom she must give part of her income. The latter, in turn, must give part of his income to the store manager," and so forth.

49 This point is made by Grossman (1977, p. 36), who notes the growing liquidity of Soviet consumers.

50 The Soviet Union has frequently neglected to produce complements, especially repair services and spare parts. This leads to the development of a black market and corruption. See Grossman (1977), Katsenelinboigen (1978), and Radio Liberty Research: "The Dawn of the Automobile Era Gives Boost to the Black Market" (RL 132/75).

51 Kramer reports (1977, p. 213) that Soviet commentators "traditionally have associated political corruption with public officials in decadent capitalist systems. . . . Such commentators generally attribute instances of corruption among Soviet officials today to 'vestiges of the past' that will wither away as the Socialist system becomes even more firmly established." Katsenelinboigen (1978, pp. 165–6) notes that "for a long time the attempt was made to explain human vices in the USSR as remnants of capitalism in people's minds."

52 This is probably a realistic concern. Connor (1972, pp. 255–6) reports that many people in the USSR justify minor illegalities on the ground that everyone else does it, including party leaders and enterprise managers.

53 Several authors have pointed out that corruption may serve some of the interests of the Soviet leaders. In particular, it may "add significantly to their control of subordinate hierarchies," because almost everyone can be threat-

ened with prosecution (Grossman, 1977, p. 37). See also Kramer (1977, p. 223).

54 At the same time, the risks connected with illicit private activity are large enough that most risk-neutral or risk-averse people will not produce illegal services unless the expected gains are very large. The high risk to the supplier leaves the field open to risk-prone "adventurers" and "parasites," socially deviant types that the state would wish to curb irrespective of the activities they engaged in. This makes the authorities more apt to repress semilicit behavior than they might otherwise, thereby further raising the risk involved. The poor reputation of the "speculators," which makes ordinary citizens willing to denounce them to the police and increases the costs of illicit activities, appears to be one of many elements that maintain the system in institutional equilibrium.

# References

Amick, George. *The American Way of Graft*. Princeton, N.J.: Center for Analysis of Public Issues, 1976.

Becker, Gary. "Crime and Punishment: An Economic Approach." *Journal of Political Economy* 76 (January–February 1968): 169–217.

Becker, Gary, and Stigler, George. "Law Enforcement, Malfeasance, and Compensation of Enforcers." *Journal of Legal Studies* 3 (January 1974): 1–19.

Bergson, Abram. *The Economics of Soviet Planning*. New Haven, Conn.: Yale University Press, 1964.

Bergson, Abram. "Managerial Risks and Rewards in Public Enterprises." *Journal of Comparative Economics* 2 (September 1978): 211–25.

Bonin, John. "On the Design of Managerial Incentive Structures in a Decentralized Planning Environment." Middletown, Conn.: Wesleyan University. Mimeographed, June 1976.

Chalidze, Valery. *Criminal Russia*. New York: Random House, 1977.

Conn, David. "A Comparison of Alternative Incentive Structures for Centrally Planned Economies." *Journal of Comparative Economics* 3 (September 1979): 261–76.

Conn, David, and Bennett, Elaine. "The Group Incentive Properties of Mechanisms for the Provision of Public Goods." *Public Choice* 32 (Spring 1977): 95–102.

Connor, Walter D. *Deviance in Soviet Society: Crime, Delinquency, and Alcoholism*. New York: Columbia University Press, 1972.

Gardiner, John A., and Lyman, Theodore A. *Decisions for Sale: Corruption in Local Land-Use Regulation*. New York: Praeger, 1978.

Granick, David. "The Ministry as the Organizing Unit in Soviet Industry." *Journal of Comparative Economics* 4 (September 1980), 255–73.

Green, J., and Laffont, J. J. "On Coalition Incentive Compatibility." *Review of Economic Studies* 46 (April 1979): 243–54.

Gregory, Paul, and R. Stuart. *Soviet Economic Structure and Performance*. New York: Harper & Row, 1974.

Grossman, Gregory. "The 'Second Economy' of the USSR." *Problems of Communism* 26 (September–October 1977): 25–39.

Groves, Theodore. "Incentives in Teams." *Econometrica* 41 (1978): 20–33.

Holmstrom, Bengt. "Moral Hazard and Observability." *Bell Journal of Economics* 10 (Spring 1979): 74–91.

Hough, Jerry. *The Soviet Prefects*. Cambridge, Mass.: Harvard University Press, 1969.

Hough, Jerry. *How the Soviet Union Is Governed*. Cambridge, Mass.: Harvard University Press, 1979.

Jacoby, Neil; Nehemkis, Peter; and Eels, Richard. *Bribery and Extortion in World Business*. New York: Macmillan, 1977.

Johnson, O. E. G. "An Economic Analysis of Corrupt Government with Special Application to Less Developed Countries." *Kyklos* 28 (1975): 47–61.

Kaiser, Robert G. *Russia: The People and the Power*. New York: Atheneum, 1976.

Katsenelinboigen, Aron. *Studies in Soviet Economic Planning*. New York: M. E. Sharpe, 1978.

Knapp Commission (Commission to Investigate Allegations of Police Corruption and the City's Anti-corruption Procedures). *Commission Report*. New York, 1974.

Koopmans, T. C., and J. M. Montias. "On the Description and Comparison of Economic Systems," in *Comparison of Economic Systems: Theoretical and Methodological Approaches* (A. Eckstein, ed). Berkeley, Calif.: University of California Press, 1971.

Kornblum, Allan N. *The Moral Hazards*. Lexington, Mass.: D. C. Heath, 1976.

Kramer, John. "Political Corruption in the USSR." *Western Political Quarterly* 30 (June 1977): 213–24.

Krueger, Anne O. "The Political Economy of the Rent-seeking Society." *American Economic Review* 64 (June 1974): 271–303.

Kushev, Eugenii. " 'Lumpen-Intelligentsia' in the Soviet Union: A Look at Drop-outs from the System." *Radio Liberty Special Report* (RL 187/75), May 2, 1975.

Lipson, Leon. "The New Face of 'Socialist Legality'." *Problems of Communism*. 7 (July–August 1958): 22–30.

Lipson, Leon. "Socialist Legality: The Mountain Has Labored." *Problems of Communism* 8 (March–April 1959): 15–19.

Lipson, Leon. "The Criminal Reconsidered." *Problems of Communism*. 10 (July–August 1961): 58–60.

Loeb, Martin, and W. A. Magat, "Success Indicators in the Soviet Union: The Problem of Incentives and Efficient Allocation. *American Economic Review* 68 (March 1978): 173–81.

McNeill, Robert K. *Democratic Campaign Financing in Indiana, 1964*. Bloomington, Ind.: Institute of Public Administration and Citizens Research Foundation, 1966.

Montias, John Michael. *The Structure of Economic Systems*. New Haven, Conn.: Yale University Press, 1976.

Pennsylvania Crime Commission. *Report on Police Corruption and the Quality of Law Enforcement in Philadelphia*. Saint Davids, Pa.: The Commission, 1974.

Powell, Raymond, "Plan Execution and the Workability of Soviet Planning." *Journal of Comparative Economics* 1 (1977): 51–78.

Pryor, Frederic L. *Property and Industrial Organization in Communist and Capitalist Nations*. Bloomington, Ind.: Indiana University Press, 1973.

Rose-Ackerman, Susan. *Corruption: A Study in Political Economy*. New York: Academic Press, 1978.

Scott, James C. *Comparative Political Corruption*. Englewood Cliffs, N.J.: Prentice-Hall, 1972.

Shavell, Stephen. "Risk Sharing and Incentives in the Principal and Agent Relationship." *Bell Journal of Economics* 10 (Spring 1979): 55–73.

Simis, Konstantin, "The Machinery of Corruption in the Soviet Union." *Survey* (1979): 36–55.

Smith, Hedrick. *The Russians.* New York: Quadrangle Books, 1976.

Stern, Mikhail, defendant. *The USSR vs. Dr. Mikhail Stern.* New York: Urizen Books, 1977.

Stigler, George J. "The Optimum Enforcement of Laws." *Journal of Political Economy* 78 (May–June 1970): 526–36.

Weitzman, Martin. "The New Soviet Incentive Model." *Bell Journal of Economics and Management Science* 7 (Spring 1976): 251–8.

Wilensky, Harold. *Organizational Intelligence.* New York: Basic Books, 1967.

# 4 Soviet use of fixed prices: hypothesis of a job-right constraint

*David Granick*

The Soviet Union's system of resource allocation combines the method of direct determination of outputs by the center with the method of central determination of parametric prices and rules of behavior. Direct allocation is used for subaggregates of products, and centrally determined prices – which, because of their considerable stickiness, cannot constitute a "dual" – are used parametrically to determine the product mix of these subaggregates. Why this reliance by the center on *both* physical planning and centrally determined parametric pricing?

The answer which first suggests itself is that parametric prices are used to deal with a level of disaggregation that cannot be handled by physical planning. Thus, the two methods complement one another. However, given that their stickiness prevents centrally determined prices from acting as a "dual," why does the center not allow the parametric prices that determine the demand and supply of individual items within each subaggregate to be determined on the marketplace? Not only would this procedure have certain optimizing features currently absent, but it could also be used – if this were desired – to increase the degree of planners' sovereignty over the product mix of consumers' goods.

The explanation that is offered in this chapter for the continuation since the beginning of the 1930s of the foregoing features of the Soviet planning system is that there exists a set of constraints, embodied in the center's objective function, which has not been considered in either the Soviet or Western literature. This set is built around job rights for the individual worker. Within this set, it is (4d) of Section II that is critical in requiring the use of centrally determined rather than market prices.

This paper was written with the aid of the Kennan Institute for Advanced Russian Studies of the Woodrow Wilson International Center for Scholars and of the Graduate School of the University of Wisconsin – Madison.

85

## I. The problem

Modern modeling of socialist allocation of resources began with an approach in which the center sets parametric prices and the rules of behavior for enterprise managers, and in which these managers decide on physical outputs and inputs as a function of such prices and rules (Lange, 1936–7). The implications of this approach with regard to socialist managers' behavior was worked out in some detail by Abram Bergson in two essays, "Socialist Economics" and "Socialist Calculation" (Bergson, 1966). The principal line of such modeling has continued along this path, substituting incentive systems for rules of behavior. An efficiency objection to such allocation through pricing instruments is that of Weitzman (1974). But the basic objection to such theoretic development of the use of the "dual" is that of irrelevance: in no socialist economy has the center in fact attempted to control the economy in this fashion.

The alternative approach has been to model an allocation system in which the center determines directly, through one or another iterative approach, the outputs of all products (e.g., Malinvaud, 1967). On the face of things, this approach would appear to be much more relevant to the working of the Soviet economy.

Let us begin an analysis of its relevance with two assumptions that appear to fit the facts of the current Soviet economy.

> Both consumer-goods and producer-goods prices are set
> centrally, but the price-setting task is so large that prices in
> general can be changed only at very long intervals.     (1)

> Central authorities have the objective of balancing the
> supply and demand of consumer goods (or, at a minimum, of
> subaggregates of such goods) at existing prices.[1]     (2)

Given that consumer demand functions for the various subaggregates change over time, and that they have different income elasticities, these assumptions imply that the center is extremely restricted in its freedom to plan the quantities of consumer goods to be produced in intervals between major price changes. True, it is fairly free in determining the monetary value of the total amount of consumer goods to be produced; this freedom arises from the center's control over the monetary income distributed to the population. However, as long as it respects condition (2) and also avoids unnecessary accumulation of stocks of consumer goods, it has thereafter no power of choice over the relative quantities of different subaggregates to be supplied. This implies that central determination of consumer prices constrains the center to accept a limited but still significant form of consumers' sovereignty – as opposed to the traditional Western thesis, originally proposed by Bergson, of planners' sovereignty combined with consumers' choice – during the long intervals between major price reforms. Moreover, owing to the existence both of physical input–output relations and capital/output relations, central determination of the relative supply of intermediate products and of capital goods is also somewhat restricted.

Although this result is important for the degree of planners' sovereignty implied by a system of centrally determined consumers' prices, it has no bearing on the relevance to the Soviet economy of models in which the center directly determines the outputs of all goods. In Lange's original basic system of central determination of parametric prices, the center is fully constrained in its choice of relative prices, with the single exception of the time rate of discount; with this exception, planners' sovereignty is exercised exclusively through the center's use of fiscal powers as a final purchaser of certain goods, and through its highly constrained choice of a rule for allocating the "social dividend." The two types of models are comparable in that the effectiveness of the center's use of its powers to fix relative consumer-goods outputs (or all prices in the other model) can be evaluated exclusively on efficiency grounds because this aspect of the center's task is purely technical and involves no employment of welfare criteria.[2]

More pertinent is the following condition, which shares with (1) the feature that it represents limitations, binding upon Soviet planners, which arise exclusively from administrative considerations.

> The number of products, when fully disaggregated, is so
> large that the center (including its representatives at
> ministerial and *glavk* levels) can both plan and set production
> targets for enterprises only in terms of subaggregates.     (3)

The significance of (3) is that, within any subaggregate for which a supply target could be set, the supply of the disaggregated individual products cannot be equated to their demand through direct determination of output by the center. An optimizing system that used central determination of physical quantities as its sole instrument would be equally impossible to implement administratively as would its "dual"; neither is capable of handling the large number of individual products produced in the economy. Both approaches could be restricted to subaggregates but would yield determinate results at the level of the individual product only if complemented in some fashion. Thus, the direct quantitative approach might be made determinate through the use of fixed prices as arguments in behavioral rules for determining the production mix within a given subaggregate; the "dual" approach could rely on fixed ratios between the prices of individual products within a subaggregate, with the subaggregate price being set by the center in each planning period. Neither approach, thus modified, would equate supply to demand at the level of the individual product.

Soviet physical allocation does indeed deal in subaggregates. Both Soviet constant prices (used in weighting the relative output of individual products produced by an enterprise, and thus determining its labor productivity) and current prices (used in expressing the enterprise's sales, profits, rate of cost reduction, and level of profitability) remain fixed for long periods [by (1)]. Thus, no maximization by suppliers of a function of any one of these indicators or of a weighted average of them can be used as a device for equating the supply and demand of individual disaggregated consumer products between years of major price reform. If demand functions for disaggregated consumer products, within a given subaggregate of such goods, change during these lengthy periods – or even if they are stable but have different income elasticities – no mechanism is available to cause movement along the demand curves so as to bring about equilibrium at the level of the disaggregated products.

At least as serious, there is the same absence of equilibrating forces at the level of disaggregated products in the realm of intermediate products and capital goods. Here, the Soviet materials allocation system determines the quantity demanded of each subaggregate, and the system of production targets determines the quantity supplied of each subaggregate. But as the opportunity cost to the suppliers of one final disaggregated product in terms of foregone production of other disaggregated products changes during the interim between price reforms, the relative supply of these disaggregates within a given subaggregate varies from its original proportions; for a similar reason, the relative demand for these disaggregates also varies.

The conclusions from assumptions (1), (2), and (3) can be summed up as follows:

1    A model of central determination of outputs has relevance to the Soviet economy only at the level of subaggregates, but not at the level of individual products. The "dual" has no direct relevance whatsoever.

2    Soviet central authorities have no means available to exercise planners' sovereignty as among different consumer-goods subaggregates during the periods between major price reforms.[3]

3    If we assume that individual enterprises engage in some form of maximizing under constraints, then disequilibrium of supply and demand at the individual-product level is inevitable for all goods during the interims between price reforms. More serious, no equilibrating forces are at work during these interims.

When we add to these three summary conclusions a fourth – (4) that implementation of research and development in new products and in major process change is made peculiarly difficult by the system of fixed prices (Granick, 1978) – one must ask why Soviet authorities not only choose to operate with a system of centrally determined prices, but have chosen to do this over a sufficiently long period so that this choice can be viewed as an equilibrium rather than a transitional selection.

It is important to recognize that a system of market prices could be instituted that would overturn the second, third, and fourth conclusions drawn above without otherwise fundamentally altering the Soviet economic system. Production and materials allocations could continue to be planned at the level of subaggregates in constant prices, whereas current prices both paid and received for consumer products, intermediate goods, and capital goods were left to be determined on the marketplace. Although this would require a two-price system, Soviet administrators already employ two sets of prices – one set being used to measure labor productivity and to determine the enterprise's wage fund, and another for all other purposes. It is true that the suggested change to a two-price system in which one set is market-determined would do little good unless subaggregate output (productivity) targets were relatively loose;[4] but this is already the case for output at the level of aggregation of the industrial ministry[5] and must also be true for at least a considerable majority of the individual enterprises. The suggested change would permit the center to employ, if it wished, planners' sovereignty as to output among different subaggregates of consumer goods, and would both create an equilibrating force, and eliminate the current obstacle to incentive for implementation of product innovations, for individual products within a given subaggregate of goods of any type. Although such a change would do nothing to remove other blemishes of the Soviet administrative system – this requiring more fundamental change – it would offer substantial gross advantages to Soviet planners.

Various approaches to answering the question of why Soviet authorities have chosen over an extended period to operate exclusively with centrally determined product prices are open to political scientists, sociologists, historians, and perhaps even to economists other than those of the neoclassical variety. For the neoclassical economist, however, it would seem to the writer that the question can be properly approached in only one way: by elaborating a planners' welfare function which both appears consistent with the known facts concerning the Soviet economy and whose maximization is consistent with the central determination of prices. The necessity for taking this approach derives from the basic assumption of neoclassical economics: that all decision makers are rational, and that their behavior can be characterized by maximization under constraints.

Consistent use of this assumption requires that it be applied not only to individual consumers and to suppliers of factors and products, but also to the authorities who shape the specific elements of the institutional structure within which individual and managerial maximization occurs.[6] Although such an application of the rationality assumption to institutional structure is not obligatory for all elements of the structure – certain fundamental elements may be determined by sociopolitical considerations that transcend the domain of economic rationality – it would seem that the choice of a particular form of pricing mechanism in a centrally planned socialist economy epitomizes the sort of narrow institutional decision that the neoclassical economist is obliged to incorporate into his Weltanschauung.

Section II elaborates and justifies the relevant aspect of the planners' welfare function. This aspect is incorporated in (4) and more particularly in (4d). It is argued that this job-rights set of constraints within the welfare function is a *sufficient* condition for explaining central determination of prices. It is not argued that it is a necessary condition; such an argument would require the examination of alternative economic explanations and would transcend the limits of this paper.

## II. The job-right hypothesis

In specifying the Soviet planners' welfare function, the novelty to be introduced is a set of four conditions – all emanating from a particular concept of a worker's right to his job – which are embodied in the planners' welfare function as constraints upon the maximization of an objective function containing other arguments. These conditions are as follows:

$$\text{Pr} \left\{ \begin{array}{l} \text{individual}_i \text{ is dismissed from his current} \\ \text{enterprise} \end{array} \right\} \leq e_1 \quad (4a)$$

$$\text{Pr} \left\{ \begin{array}{l} \text{individual}_i \text{ is compelled involuntarily to change} \\ \text{the type of work done within his current} \\ \text{enterprise} \end{array} \right\} \leq e_2 \quad (4b)$$

$$\text{Pr} \left\{ \begin{array}{l} \text{total annual income of manual worker}_i, \text{ while} \\ \text{he continues to work in his current enterprise} \\ \text{and in his current type of work, declines by} \\ > x \text{ percent} \end{array} \right\} \leq e_3 \quad (4c)$$

$$\text{Pr} \left\{ \begin{array}{l} \text{individual}_i \text{ is kept idle within his current} \\ \text{enterprise for} > y \text{ working days per annum} \end{array} \right\} \leq e_4 \quad (4d)$$

where $e_1, \ldots, e_4$ are very small, $x$ is modest (e.g., 10 percent), and $y$ is a moderately substantial number (e.g., 30).

Constraints (4a) and (4b) appear to reflect both Soviet law (Ruble, 1977) and practice. Constraint (4c), operating in an environment of little or no inflation, prevents enterprises from compelling "resignation" of workers by drastically reducing their earnings. Constraint (4d) is introduced to ensure against disguised unemployment taking a form in which the individual worker obtains the impression that he is receiving a dole rather than an earned wage. It can be used to distinguish between supply-created and demand-created disguised unemployment. The Soviet system of materials allocation, particularly when, as now, there is disequilibrium of supply and demand within any subaggregate subject to such allocation, is bound to lead to idle worktime in a high proportion of enterprises; but such idleness can be distributed among individual workers in a fashion approaching randomness provided that deviations of actual from planned deliveries are themselves reasonably random. Demand-created idleness, in contrast, is much more likely to be bunched in its effects on individual enterprises and on product lines within an enterprise.

Let us now explore the implications of (4) in determining those institutional arrangements which are compatible with these constraints embodied in the planners' welfare function.

A. *Allocation of resources through the setting of parametric prices for individual products by the center*. Given assumption (1), this type of allocation system is impossible to realize (as explained above) for administrative reasons.

B. *Use of market-determined prices, no output targets of materials allocation, and the objective function of producers being established as profit maximization*. This institutional arrangement represents more or less the original goal of the Hungarian reform of 1968. The center, as in the basic Lange system, exercises planners' preference primarily as a final purchaser of certain goods and by determining the social rate of time discount (i.e., the allocation of national income between aggregate consumption and aggregate investment); it may also exercise a strong influence on the distribution of disposable income, and may make decisions disaggregating investment at a minimum for cases considered to be of particular importance. (This last role consists of reducing the effects of uncertainty on decision making rather than of exercising a greater degree of planners' preference than would exist without such investment control.[7]

Institutional arrangement B provides no means of enforcing the set of constraints (4) at any time of disequilibrium; in this regard, it shares the disadvantage of any market system. [See Granick (1976, chaps. 8–10) for a discussion of this issue with regard to post-1967 Hungary.] The obvious solution to this difficulty is for the center to try to impose upon the individual enterprises a set of rules that embody these constraints.

Constraints (4a) to (4c) would not appear to present any serious problem in this regard.[8] But it seems to the writer that constraint (4d) is incapable of enforcement by the center under this institutional arrangement. Sharp changes in demand may well cause the objective function of enterprise$_j$ to be maximized by keeping individual$_i$ on the payroll but idle for many more than $y$ working days annually. (Such reduction of the product of the marginal worker to less than zero can be inferred in the case of those large Japanese enterprises that have laid off permanent workers at virtually 100 percent of their normal earnings, with these expenses being borne by the enterprise itself.) "Idleness" is too subjective a concept for it to be feasible for the center to enforce constraint (4d) directly in the same fashion as it could enforce constraints (4a) to (4c).

C. *Institutional arrangement B combined with the constraint on the enterprise of subaggregate output targets measured in market-determined prices.*

If the output targets are loose, even though not so loose that they are totally nonbinding, we return to institutional arrangement B as far as the set of constraints (4) is concerned. Thus, the output constraints must be taut if we are to have a genuinely different case.

However, if output targets measured in market-determined prices are taut, the quantity of a particular subaggregate supplied moves perversely to the demand for that subaggregate. A reduction in demand for subaggregate$_a$, given a constant supply measured in market-determined prices, leads to a reduction in the prices of its component products; this in turn forces an increase in the physical quantities supplied of the subaggregate and increases the utilization in subaggregate$_a$ of material and labor inputs expressed in physical terms. In contrast, physical production of subaggregate$_b$ – for which demand and thus prices have risen – can fall without violating the output constraints placed on the individual enterprise. Since, short of enterprise bankruptcy, an enterprise will always be willing to pay higher prices for inputs necessary to meet constraints than for those useful only in maximizing an objective function, inputs entering into the production of both subaggregates$_{a+b}$ will be diverted to subaggregate$_a$ and the physical output of subaggregate$_b$ will decline. Thus, institutional arrangement C is thoroughly inappropriate.

D. *Institutional arrangement C with the substitution of subaggregate output constraints being measured in constant prices rather than in current market prices.*

For the same reason as under case C, the output constraints must be taut if we are to depart from case B. But extremely taut output constraints imply that the objective function is irrelevant; the enterprises can do no better than meeting their constraints. Thus, in the extreme, demand-determined price variations play no role in allocating resources. Although the set of constraints (4) can be satisfied, there is no improvement in the allocation process over the current Soviet system of maintaining centrally determined prices (case F). A sufficient degree of tautness to escape case B will come uncomfortably close to this extreme-tautness position. Because of changing supply conditions over time, a system of materials allocations might well have to be reintroduced, returning the situation even more closely to the status quo.

E. *Institutional arrangement B with the addition of an enterprise constraint of profits measured in constant prices for both inputs and outputs.* Here we have a profit constraint measured in constant prices combined with an objective function of profits measured in current market prices.

Case E is an uninteresting variant of case D. If the profit constraint in constant prices is taut, the introduction of market prices for the objective function becomes irrelevant. If the constraint is loose, we return once more to case B.

F. *The current Soviet institutional arrangement.* [9] The critical features of this arrangement are as follows:

1   The use of one or more sets of centrally determined prices as measures both of constraints and of arguments in the producer's objective function. The single important exception to this (apart from the collective farm market) is the price of labor (see F3 below).

2   The use of a system of materials allocation of subaggregates of inputs other than labor. Unless the center is willing to renounce planners' sovereignty over all output targets for subaggregates (as we have seen is already effectively the case for the subset of consumer goods), centrally determined prices of intermediate and capital goods must at best depart quickly from their shadow prices as supply functions evolve during the years following the imposition of such prices. Without permitting such departures, the quantities–prices system would be overdetermined. Thus, some type of physical rationing appears indicated.

3   The use of a financial (wage fund) constraint on the ability of producers to compete for labor – the single nonallocated input. The constraint does not take the form of profit or cash flow, but of the total amount of funds available within a period to the producer for the hiring of labor of all sorts. [10]

The relative prices of different types of manual labor are set centrally at the moment of a wage reform, but thereafter are increasingly determined as market prices within the constraints of minima set by the centrally established basic wages for each type of labor and of maxima arising out of the centrally provided wage fund for each producer. The relative basic wages determined by a wage reform may well be close to an equilibrium level for the current distribution of different types of manual workers as between the various producers; the finding by the center of such equilibrium basic wages is greatly simplified by the fact that the basic wage for a given job is set so as to incorporate most of the difference between the total wage payment and the basic wage previously paid. Whether or not these immediate postreform wages are indeed close to equilibrium, equilibrium of total wage payments is thereafter maintained (or approached) through reductions in the average ratio of the basic wage to total wage payments as the period lengthens since the last wage reform.[11] The mechanism for maintaining (or approaching) such equilibrium is the competition among individual suppliers for a mobile labor force; equilibrium occurs where the ratios of marginal products of different kinds of labor are the same in the various enterprises, where these ratios are equal to the wage ratios of the different kinds of labor, and where the wage for a given type of labor working under given conditions is the same in all enterprises.

4    The use of output constraints (normally only minima) by product subaggregates. These constraints are set at least sufficiently high to supply the allocations of such subaggregates to other producers or, when insufficient for this, to permit excesses of such allocations over actual deliveries to be of a fairly random nature as among subaggregates.

5    The guarantee to producers of markets for their outputs. For intermediate and capital goods, this guarantee is implemented by assuring a seller's market. For consumer goods, where assumption (2) provides for the central objective of market-clearing prices, the trade sector absorbs excesses.

6    The use of an objective function to be maximized by the producer. This objective function is expressed in terms of various indicators, which share the following common features: (a) both outputs and costs are expressed in aggregative terms rather than in terms of product subaggregates; (b) outputs and all inputs except labor are combined by the use of fixed weights (normally prices); labor weights are partly fixed (for the indicator of labor productivity) and partly changing (market prices of labor for the indicator of profitability).

7    Partly legislation, but primarily custom, imposes constraints (4a) to (4c) upon the individual producer.

To the degree that all prices are constant and that deviations of deliveries of inputs from materials allocations are random, there would seem to be no incentive for the individual producer to violate constraint (4d). The number of different types of workers within the producer's labor force, and the amount of labor assigned to different product subaggregates, can be adjusted over time by the managers of producing units through their reaction to normal attrition occurring by means of resignations, retirements, and so on. Since the environment to which these managers react remains relatively constant – partly because of constant prices, but also because of the slowness of introduction of new technology – one would expect that respect for constraint (4d) would follow from maximization of the objective function.[12]

To be sure, a problem is introduced with regard to constraint (4d) to the degree that the relative prices of different types of labor are variable. If enterprise$_j$ produces subaggregates$_{a+b}$, then to the extent that product subaggregate$_a$ requires labor-skill types (1 + 2) in fixed proportions, that subaggregate$_b$ requires only labor type (3), and that the market price for labor type (2) rises sharply relative to (1) and (3), profit maximization by enterprise$_j$ may dictate reduction of production of subaggregate$_a$ to the level of the output constraint imposed by the center and – therefore – forced idleness of part of the type (1) labor force.

The degree of this problem is, however, much less than if all prices were free, as in case B above. Respect for constraint (4d) is threatened by changes in relative wages and by varying quit rates for different types of complementary labor; these threats cannot be avoided if a free labor market between enterprises is to be preserved. [The existence of a free labor market should be taken as constraint (5) embodied in the planners' welfare function. Constraint (5) can be viewed as imposing a set of lower limits to $y$ and to $e_4$ in constraint (4d).] However, such threats are not supplemented by those emanating from changes in product prices and nonlabor input prices.

The conclusion of this analysis is that, of the six different types of institutional arrangements examined, only the current Soviet one (case F) is consistent with respect for constraint (4d), which was hypothesized to be embodied in the Soviet planners' welfare function. This is the proposed solution to the puzzle stated in Section I.

## III. Three aspects of the current Soviet system

### A. Production of individual products within planned subaggregates

The problem of supply and demand of individual products, which constitute the disaggregated elements of planned output and planned materials allocations, could well be interpreted from Section I as being so serious as to be beyond the realm of belief. It is my purpose here to suggest how the dimensions of the problem are reduced to a level with which Soviet administrators can live.

Given assumptions (1) and (3), and a system of maximization under constraints as outlined under F in Section II, one might expect the produced product mix of each subaggregate to evolve during the interim between general price reforms in the direction of a single product. Suppose that a given factory began by producing a wide range of products, all included within the same production subaggregate and thus subject only to a joint output-plan constraint, with each product produced at constant returns and using an identical proportion of inputs of different types (including capital capacity). In this case, one might expect the factory to cease production of all those products within the subaggregate whose price/cost ratio is less than the highest ratio found among these products.

Of course, our conditions above are quite strong. Normally, one would expect different products within a given subaggregate to have changing marginal costs as their relative outputs varied. Second, Soviet enterprises are judged according to two sets of fixed prices (constant and current prices); one product may be favored by one set of prices and a second by the second set; the relative importance of these two different product evaluations can change from year to year (e.g., through alteration by the center of the relative weight in the enterprise objective function of labor productivity versus sales or profitability); thus, there may be annual changes as to the particular products within the given subaggregate which the producer prefers. Third, labor inputs are paid for at prices that vary over time; therefore, different products within a given subaggregate may have changing relative profitability and may make changing contributions to sales and to the factory's labor productivity index for a given usage of the constrained total wage fund. These three considerations suggest both that the production of an assortment of products – rather than a single product – within a subaggregate may well be dictated by the consideration of maximizing the enterprise's objective function, and that this assortment is likely to change over time. But there is no reason in our analysis to this point why such an assortment, or the direction of its change over time, should be at all influenced by purchaser demand. (In this statement, we assume general conditions of a seller's market for sales by producing units.)

The saving feature here is an administrative one. Producing and purchasing units are expected in the Soviet system to negotiate between themselves as to the product mix within each subaggregate that is specified both in the producer's output plan and in the purchaser's materials-allocation plan. The negotiations result in a contract. Arbitration exists not only as to the carrying out of the contract, but also as to the original negotiation of the contract itself. Although it is true that the producer has the whiphand in both negotiations and arbitration (Kurotchenko, 1975, pp. 164–5), the negotiating power of a nonmonopolistic supplier is at its greatest when its reputation with purchasers, relative to the reputation of possible alternative suppliers, is high. It is under these conditions that purchasers are most willing to accept producer decisions as to product mix, packaging, delivery dates, and so on.

It is because of this system of precontract and postcontract arbitration that the medium-run objective function of the Soviet enterprise should include as an argument its reputation with purchasing organizations. It is here that we find some constraint on the purely supply-directed narrowing and shifting of product mix that would otherwise occur within any given subaggregate. A parallel in capitalist economies is the constraint on the speed and degree of change of relative prices among products within a given product line of a company; under conditions of imperfect competition, capitalist competition includes reputation for stability and not solely price competition.

## B. Prices for units of effort

Since the 1965 industrial reform, the bonuses to be shared at the enterprise level among the labor force of the enterprise (but particularly among white-collar personnel) have been set as a weighted function of realized versus planned results of several indicators. For simplicity's sake, let us consider the situation for an enterprise with only two indicators: sales and level of profitability. The determination of bonus rates seems to be as follows (Granick, 1978).

For enterprise$_j$, planned total bonus ($B$) in year ($t$) is determined by the center as a function of the number of personnel planned for year ($t$), the composition of these personnel, the rate of bonus currently paid in enterprise$_j$, and similar factors that are all independent of the degree of success in year ($t$) of enterprise$_j$. The rates are set for planned percentage improvement in sales ($I_s$) and planned percentage improvement in the rate of profitability ($I_p$) over the current level. These three figures can be taken as exogenous, having been decided prior to determining the relative importance of the two indicators in determining the actual bonus to be paid out.

Defining $B_s$ as the number of rubles bonus to be paid for each percentage improvement in sales, and defining $B_p$ comparably for profitability, we then have the equation $B_s(I_s) + B_p(I_p) = B$.[13] We thus have one equation and two unknowns, with $B_s = B/I_s - (I_p/I_s)B_p$. How is the center to determine $B_p$ for enterprise$_j$?

An example of such determination would be the following. Assume that the center believes that it has set $I_s$ and $I_p$ at levels that require twice as much marginal effort by enterprise$_j$ to achieve the last bit of planned improvement in the sales compared with the profitability indicator. Second, assume that the center wishes to reward equally marginal effort (at

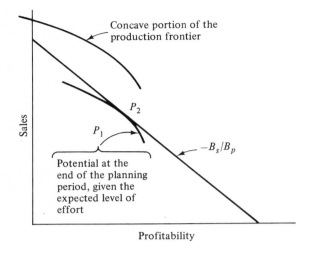

Figure 1. Guidance of enterprises through a bonus system of "prices."

the level of plan fulfillment) regardless of the indicator to which it is directed. Then $\partial B/\partial I_s$ should be set equal to $2(\partial B/\partial I_p)$, making the ratio $B_p/B_s = \frac{1}{2}$. If, on the other hand, the center feels that it is more important to achieve the $I_s$ plan than the $I_p$ plan, the $B_p/B_s$ ratio should be set at less than $\frac{1}{2}$.

Note that the foregoing system of setting the $B_p/B_s$ ratio amounts to setting a price (with bonus payments to the enterprise work force being the *numéraire*) per unit of attainment according to each of various criteria of effectiveness. This is far from an effective substitute for the missing system of market prices of individual products and inputs. Although it might indeed be used as a device for the center to guide enterprises to make both product and input choices to the degree that this is feasible within the constraints set by planning, it is difficult to believe that a system of prices which is restricted to criteria rather than to specific outputs and inputs would be a very effective guide.

On the other hand, if it is assumed that enterprises are always operating well within their production frontiers, and if the principal microeconomic problem is viewed as that of motivating them to move toward the frontier in the proper direction, this system may well be useful. Here the axes of the production frontier are composed of different success indicators, each of which reflects both output and opportunity-cost elements; the relevant portions of the production frontier are concave, embodying trade-offs (as shown in Figure 1). The individual enterprise is currently at point $P_1$, and the expected degree of total labor force effort during the planning period is expected to be able to advance it to some point on the relevant portion of the inner curve. The bonus ratio $B_p/B_s$ is intended to guide the enterprise to the point $(P_2)$ on this curve that is tangent to the center's welfare function.

There is one attractive feature inherent in the partial guidance of the economy by the $B_p/B_s$ system of prices. This feature consists of the fact that, although these are centrally determined prices just as are the prices of specific inputs and product outputs, unlike the latter it is administratively feasible to change them annually. The number of such bonus prices = (number of enterprises) × (average number of indicators per enterprise). If only the two indicators of sales and profitability were used, the central setting of no more than 100,000 bonus prices a year (50,000 more than the number of $B$'s that would in any case have to be determined) would permit the center to use bonus prices that change annually rather than product and input prices that remain fixed for an average of 10 years. By Soviet standards, this administrative task is substantial but by no means inordinate.

## C. Externalities

It is sometimes thought that a socialist economy should be immune to the problem of externalities, because all relevant economic matters are internalized in the planners' welfare function. However, once the producing unit's management is given a set of constraints and is set the problem of maximizing an objective function (assumed here to be bonus per member of the labor force, with the latter standardized by a procedure in which each individual employee is weighted according to his share in the unit's bonus earnings), then elements entering into the planners' welfare function can be internalized to the producing unit only to the degree that they can be incorporated into either the constraints or the objective function of such management.

Given the system described above for setting bonuses, the center cannot internalize to the producing unit any desiderata that are incapable of accurate measurement in the form of success criteria. Such desiderata constitute a large class, currently apparently including the introduction on a substantial production scale of minor desirable product innovations. Because of fixed prices and the existence of a pronounced sellers' market in the Soviet economy, it is very difficult to incorporate into the producing unit's objective function nonquantifiable features that are believed to enhance the attractiveness of a product to potential customers; in this regard, the problem of externalities in industry is much greater in the Soviet economy than in a capitalist economy.

A second feature of the Soviet economy further aggravates the problem. For any period, planned bonus is determined independently of the planned level of output–input relations for the producing unit during this period. If one makes the customary assumption that the planned outputs and inputs are set at levels reflecting the center's conception as to the producing unit's current attainments and as to its potential for improvement during the period, any improvement achieved during period $t$ will be reflected in an increase of the plan for period $(t + 1)$. The significance of this assumption is that the producing unit's objective function should incorporate an infinite rate of time preference to be applied to those improvements achieved in period $(t + 1)$ as a result of costs incurred by the producing unit itself during period $t$.

To the degree that the foregoing assumption is correct, and that the producing unit's objective function is properly measured by bonus per standardized member of the labor force (see the discussion in Granick, 1978), any results occurring during $(t + 1)$ as a result of activities during $t$ must be considered as externalities.

### IV. Summary

This chapter begins with the puzzle of why Soviet central administrators have designed a planning system for industry based on two different sets of fixed prices rather than on a dual-pricing system in which one set consists of market prices. The costs to Soviet administrators both in terms of limitations on planners' sovereignty and of the absence of equilibrating mechanisms at the micro-product level are expounded, and the nature of a neoclassical solution to the puzzle is explained as consisting of the elaboration of a planners' welfare function whose maximization is consistent with the central determination of all product prices.

Section II suggests that a solution to the puzzle lies in the fact that the planners' welfare function contains a job-rights constraint. The critical feature of this constraint is that the probability of a given individual being de facto idle for a long time while kept on his enterprise's payroll is very small. However, even with the existing Soviet reliance in pricing exclusively on fixed prices, the ability of the system to satisfy the foregoing feature is limited by an additional constraint within the planners' welfare function, consisting of the maintenance of a free labor market.

Section III is concerned with three residual problems from Section II. It attempts to explain how the degree of disequilibrium of individual products within a planned subaggregate of products is kept within limits acceptable to Soviet administrators without the existence of any formal equilibrating mechanism. Second, it describes the sense in which a peculiar type of market price, whose *numéraire* is bonus, exists within the framework of fixed product and input prices. Third, it discusses the unusual nature and degree of externalities created by the Soviet system of maximization by enterprises.

## Notes

1 Soviet treatment of a few items of consumption – cars constitute the most important example – clearly falls outside the scope of assumption (2).

2 This last statement abstracts from the relative importance given to type I and type II errors in satisfying demand.

3 One means does exist for Soviet central authorities to exercise this form of planner's sovereignty, but it is a means they have never employed. Rather than fixing the prices of individual consumer products at the time of a price reform, they might at that time instead fix the ratios of all products within a given consumer-goods subaggregate to the average price of that subaggregate. They could then annually change the average price of each such subaggregate at the same time that they fixed the output plans. This mechanism for liberating the central planners from the constraint of consumers' demand would appear to be administratively practical, because there are only a limited number of consumer-goods subaggregates that would require such annual repricing. (This mechanism is an elaboration of a suggestion by Herbert S. Levine.)

4 Since the degree of looseness in planning targets can only be represented on a continuum, it is the two ends of the continuum that must be defined. Viewing targets as a set of constraints on enterprise behavior, within which the enterprise management attempts to maximize a utility function, the "looseness" end of the continuum is one in which the targets are always nonbinding constraints. The "tautness" end is one in which there is no room for any process of maximization by the enterprise management. When targets are taut, we would expect that many organizations would fail in their efforts to remain within the targeted constraints.

5 During the most recent period for which we have data as to fulfillment of annual sales plans by ministries (1969–77), the rule has been that all industrial ministries – excluding those processing food which are much more at the mercy of acts of God – fulfilled at least 100 percent of their annual plans. With data available for 21 to 23 ministries in each year, all fulfilled their annual plans during six years and all except one (iron and steel) during the seventh. It is true that there were two years (1969 and 1972) in which 29 percent of the ministries missed their plans, but clearly these were years in which the central authorities were carried away in their planning. [Data also exist for 1978, but these are not comparable to those for earlier years. In 1978, for the first time, counterplans are included as part of the annual sales plans (Rzheshevskii, 1978, pp. 7–9).]

This period, in which for seven out of nine years there was only one ministerial underfulfillment out of 157 ministerial observations, differs radically from the previous period of ministerial organization of industry, in which there were underfulfilling ministries during all but one of the 1949–56 years. At least at the ministerial level, a radical change had occurred between the first half of the 1950s and the 1970s in respect to the degree of tautness of annual production planning in normal years.

6 Alfred Chandler's historical treatment of the changing structure of large American corporations, so as to allow micro decisions within the individual

corporation to adapt to a changing business environment, can be regarded as a testing of this neoclassical assumption as applied to institutional change (Chandler, 1962).

7 Alternatively, investment control as among capacities for producing various consumer goods (and for producing their direct and indirect inputs) might also be exercised as a means of asserting planners' preference for a future, as opposed to a current, consumer-goods mix. Investment control directed to this second objective would have the same effect as the use of different rates of time discount for various sectors in application to decentralized investment decisions made with the goal of maximizing discounted long-run profits.

8 For example, (4a) can be enforced by limiting enterprise$_j$ to maximum annual dismissals of $k$ employees of category $m$.

9 One might also imagine a seventh institutional arrangement which would be the dual of F, relying on the annual determination by the center of prices for subaggregates. Such an arrangement would be subject to conclusions 3 and 4 of Section I – although not to conclusion 2. For constraint (4d) to be respected, planners would have to behave "appropriately" in their annual changes of subaggregate prices; but this restriction is simply the counterpart of that required under F, as discussed in note 12.

It would appear that the Soviet preference for arrangement F to this seventh alternative must be explained on grounds other than those dealt with in this chapter.

10 This constraint was nonbinding during the 1930s, but this was also a period during which the marginal productivity of unskilled and semiskilled labor was extremely low. Despite this favorable (from the standpoint of restraining demand) labor situation, the absence of a binding wage-fund constraint resulted in a very high rate of inflation – a condition avoided since the late 1940s when Soviet administrators apparently became administratively capable of making the wage-fund constraint binding.

11 As most basic wages remain fairly constant during the long period between wage reforms, actual real earnings increase continuously over time through the expansion of the share of piece-rate earnings, bonuses, and so on, in total wages. (See McAuley, 1979, pp. 247–51.)

12 The distinction with respect to constraint (4d) between the current institutional arrangements and case B flows from the absence in the current arrangements of changes in the relative prices of the outputs and inputs of the individual producer. Thus, changes in the relative demand for different types of labor within a given enterprise arise primarily from variations in the relative size of output targets set for different subaggregates [here planners themselves must be constrained if (4d) is to be respected], by changes in the production functions (changes relevant only for existing as opposed to new enterprises) of the disaggregated products, and by the effects of enterprises altering their scale of output or moving along the learning curve of the product group. Assuming both appropriate behavior by planners and normal labor attrition, respect for constraint (4d) seems unlikely to be threatened under the current institutional arrangements except in some instances by movement of the enterprise along its learning curve.

13 Percentage improvements in either of the indicators which are other than planned are supposed to yield bonuses at a rate of 70 percent of $B_s$ or $B_p$ (as appropriate) for that portion of indicated results which differs from plan. Thus, the provision of bonus reward for nonplanned results required the introduction of no additional variable.

# References

Bergson, Abram. 1966. *Essays in Normative Economics.* Harvard University Press (Belknap Press), Cambridge, Mass.

Chandler, Alfred D. 1962. *Strategy and Structure: Chapters in the History of the Industrial Enterprise.* MIT Press, Cambridge, Mass.

Granick, David. 1976. *Enterprise Guidance in Eastern Europe.* Princeton University Press, Princeton, N.J.

Granick, David. 1978. "Soviet Research and Development Implementation in Products: A Comparison with the G.D.R.," in F. Levcik (ed.), *International Economics – Comparisons and Interdependences* (Festschrift für Franz Nemschak). Springer-Verlag, New York.

Lange, Oscar. 1936–7. "On the Economic Theory of Socialism." *Review of Economic Studies,* 4, 1 and 2.

Kurotchenko, V. S. 1975. *Material'no tekhnicheskoe snabzhenie v novykh usloviiakh khoziaistvovaniia.* Ekonomika, Moscow.

McAuley, Alastair. 1979. *Economic Welfare and Inequality in the Soviet Union.* University of Wisconsin Press, Madison, Wis./George Allen & Unwin, London.

Malinvaud, E. 1967. "Decentralized Procedures for Planning," in E. Malinvaud and M. O. L. Bacharach (eds.), *Activity Analysis in the Theory of Growth and Planning.* I.E.A./Macmillan, London.

Ruble, Blair A. 1977. "Full Employment Legislation in the U.S.S.R." *Comparative Labor Law,* 2, 3 (Fall).

Rzheshevskii, V. 1978. *Sotsialisticheskii trud,* 6.

Weitzman, Martin L. 1974. "Prices vs. Quantities," *Review of Economic Studies,* 41, 4 (October).

# 5 Technological progress and the evolution of Soviet pricing policy

*Joseph S. Berliner*

The basic structural features of the Soviet planned economy emerged in the period following the termination of the New Economic Policy (NEP) and the launching of the First Five Year Plan. With respect to the structure of prices, three principles were formulated as a guide to the formation of industrial wholesale prices. The first is the principle of average cost pricing; the price of a product is based on the average cost of its production in all the enterprises in that branch of industry, plus a normal profit markup of 4 to 5 percent over cost. The second is the principle of permanent prices; once the price is assigned to a product, it endures without limit of time, although from time to time prices are revised. The third is the principle of uniformity; the price of a given product is the same for all sellers and all purchasers. For decades these three principles have been presented in the general literature as the basis of price formation. In fact, certain departures were introduced in the very first years in which they were being formulated, but in the course of time the departures became increasingly massive, and the three principles have become less and less useful as a guide to the actual basis of price formation.

A variety of considerations have contributed to the evolution of price policy. There is, however, one common thread that unifies much of the history of that evolution. That thread is the effort to grapple with the problems encountered in the promotion of technological progress.

## I. Assumptions regarding technological progress

A structure is normally designed with certain functions in view. With the termination of NEP, there were two functions for which the new economic

I am grateful to Barney K. Schwalberg for his careful reading and insightful criticism of an earlier draft of this paper, and to the editor, Steven Rosefielde, for his valuable comments.

105

structure was designed. The first was to serve as a resource allocating mechanism, to replace the market mechanism that had served that function in the past. The second was to facilitate the attainment of the government's objective of generating a high rate of growth. It was in that context that the structural features of the new economic system took shape.

The choices of structural arrangements that were made for the purpose of promoting economic growth are those that are now thought of as the distinctive features of the Soviet economy: collectivized agriculture, for the purpose of generating a large and secure marketed surplus; an exceptionally high rate of investment; the predominance of heavy industry; and so forth. One can detect in this set of choices the predominance of the view that the source of rapid growth is the building up of the capital stock. On the other hand, one finds little evidence in these early structural choices that much thought was given to the second source of growth, technological progress.

That technological progress contributes to growth was, of course, widely appreciated at the time. If that appreciation did not find reflection in the economic structure then taking form, the reason may lie in the current views about the nature of technological progress and its relationship to socialism.

The architects of the structure of the Soviet socialist economy approached their task from two perspectives: that of the Marxian conception of the nature of capitalist development and that of the government of an economically underdeveloped country. From these perspectives one may identify four assumptions that characterized their views about the nature of technological progress under socialism. Those assumptions are expressed somewhat starkly below, but they do capture the thrust of widely held views.

### A. The Superiority Assumption

It was generally assumed that the rate of technological progress would be higher under socialism than under mature capitalism.[1] That view follows from the Marxian theory of the contradictions of capitalism. In its progressive stage, capitalism releases a great flood of technological advances, but as the system matures technological progress slows down under the influence of the growing contradictions. With increasing concentration of industry, for example, the spur of competition no longer compels capitalists to seek new technologies for invading each other's markets, and monopolies are increasingly successful in suppressing inventions that threaten the loss of capital values. In the most advanced stage, technological progress virtually ceases, which hastens the arrival of the general crisis. Following the revolution technological progress flourishes again, at a rate limited only by the scientific and technological prowess of the population, and unimpaired by the contradictions inherent in the preceding social system.

## B. The Investment Assumption

The basis of Marxian growth theory is the model of expanded reproduction. That model was generally accepted as the basis of the controversies during the Industrialization Debate of the 1920s, and the growth process with which it dealt underlay the structural design of the economy in the early 1930s. The purpose of the model was to illuminate the structure of the growth process, the crux of which was the requirement that the capacity of the capital-goods sector exceed the replacement rate of the total capital stock. But to the extent that it established the terms of the analysis, its effect was to focus attention on investment as the primary source of growth. "And although the Marxian model taken by itself did not yield any policy recommendations one way or another, people whose minds were set on industrialization at the greatest possible speed could derive from the construct a powerful support for their contention that in order to secure a rapid and smooth advance in the future a discontinuous jump was needed now."[2]

The promise of technological progress also figured prominently in the debate. But in the context of the times, that term referred not to advancing the frontiers of knowledge, but to equipping the economy with the kind of technology currently employed in the most advanced countries. Technological progress was therefore synonymous with investment, and the higher the rate of investment, the more rapidly an economy could appropriate the fruits of technological progress. Hence, the first order of business in designing the planned economy was to provide for a high rate of investment.

## C. The Product Innovation Assumption

From a Marxian perspective, the decline of technological progress under capitalism is a consequence of the structure of the system. Private ownership, production for profit, and competition result in a squandering of resources devoted to innovation; commercial secrecy leads to a wasteful multiplication of research efforts in competing firms; and scientists in different industrial laboratories work in ignorance of the results produced elsewhere. Since these practices are consequences of the capitalist structure, once that structure is replaced by socialism, these sources of inefficiency and restraints on technological progress will be removed. Instead of several small research units in the individual firms in each industry, a single centralized research institute could be established in each industry, thus taking advantage of economies of scale and eliminating the waste of duplication. The abolition of commercial secrecy will further spur the growth rate of new technological knowledge. Hence, new products will be developed at a rate never before attained under capitalist conditions. And in the absence of monopolistic restrictions the socialist enterprises, producing for use rather than for profit, will readily introduce into production those new products certified as ready for production by the central planning agency.

The essence of the Product Innovation Assumption, then, is that the process of new product invention and innovation proceeds more or less automatically under socialism. The only structural provision that needs to be made is the establishment of the centralized research and development institutes. Once they are in place, the rate at which new products appear is limited only by the quality of the nation's scientific and engineering manpower and the volume of resources placed at their disposal. No other special provision needs to be made in the economic structure – incentives, or prices, or organizational arrangements; or otherwise put, the rate of product innovation under socialism is invariant with respect to economic structure. As that rate depends primarily on the volume of resources allocated for the purpose, and the planning agency controls the allocation of resources, the rate of product innovation is uniquely determined by central planning policy.

The Soviet leadership was not so naive as to expect that all managerial officials were devoid of personal ambitions that might on occasion present obstacles to product innovation.[3] But such manifestations were very likely thought to be transitory, and in any case not of such magnitude as to require any major attention in the overall design of the structure of the economy.

### D. The Process Innovation Assumption

The argument with respect to new processes is substantially the same as that regarding new products. There are no elements of socialist economic structure that would deter enterprises from changing over to improved production processes that have been certified by the planning agency as ready for application. Hence, new processes will move fairly automatically from the laboratory into the production operation. The rate of process innovation is therefore also invariant with respect to economic structure and is uniquely determined by the planning agency.

It followed from the foregoing assumptions that the primary function of the new economic structure was allocative. The static allocative task was to manage the mobilization and direction of resources toward the production of the desired outputs, for which the planning method of material balances was developed. The dynamic allocative task was to direct the flow of output so as to attain a high rate of investment. It was for the fulfillment of these allocative tasks that the elements of economic structure were designed. As for technological progress, all that was required was that appropriate provision be made for the establishment of centralized research and development institutes adequately supplied with trained personnel and materials and equipment. Beyond that, no special provision needed to be made in the design of economic structure for the promotion of technological progress. Given the assumptions about technological progress under socialism, once the allocative mechanism was securely in place, the rate at which new products and processes would be incorporated into the economy would be limited only by the availability of resources for investment.

It was in that context that the basic decisions regarding the new economic structure were made and that the principles generating the price structure were formulated. In the course of time, however, the pricing system underwent an extensive evolution. It is our thesis that a central feature in the explanation of the evolution of price policy is to be found in the continuous effort to come to grips with the accumulating evidence that the assumptions are not valid. Each of the major changes in price policy discussed below reflects the abandonment of one or more of those assumptions.

## II. Subsidies for new technology, 1930–6

The massive investment program launched under the First Five Year Plan led rapidly to the emergence of inflationary pressures. Industry felt the pressure initially from the rising wage payments that resulted from enterprise efforts to attract and hold the labor required to meet excessively high production targets. Rising wage costs reduced profit margins and enabled enterprises to press for higher wholesale prices. Rising wholesale prices added further to production costs and the wholesale price level began to spiral upward in typical inflationary fashion.

It would have been possible for the state to respond to the inflationary pressures by authorizing price increases just large enough to maintain all prices at the average-cost level. That was not done, however. Instead, prices were permitted to rise at differential rates in such manner as to produce different profit rates. Some prices were permitted to rise to levels required to return a normal profit. But others were either held constant or permitted to rise slowly at a rate insufficient to maintain normal profit levels. Enterprises producing the latter kinds of products received subsidies from the state budget to cover the difference between their prices and their rising costs.

The episode was the first major departure from the formal principle of average-cost pricing. The inflation itself, of course, violated the principle of permanent prices, but the cause in this case was not related to the matter of technological progress. It was in the policy of subsidies that one finds the first effort to cope with that issue. The major reason for that departure was to encourage the adoption of new technological processes.

The massive investment program of the early 1930s entailed the production of large quantities of new types of materials and equipment and the appearance of new production processes. One would not be surprised if, under capitalist conditions, such rapid technological change would meet with some resistance, particularly by workers and lower-level managers threatened by the obsolescence of their skills and possible redundancy. But the Process Innovation Assumption led the Soviet leadership to expect that there would be no significant structural basis for such resistance to appear under socialism. In fact, the evidence mounted that such resistance did appear, and was sufficiently widespread to require a response. In view of the state of overfull employment in labor markets, it may be thought that workers had no serious reason to fear technological displacement. But the loss of a job nevertheless involved considerable private costs to workers. A certain amount of time was required for job search, especially since the labor exchanges had been abolished. Having to leave one's friends – the "collective" – and perhaps move to another city, is still identified in the sources as one of the bases of resistance to technological redundancy.[4] As regards foremen and lower-level management, the introduction of complex new mechanical and electrical equipment of which they had little understanding undermined their authority and weakened their competence to manage their section. They were, moreover, increasingly dependent on the new young servicing technicians, who knew so much more than they did. Senior management had the same concerns, and in addition had to face the difficult problems of production startup. Under the best of circumstances, startup operations are uncertain, unexpected problems arise, and unanticipated costs are incurred. Under the specific Soviet conditions of the 1930s, when the major political slogan was "tempo," the uncertainty was all the greater.

Under the pressure of mounting evidence of resistance to the adoption of new technology, the Process Innovation Assumption had to be abandoned. Once it was acknowledged that the rate of process innovation is not invariant with respect to economic structure, the task was then to introduce the appropriate structures. In the case of price structure, prices were now to serve a new function that would not have been required had the Process Innovation Assumption been valid – as an incentive to motivate process innovation. "During the period covered by the First Five Year Plan it was necessary in the interest of industrialization to maintain low prices for the production of heavy industry. Low prices for metal and coal meant low prices for machines, thus creating an additional stimulus to the adoption of machinery in all branches of the national economy."[5]

The decision to maintain low prices on such products as coal, metals, and machinery constituted the first major departure from the principle of average-cost pricing. As costs rose, the losses sustained by the enterprises that produced those products were covered by state subsidies. The intent was to encourage other enterprises to replace their older technology by new, with the prospect of lower costs of production and larger profits. Since the principal criterion of enterprise performance and reward was not financial performance but rather output-plan fulfillment, the subsidization of input prices was not the strongest incentive that might have been designed. Profit, however, was an important secondary criterion of performance, and it also served as a source of working capital, which greatly increased management's ability to acquire resources for fulfilling output plans.[6] Hence, a manager who would hesitate to mechanize a production process because it would reduce output-plan fulfillment in the short run during the startup period might nevertheless proceed with the innovation if it promised a sufficiently large profit in the long run.

As the general price level continued to climb, the volume of subsidies required to maintain the low-price policy on machinery, coal, and metals grew continuously. At the same time, as the experience with subsidized pricing accumulated, the negative effects of large-scale subsidies became increasingly evident. In April 1936 the government decreed that subsidies be phased out and prices restored to average-cost levels. The major reason for that decision was the growing magnitude of the distortions in relative prices that developed as the effects of subsidized inputs percolated through the price system. In some of the other criticisms leveled against subsidies, however, one can see the growing awareness that, contrary to the Product and Process Innovation Assumptions, managerial behavior is highly responsive to variations in economic structure. "The system of budget subsidies fostered, on the one hand, an irresponsible attitude among certain managers of economic organs. . . . Budgetary subsidies encouraged some managers to be irresponsible and negligent about finance: on the principle that 'anyway the budget will refund.' "[7]

Following the decree of April 1936, the government launched a process of price reform designed to restore the average-cost principle as the basis of the price structure.[8] The process of reform was interrupted by the outbreak of the war. During the war subsidies again grew to very large magnitudes, and in 1949 the government once again undertook an extensive price reform to eliminate subsidies. The task proved to be more complicated than anticipated, and it required several subsequent price reforms to accomplish that end. The last of that wave of reforms occurred in 1955, and the prices finally established at that time are thought to constitute a close approximation of average cost.[9]

### III. Temporary prices, 1955–64

The restoration of average-cost pricing in 1955 concluded the first episode in the evolution of pricing policy. The elimination of subsidies, however, generated a new set of problems that launched a second wave of changes in pricing policy. In this case the changes consisted of departures from the principles of permanence and of uniformity of prices. The source of the changes was again the incompatibility of those pricing principles with the requirements of technological progress. In particular, the accumulated evidence required the abandonment of the Product Innovation Assumption.

The principle of permanent prices is that once a price is established, it is regarded as undated, in the sense that it is expected to endure for a long period of time. The principle of permanence is the source of the stability of Soviet prices, which was thought to demonstrate the superiority of a planned socialist economy over a capitalist market economy, in which prices fluctuate continuously in response to the "anarchy of the marketplace." Price stability also eases the tasks of economic planning and of the evaluation of enterprise performance.

The specific problem that arose derives from a special feature of the cost behavior of new products. In all economies the real cost of production of new products tends to decline over time following the first production run. Among the reasons for the high initial production costs are the small scale of output and the costs of startup and learning. As production experience accumulates, startup costs decline because of learning by doing and because of economies of scale. In the course of time, average cost declines until it levels off and stabilizes thereafter at what may be regarded as long-run average cost. Given this pattern of cost behavior over time, if the price of a new product is set at its initial average-cost level and is unchanged thereafter, the earned profit rises as the product grows "older" and cost approaches its long-run minimum. Hence, an enterprise that drops an older model from its product line and starts up the production of a new model suffers a decline in both its total profit and its average profit rate. If the new product is added without reducing the output of older products, total profit increases but the profit rate declines, and profit rate is one of the indicators of performance. A mass of empirical evidence has been published by Soviet analysts showing that profit rates are higher on older products than on new, and that the more innovative the enterprise, as measured by the proportion of new products in its total output, the lower its rate of profit.[10]

Had the original assumptions about the nature of socialist technological progress proven to be valid, the post-1955 price structure would have posed no serious problem. In particular, if the Product Innovation Assumption adequately described innovative behavior, the rate of product innovation would not have responded to the new price structure. New products would have been introduced at a rate predetermined as optimal by the central planners, irrespective of the penalty that the price structure placed upon product-innovating enterprises. In fact, evidence abounded that the price structure did exert a significant influence on product-innovation decisions of enterprises. New products were referred to by such terms as "disadvantageous" and "noncompetitive," and managers did in fact discriminate against the introduction of new products in the many ways, both formal and informal, in which they were able to exercise that choice. When it became clear that the rate of product innovation did in fact vary with the price structure, contrary to the Product Innovation Assumption, the task at hand was to modify that structure in such ways as to eliminate the source of that bias.[11]

The modification that was selected was the rejection of the principle of permanent prices in the case of new products and the substitution in its place of the principle of "temporary" prices.[12] The new principle was first introduced in the engineering industries and later extended to others. Under the new principle, products first introduced into production after 1955 were assigned not permanent prices that endure without limit of time, but temporary, or "dated" prices. The temporary price was to be high enough to cover the high initial costs of production plus the normal profit rate for the industry. After a period of time, however, when the new product's average production cost had declined and had begun to approach its long-run level, the temporary price was to be dropped and a lower permanent price assigned. The assignment of the permanent price transformed the product, as it were, from the category of "new" to "old." This new pricing method was designed to eliminate the high profits that would otherwise have been earned by older products and thus to reduce the bias against the introduction of new products.

One of the reasons for the original formulation of the principle of permanent prices was its convenience as an instrument of central planning and control. That there was merit in that view was demonstrated by the events that followed the discarding of that principle in favor of temporary prices for new products. It was anticipated that the number of products eligible for temporary prices would be relatively small and the system therefore easily administered. In fact, enterprises seized upon the temporary price arrangement with enthusiasm and the number of products selling at temporary prices expanded rapidly, far beyond what was intended. In 1964, 40 percent of the output of mining machinery, 41 percent of textile machinery, and 47 percent of forging and pressing equipment were selling at temporary prices. In some enterprises the percentage reached 70 percent and higher.[13] In 1966 the price catalogs, which list only permanent prices, contained price listings for only about half the value of all equipment output.[14] The prospective customer or project designer who needed a price quotation on the unlisted equipment had to call the producing enterprise to find out what the temporary price was.

One reason for the explosion of temporary prices was administrative complexity. The agencies of price administration were unable to process all the applications for temporary prices and to monitor the conversion of temporary prices to permanent prices. Consequently, many products continued to sell at their high temporary prices long after they should have been replaced; they were "simply transformed into permanent prices, in effect."[15] A second reason was that enterprises took advantage of the temporary-price regulations to secure higher prices for those of their older products that earned low profit rates.[16] By making some minor modifications in an older product, it could be represented to the price-administration agency as a "new" product, and if the application was successful it could receive a new high temporary price, higher than the old permanent price. The increase in the volume of "simulated innovation" was one of the serious consequences of temporary pricing.

The discussion has concentrated on the influence of technological progress on the principle of permanent prices. Temporary prices, however, also led to extensive incursions into the principle of uniform prices as well. The objective of that principle is that the same price should be paid for the same product by all purchasers. That objective clashed, however, with the objective of the temporary-price regulations, which was to encourage new product innovation. There was no problem in the case of a product that was new in the sense of not having been produced before in the USSR. The problem arose, however, in the course of the diffusion of that product among other producers. In the case of the second, third, and later enterprises to introduce the same new product, the question was whether each of them should be entitled to apply for new temporary prices. According to the principle of uniform pricing, they should not; their prices should be the same as that of the identical product innovated by the pioneering producer. If the objective is to promote the diffusion of the production of new technology, however, they should be; for each enterprise faces its own startup costs, even in the case of new products already produced elsewhere. Again, it was under the impact of the requirements of technological progress that the principle of uniform prices was abandoned. The temporary-price regulation was interpreted to mean that a product was "new" if it was produced for the first time in a given enterprise, and was therefore entitled to a temporary price based on the initial average cost of production in that enterprise. The result was a growing number of instances in which the same product was selling at different prices.[17]

Thus, the realization that the Product Innovation Assumption could not be counted on to promote technological progress led to departures from both the principle of permanent prices and the principle of uniformity. The cure, however, proved to be worse than the disease, and the price-administration agencies virtually lost control of the price system as the number of temporary-priced commodities spread far beyond what was originally intended. The price structure that had been put together with such difficulty between 1949 and 1955 had begun to come apart once again, and it required another major price reform in 1967 to put it back together. To prepare the ground for that reform, a decree of June 1966 required that the use of temporary prices be greatly restricted.[18] They could be used, for example, only for products that are new in the strict sense of having been "introduced for the first time in the USSR." That requirement restores the principle of uniformity, but the use of temporary prices continues to exclude a certain range of new products from the principle of permanent prices.

A more significant legacy of the episode, however, is that the terms in which discussion of price policy are conducted have been greatly modified. Price stability, which was seen originally as one of the advantages of the planned economy, is now generally conjoined with price flexibility as a desideratum of price policy. In the interest of greater flexibility the current policy is to conduct more frequent general price revisions and partial revisions of groups of prices. New instruments of price flexibility such as stepped pricing have come into vogue. Under stepped pricing a new product is assigned not a single temporary price but a schedule of prices that decline in predetermined steps at specified future dates.[19] Thus, the requirements of technological progress have dislodged the principle of permanent prices from its paramount position and replaced it by the notion of an optimal combination of stability and flexibility.

## IV. The New Products Fund, 1960

The decline in cost over time is one respect in which the cost behavior of new products differs from that of established products. There is another respect, however, in which the cost behavior of new products is distinctive. Because of this latter feature, it proved to be impossible to maintain the average-cost principle that was restored in 1955 after the elimination of subsidies.

Soviet analysts distinguish two stages of production startup of new products. The first, called the production-preparation stage, consists of costs incurred before the first full production run. It includes enterprise-financed design and development, labor training, prototype construction, sometimes the acquisition of specialized equipment, and testing. The second, called the break-in stage, consists of costs that are incurred after production has commenced and that diminish in time and eventually vanish when the technique for producing the new product is fully mastered. These are primarily the aforementioned learning costs. It was the learning costs of new-product production that led to the temporary-price episode. It was the production-preparation costs that led to the next period in the evolution of price policy.

The intention of the elimination of subsidies was that the price be high enough to enable the enterprise[20] to recover all costs of production out of sales revenue. That requirement poses no particular problem for the producer of established products because in an ongoing production operation, current outlays can be covered out of current sales or out of short-term commercial credit. The product innovator, however, incurs production-preparation costs in the period before production begins. During that period there is no sales revenue out of which those costs can be defrayed.

Before 1955 the problem was dormant because startup costs were presumably covered by the subsidies for new technology. After subsidies were eliminated, however, startup costs were to be included in the price of new products by capitalizing them over a specified number of years; two to three years in the case of machinery products, for example.[21] Thus, production-preparation costs, the first of which might be incurred months or years before the first production run, would not be fully recovered until two or three years after the first production run. During that long period of time those expenses had to be financed either out of the enterprise's working capital or by bank credits. Because of the inherent uncertainty of the innovative process, product innovators often faced the prospect of running up unanticipated debts or having to deplete their working capital with potentially serious consequences for their main lines of established products.[22] One consequence of these financial pressures was that managers contrived to recover their outlays more rapidly by reducing the capitalization period of startup costs, often to one year, and in some reported cases they were loaded on to the cost of the first few production runs.[23] The shortening of the capitalization period is one of the reasons for the sharp increase in the relative prices of new products during the temporary-price period.

As the nature of the problem began to emerge in the writings of Soviet analysts, it became evident that both product innovation and process innovation were adversely affected. The financial difficulties that production-preparation costs entailed tended to bias management against product innovation, and the sharp rise in new-product prices due to the elimination of subsidies and the excessively rapid capitalization of startup costs biased management against the adoption of new machinery and equipment for incorporation into their own production processes. Hence, both the Product Innovation Assumption and the Process Innovation Assumption proved again to be deficient as guides to managerial behavior with respect to technological progress.

Once it is clear that behavior is responsive to economic structure, one can proceed to search for that structural arrangement that would elicit the desired behavior. The change in price structure that was eventually introduced in this case involved a return to subsidies. Thus, the principle of average-cost pricing gave way again in response to the imperatives of technological progress.

A decree of 1960 authorized selected ministries to establish a New Products Fund (*fond osvoeniia novoi tekhniki* – literally, "fund for the mastery of new technology").[24] The fund is financed by what is essentially a tax on the ministry's enterprises, amounting to 0.3 to 3.0 percent of the enterprise's total cost of production. Enterprises preparing to introduce new products apply to the ministry for a subsidy to cover production-preparation costs. The subsidized costs are not included in the producer's full cost of production, nor in the average unit cost of the new product on the basis of which the price is established. The subsidies cover roughly 15 percent of the production costs of new machinery products and to that extent the fund has contributed to a reduction in the wholesale prices of new products.

The fund has very likely succeeded to some degree in its twin objectives. By reducing the strain on the enterprise's working capital in financing startup costs, it has reduced one of the sources of bias against product innovation.[25] And by reducing the prices of new products, it has increased the returns to process innovators who purchase those products for incorporation into their own manufacturing processes. The structure of prices is therefore now somewhat more supportive of technological progress, but at the cost of the abandonment of the principle of average-cost pricing in the case of new products.

## V. Productivity pricing, 1965

The use of subsidies is a modification of the principle of average-cost pricing in the sense that some costs are excluded in determining what the price should be. Subsidization does not, however, violate the broad principle that the cost of producing the product should be the basis of price determination. In 1965, however, a major decree of the government authorized a new set of pricing principles that virtually dislodged cost of production as the basis of new-product pricing.

The source of the problem is that when prices are based solely on cost of production, relative prices cannot reflect differences in productivity. A typical instance of technological progress, however, is the development of a new model of a product that is more productive than an older model in some or all of the uses in which the latter had been employed, after the cost of production of the two models is taken into account. Relative prices, however, will reflect only the difference in their costs of production, not the larger difference between their net marginal productivities. The significance of this consequence of cost-based pricing depends upon the extent to which decision making with respect to product innovation is influenced by economic structure – specifically price structure in this instance. In a world of perfect planning, for example, the omniscient planners would increase the output of the new model from year to year and correspondingly reduce the output of the older model. As the output of the new model increased, it would replace the older first in those uses in which its net marginal productivity was highest, and then in successively less productive uses. The new model would continue to replace the older one at the optimal time rate, until in equilibrium the ratio of the marginal productivities of the two models was equal to the ratio of their costs. Throughout this process the prices of the two models serve only to establish the financial terms at which products are transferred from those who produced them to those who purchased them. In particular, producers are not deterred from introducing the new models into their product lines by a price structure that conveyed to them none of the "fruits" of their innovativeness; none, that is, of the quasi-rent generated by the higher productivity of the new models.

The four assumptions about technological progress held by the designers of the Soviet economic structure appear to refer to a world substantially like that described above. The Superiority Assumption provided reason to expect that whatever the potential for technological progress in the state of the art, it would be fully exploited in a socialist planned economy in which the capitalist barriers to technological progress had been eliminated. Under the Investment Assumption it could be taken for granted that the technology incorporated in the rapidly growing new capital stock would be the world's most advanced, although suitably adapted to Soviet factor proportions and other special conditions. And the assumptions regarding product and process innovation sustained the view that such elements of economic structure as the structure of prices are unlikely to restrain the innovative enthusiasm of socialist managers.

Although it may have been possible to accept these assumptions in the early 1930s, it was no longer possible to do so in the 1960s. The several episodes in the evolution of price policy set forth above reflect the fact that the Product and Process Innovation Assumptions had already been called into question in the prewar period and had been further undermined later. The other two assumptions, however, did not face serious challenge until the postwar period. The history of the 1930s gave no reason to challenge the Superiority Assumption; on the contrary, the juxtaposition of the capitalist depression against the rapid expansion of Soviet industry appeared to strengthen it. It was the remarkable postwar technological advances in the capitalist world that made it increasingly difficult to accept that assumption. By the 1960s no responsible Soviet official could continue to believe that the laws of history could be counted on to project the Soviet economy into technological superiority. If superiority were to be attained, something had to be changed within the economy and the society. As for the Investment Assumption, it was dealt a mortal blow by the development in the 1950s of econometric techniques for measuring the contribution of technological progress to growth relative to the contribution of increasing capital and other inputs. The cumulating research made it clear that technological progress has accounted for a much larger proportion of the growth of capitalist countries than had formerly been guessed. During the period 1955–70, for example, gross domestic product grew in the USSR at an annual rate of 5.7 percent, about the same rate as that of France (5.4 percent), West Germany (5.4 percent), and Italy (5.6 percent). Abram Bergson has calculated, however, that real national income per worker, adjusted for capital stock, grew at an annual rate of 2.4 percent in the USSR, substantially less than in France (3.9 percent), West Germany (3.4 percent), and Italy (4.4 percent).[26] The findings suggest that over half of the growth of those countries has been due to technological progress, and that the rate of technological progress in those countries has been 50 to 100 percent more rapid than that in the USSR. The implication is that the thing the Soviet economy does best – mobilizing capital and other factors of production – is not that decisive after all in promoting modern economic growth. The weight of the accumulating evidence demanded the rejection of a policy that was based on the assumption that a high rate of investment was a sufficient condition for the task of promoting rapid growth. The new attention given to the independent role of technological progress can be seen in the growth of a large volume of Soviet writings seeking to understand the nature of what has been called the "scientific–technical revolution."

With the abandonment of all four original assumptions about technological progress, the way was clear for that general review of the structure of the Soviet economy that is referred to as Economic Reform, one of the chief purposes of which is to promote technological progress. All the major elements of economic structure have come under review: incentives, organizational arrangements, and prices. It was in that context that criticism finally turned to the central principle that prices should be based solely on cost of production.[27]

The 1965 pricing statute established a complex set of procedures for incorporating productivity into the pricing of new products.[28] Two such procedures will serve to illustrate the new approach.

The first procedure is applied in the pricing of a new product that was designed as an advance over an older product, called the "analogue," and was intended to serve as a partial substitute for the analogue. The procedure in analogue pricing involves three steps. The first step consists of the calculation of an "upper limit" price, which is the price at which a user would be indifferent between purchasing the new product or the analogue.[29] The method involves the calculation of the maximal increase over the price of the analogue product that a purchaser would be willing to pay for the new product because of its greater productivity. The formula consists of the present discounted value of the stream of additional net output produced by the technological advances incorporated in the new product (durability, reliability, fuel economy, etc.).

The second step involves the calculation of a "lower-limit" price, which is the price at which a producer would be indifferent between producing the new product or the older analogue. This price is calculated in the traditional manner; it equals the sum of average cost of production plus the normal profit rate in the industry. The third step involves the determination of the final wholesale price. The general instruction is that the wholesale price is to be set somewhere between the upper- and lower-limit prices in such manner that the quasi-rent produced by the innovation is divided "equitably" between the producer and the user of the new product.

Since the instructions skirt the question of what an equitable sharing should be, that question has generated an extensive controversy. The indecisiveness of the authorities on this crucial issue opened the way for efficiency-minded economists to urge that the wholesale price be set at the market-clearing level.[30] Under this operating rule, at the start of production when the rate of output of the new product is still low, the wholesale price would be set close to the upper-limit price in order that the restricted supply be allocated to the product's most productive uses. In the course of time output expands and the wholesale price would be gradually reduced as the new product is allocated toward successively less productive uses. Finally, when the long-run optimal rate of output is attained, the wholesale price would approach the lower-limit price. Thus, the quasi-rent generated by the new product would be appropriated initially by the product innovator in the form of above-normal profit, but the profit rate would diminish over time, falling finally to the normal-profit level when the new product ceased to be "new."

Critics of this market-clearing rule regard as inequitable an arrangement in which all the quasi-rent accrues to the producer of the new product and none to the user. They have proposed as an equitable rule of thumb that the wholesale price be set at a level at which the producer receives 30 to 50 percent of the quasi-rent and the user receives the balance.[31] The authorities appear not to have taken a position on this issue. Evidently, the market-clearing rule is used in the case of new products that are regarded as in very short supply, but the equity rule seems to be the most widely employed. Meanwhile, the price administration agency has been grappling with a series of complicated administrative problems that analogue pricing entails. One such complication is that in the case of major technological advances, the spread between the lower- and upper-limit prices is very large and both the market-clearing and equity rules yield very large profits to producer or user or both. The authorities appear to hold the view that, beyond a certain level, above-normal profits cannot be justified, regardless of the nature of their origin. Accordingly, a regulation has been introduced which limits the wholesale price to a level that would yield the producer an earned profit rate no larger than 50 percent more than the normal profit rate for the industry.[32] That strong limitation serves as a reminder that although the authorities are prepared to make structural changes in the interest of technological progress, some structural changes are still regarded as out of bounds even though they may contribute to technological advance.

The second pricing procedure in the 1965 statute applies to new products that involve no significant technological advance but are designed to fill in or extend an established product line. Suppose that a certain type of pump is produced in three sizes, capable of delivering 10, 50, and 100 gallons per minute. It has been decided that there is a sufficient number of uses in which it would be economical to produce a pump of the same type with a capacity of 30 gallons per minute. Under the traditional pricing principles, the new pump would be priced at its average cost plus normal profit, without regard to the prices of similar models with varying technical parameters. The 1965 statute requires that new products that are part of a "parametric series" be priced not at their cost but in a manner consistent with the prices of other models having different technical parameters.

Several methods are employed for calculating parametric prices, the principal one being a form of hedonic index. Price is regressed statistically upon the major technical parameters, such as capacity, durability, and weight, with data derived from the established line of products. The multiple regression coefficients then measure the economic value, as it were, of each of the parameters. Applying the regression equation to the parameters of the new product yields the price. Thus, parametric pricing ignores entirely the cost of producing the new product; the price depends solely on its productivity relative to that of the other models in the product line.

Neither analogue pricing nor parametric pricing are entirely new in the USSR. Abram Bergson has pointed out that "while average cost pricing did become the rule with the latter reform [1949:JB], the government again and again has departed from it." One such departure was the pricing of different grades of iron ore, in which production costs were subordinated to ore content and other qualities in the manner of present-day parametric pricing. A second was the pricing of close substitutes such as the major fuels. The price of petroleum has been disproportionately high not only in relation to its cost but also to its caloric content relative to that of other fuels. The reason was that the productivity of petroleum to the user was so much higher than that of other fuels that the implicit demand would have greatly exceeded the supply at a cost-based price or even at a parameter (caloric content)-based price.[33] The pricing of petroleum on the basis of its productivity resembles the current procedures of analogue pricing, including the market-clearing rule for allocating the quasi-rent. These earlier departures from cost-based pricing, however, were the exception rather than rule; they were employed only in those cases in which the static inefficiency of average-cost pricing was exceptionally large. The pricing statute of 1965, however, mandated the adoption of productivity-based pricing as the normal rule in the case of new products generally. Hence, in the domain of products that are central to technological progress, relative prices have ceased to bear any relationship to cost of production.

The argument of the chapter may be summarized by imagining that, contrary to fact, the original assumptions about technological progress had proven to be valid. Had enterprises adopted new processes at the optimal rate even though the social benefits exceeded the private benefits (or losses) accruing to them, there would have been no reason to undertake the subsidy policy of the 1930s. Had enterprises been willing to introduce new products at the optimal rate even at the cost of a decline in their profit rates, there would have been no resort to the use of temporary prices in 1955 or to the New Products Fund subsidy program of 1960. Suppose, in addition, that technology had indeed stagnated in the postwar capitalist world and that technological advance had contributed very little toward economic growth relative to capital investment. Under these conditions it is unlikely that the USSR would have undertaken that critical and no doubt painful reexamination of its economic structure that led to the introduction of productivity pricing in 1965. Thus, had all four assumptions proven to be valid, the Soviet price structure today might very well be based on the principles first adopted four decades ago.

This chapter has examined the influence of technological progress on the evolution of only one aspect of economic structure – that of prices. A similar examination of the evolution of organizational structure and incentives structure would very likely support the view that the need to accommodate to the requirements of technological progress has been a major influence in the shaping of the Soviet economy overall.

## Notes

1 On the Superiority Assumption during the Industrialization Debate, see Alexander Erlich, *The Soviet Industrialization Debate, 1924–1928* (Cambridge, Mass.: Harvard University Press, 1960). p. 19. The assumption was also widely held outside the USSR. For example, Alexander Baykov wrote in *The Development of the Soviet Economic System* (Cambridge: Cambridge University Press, 1946):

> The abolition of proprietary rights over inventions and of secret patents and improvements in manufacturing processes, together with the mutual exchange of industrial information among enterprises, cannot but contribute to a fuller and more timely use of the creative initiative of those actually working for industrial progress, and remove anomalies in the utilization of industrial inventions which often occur under the competitive system. . . ." [P. 302]

2 Erlich, *Soviet Industrialization Debate,* p. 147.
3 The experience with price administration in the 1920s provided the first evidence that managers of socialized enterprises find it advantageous to raise their prices far above normal profit levels when they can [R. F. D. Hutchings, "The Origins of the Soviet Industrial Price System," *Soviet Studies,* 13 (July 1961), pp. 2–5, 11]. At that time, however, prices were not set by higher government organs and that price behavior was not illegal, nor was the economy yet controlled by overall central planning.
4 *Ekonomicheskaia gazeta,* no. 46, 1967, p. 30; *Voprosy ekonomiki,* no. 10, 1969, p. 38.
5 *Planovoe khoziaistvo,* no. 5, 1936, pp. 76–77, quoted in Baykov, *Development of the Soviet Economic System,* p. 294.
6 Joseph S. Berliner, *Factory and Manager in the USSR* (Cambridge, Mass.: Harvard University Press, 1957), chap. 5.
7 *Planovoe khoziaistvo,* no. 5, 1936, pp. 76–77, quoted in Baykov.
8 The continued upward wage drift after 1936 led again to a rise in the volume of subsidies. In 1939–40, prices were increased once more to restore average-cost prices [S. G. Stoliarov, *O tsenakh i tsenoobrazovaniia v SSSR* (Prices and Price Formation in the USSR) (Moscow: Statistika, 1969), p. 57.
9 Richard Moorsteen, *Prices and Production of Machinery in the Soviet Union, 1928–1958* (Cambridge, Mass.: Harvard University Press, 1962), p. 10.
10 Joseph S. Berliner, *The Innovation Decision in Soviet Industry* (Cambridge, Mass.: MIT Press, 1976), pp. 249–54.
11 David Granick found that during the First Five Year Plan there was little evidence of managerial resistance to the introduction of new Western product designs into production in Soviet plants. He explains this in part by the fact that many of the plants in that period were newly built and produced only a few complex products. In enterprises that produced both the old and new products, he suggests that such resistance may have been possible [*Soviet Metal*

*Fabricating and Economic Development* (Madison, Wis.: University of Wisconsin Press, 1967), p. 236]. This explanation is consistent with the evidence that not until the postwar period did the problem of resistance to product innovation come to fore. In the later period new product designs were primarily of Soviet rather than Western origin, and the proportion of new products produced by newly built enterprises was much smaller; hence, more managers confronted the issue of the conflict between new and old products.

12   Temporary prices were employed during the 1930s as well (Hutchings, "Soviet Industrial Price System," p. 20). That they did not become a matter of serious concern until the 1950s was due to the availability of subsidies. It was only after the 1955 price reform, which finally eliminated branch subsidies, that temporary prices were given a formal place in the pricing system. A. I. Komin, *Problemy planovogo tsenoobrazovaniia (Problems of Price Formation)* (Moscow: Ekonomika, 1971), p. 150.

13   Komin, *Problemy,* p. 150.

14   *Planovoe khoziaistvo,* no. 10, 1966, p. 3.

15   Komin, *Problemy,* p. 150.

16   Permanent prices were reviewed from time to time, to eliminate the disparities in earned profit rates that arise when relative prices are constant but relative costs change. On these occasions some permanent prices were revised downward, to restore the normal profit level for the industry. It was these products whose prices had been reduced to normal profit levels that are referred to in the text, not those older products that were still selling at their original permanent prices and therefore earning large profits because of the reduced production costs.

17   Berliner, *Innovation Decision,* pp. 280–1. Certain departures from uniform pricing have been permitted in activities in which variations in natural resource endowment greatly influence unit costs of different producers, as in petroleum extraction and agriculture. In those cases, different producers receive different prices for, say, a ton of oil or a ton of wheat, but all purchasers of oil or grain pay the same price, except for regional differentials. In the case of temporary prices, however, purchasers could buy the same product from different producers at different prices.

18   K. N. Plotnikov and A. S. Gusarov, *Sovremennye problemy teorii i praktiki tsenoobrazovaniia pri sotsializma* (Current Problems of Theory and Practice in Socialist Price Formation) (Moscow: Nauka, 1971), pp. 124–8.

19   Berliner, *Innovation Decision,* pp. 293–8. The problems of administering stepped prices are also discussed by Gregory Grossman, "Price Control, Incentives and Innovation in the Soviet Economy," in Alan Abouchar (ed.), *The Socialist Price Mechanism* (Durham, N.C.: Duke University Press, 1977), pp. 163–4.

20   More precisely, it is the branch of industry that is expected to cover the costs out of revenues. Hence, it is the average cost of the branch that serves as the basis of price. Enterprises whose costs are above the branch average continue to be subsidized by the branch ministry out of the profit earned by lower-cost enterprises. These subsidies, however, do not appear in the state budget. [Abram Bergson, *The Economics of Soviet Planning* (New Haven, Conn.: Yale University Press, 1964), p. 162].

21   Plotnikov and Gusarov, *Sovremennye problemy,* p. 371.

22   Innovation is often characterized by cost overruns and by scheduling delays. Among the reasons are imperfections in the working drawings prepared by

the research and development staff, requiring redesign of the product; production engineering problems that arise in the course of startup; unfamiliarity with new materials and components; procurement problems because relations have not yet been established with new suppliers; and marketing problems because of user resistance to untested technology.

23  P. S. Mstislavskii, M. G., Gabrieli, and Iu. V. Borozdin, *Ekonomicheskoe obosnovanie optovykh tsen na promyshlennuiu produktsiiu* (The Economic Basis of Wholesale Pricing of New Industrial Products) (Moscow: Nauka, 1968), pp. 113–14.

24  Berliner, *Innovation Decision,* pp. 198–204, 217–4.

25  The size of the fund is not sufficient to cover all the production-preparation costs of all product innovators. The balance continues to be financed primarily out of the enterprises' own working capital. *Planovoe khoziaistvo,* no. 3, 1971, p. 36.

26  Abram Bergson, *Soviet Post-war Economic Development,* Wicksell Lectures 1974 (Stockholm: Almqvist & Wiksell, 1974), pp. 70–8.

27  Several other lines of development in Soviet economics converged around this time, all tending to discredit the principle of cost-based pricing. Gregory Grossman noted that in the post-1956 theoretical debates on pricing in general, virtually all the participants rejected the average-cost-plus-normal-profit formula ("Price Control," pp. 129–30). The earlier debate on the choice among investment alternatives also contributed to the rejection of that principle and provided the basis for the analogue-pricing method discussed below (Berliner, *Innovation Decision,* pp. 306–7).

28  The 1965 statute was supplemented in 1969 by a more detailed document entitled *Manual for Determining Wholesale Prices on New Industrial Products.* The following description is based on the latter document as presented in Berliner, *Innovation Decision,* chap. 11. Further analysis of the new procedures may be found in Grossman, "Price Control," pp. 158–64, and in Michael J. Lavelle, "The Soviet 'New Method' Pricing Formulae," *Soviet Studies,* 26 (January 1974), pp. 81–97.

29  The procedure assumes that there is a single use for the product, and does not deal with the case in which the product has alternative uses in which its productivity differs. That more general case underlies the views of the proponents of the market-clearing rule discussed below.

30  For example, *Voprosy ekonomiki,* no. 5, 1967, pp. 34–5.

31  *Ekonomicheskaia gazeta,* no. 31, 1969, p. 11.

32  Plotnikov and Gusarov, *Sovremennye problemy,* p. 372. This maximum may be the reason for the finding reported by Grossman ("Price Control," p. 161) that in the case of most new products the producer gets no more than 10 to 12 percent of the quasi-rent. Although this limit on the wholesale price places a ceiling on the profit that the product innovator may earn, in essence it merely shifts the profit to the purchaser of the new product, who captures the balance of the economic rent. It is not clear why that is regarded as less objectionable. The policy is consistent, however, with a long-standing tendency to regard the encouragement of the adoption of new products and processes as more important than the encouragement of the production of new products and processes. See Granick, *Soviet Metal Fabricating,* p. 235.

33  Bergson, *Economics of Soviet Planning,* pp. 163–4.

# 6　Earning differentials by sex in the Soviet Union: a first look

*Gur Ofer and Aaron Vinokur*

## I. Introduction

At work, women in the USSR earn on the average less than two-thirds of a man's wage; at home they spend more than twice as much time on household chores as do their spouses. In these two respects Soviet urban society resembles urban societies in most developed market economies. However, Soviet women are much more active in the labor force. When coupled with unusually high participation in the labor force, undiminished, perhaps even greater, work at home imposes on women in the Soviet Union an exceptionally heavy double burden.

For women to bear such a heavy work load and then to receive low pay – compared to men – would appear to be in direct conflict with the egalitarian principles of socialist ideology.[1] The obvious embarrassment created by this conflict may be one reason for the shyness of Soviet sources to provide data on male/female wage differentials.[2] On the other hand, the broader questions of the status of women in the family and in society, the double burden of married women, restricted access to various occupations, high participation in the labor force – together with the possible demographic effects of these phenomena – are dealt with in dozens of books and scores of articles by Soviet scholars.[3] Many of these studies emphasize how greater equality for women has been achieved with respect to education, occupational choice, income independence, and social and political activity. They also discuss rather frankly areas in which

The study is supported by a grant from the Ford Foundation and is part of a larger project on the Economics of the Soviet Urban Household in the Seventies (temporary title), which will be published in a forthcoming book by MIT Press. We would like to thank Reuven Bisk and Yechiel Bar-Chaim, who assisted in the research, and Ruth Vainstein and Maggie Eisenstaedt at the Falk Institute for Economic Research in Israel, who typed and retyped many successive drafts.

127

inequality is still significant. In this respect, reasons for wage inequality are in most cases treated qualitatively, not quantitatively.

The recent upheaval in the West regarding the status of women has now directed even more attention to the place of women in Soviet society. Some very good surveys and studies covering the available Soviet data as well as Soviet views on many of these issues have been produced in recent years by Western scholars. New tools of analysis have also been used to further analyze the issues, sometimes in a comparative setting.[4] The main factors contributing to earning differentials by sex have been discussed and their consequences analyzed, within the above-mentioned limitations of the available data. In only one case, however (Swafford, 1977), could the analysis of earning differentials be carried to the level of multivariate analysis based on (semi)micro data on earnings of individuals. The general lack of such micro data has prevented Western students of the Soviet Union from performing the kind of multivariate analysis that is so common in similar studies in the West.

Such micro data are now available to us through a family budget survey of families of Jewish emigrants from the Soviet Union who have come to live in Israel. The main purpose of this chapter, therefore, is to use these data to analyze earning differentials by sex in the urban sector of the Soviet Union and to study and compare the earning functions of men and women. The abundance of recent studies on the status of women, mentioned above, allows us to present only short summaries of the broader issues and concentrate mostly on the empirical analysis and its implications.[5]

In Section II we formulate our hypotheses on expected earning differentials by sex in the Soviet Union, based on theories of earning functions, intrafamily distribution of labor and household roles, and discrimination. The data are described in Section III, where the variables and estimated equations are also defined. Section IV presents and analyzes the results. This chapter presents only our initial findings and analysis and leaves many questions for further research.

## II. The theory of earning differentials by sex

### A. *A summary of Western and Soviet theories*

Broadly speaking, there are three bodies of theory to explain observed earning differentials by sex: the human capital approach, the theory of comparative advantage, and the theory of discrimination. These three approaches compete with each other in some aspects, but are complementary – and even overlapping – in others. The human capital approach attributes wage or earning differentials to differences in formal education, experience or on the job training, the depreciation of human capital, and, one might add, hours of work, intensity of work, and so on. The lower pay received by women is thus to be explained in part by lower investments in all forms of human capital, less intensity of work, and shorter hours.[6] An additional manifestation of these features would be the small proportion of women holding managerial jobs and other positions demanding great responsibility, extensive involvement, and a good deal of time.

A major explanation of why women invest less in human capital – both formally and on the job – choose less intensive jobs, work fewer hours, and so on, and get paid less for work is that they devote much more of their time than do men to family affairs and responsibilities. Some believe that this division of roles is due to the (alleged) comparative advantage of women in performing family-type tasks. Women are said to be more fit, and perhaps more inclined, than men to bring up children and execute various other household chores. If optimal behavior requires women to award first priority to managing their family affairs, they naturally participate less in the labor force, thus investing less on the job. Shorter and more frequently interrupted work careers also make investment in human capital less attractive. Women therefore tend to choose less demanding (and thus lower-paying) jobs closer to home, with shorter hours, and so on. Because, in this system, the man becomes the principal earner, his choice of a workplace takes precedence within the family; his wife must then restrict her job search, which in turn obliges her in many cases to select less suitable jobs for which she tends to be, on the average, relatively overqualified and underpaid compared to her husband (Frank, 1978).

The theory of comparative advantage by sex is also extended to include market jobs. Alleged differences between men and women in ability and inclination to perform different tasks are thus said to explain part of the occupational segregation by sex observed to varying degrees in most societies. No doubt some "natural" differences between the sexes do enhance the performance of one or the other at a given job. The comparative advantage of men in performing hard physical labor is perhaps the most natural example. Yet at present there is no general agreement as to how much of the observed occupational segregation can be explained in this way.[7]

Third, sex discrimination can explain part of the observed earning differentials, either directly or indirectly, by being the underlying and ultimate reason for some of the explanatory factors mentioned above. First, it may exist openly in the labor market: lower wages may be paid to women performing identical work as men, or less money may be paid to women for what is essentially the same job but which has been disguised as a different (inferior) job, role, or occupation. Discrimination in the labor market can also take the form of blocking the entry of women into certain occupations or roles (management) or denying them equal opportunities to invest in certain forms of human capital. Both means constitute an alternative explanation for occupational segregation as opposed to the theory of comparative advantage.

On a deeper level, it is claimed that the lopsided distribution of family burdens, which is responsible for so much of the wage differential, is a direct result not of comparative advantage, but mostly of social or family norms created by men in a world dominated by men.[8] Even without open discrimination in the labor market or the family, women themselves are said to "freely choose" to behave in such a way as to create wide pay differentials, this "choice" being determined by and conditioned upon a system of "role segregation" deeply entrenched in the values, traditions, and educational systems of most societies to the benefit of men (Fuchs, 1971, pp. 14–15).

The actual mix of factors explaining the earnings gap varies among societies, over time, and even by the approach of the student who studies it. In all cases, however, there is a high degree of complementary interaction between most of the explanations listed: some discrimination in the labor market raises the relative advantage (per hour) of women in family work, which in turn reduces their incentive to invest in human capital, and so on.

It is interesting to note that although the human capital approach is formally rejected by Soviet scholars (Goilo, 1971, 1976) and that discrimination as such is formally preserved to explain only earning differentials in capitalist countries (Ershova, 1979), the study of why women are paid less in the Soviet Union adopts all three approaches described above.[9]

### B. Sources of earning differentials by sex in Soviet society: a comparative approach

Even without a definitive explanation of earning differentials by sex, it seems possible to hypothesize on the relative size of this differential under Soviet conditions compared with developed market economies. As the data available are limited to the urban sector, the discussion here does not enter into the additional complexities involved in dealing with rural communities. Three possible sources of the male/female wage differential specific to the Soviet system are treated: ideology, Soviet growth strategy, and the system of wage determination.[10]

#### Ideology

All other things being equal, the ideological principles of Soviet society, if implemented, should considerably narrow the earnings differential by sex. The official doctrine on wages is to pay everyone according to his or her contribution – that is, on the basis of productivity. If, on the one hand, there is little room for preferential treatment for women within the wage system, on the other hand, this principle does guarantee equal pay for equal work; it rejects any form of irrelevant wage discrimination.[11] Women are granted equal access to almost all jobs and occupations, and there is no sex barrier to their entry into educational institutions. The ideological principles call, moreover, for women to enjoy equal status in the home and in society at large; a woman's personal and economic independence is to be on a par with that of men. Although these ideological principles – calling for deep changes in perceptions, values, and cultural traditions – could not be fully implemented even during the 60 years of Soviet rule, efforts to adopt most of them have raised the status of women in many respects and thus should have worked toward more equal pay.

There is, however, one major exception to this tendency: the equalization of the status of women within the family has lagged behind. At the same time that the proportion of women in the labor force and in the educational system increased rapidly, the status of women at home changed slowly, if at all. Working women in the Soviet Union still shoulder more than two-thirds of the household tasks (Kolpakov and Patrushev, 1971, pp. 83, 89), a burden that significantly reduces their relative productivity in the labor market. Apparently, it is much easier to create changes in the social sphere than to alter basic mental and cultural values within the family unit. As demonstrated below, under this state of affairs, even the (net) effect of ideology on the relative pay of women is not clear.[12]

### Soviet growth strategy

The specific growth strategy adopted by the Soviet Union has also contributed to the asymmetrical change in the status of women and, in this respect, has aggravated its consequences with respect to their relative pay. Rapid growth, especially via the "extensive" model, meant, first of all, enlisting most women into the labor force. This pressure gained further momentum during the 1960s and 1970s, and today some 86 percent of all women of working age (15 to 54) are employed (Turchaninova, 1975, p. 254), a figure 15 to 30 percentage points higher than in most Western societies (based on ILO, 1977, table 1, and *OECD Observer*, 1979, p. 28). The actual difference between the Soviet Union and the West is even wider, however, because there is very limited opportunity for part-time work in the Soviet Union.

On the other hand, efforts to maximize the rate of investment call for low consumption levels, especially with respect to consumer goods and services, but also regarding housing, household appliances and pre-school children's institutions.[13] Under such conditions, household tasks demand not only more time but also much more mental and physical effort. Were these tasks equally distributed within the family, they would not affect relative pay for women; but since they are not – as is so well documented by Soviet time-budget studies – most of the extra burden is shouldered by women, further reducing their ability to demonstrate equal productivity and thereby obtain equal pay in the labor market.

The coexistence of a heavier household burden with a higher rate of participation in the labor force adds further to the negative effect on women's pay. Among the nonworking women in Western societies are those with higher-than-average family obligations. As their counterparts in the Soviet Union do work, the average negative effect of household tasks on women's pay in the Soviet Union is intensified; the almost complete absence of part-time work opportunities makes the situation even worse. Some of this pressure on the Soviet woman is relieved by raising fewer children (Berliner, 1977, pp. 13–22; Lapidus, 1978, pp. 262–3, 292–309) and/or children of "lower quality" (Berliner, 1977, pp. 23–39). Other possible consequences include the breaking up of families or the avoidance of family life altogether (Berliner, 1977, pp. 8–12; Lapidus, 1978, pp. 236–40). The present study, however, is limited to women in families. As long as there is little change in the intrafamily distribution of household work, Soviet growth strategy will continue to be in direct conflict with the goal of achieving equal productivity and thus equal pay for women.

But the planner may be interested in going even further and pay women less than their marginal product. This will be the case when he tries to maximize not total product but the "public surplus" of each worker above and beyond his private consumption. To engage a second family member in public-sector work, the planner must relieve the family of certain household tasks by supplying them through the market. This provision of additional services is considered by the planner as a cost that should be subtracted from the wages he would otherwise be willing to pay a second worker.[14] Given that families consider women members to be secondary earners (whether because of discrimination or on grounds of comparative advantage), the planner will want to pay women even less than their marginal product. If there is a reasonable amount of occupational segregation, such a policy may even be implemented, but we do not have any direct evidence to show that this is indeed attempted.[15]

A rapid rise in the number of women in the labor force in conjunction with a limited and slowly expanding supply of women-oriented jobs – as indeed is the case in the Soviet Union – can also negatively affect the relative pay for women. By emphasizing heavy industry and construction and by limiting the extent of mechanization and automation of auxiliary and low-priority production processes, the Soviet growth strategy creates at each stage of development many more "male" jobs. It creates fewer "female" jobs by constraining the development of the service industries. Women who join the labor force may simply be obliged to take jobs in which they have a comparative disadvantage, such as work involving hard physical labor.[16]

Even with normal availability of female jobs, the higher-than-normal influx of women into the labor force may affect their relative pay. To the extent that the prevailing occupational segregation of the sexes is based on comparative advantage and on the assumption that the penetration of women into additional occupations – and jobs – proceeds according to this principle, a higher proportion of women in any given profession means lower average productivity. On the other hand, to the extent that the initial occupational segregation results from discrimination, with men monopolizing for themselves the best jobs, the penetration of more women into high-paying jobs raises their average productivity. This process of rising productivity may be delayed, however, if the occupational segregation is achieved through well-developed social norms and perceptions. In such cases, women do not train themselves for male jobs and thus appear as if they actually did have a natural disadvantage in performing them. In this way, actual comparative disadvantage may, in fact, be simply conditional upon accepted norms and values.

In reality, it seems to us that both discrimination and comparative advantage, part of which is not really natural but learned, account for occupational segregation. But even if discrimination is important in occupational segregation, the rapid entry of women into the labor force does not necessarily mean higher relative productivity or rate of pay, at least in the short run.

The higher priority given to heavy industry and the lower priority enjoyed by light industry, the service sector, and white-collar jobs in general may also result in lower pay for women, who concentrate more in the latter group. The preferential pay awarded to important sectors may reflect an allocative goal – a premium above actual productivity – or it may enter into the concept of productivity as seen by the planners. Priority treatment (in investment allocation), coupled with less-than-free movement among sectors, can also create the same effect of higher marginal productivity in some branches.

A final aspect of Soviet growth strategy, but by no means the least important, is to raise – as rapidly as possible – the level of education, qualifications, and training of the labor force. The fast growth of the Soviet educational system has made it possible for women to close the rather vast educational gap with men that had existed and to prepare themselves better to enter the labor force on an equal footing. Here, too, ideology and economic growth have converged to bring urban women more or less to equality with men in terms of the average length of their formal schooling. This should clearly reduce earning gaps resulting from different educational levels or from quasi-rents of holders of scarce skills.[17] It should also open up certain traditional male jobs to women. According to human capital theory, increased participation in the labor force, expressed here in the form of longer work careers for women with fewer and shorter interruptions, is complementary with a greater demand for education. In this sense the two reinforce each other to reduce male/female earning gaps.

### The Soviet wage system

How are all the aforementioned factors translated into actual wages? How does the Soviet system of wage determination affect the relative pay of women? The major difference between the Soviet system and the market economy in this respect is that wage rates in the former are determined from above by the planning organs. Wages are based on such factors as output, working conditions, and the priority awarded to a particular industry or occupation.[18] The system ostensibly precludes, therefore, any direct discrimination, but it does prescribe lower pay for lower productivity, even if the latter results from indirect discrimination. Both Chapman and Lapidus – as well as many Soviet scholars – cite the allowances for conditions of work and the high rates of pay for preferential sectors as at least indirect sources for lower pay for women (see note 15). Even so, one is left with questions concerning the relation between officially prescribed wage rates and actual wages paid or the extent to which actual wages are determined by market forces.

Following the pioneering lead of Bergson (1944), most observers tend to believe that actual relative wages paid have a tendency to move toward labor market equilibrium levels[19] – that the household supply of labor and the demand for labor by managers are strong enough to mold wage rates to wages reflecting market conditions. In periods between wage reforms this is done with the help of various wage supplements – bonuses, premiums, changes in job definition, piece rates, and so on – which are more flexible than basic wage rates. Furthermore, changes in wages that take place between wage reforms due to market forces eventually find expression in various ways in the new wage scales determined by the next wage reform. The adjustment toward equilibrium does not have to take the form of changing wages, however; it can be achieved by the movement of people of different quality and commitment from one job to another to obtain wages suiting their qualifications. If we assume that market forces prevail, the existing overall wage differentials by sex and those within occupations and industries represent (1) measurable differences in labor quality – education, experience, hours, and so on; (2) differences in labor quality that cannot easily be measured, such as the degree of responsibility, intensity of work, and actual amount of on-the-job training required (as distinct from years of working experience); (3) differences in conditions of work or degree of disutility from work; (4) occupational barriers; and (5) elements introduced to promote dynamic adjustments toward equilibrium.

Applying all these factors to the question of wage differentials by sex, we believe that, first, occupational barriers external to women's own tastes do exist but to a lesser degree than in Western societies. This follows from both the doctrine and growth needs of the system; it was further enhanced by the relative shortage of men during the last generation because of the war. Even with fewer barriers, however, the pay differentials may be just as large as in the West if the labor supply of women is relatively abundant. Second, we expect to find greater equality between the sexes with respect to the measurable quality variables, especially the level of education, length of experience, and hours of work. Third, we expect to find relatively wider wage differentials caused by items (2) and (3) above as women try to lighten the quantitative pressures on their time by reducing the quality and intensity of their work. In this way women develop tastes for less demanding jobs – with less on-the-job training, in low-priority industries, closer to home, with shorter regular hours and lighter physical and mental strain. There is, indeed, plenty of evidence in the Soviet literature on these qualitative adjustments to quantitative pressures (a common phenomenon in many other areas of economic activity).[20] This inclination to take lighter jobs increases the supply pressure on relatively low-level white-collar jobs, which, as we have seen, are in limited demand, and thus acts to reduce even further the wages paid there.

The lopsided development of more equality and opportunity for women in the labor market on the one hand, but heavier household pressures on the other, locked together in a system in which almost every woman is made to work but with fewer female jobs, creates a situation under which it is not clear whether the relative pay for women should be higher or lower than under a system of possibly greater labor market discrimination but with smaller household burdens, a much lower labor participation rate for women, and a more ample supply of female jobs. As a minimum we think there are enough good reasons to assume that pay differentials by sex in the Soviet Union should not be significantly narrower than in the West.

## III. Equations, variables, and data

### A. The sample population

The data consist of returns from a family budget survey of 1,016 families of Soviet emigrants [dubbed the "survey population" (SP)]. Every family member 17 years old and older reported on his education, work, and earnings during the last "normal" year of his life in the Soviet Union. Other information on the family was also provided.[21] About one-third of the families reported for 1972, more than one-third for 1973, and slightly less for 1974, with a few families reporting for other years. In what follows, the findings will be compared to Soviet data for 1973.

The sample consists of urban families only, all Jewish, from the European republics of the USSR. It is also limited to two-parent families, in which at least one of the parents was active in the labor force during the normal period.[22] Our analysis thus excludes the rural sector as well as the population of the Asian republics, two sectors where one expects to find lower relative earnings of women. It also precludes the possibility of comparing the relative earnings of married women with those of single independent women.[23] This is unfortunate, because this last comparison is often used in Western studies to estimate the effect of family responsibilities on the productivity and earnings of women. On the basis of the previous discussion and Western findings, single (career) women should earn more than married women, but it is not clear if this should be the case for single mothers.

In addition to these omissions, the survey does not represent accurately its "target population" – the urban European segment of Soviet society [designated as "urban population" (UP)]. First, specific biases may be created by the Jewish and emigrant character of SP. Although important direct effects relating to the question of origin are not easy to determine, some biases may be created if Jewish husbands share more in household tasks, if Jewish mothers devote more time to family affairs, or if emigrant (or Jewish) families are less conservative and more open to new ideas, as, for example, that of women's liberation. We have no control group against which to test these possibilities. Second, biases may be due to the many structural or compositional differences between SP and UP. (To illustrate: two-thirds of SP are white-collar families, whereas UP is two-thirds blue-collar.) Similarly, there are differences in levels of education, industrial and occupational structure, geographical location, and in other characteristics as well.

These differences, or most of them, can be accounted for or corrected simply by reweighting the findings on any given phenomenon by the relevant structure of UP instead of SP. Thus, if the relative earnings of blue-collar women are lower than those of university graduates with respect to the corresponding groups of men, SP will show a higher overall relative women's earnings figure because blue-collar workers are underrepresented. This bias can be corrected by multiplying the two specific relative earnings by UP weights. The findings presented in this chapter have not yet been so corrected, but work in this direction is in progress. Until it is completed, no final judgment on the extent of the bias can be established, but preliminary checks seem to indicate that it is rather small.[24] It should be noted, however, that the structural differences do not affect, under reasonable conditions, the results of estimates based on multivariate (regression) analysis.

### B. The model, equations, and variables

The main analytical approach used in this chapter is that of earning functions in which earnings and earning differentials are determined or explained by hours of work, level of education, experience, type of job (industry, role), and a number of other variables. Following Oaxaca (1973), Malkiel and Malkiel (1973), Mincer and Polachek (1974), and others, earning differentials by sex are explained by male/female differences in the foregoing characteristics and an unexplained residual representing missing variables, errors in variables, and/or direct discrimination. The general form of the earning functions following Mincer is

$$\ln W = a + (b \text{ sex}) + \sum_i c_i X_i + U_i$$

where $W$ is earnings and $X_i$ the explanatory variables. Such equations can be estimated for all workers with a dummy variable representing sex (as in Swafford, 1977) or for males and females separately. We have performed both estimates but present here only results based on separate equations. The gross earning differential can be attributed to the various factors and to the unexplained residual by multiplying the sex differential in any given variable by the coefficient of the same variable estimated by either the corresponding male or female earning function (Oaxaca, 1973, pp. 695–8).

The main earning variables and the variables used to explain earning differentials are as follows:

#### Earning variables

The analysis uses four different concepts of earnings (each with a corresponding male/female ratio), all net of direct taxes, per month:

W0 (W0R)    Basic wages or salary from the main place of work, that is, excluding bonuses or premiums, pay for overtime, and so on.

W1 (W1R)    Total wages and salaries from the main place of work, including bonuses, and so on.

W2 (W2R)    Total earnings from the public sector, that is, W1 plus all earnings from extra jobs in the public sector.

W4 (W4R)    Total earnings, that is, W2 plus any private earnings reported by the respondents.

Of all of these, gross W1 is closest to the wage concept published in official Soviet publications.

*Explanatory variables*

Earnings ratios by sex are explained by the following variables:

1  *Hours of work:* The present analysis is carried out for full-time workers only, so that differences in regular hours worked (HO) represent differences in what constitutes "full time" (hours per week) in different jobs. The values of the other variables – H1, H2, and H4 – which correspond to W1–W4, vary, of course, according to the amount of extra work performed.

2  *Education:* Two sets of variables are used: years of formal schooling and level of schooling completed. The regressions include mostly the former, with a small correction for the type of school (regular, night, or by correspondence) in the case of university studies:[25] RS, years in regular school (up to 10 years); PS, years in secondary vocational (professional) schools; US, years to obtain first university degree; and AS, advanced university studies.

3  *Experience (EX):* A proxy for on-the-job training is estimated by using the actual number of years worked (not life following formal schooling, as in many Western studies). Following conventional theory, both EX and $(EX)^2$ are introduced into the equations.

4  *Age (Age):* When both schooling (by years) and experience are present in the regression, Age measures years of neither work nor school, the depreciation of human capital, and the quality (vintage) of formal education. *Experience* and *age,* however, are closely correlated and so are their respective coefficients.

5  *Branch and role:* The introduction of such characteristics into earning functions as independent variables is controversial, especially when near-perfection in the labor market is assumed. We introduce them in the following analysis as proxies for differences in labor quality unaccounted for by other variables and/or as estimates of the effects of occupational segregation under conditions of market imperfection, as explained above. The variables included are for industry, IND1 to IND12, with IND1 for manufacturing as the reference variable, and IND2, agriculture; IND3, construction; IND4, communications; IND5, transportation; IND6, communal and housing services; IND7, trade; IND8, health services; IND9, education and culture; IND11, science; and IND12, administration and social security.

   The dummy variables for ROLE are ROLE1, managerial jobs; ROLE2, high professional jobs (jobs which require university education) – the reference role; ROLE3, low professional jobs (those demanding secondary vocational education); ROLE4, nonprofessional white-collar jobs; ROLE5, skilled blue-collar workers; ROLE6, semiskilled workers; ROLE7, unskilled workers; and ROLE8, service blue-collar workers of all skill levels.

A dummy variable for nonmarried status was added to some of the equations but, as mentioned earlier, the nonmarried in SP belong to active families and are typically either young or old and thus earn less than their married counterparts, who are normally heads of families or wives of prime working age.

Other variables that were included in the analysis but did not contribute to the explanation of wages or wage differentials include location variables, health information, and the number of children of various ages. The effect of the number of children and their ages on earnings at a certain point in time is not straightforward and needs to be studied further.

## IV. Results and interpretation

The results are presented in two forms. In Tables 1, 4 to 7, and in Figure 1, we present results on wages and wage differentials by sex, classified by one or more of the main explanatory variables. These results are gross in the sense that the levels of other variables are not kept constant, and they are presented mainly as source of data for the interested reader. The regression, multivariate results are presented in Tables 2 and 3. Table 2 contains results of four earning functions, two for men and two for women, with ln W1 as the dependent variable. In each case, one regression, "short," excludes and a second one, "long," includes the variables for role, industry, and nonmarried status. The levels of the relevant variables are also shown for men (column 1), women (column 2), and the differences between them (column 3). Table 3 contains an analysis of the male/female earning difference according to the variables included in the long earning functions. The entire earning differential[26] is broken down into "explained" and "unexplained" segments. The explained segment, which appears in Table 3, is calculated as the sum of the products of the male/female differences in levels of the variables (Table 2, column 3) multiplied by the corresponding (male or female) regression coefficients (Table 2, columns 6 and 7). This is equivalent to calculating the hypothetical earnings of women (men) had they received payments according to the men's (women's) earning function and comparing them to actual earnings (see Gronau, 1979; Malkiel and Malkiel, 1973; and Oaxaca, 1973). The explained portion of the earning differential is attributed to the several

Table 1. *Earnings and hours of work by sex*

|  | (1) All | (2) Male | (3) Female | (4) Female/male ratio |
|---|---|---|---|---|
| 1. Number | 2,106 | 1,117 | 989 | 0.47[a] |
| 2. Earnings per month (rubles) |  |  |  |  |
|   a. Basic wage (W0) | 130.5 | 153.6 | 104.6 | 0.68 |
|   b. Main workplace (W1) | 153.8 | 185.1 | 118.8 | 0.64 |
|   c. Public sector (W2) | 160.2 | 194.8 | 120.9 | 0.62 |
|   d. All work (W4) | 168.8 | 208.5 | 123.8 | 0.59 |
| 3. Hours per week |  |  |  |  |
|   a. Regular hours (H0) | 38.1 | 39.0 | 36.6 | 0.94 |
|   b. Main workplace (H1) | 39.9 | 41.1 | 37.6 | 0.91 |
|   c. Public sector (H2) | 41.1 | 42.4 | 38.2 | 0.90 |
|   d. All work (H4) | 41.9 | 44.1 | 38.6 | 0.88 |
| 4. Wage per hour (rubles) |  |  |  |  |
|   a. Basic wage (WPH0) | 0.79 | 0.91 | 0.66 | 0.73 |
|   b. Main workplace (WPH1) | 0.89 | 1.04 | 0.73 | 0.70 |
|   c. Public sector (WPH2) | 0.90 | 1.06 | 0.73 | 0.69 |
|   d. All work (WPH4) | 0.93 | 1.09 | 0.74 | 0.68 |
| 5. Level of education (years) | 13.0 | 12.9 | 13.0 | 0.1[b] |
| 6. Work experience (years) | 17.2 | 19.6 | 14.4 | −5.2[b] |
| 7. Age (years) | 37.2 | 38.7 | 35.5 | −3.2[b] |

[a] Proportion of women in labor force.
[b] Female/male difference in years.

variables in an aggregated form. Table 3 contains an analysis of earning differentials for the entire population (as in Table 2) and for three sub-groups thereof: those with university degrees or more, those with secondary professional diplomas, and those possessing a lower level of education (the corresponding equations are not shown). Since our main interest is in the earning differentials, the discussion will follow the findings of Table 3, referring back to Table 2 when necessary. A few remarks will also be added on the results obtained for the other earning variables discussed above, which are not shown here.[27] In comparing the results in the other tables with those in Tables 2 and 3, the reader is reminded that in the former the earning differential is defined by $W_{female}/W_{male}$, whereas in the latter we use $\ln W_{male} - \ln W_{female}$.[28]

Data on the overall earning differentials by sex are presented in Table 1. Net monthly earnings from the main job average 185.1 rubles for men and 118.8 rubles for women, 64 percent that of men (line 2b). Since W1 is the (net) wage category closest to that published in official Soviet data, given the small effect of the structural difference between SP and UP (see p. 136 and note 24), this earning differential should not be too different from the one that would have been observed from Soviet data on net wages.[29]

Wage rates (W0) are more equal than monthly main-job earnings (W1), but total earnings, including extra public (W2) and private (W4) jobs, show wider gaps. Thus, in terms of basic wage, women earn 68 percent of what men do, but the rate falls to 59 percent when all earnings are taken into account (Table 1, line 2d). Part of the growing gap is explained by the widening hours gap over the range from H0 (basic hours) to H4 (total hours). At their main job women work fewer regular hours than men do (36.6 versus 39.0) because they are highly concentrated in jobs with short work weeks, especially as teachers and nurses. On top of their regular workweek, women also work fewer additional hours both at their main place of work (H1) and in extra public (H2) or private (H4) jobs. When all hours of work are accounted for, women work 38.6 hours per week, only 88 percent of the 44.1 hours that men work weekly. The second part of the growing gap is due to the higher pay per hour received for extra work in general and by men in particular. For this reason, women's wages per hour go down from 73 percent of men's for basic hours to 68 percent for all hours. The widening of the gap between W0 and the other wage concepts may reflect in particular the influence of the market forces on the wage rates determined by the planners.

A side implication of the data in Table 1 is that, in addition to being employed for a longer regular workweek, men engage much more than women in extra work of all kinds (5.1 hours per week for men and 2.0 hours for women). In this way, part of the observed imbalance in household work in the other direction is offset.

Additional information on the overall earnings gap, this time for subgroups of the population, is included in Table 3. The wage gap (based on W1) is narrowest for academics, the male advantage being only 35.7 percent compared to the average advantage of 41.3 percent, and widest for semiprofessionals (47.1 percent). It is somewhat narrower (44.0 percent) for those with general education or less (line 1).[30] The high inequality of the middle group is somewhat surprising, as one would expect inequality to be negatively correlated with the level of education. We shall come back later to this special feature.

Roughly half of these earning differentials are explained by the independent variables included in the analysis according to the male equations – only about 40 percent when the female equations are used (Table 3). The unexplained part of the pay differentials represents lower pay for women of the same age, education, and experience as men, who work the same number of hours, in the same industry, and at the same job level. This unexplained difference may result in principle from lower quality (rather than quantity) of experience or education, from lower productivity, or from other factors, such as the second burden at home or comparative advantage or discrimination. We tried, without success, to

Table 2. Earning functions of males and females

| | (1) Level of variables | | (3) | (4) (5) Regression coefficients Short equations | | (6) (7) Long equations | |
|---|---|---|---|---|---|---|---|
| | Males | Females | Male/female difference | Male | Female | Male | Female |
| 1. Monthly earnings from main job ln W1 | 5.1297 | 4.7165 | 0.4132 | — | — | — | — |
| 2. $\bar{R}^2$/standard error of estimate | — | — | — | 0.32/0.35 | 0.31/0.29 | 0.39/0.33 | 0.43/0.26 |
| 3. Regression constant | — | — | — | 2.799 | 3.584 | 2.830 | 3.900 |
| *Independent variables* | | | | | | | |
| 4. Regular hours ln H1 | 3.7193 | 3.6600 | 0.0593 | 0.440 | 0.139 | 0.425 | 0.086[a] |
| 5. Regular school RS (years) | 9.24 | 9.57 | −0.33 | 0.023 | 0.024 | 0.028 | 0.031 |
| 6. Profession school PS (years) | 1.09 | 1.15 | −0.06 | 0.027 | 0.019 | 0.031 | 0.021 |
| 7. University US (years) | 1.93 | 1.88 | 0.05 | 0.050 | 0.065 | 0.047 | 0.052 |
| 8. Advanced studies AS (years) | 0.26 | 0.06 | 0.20 | 0.063 | 0.076 | 0.070 | 0.090 |
| 9. Experience EX (years) | 19.58 | 14.41 | 5.17 | 0.051 | 0.026 | 0.036 | 0.017 |
| 10. (Experience)² (EX)² | 507.59 | 282.96 | 224.63 | −0.0007 | −0.0004 | −0.0005 | −0.0002 |
| 11. Age (years) | 38.69 | 35.51 | 3.18 | −0.0077 | −0.0006[a] | −0.0030[a] | 0.0011[a] |
| 12. Unmarried | 0.099 | 0.117 | −0.018 | — | — | −0.006[a] | −0.063[b] |
| *Roles* | | | | | | | |
| 13. Managerial | 0.235 | 0.068 | 0.167 | — | — | 0.119 | 0.181 |
| 14. High-level professional (ref.) | 0.321 | 0.418 | −0.096 | — | — | — | — |
| 15. Semiprofessional | 0.057 | 0.290 | −0.233 | — | — | −0.092[b] | −0.124 |
| 16. Other white collar | 0.014 | 0.032 | −0.018 | — | — | −0.018[a] | −0.285 |

| | | | | | | | |
|---|---|---|---|---|---|---|---|
| *Blue collar* | | | | | | | |
| 17. Skilled | 0.120 | 0.004 | 0.116 | — | — | — | 0.162 | −0.103[a] |
| 18. Semiskilled | 0.121 | 0.030 | 0.091 | — | — | — | 0.087[b] | 0.040[a] |
| 19. Unskilled | 0.049 | 0.036 | 0.013 | — | — | — | −0.107[b] | −0.017[a] |
| 20. Service | 0.082 | 0.121 | −0.039 | — | — | — | −0.085[a] | −0.134 |
| *Industry* | | | | | | | | |
| 21. Manufacturing (ref.) | 0.349 | 0.260 | 0.089 | — | — | — | — | — |
| 22. Agriculture | 0.025 | 0.013 | 0.012 | — | — | — | −0.070[a] | −0.109[a] |
| 23. Transport | 0.063 | 0.016 | 0.047 | — | — | — | −0.056[a] | −0.138[b] |
| 24. Communications | 0.007 | 0.013 | −0.006 | — | — | — | −0.305 | −0.124[a] |
| 25. Construction | 0.106 | 0.035 | 0.072 | — | — | — | 0.007[a] | −0.037[a] |
| 26. Trade and catering | 0.084 | 0.107 | −0.023 | — | — | — | −0.147 | −0.085 |
| 27. Communal services | 0.123 | 0.090 | 0.033 | — | — | — | −0.041[a] | −0.025[a] |
| 28. Health services | 0.068 | 0.189 | −0.121 | — | — | — | −0.227 | −0.216 |
| 29. Education and culture | 0.091 | 0.176 | −0.085 | — | — | — | −0.027[a] | −0.166 |
| 30. Science | 0.071 | 0.056 | −0.015 | — | — | — | −0.108 | −0.209 |
| 31. Administration and banking | 0.013 | 0.045 | −0.031 | — | — | — | −0.111[a] | −0.038[a] |

*Note:* Except where otherwise indicated, coefficients are significant at 1%.

[a] Not significant at 5%.

[b] Significant at 5%.

Table 3. Sources of earning differentials by sex

| | (1) | (2) | (3) | (4) | (5) | (6) | (7) | (8) |
|---|---|---|---|---|---|---|---|---|
| | Entire population | | University graduates | | Secondary professional | | General schooling or less | |
| | Male equation | Female equation | Male equation | Female equation | Male equation | Female equation | Male equation | Female equation |
| 1. Wage differential[a] | 41.32 | 41.32 | 35.71 | 35.71 | 47.08 | 47.08 | 43.98 | 43.98 |
| 2. Explained[b] | 20.35 | 16.24 | 17.17 | 15.39 | 21.74 | 19.08 | 23.84 | 12.97 |
| 3. due to: Hours | 2.48 | 0.50 | 3.61 | 1.22 | 2.74 | 1.22 | 1.34 | -0.27 |
| 4. Education | 0.49 | 0.80 | 3.20 | 3.81 | 0.85 | 1.63 | -0.25 | -0.93 |
| 5. Experience | 7.73 | 4.14 | 2.94 | -0.25 | 5.53 | 9.03 | 11.99 | 3.27 |
| 6. Age | -1.04 | 0.35 | 2.29 | 2.26 | -0.30 | -1.39 | -2.46 | 0.26 |
| 7. Role | 7.03 | 6.35 | 4.35 | 6.42 | 5.56 | -1.10 | 7.34 | 8.07 |
| 8. (Managerial) | (1.98) | (3.04) | (3.95) | (6.69) | (-0.08) | (-0.10) | (1.43) | (0.68) |
| 9. (Semiprofessional) | (2.15) | (2.92) | (0.42) | (0.10) | (-4.07) | (5.14) | (2.24) | (5.66) |
| 10. Industry | 3.66 | 4.10 | 0.82 | 1.88 | 7.42 | 9.68 | 5.30 | 2.12 |
| 11. (Health services) | (2.77) | (2.60) | (1.13) | (1.01) | (10.26) | (6.85) | (1.28) | (0.76) |
| 12. Unexplained | 20.97 | 25.08 | 18.54 | 20.32 | 25.34 | 28.00 | 20.14 | 31.01 |
| *Percentages:* | | | | | | | | |
| 13. Total wage differential | 100.0 | 100.0 | 100.0 | 100.0 | 100.0 | 100.0 | 100.0 | 100.0 |
| 14. Unexplained | 50.7 | 60.7 | 48.1 | 43.1 | 46.2 | 40.5 | 54.2 | 70.5 |
| 15. Explained[c] | 49.3 | 39.3 | 51.9 | 56.9 | 53.8 | 59.5 | 45.8 | 29.5 |
| 16. Explained percent | 100.0 | 100.0 | 100.0 | 100.0 | 100.0 | 100.0 | 100.0 | 100.0 |
| 17. by: Hours | 12.2 | 3.1 | 21.0 | 7.9 | 12.6 | 6.4 | 5.6 | -2.1 |
| 18. Education | 2.4 | 4.9 | 18.6 | 24.8 | 3.9 | 8.5 | -1.0 | -7.2 |
| 19. Experience | 38.0 | 25.5 | 17.1 | -1.6 | 25.4 | 47.3 | 50.3 | 25.2 |
| 20. Age | -5.1 | 2.2 | 13.3 | 14.7 | -1.4 | -7.3 | 10.3 | 2.0 |
| 21. Role | 34.5 | 39.1 | 25.3 | 41.7 | 25.6 | -5.8 | 30.8 | 62.2 |
| 22. Industry | 18.0 | 25.2 | 4.8 | 12.2 | 34.1 | 50.7 | 22.2 | 16.3 |
| 23. Number of observations | 1117 | 989 | 448 | 376 | 244 | 319 | 425 | 294 |

[a] In $W1_{male}$ − In $W1_{female}$; see note 30 for correspondence with arithmetic ratios of $W1_{female}/W1_{male}$.
[b] The figures in columns 1 and 2 are calculated on the basis of the unrounded figures underlying those shown in columns 3, 6, and 7 in Table 2.
[c] Small effect of being unmarried included in total but not shown.

144

estimate directly the possible effects of having small children and sickness-related absenteeism from work.[31] The pure children effect may show up in earning functions for women in those age groups, such as 25 to 45 (not estimated yet), where their presence should hurt most. We believe that the household burden is very important in the unexplained portion of the gap, but at least until further work is done one cannot exclude the influence of other factors.

The impacts of the main independent variables on the explained part of the earning gaps are as follows:

1. Differences in the *number of hours* worked account for only a small part of the explained segment, at most one-fifth for academics according to one equation, but usually less than 10 percent. Although the difference in hours by sex is itself relatively small, this result is also due to the low coefficients for hours estimated by the equations – 0.425 for men and (nonsignificant) 0.086 for women (Table 2, long equation). Part of the hours' effect is due to the shorter workweek prevailing in a number of sectors; as a result, the elasticity of hours in the short equations is slightly higher. The lower elasticities of hours in the female equations probably result from the higher pay per hour received by women in jobs that require fewer hours. The relative importance of hours does increase, however, as we move to more inclusive earning concepts. This results from a widening of the male/female difference in the number of hours worked and from a rise in the elasticity of earnings with respect to hours.[32] But even when we account for the larger contribution of hours in explaining the gap of total wages (W4), there remains a difference in the earning gap between W4 and W1: For the entire population, based on the men's equation, the differentials are 42 percent for the former and 39 percent for the latter.

2. The contribution of *education* to earning differentials by sex is on the average very small, less than 1 percent (Table 3). This is a combined result of the overall equality in the level of education between the sexes (Tables 2 and 4) and the relatively low rates of return to formal education in the Soviet Union (Table 2). The latter average 2 to 3 percent per year for regular schooling and for secondary professional training, but reach 6 to 9 percent a year for advanced studies. These should be compared to rates on the upper side of 10 percent in the West (see, e.g., Mincer, 1974, pp. 92–3).

For a number of reasons the picture is somewhat different when education is broken down into its various stages. First, women are underrepresented in groups of both high and low educational attainment and overrepresented in the group possessing secondary vocational education. Whereas they constitute less than one-fifth of those with advanced degrees (less than half their average proportion), women account for almost three-fifths of those with secondary vocational training (Table 4). An im-

Table 4. *Earning differentials by sex according to education, age, and experience*

| | (1) | (2) | (3) | (4) | (5) |
|---|---|---|---|---|---|
| | | | Female/male ratios | | |
| | Women in group (%) | Monthly wages | | Hourly wages | |
| | | W1 | W4 | WPH1 | WPH4 |
| All | 47.0 | 0.64 | 0.59 | 0.70 | 0.68 |
| *A. Level of education* | | | | | |
| Advanced degrees | 18.2 | 0.64 | 0.59 | 0.70 | 0.69 |
| University degree | 48.0 | 0.70 | 0.67 | 0.80 | 0.80 |
| University noncomplete | 46.0 | 0.64 | 0.61 | 0.71 | 0.70 |
| Secondary professional | 58.6 | 0.59 | 0.53 | 0.62 | 0.58 |
| Secondary general | 43.5 | 0.62 | 0.57 | 0.66 | 0.63 |
| 7–9 years | 41.3 | 0.63 | 0.57 | 0.66 | 0.63 |
| 6 years and less | 31.6 | 0.65 | 0.57 | 0.71 | 0.68 |
| *B. Age groups (in years)* | | | | | |
| 17–24 | 55.3 | 0.72 | 0.69 | 0.79 | 0.76 |
| 25–34 | 50.3 | 0.71 | 0.63 | 0.77 | 0.73 |
| 35–44 | 48.3 | 0.60 | 0.56 | 0.67 | 0.66 |
| 45–54 | 44.0 | 0.63 | 0.59 | 0.64 | 0.63 |
| 55+ | 20.3 | 0.68 | 0.68 | 0.75 | 0.75 |
| *C. Experience groups (in years)* | | | | | |
| 0–5 | 63.0 | 0.82 | 0.78 | 0.86 | 0.84 |
| 6–10 | 49.0 | 0.70 | 0.64 | 0.75 | 0.71 |
| 11–15 | 55.0 | 0.65 | 0.57 | 0.77 | 0.72 |
| 16–20 | 54.7 | 0.61 | 0.57 | 0.66 | 0.65 |
| 21–25 | 43.1 | 0.62 | 0.59 | 0.69 | 0.68 |
| 26–30 | 37.6 | 0.70 | 0.63 | 0.73 | 0.70 |
| 31+ | 18.2 | 0.69 | 0.70 | 0.67 | 0.70 |

plication of this structural difference is that although women study only slightly more than men, they spend on the average more time in regular and secondary professional schools and less time in universities, especially in advanced studies (0.26 year per man and 0.06 year per woman, and 0.65 and 0.49 year, respectively, for academics; see Table 2). For this reason, education reduces the sex earning differentials for the low educational group, but raises them considerably for university graduates.[33] The male advantage created by education in the semiprofessional group (Table 3) results from more professional schooling for men who belong to this group.

Second, for higher levels of education, especially for advanced studies, female rates of return are higher than those for males. This differential might reflect the existence of a comparative advantage for women in jobs that require high education as well as the operation of a selection process

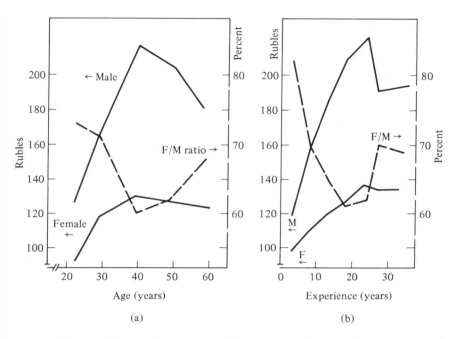

Figure 1. Wage profiles by sex and (a) age groups; (b) experience groups.

in which only the most highly skilled women can overcome the difficulties involved in obtaining jobs demanding such advanced training. The difficulties of penetrating into jobs requiring advanced degrees are demonstrated by both the low proportion of women found in such jobs and their low relative pay (Table 4). Comparative advantage seems to play a greater role for university graduates without advanced degrees, because there women are adequately represented and their relative pay is high.

3. The female/male ratios by *age* and *experience* show rather definite U-shaped forms (Table 4 and Figure 1): The relatively high ratios for young age and experience groups decline with rising age and experience but begin to increase again at older ages and after long experience. The earning ratio patterns correspond to an inverted U-shaped development of male and female earnings through the age groups and a logistic or parabolic shape of the experience–wage profiles. At least the form of all these patterns are well established by human capital theory and closely resemble findings in the West. At young ages (and low experience) women earn 72 (82) percent of an average man's wage – 79 (86) percent per hour (based on W1 and WPH1). These ratios decline to 0.60 (0.67 per hour) at 35 to 44 years of age, and to 0.61 (0.66 per hour) after 16 to 20 years of

experience. They climb back to 0.68 (0.75 per hour) at higher ages and to 0.70 (0.73 per hour) for the group with long experience (26 to 30 years). The U-shaped patterns of the male/female wage ratios reflect a situation in which the intensive accumulation of human capital by men during work is offset at older ages and long experience by a selection process in which (mostly) women of lower earning capacity leave the labor force. This process can be observed by the declining proportion of women in high-age and long-experience groups. Part of the initial rise in the ratios may also reflect a time trend of declining direct and indirect discrimination against women. Another part of the pattern is explained by a sharper decline in number of hours (relative to men) worked by women of prime working age with relatively long experience.

When translated into the regression analysis, sex differences in work experience are found to be a major source of pay differentials for all groups with the exception of academics (Tables 2 and 3). They explain between 5.5 and 12 points of the total differential for the other groups but only 2.9 for academics[34] (male equations), or between one-fourth and one-half of the entire explained part. As can be seen from Table 2, the EX coefficients are in general not very different from those for education, although unlike education, they decline, as expected, over time and flatten out completely after 32 to 36 years.[35] They seem, however, to be higher than those found in most Western studies, but this may result from the direct estimate of experience in our study in contrast to the "years follow-ing schooling" used in many Western ones.[36] In all cases the EX coeffi-cients in the female equations are much lower than the corresponding ones for males, not only initially but – with only one major exception – at all relevant experience levels. Since the rates of return on investment in education are not lower for women, this would seem to indicate that the rate of investment in human capital per year of work is lower for women than for men. That such is indeed the case is fully documented in Soviet sources; the main reason given there is that women have less available free time because of family responsibilities (Parkhomenko, 1972, p. 78).

The difference of more than 5 years in work experience between the sexes contributes, of course, to the experience part of the earning differen-tial. By Western standards, however, this is a small experience gap. Analytically, it can be divided into one gap resulting from the lower aver-age age of women – 3.2 years in SP – and an experience gap between persons of the same age. Controlling for age, the experience gap narrows by almost half, to 2.6 years.[37] The pure experience effect is thus only about half of what is shown in Table 3; the rest should be added to the age effect. It may be, however, that because of the high correlation between age and experience, there is some shifting of effects between them; the results should be viewed in this light.

Table 5. *Earning differentials by sex: status and role*

|  | (1) | (2) | (3) | (4) | (5) |
|---|---|---|---|---|---|
|  |  | Female/male ratios | | | |
|  | Women in group (%) | Monthly wages | | Hourly wages | |
|  |  | W1 | W4 | WPH1 | WPH4 |
| 1. All | 47.0 | 0.64 | 0.59 | 0.70 | 0.68 |
| 2. Employees: all | 51.9 | 0.62 | 0.58 | 0.67 | 0.66 |
|   a. Managers | 20.4 | 0.75 | 0.70 | 0.74 | 0.72 |
|   b. High-level professionals | 53.5 | 0.72 | 0.66 | 0.82 | 0.80 |
|   c. Semiprofessionals | 81.8 | 0.67 | 0.64 | 0.67 | 0.67 |
|   d. Other white-collar employees | 66.7 | 0.55 | 0.49 | 0.55 | 0.52 |
| 3. Workers: all | 31.4 | 0.61 | 0.57 | 0.66 | 0.63 |
|   a. Managers | 2.9 | 0.57 | 0.49 | 0.56 | 0.52 |
|   b. Skilled workers | 18.2 | 0.75 | 0.66 | 0.76 | 0.71 |
|   c. Low-skilled workers | 39.6 | 0.85 | 0.75 | 0.86 | 0.81 |
|   d. Service workers | 56.6 | 0.70 | 0.65 | 0.72 | 0.71 |

The age coefficients in earning functions are expected to represent depreciation of human capital and obsolescence of old vintage education, as well as interruptions during schooling or working careers. They are thus expected to be negative, as indeed they are in three of the four equations of Table 2. The age coefficient is positive, however, in the equations for academics and in some other female equations. Positive or nonsignificant values may reflect the collinearity with experience, mentioned above.

As mentioned above, up to one year of the age difference – and a resulting 0.7 year of experience gap – may be due to a bias of SP. This may account for up to one point of the earning gap by sex.

In the short equations the coefficients for hours, experience, and advanced studies are higher than in the long equations, so that despite lower coefficients for the other schooling stages, the variables of the short equations explain more of the earning gap in the short than in the long equations. Part of the impact of hours, experience, and so on, is absorbed in the long equations by roles and industries correlated with the main variables: such as a positive correlation between managerial roles and experience.

4. That *role* is an important explanatory factor is shown by the gross female/male earning ratios by role (Table 5), the relevant regression coefficients (Table 2), and the contribution of role in explaining the earning gap (Table 3). To put it concisely, women are underrepresented in high-level roles that pay well and overrepresented in low-level roles that pay

less. The product of this negative relationship explains between 6.35 and 7.03 points of the entire earning gap, between 34 and 40 percent of the explained portion (Table 3). The most important contributors to this large role effect are as follows.[38] First, only 7 percent of all women fill managerial roles that pay a 12 (men's equation) to 18 (women's equation) percent premium over wages of high professional workers (which is the reference group, see Table 2, line 14). The results on the earning gap, as shown in line 8 of Table 3, demonstrate that this factor alone absorbs more or less the entire role effect for academic workers. Second, 29 percent of all women are semiprofessionals against only 6 percent of the men, and here there is a negative premium of 9 to 12 percent. This factor alone reduces women's wages for the two schooling groups of workers by between 2.2 and 5.6 points, a major part of the total role effect. Third, skilled workers, and to a lower degree semiskilled workers, earn wage premiums of up to 16 percent (over high professionals' wages!), but women are almost absent among their ranks (Table 2).[39] Finally, women are overrepresented among service workers who earn a negative premium of between 8.5 and 13.4 percent. The last two factors affect predominantly the lowest schooling group, mostly blue-collar workers, accounting together for 4 points of the earning gap. Again we find that the role coefficients in the female equations are usually positive and higher than those for men for roles in which men predominate; they are negative and larger (in absolute terms) for roles where women predominate.

The importance of role as an explanatory variable is also demonstrated in Table 5 in that intrarole earning ratios (with two unimportant exceptions) are much higher than the average ratio. Table 5 also demonstrates a rather complicated relationship between the proportion of women in a certain role and their relative pay: Among employees (with one exception) this relationship is negative, whereas among workers (again with one exception)[40] it is positive. We shall come back to investigate this relationship for a more detailed breakdown by occupation.

5. The different *industrial structure* of the sexes is less important than role for the entire group as well as for all subgroups, except for those with secondary professional schooling (Table 3). Its effect is very small for the academic group, where none of the industry coefficients in the male equation are significant. Academic salaries apparently vary least between branches. But for those with secondary professional schooling, industrial structure is the most important explanatory factor. As can be observed from line 28 in Table 2, the branch that is mostly responsible for the industry effect is that of health services. All the equations have large negative coefficients for this branch (as compared with salaries in manufacturing) – and in every group of workers women are represented in this branch to a much higher degree than men.[41] A high concentration of

Table 6. *Earning differentials by sex and industry* [a]

| Industry | (1) Women in group (%) | (2) Female/male W1 wage ratio | (3) Monthly wages from main workplace W1 (rubles) |
|---|---|---|---|
| All | 47.0 | 0.64 | 185.1 |
| 1. Manufacturing: all | 39.7 | 0.68 | 190.0 |
|    a. Workers | (31.8) | (0.68) | (166.9) |
|    b. Employees | (45.2) | (0.65) | (209.7) |
| 2. Transportation | 18.6 | 0.56 | 179.7 |
| 3. Construction | 22.9 | 0.71 | 199.4 |
| 4. Trade and catering: all | 53.0 | 0.65 | 160.6 |
|    a. Workers | (53.8) | (0.64) | (139.5) |
|    b. Employees | (52.5) | (0.66) | (174.3) |
| 5. Communal services: all | 39.4 | 0.69 | 162.2 |
|    a. Workers | (25.9) | (0.69) | (156.3) |
|    b. Employees | (59.3) | (0.65) | (178.3) |
| 6. Health services | 71.1 | 0.64 | 174.6 |
| 7. Education and culture | 65.3 | 0.63 | 189.4 |
| 8. Art | 21.4 | 0.47 | 242.1 |
| 9. Science | 41.8 | 0.58 | 218.8 |
| 10. Administration [b] | 71.3 | 0.68 | 162.1 |

[a] According to official Soviet classification.
[b] Includes social insurance, banking, and communications.

women plus negative coefficients for education and culture also contribute a little to the industry effect, especially for the low-schooling group. On the whole, however, much of the gross industry variation in relative pay for women observed in Table 6 seems to be absorbed by the other variables.

6. Table 7 includes data on the proportion of women, female/male earning differentials, and men's wages for 35 *occupational groups* of workers. This disaggregation goes much beyond what is included in the regression equations. In deciding not to include the detailed occupational breakdown in the regressions, we shared Victor Fuchs's conviction "that if one pushes occupational classification far enough, one could 'explain' nearly all the (earning) differential" (1971, p. 14). On the other hand, such analysis may throw more light on the question of occupational segregation.

As indeed found by Fuchs and others, intraoccupational wage differentials by sex are much smaller than the overall differences. Within occupational groupings the unweighted, average male/female monthly pay ratio is 0.82; per hour the ratio rises to 0.85. This implies a significant degree of occupational segregation, with women being concentrated in lower-paying occupations. In 17 occupations, comprising 41.6 percent of all those em-

Table 7. *Relative earnings and the proportion of women: 35 occupations*

| Occupational group[a] | (1) Women in group (%) | (2) Female/ male wage ratio | (3) Average male wage (rubles per month) | (4) Total number in group |
|---|---|---|---|---|
| Average 35 occupations | 46.2 | 0.82 | 180.5 | 2106 |
| 1. Enterprise managers | 0.0 | — | 387.4 | 5 |
| 2. Highly skilled workers, heavy industry | 0.0 | — | 198.1 | 96 |
| 3. Skilled workers, heavy industry | 4.3 | 0.71 | 167.4 | 116 |
| 4. Senior faculty members | 5.9 | 0.66 | 350.9 | 16 |
| 5. Highly skilled workers, light industry | 9.5 | 0.59 | 188.4 | 42 |
| 6. Unit production managers | 11.7 | 0.81 | 232.7 | 60 |
| 7. Head engineers | 13.2 | 0.72 | 253.3 | 53 |
| 8. Senior research people | 18.4 | 0.62 | 316.7 | 38 |
| 9. Department managers | 18.7 | 0.84 | 213.7 | 75 |
| 10. Artists | 19.4 | 0.66 | 233.0 | 31 |
| 11. Low-skilled workers, light industry | 25.0 | 0.82 | 127.2 | 44 |
| 12. Chief engineers | 32.9 | 0.76 | 192.9 | 79 |
| 13. Employees in services | 33.3 | 0.87 | 137.8 | 18 |
| 14. Senior trade employees | 35.9 | 0.76 | 166.3 | 59 |
| 15. Engineers | 39.8 | 0.75 | 174.1 | 216 |
| 16. Chief doctors | 40.0 | 1.01 | 210.4 | 25 |
| 17. Dentists | 43.5 | 0.78 | 123.5 | 23 |
| 18. Skilled workers, light industry | 51.0 | 0.85 | 145.0 | 49 |
| 19. Chief planners, economists | 52.6 | 0.84 | 188.1 | 57 |
| 20. Low-skilled workers, light industry | 53.2 | 0.90 | 115.5 | 47 |
| 21. Junior faculty members | 56.2 | 0.97 | 153.6 | 16 |
| 22. Service workers | 56.6 | 0.70 | 139.0 | 212 |
| 23. Junior trade employees | 58.3 | 0.52 | 172.0 | 24 |
| 24. Junior research people | 60.6 | 0.90 | 133.3 | 33 |
| 25. Chief editors, writers | 60.9 | 0.61 | 190.7 | 23 |
| 26. Editors, writers | 62.2 | 0.63 | 142.4 | 37 |
| 27. Technicians | 62.3 | 0.73 | 154.5 | 77 |
| 28. Medical doctors | 71.3 | 0.77 | 188.6 | 80 |
| 29. Teachers | 74.8 | 0.79 | 162.0 | 155 |
| 30. Planners, economists | 85.2 | 0.91 | 139.8 | 27 |
| 31. Accountants | 86.8 | 0.61 | 177.3 | 136 |
| 32. Pharmacists | 87.5 | 1.18 | 78.3 | 32 |
| 33. Laboratory assistants | 91.3 | 1.29 | 75.0 | 23 |
| 34. Nurses | 92.4 | 0.81 | 106.8 | 66 |
| 35. Secretaries | 100.0 | — | — | 16 |

[a] In increasing order of female representation.

ployed, the proportion accounted for by one sex is at least 75 percent of the total. Included here are three single-sex occupations – enterprise managers and highly skilled workers in heavy industry on the one side and secretaries on the other. The predominantly male occupations are either characterized by high managerial content and the need for advanced studies or call for skilled work in (heavy) industry; the predominantly female occupations are nurses, pharmacists, planners, economists and accountants, teachers, and doctors. (Only the last group differs from the pattern commonly found in the West.) Another 38.1 percent of all workers and employees work in occupations with 60 to 75 percent majorities for one sex or the other, and only 20.3 percent (seven occupations) work in balanced groups.[42]

That women concentrate in low-paying occupations can be seen by comparing the proportion of women (column 1) with the level of wages paid to men (column 3). The simple correlation between the two (for 34 occupations) is $-0.66$; the regression coefficient of the latter with respect to the former – controlling for education, hours, and experience, is $-0.346$ ($t = -4.6071$).[43]

A second observation from the table is, however, that the relative pay of women is positively correlated with the proportion of women in a given occupation. The simple correlation between the two (for 32 occupations) is 0.39, and a regression coefficient of the latter with respect to the former is 0.24 ($t = 2.3398$). This second finding may be partially dependent on the first (the male wage is the denominator of the pay ratio), but it also has independent significance. The two together are consistent with most of the findings on segregation by role and with all the theories explaining occupational segregation.

The concentration of women in low-paying jobs may result from heavy family burdens with all that they imply, whereas the high relative pay may reflect derived or genuine comparative advantage and/or the consequences of the "overqualification" of women in the jobs they perform. Also, the large demand by women for such jobs may force a decline in average wages for everybody, crowding out the more qualified men. But the same pattern of concentration of women may just as well reflect artificial entrance barriers to the best-paying jobs and all the rest follows. In both cases it is possible to use the existing occupational segregation to artificially reduce wages in women's jobs below productivity. Again we tend to believe that the first set of factors dominate, but more study is needed to prove this claim.

The figures in Table 7 as well as the findings in Tables 2 and 3 point to a large cluster of women with inferior pay, which is "responsible" for a major part of the earning differential. These are women with secondary vocational education working in semiprofessional roles and occupations in economic branches (such as health and education) with great demand for such workers. These women constitute the majority of the middle-educational group in Table 3, where the earning differential is the widest. This situation symbolizes best the problems of the Soviet working woman – who tries to avoid physical work on the one side and for whom many jobs with high professional training are too demanding under the circumstances. The relative scarcity of such jobs creates the pressure that helps to reduce relative wages in these areas and branches.[44] The most striking example on the border of this group is that of medical doctors: Unlike anywhere in the West, women make up about 70 percent of this group in the Soviet Union, but unlike anywhere in the West, doctors in the Soviet Union are paid very low salaries. Finally, because medicine is public, the burdens of the job are much lighter than typically in the West. In short, the medical profession was opened to women and adapted to their needs; the rate of pay was reduced accordingly.

## V. Concluding observations (in a comparative context)

The main conclusions to be drawn from the foregoing analysis is that by and large both the levels of the pay differential by sex and the main explanatory factors are similar to those in the developed Western economies. A full-scale comparative analysis is beyond us at this point, but the following observations on the major similarities and possible differences may be offered.

First, as stated in the introduction, the average differential for the Soviet population is rather similar to what is found in other countries; it may be slightly smaller than in the United States. For 1969, Oaxaca placed the relative hourly pay of women for the urban white population at 0.65, compared to our figure of 0.70 to 0.68 (WPH1 and WPH4, respectively) percent; Malkiels's yearly figure for university graduates was 0.66 percent, whereas our monthly measure for the same group was 0.65 or 0.64.[45] The Soviet ratio seems, however, to be lower than in other East European countries and in a number of countries in northern and western Europe.[46] The similarity of the Soviet ratio to that of the United States stands out all the more, given the extreme difference between the two countries with respect to overall wage equality.[47] This indicates that some of the factors causing higher inequality by sex operate outside the general labor market, affecting women in particular – especially household responsibilities.

A second observation is that by and large, and within the limitations imposed by the data, the direct factors explaining the wage gap by sex in the Soviet Union do not differ, either qualitatively or even quantitatively, from those found in the United States.

a. In the more recent studies on the United States, the levels of education for the sexes are found to be more or less equal, so that even if the rates of return are lower in the Soviet Union, the contribution of formal schooling to the wage gap is not typically or significantly higher than in those studies.[48] This may not be the case when comparisons are made between the Soviet Union and other countries of the same level of development. There we expect to find larger educational gaps and higher schooling coefficients.

b. Although the differences in experience between the sexes, especially for persons of the same age, are much smaller in the Soviet Union, experience still seems to explain at least as much of the wage gap as in the West. In some cases (such as those in Oaxaca, 1973, pp. 705, 706), it results from the much higher experience and age coefficients in the Soviet earning functions. However, where the estimated experience coefficients are high, as in Mincer and Polachek (1974, p. 423), experience accounts for a higher proportion of the gap than in our study. In all studies the experience coefficient is significantly higher for men than for married women: According to Mincer, the results in the West reflect women's lower attachment to work and greater household responsibilities (Mincer and Polachek, 1974, pp. 424–5). With the much greater relative attachment to work of Soviet women (measured in years of work), more explanatory burden is shifted to lower intensity of attachment and lesser ability to devote time and energy to job advancement due to their relatively heavier family responsibilities.

c. The Oaxaca study, which includes industry and role variables in a way similar to our study, gives higher explanatory power to industry and less to role than do our results, but we are not in a position to attribute this difference to underlying factors.

d. Finally, with a list of variables that is more or less similar to that of Oaxaca and the Malkiels, our study also explains up to half of the wage gap. The rest of the gap remains in the darkness of missing variables and qualitative dimensions of existing ones.

Third, the general similarity in the pattern of the gaps across countries, when viewed through the prism of the explanatory variables, does not, however, lead to the conclusion that the underlying intrinsic factors responsible for the gaps are the same. As we have shown above, the difference explained by experience may be caused in one country by the lower labor force participation of women, and in another by low ability of women to take advantage of training. As in many other areas in the Soviet Union, women find shelter against heavy quantitative pressures under an umbrella of lower-quality response.

In a review article, Barbara Jancar claims that industrializing societies, both capitalist and communist, have encouraged women to assume male roles while losing none of their "female" roles, by entering men's industrial world. "But adoption of male roles in many ways is a step backward for sexual equality" (1976, pp. 71–2), mainly because of the handicap created by the family role, which although now degraded in status, still carries its unlightened burden.

One does not have to subscribe fully to these views to see that at some stages "half" or one-sided equality may not bring more equality. In Jancar's terms, the Soviet system is very intensively industrialized, overemphasizing industrialization on the one hand and neglecting leisure-augmenting development and changes in family roles on the other. At least temporarily, it thus accelerates the one-sided equality that helps to preserve both a wide pay gap and a heavy double burden on women.

## Notes

1 It is our impression that the Soviet record with respect to earning inequality by sex is less favorable, when compared to other countries, than that of the overall income inequality. This is definitely true in comparisons with the United States. See, for example, Chapman (1978a, pp. 45–7 and table 11) and p. 155.
2 Almost exhaustive lists of such citations are to be found in Lapidus (1978, pp. 190–4) and McAuley (1978, pp. 10, 13).
3 A partial list should include Danilova (1968), Gordon and Klopov (1972), Kharchev and Golod (1971), Kotliar (1973), Kotliar and Turchaninova (1975), Kotliar et al. (1973), Mikhailiuk (1970), Novikova et al. (1978), Pimenova (1966), Porokhniuk and Shepeleva (1975), Sakharova (1973), Shishkan (1976), Sonin (1973), Trifanov (1973), and Turchaninova, (1975). More complete lists are to be found in Atkinson et al. (1978) and in Lapidus (1978).
4 Some of the main and most recent Western studies are Atkinson et al. (1978), Berliner (1977), Desfosses Cohn (1973), Geiger (1968), Lapidus (1978), McAuley (1978), Mandel (1975), and Sacks (1976).
5 We have therefore economized on citations in all places where the studies cited above have sufficiently covered the specific points discussed. In most cases Soviet references are cited only if they have not been covered by the above-mentioned studies.
6 See Fuchs (1971), Gronau (1979), Malkiel and Malkiel (1973), Mincer (1974), Mincer and Polachek (1974), and Oaxaca (1973), to mention only a few studies of this type.
7 The feminist school tends, of course, to minimize the scope of natural differences between the sexes in this respect. A presentation of the theoretical discussion in the West and in the Soviet Union is found in Lapidus (1978, pp. 322–34).
8 It is interesting to note that most studies that estimate earning functions take the intrafamily division of labor and roles as given, whereas most studies that analyze intrafamily optimizing behavior assume a wide earning gap between men and women as one determinant of their dependent variable. See, for example, Mincer and Polachek (1974) vs. Gronau (1973).
9 See Chapman (1978b), Kotliar and Turchaninova (1975), Lapidus (1978, chap. 5), and Parkhomenko (1972, pp. 77–8).

10 The following discussion is based partly on Ofer (1973, pp. 64–7) and on the literature cited in note 4.

11 Women are entitled to maternity leaves of 112 days and to some other privileges during pregnancy and while the children are in their infancy. Women are also entitled to a retirement pension 5 years earlier than men are. They also benefit most from the legislation on minimum wage, because they are overrepresented in the lowest-paid groups. As pensions and maternity leave benefits are paid by social security, the employer directly bears only the burden of minimum wage payments and the work interruptions in connection with birth. See more in Lapidus (1978, pp. 125–6) and Madison (1978).

12 Even William M. Mandel, who has more praise for the achievements of Soviet women than do many Soviet students, admits that inequality within the family is a main obstacle to achieving full equality (1975, chaps. 10, 11).

13 Although there may indeed be more places for preschool children per 1,000 children in the Soviet Union than elsewhere, it is quite clear that there are not more of them per 1,000 working mothers who have children. See Lapidus (1978, pp. 128–35).

14 We assume that the planner has recourse to other policy tools (such as the husband's pay level or social pressures) to encourage women to work.

15 Janet Chapman claims that there is no evidence for any official policy along such lines (Chapman, 1978b, p. 236). But both she and others indicate that premiums paid for difficult working conditions are lower in women's jobs (p. 229), that women's jobs offer fewer bonuses (p. 233), and that production norms for women are more demanding (Sakharova, 1973, p. 25). Other examples may be found in Lapidus (1978, chap. 6). All these may, however, be responses to market forces, as we claim below.

16 Although this phenomenon is still pronounced in agriculture, which we do not cover, it is very important in the urban sector. See McAuley (1978, pp. 20–1).

17 The rapid growth of the educational system is considered to be one of the major factors contributing to the greater equalization of earnings in the Soviet Union, at least since the 1950s. For women the educational level has risen faster than for men (Chapman, 1978a, p. 238). See also Lapidus (1978, pp. 134–60).

18 The most recent description of the system can be found in Chapman (1978a), and its relation to the wages of women is discussed in Chapman (1978b) and Lapidus (1978, chap. 5).

19 The absolute wage is determined at such a level that, with the help of social and legal pressures, every able-bodied person will tend to seek a job.

20 Among others, see Dubovoi (1969), Gordon and Klopov (1972, p. 11), Iuk (1972, pp. 40–4), Kharchev (1969, pp. 441–3), Kolpakov and Patrushev (1971, pp. 110, 112, 149), Lebin and Leiman (1972, pp. 136–41), Pankratova and Iankova (1978, p. 26), Parkhomenko (1972, p. 78), Riurikov (1977, pp. 118–19), Sakharova (1973, p. 46), Slesarev and Iankova (1969, p. 423), Turchenko (1972, pp. 141–5), Velichkene (1970, p. 96), Zdravomyslov (1967, pp. 265), and many, many more.

21 For more details, see Ofer et al. (1979).

22 There were five families in which the head of the family did not work.

23 Included in the sample are 116 unmarried working women, but they are typically young and reside within an active family.

24 The wage of all full-time working women relative to that of men in SP is 0.64296; when reweighted by work status (white collar/blue collar) it comes to 0.64120, and when reweighted by work status and level of education (three

to four groups within each work-status group) it comes 0.63020 (Ofer et al., 1979, table 16, p. 41; data on structural differences are given on pp. 23–33).

A second possible source of structural bias is that the age difference between the sexes in SP may be somewhat wider than that for UP and thus exaggerate the true effect of work experience and age on earning differentials. The 1970 census does not provide any data on the average age of the Soviet urban civilian labor force, but statistics from the 1959 census and the more general data for 1970 lead us to believe that women in UP are younger by at least 2 years, and possibly 3, than men as compared with the 3.2-year gap in our sample.

For 1959, the average age of working men in the nonagricultural sectors (excluding the army) is estimated at 35.5 years and that of working women at 33.3 years (based on Soviet Union Ts.S.U., *1959 Census,* tables 33 and 39, and the discussion on armed forces figures in Rapaway, 1976, table 9, pp. 19–25). Demographic development since then, especially the retirement of working cohorts of advanced age, with a high proportion of women, and the introduction of more balanced cohorts of younger age should have widened this gap by raising the average age of working men. The implication of this possible bias is discussed below.

25 The correction was made only when the coefficients for the different types of schooling differed significantly from each other. The correction for university studies is to assign 0.6 year for every year of night or correspondence studies toward the first university degree.

26 In $W1_m$ − In $W1_f$ or the percent increase of men's wages over women's estimated by the respective geometrical averages.

27 Results not presented here can be obtained from the authors by request. They also include regression results for the entire working population, with sex as a dummy variable as in Swafford (1977, table 5).

28 On the basis of data for W1, the first ratio is 0.64 (Table 1, line 2b) and the second is 0.4132 (Table 2, line 1).

29 The corresponding female/male ratio of gross wages is roughly calculated to be 0.63, slightly lower because of the progressiveness of income taxes.

30 Based on the geometrical average, the corresponding female/male ratios are 0.71 on the average and 0.74 for academics, 0.68 for semiprofessionals, and 0.69 for the low educational group. The corresponding ratios based on arithmetic averages are 0.64, 0.67, 0.60, and 0.63, respectively.

31 Women in SP did report higher absenteeism rates for health reasons than men did. Presumably, this is due in part to illness in the family.

32 For In W4 and the entire population, hours contribute (according to the male equation) 7.4 points to a male earning advantage of 48.3 percent, or more than 30 percent of the total "explained" segment.

33 Which in Tables 2 and 3 include all those with advanced degrees. Almost the entire explanation of education comes from the stage of advanced studies.

34 Together with age the difference in experience explains more than 5 points. Since there is high correlation between age and experience, their respective effects may have shifted from one to the other.

35 The marginal rates of experience per year go down for males from 5.1 percent in the first year (3.6 percent according to the long equation) to 3.7 (2.6) percent after 10 years, 2.3 (1.6) percent after 20 years, and 0.9 (0.6) percent after 30 years. The corresponding figures for women are 2.6, 1.8, 1.0, and 0.2 percent, respectively, according to the short equation, and 1.7, 1.5, 1.3, and 1.1 percent according to the long one.

36  Thus the initial experience coefficients estimated by Oaxaca are approximately 2 percent for men and 15 percent for women (1973, pp. 700, 703). When experience is estimated directly, the coefficients are much higher, as in Mincer and Polachek (1974, p. S102), where the average rate for males 30 to 44 years old is estimated at 3.4 percent.

37  The calculation is based on a weighted average of differences in experience in the various age groups. The experience gaps for specific age groups go up from 1.1 years for those younger than 25 to 4.6 years for the 45- to 54-year age group, indicating the accumulative effect of raising children.

38  All the following observations on the effects of specific roles are additional to and relative to the reference differential between the sexes that exists for high-professional workers in manufacturing.

39  There are only four such women who obtain a negative premium of academic workers. This result may be typical, but we cannot judge on this basis; in this case the results based on the female equations should not be relied upon. The same problem creates a negative role effect on the advantage of males with respect to semiskilled in the semiprofessional group of workers.

40  The exceptions are for white-collar employees and service workers, in both cases a rather diverse collection of occupations with women at the lower range in both.

41  Among academics, 20.7 percent of women but only 10.5 percent of all men are engaged in health services. The corresponding figures for secondary professionals are 27.6 and 7.0 percent; they are 7.1 and 2.8 percent for the low-schooling group.

42  If engineers, with 39.8 percent women, were shifted from the second to the third group, each group would contain approximately 30 percent of the sample labor force.

43  These results are generally very similar to those obtained by McAuley (1978, pp. 18–41), Sacks (1976, pp. 79–92), and others.

44  See also the discussion on these points in McAuley (1978, pp. 33–41).

45  See also Mincer and Polachek (1974, p. S102), where the hourly wage gap for the 30 to 44-year age group is 0.66 (p. S101).

46  See Galenson (1973, various places), Kýn (1978, pp. 280–8), McAuley (1978, pp. 11–12), MEMO (1974, p. 156), Michal (1975, p. 267), *OECD Observer* (1979, p. 32).

47  See note 1 above. Kýn (1978, pp. 280–1) observes a similar phenomenon in Eastern Europe.

48  Fuchs (1971, p. 10) and Oaxaca (1973, p. 705) find education to explain less than 1 point of the wage gap; see also Mincer and Polachek (1974, p. S102). Malkiel and Malkiel (1973), however, show a wider gap in years of higher education for a group of academics than in our group of academics (1.7 years' difference as compared with 0.4 year in our sample).

## References

Atkinson, Dorothy; Dallin, Alexander; and Lapidus, Gail Warshovsky (eds.). 1978. *Women in Russia*. Harvester Press, Hassocks, England.

Bergson, Abram. 1954. *The Structure of Soviet Wages*. Harvard University Press, Cambridge, Mass.

Berliner, Joseph S. 1977. *Notes on Economy and Family in Soviet Russia*. A Discussion Paper. Russian Research Center, Harvard University.

Chapman, Janet C. 1978a. "Equal Pay for Equal Work?" In D. Atkinson et al. (eds.), *Women in Russia*. Harvester Press, Hassocks, England, pp. 225–39.

Chapman, Janet C. 1978b. "Recent Trends in Soviet Industrial Wage Structure." In A. Kahan and B. A. Ruble (eds.), *Industrial Labor in the USSR*. Pergamon Press, Elmsford, N.Y., 1979, pp. 151–83. (Citations based on mimeographed draft, 1978b.)

Danilova, E. Z. 1968. *Sotsial'nye problemy truda zhenshchiny-rabotnitsy*. Moscow.

Desfosses Cohn, Helen. 1973. "Population Policy in the USSR." *Problems of Communism*, 22 (July–August), pp. 41–55.

Dubovoi, P. 1969. "Uslovia truda kak faktor differentsiatsii zarabotnoi platy." *Voprosy ekonomiki*, no. 9, pp. 57–66.

Ershova, E. H. 1979. "Zhenshchina v sovremennoi Amerike." *SSha* (U.S.A.), no. 3, pp. 32–41.

Frank, Robert H. 1978. "Why Women Earn Less: The Theory and Estimation of Differential Overqualification." *American Economic Review* 68 (June) pp. 360–73.

Fuchs, Victor R. 1971. "Differences in Hourly Earnings between Men and Women." *Monthly Labor Review*, 94 (May) pp. 9–15.

Galenson, Marjorie. 1973. *Women and Work: An International Comparison*. Cornell University, Ithaca, N.Y.

Geiger, H. K. 1968. *The Family in Soviet Russia*. Harvard University Press, Cambridge, Mass.

Goilo, V. 1971. "Burzhuasnaia teoria 'chelovecheskogo kapitala'." *Voprosy ekonomiki*, no. 11, pp. 84–92.

Goilo, V. 1976. "Burzhuaznye teorii vosproizvodstva robochei sily." *Voprosy ekonomiki*, no. 2, pp. 78–90.

Gordon, L. A., and Klopov, E. V. 1972. *Chelovek posle raboty: sotsial'nye problemy byta i vnerabochego vremeni*. Moscow.

Gronau, Reuben. 1973. "The Intrafamily Allocation of Time. The Value of the Housewives' Time." *American Economic Review*, 63 (September), pp. 634–51.

Gronau, Reuben. 1979. *Participation of Women in the Labor Force and Their Wage Structure* (in Hebrew). The Falk Institute, Jerusalem.

ILO. 1977. *Yearbook of Labor Statistics*. Geneva.

Iuk, Z. M. 1972. "Tekhnickeskii progress i kvalifikatsiia zhenshchiny-rabotnitsy." In I. N. Lushchitskii et al. (eds.) *Proizvodstvennaia deiatel'nost' zhenshchin i sem'ia*. Minsk, pp. 40–4.

Jancar, Barbara W. 1976. "Women's Lot in Communist Societies." *Problems of Communism*, 25 (November–December), pp. 68–73.

Kharchev, A. G., and Golod, S. I. 1969. "Proizvodstvennaia rabota zhenschin i sem'ia." In G. V. Osipov and Ia Shchepanskii (eds.), *Sotsial'nye problemy truda i proizvodstva*. Moscow, pp. 439–56.

Kharchev, A. G., and Golod, S. I. 1971. *Professional'naia rabota zhenshchin i sem'ia*. Leningrad.

Kolpakov, B. T., and Patrushev, V. D. 1971. *Biudzhet vremeni gorodskogo naseleniia*. Moscow.

Kotliar, A. E. 1973. "Metodologicheskie voprosy izucheniia struktury zaniatosti po polu v territorial'nom razreze." In A. E. Maikov (ed.), *Problemy ispol'zovaniia trudovykh resursov*. Moscow, pp. 400–34.

Kotliar, A. E., and Turchaninova, S. Ia. 1975. *Zaniatost' zhenshchin v proizvodstve*. Moscow.

Kotliar, A. E., et al. 1973. "Professional'no-otraslevaia struktura zaniatost zhen-shchin v promishelennosti RSFSR." In A. E. Maikov (ed.), *Problemy is-pol'zovaniia trudovykh resursov.* Moscow, pp. 379–99.

Kýn, Oldrich. 1978. "Education, Sex, and Income Inequality in Soviet Type Socialism." In Zvi Griliches et al. (eds.), *Income Distribution and Economic Inequality.* Campus Verlag, Frankfurt, pp. 274–89.

Lapidus, Gail Warshovsky. 1978. *Women in Soviet Society: Equality, Develop-ment and Social Change.* University of California, Berkeley, Calif.

Lebin, B. D., and Leiman, I. I. 1972. "Zhenschchina-uchenyi, ee profes-sional'naia i semeinaia roli." In I. N. Lushchitskii et al. (eds.), *Proiz-vodstvennaia deiatel'nost' zhenschin i sem'ia.* Minsk, pp. 136–41.

McAuley, Alastair. 1978. *Women's Work and Wages in the USSR.* Department of Economics (Discussion Paper No. 111), University of Essex, (April).

Madison, Barbara. 1978. "Social Services for Women: Problems and Priorities." In D. Atkinson et al. (eds.), *Women in Russia.* Harvester Press, Hassocks, England, pp. 307–32.

Malkiel, Burton G., and Malkiel, Judith A. 1973. "Male Female Pay Differentials in Professional Employment." *American Economic Review,* 63 (September), pp. 693–705.

Mandel, William M. 1975. *Soviet Women.* Anchor Books, New York.

Michal, Jan M. 1975. "An Alternative Approach to Measuring Income Inequality in Eastern Europe." In Z. M. Fallenbuchl (ed.), *Economic Development in the Soviet Union and Eastern Europe,* vol. 1. Praeger, New York, chap. 9.

Mikhailiuk, V. B. 1970. *Ispol'zovanie zhenskogo truda v narodnom khoziaistve.* Moscow.

Mincer, Jacob. 1974. *Schooling Experience, and Earnings.* Columbia University Press (National Bureau of Economic Research), New York.

Mincer, Jacob, and Polachek, Solomon. 1974. "Family Investments in Human Capital: Earnings of Women." *Journal of Political Economy,* 72, pt. 2 (March–April), pp. S76–S108.

*Mirovaia ekonomika i mezhdu narodnye otnosheniia.* 1974. *MEMO,* no. 8 (Au-gust).

Novikova, E. E., Iazykova, V. S., and Iankova, Z. A. 1978. *Zhenshchina trud sem'ia.* Moscow.

Oaxaca, Ronald. 1973. "Male–Female Wage Differentials in Urban Labor Mar-kets." *International Economic Review,* 14 (October), pp. 693–709.

*OECD Observer.* 1979. "Equal Opportunities for Women," no. 97, March, pp. 27–32.

Ofer, Gur. 1973. *The Service Sector in Soviet Economic Growth: A Comparative Study.* Harvard University Press, Cambridge, Mass.

Ofer, Gur, Vinokur, Aaron, and Bar-Chaim, Yechiel. 1979. *Family Budget Survey of Soviet Emigrants in the Soviet Union.* Research Paper No. 32, The Soviet and East European Research Center, The Hebrew University, Jerusalem.

Pankratova, M. G., and Iankova, Z. A. 1978. "Sovetskaia zhenshchina." *Sot-siologicheskie issledovania,* no. 1, pp. 19–28.

Parkhomenko, V. F. 1972. "Nekatorye problemy ratsional'nogo ispol'zovania zhenskikh kadrov v sostave inzhenerno-tekhnicheskikh rabotnikov sotsialis-ticheskogo proizvodstva." In V. F. Medvedev et al. (eds.), *Vosproizvodstvo i ispol'zovanie trudovykh resursov Belorusskoi SSR.* Minsk.

Pimenova, A. L. 1966. "Sem'ia i perspektivy razvitiia obshchestvennogo truda zhenshchin pri sotsializme." *Nauchnye doklady vysshei shkoly: filosofskie nauki,* 3, pp. 35–44.

Porokhniuk, E. V., and Shepeleva, M. S. 1975. "O sovmeshchenii proizvodstvennykh i semeinykh funktsii zhenshchin-rabotnits." *Sotsiologicheskie issledovaniia*, 4, pp. 102–8.

Rapaway, Stephen. 1976. *Estimates and Projections of the Labor Force and Civilian Employment in the U.S.S.R., 1950 to 1990*. Foreign Economic Report No. 10, Bureau of Economic Analysis, U.S. Department of Commerce, Washington, D.C.

Riurikov, Iu, B. 1977. "Deti i obshchestvo." *Voprosy filosofii*, no. 4, pp. 111–21.

Sacks, Michael P. 1976. *Women's Work in Soviet Russia: Continuity in Midst of Change*. Praeger, New York.

Sakharova, N. A. 1973. *Optimal'nye vozmozhnosti ispol'zovaniia zhenskogo truda v sfere obshchestvennogo proizvodstva*. Kiev.

Shishkan, N. M. 1976. *Trud zhenshchin v usloviakh razvitogo sotsializma*. Kishinev.

Slesarev, G. A., and Iankova, Z. A. 1969. "Zhenshchina na promyshlennom predpriatii i v semie." In G. V. Osipov and Shchepanskii (eds.), *Sotsial'nye problemy truda i proizvodstva*. Moscow, pp. 416–38.

Sonin, M. Ia. 1973. "Aktualnye sotsial'no-ekonomicheskie problemy zaniatosti zhenshchin." In A. E. Maikov (ed.), *Problemy ispol'zovaniia trudovykh resursov*, Moscow, pp. 352–79.

Soviet Union Ts. S.U. 1962. *Itogi vesoiuznoi perepisi naseleniia 1959 g. SSSR* (Population Census, 1959). Moscow.

Soviet Union Ts.S.U. 1973. *Itogi vsesoiuznoi perepisi naseleniia 1970 goda* (Population Census, 1970), various volumes. Moscow.

Swafford, Michael. 1977. *Sex Differences in Soviet Earnings*. Mimeo.

Trifanov, I. P. 1973. *Problemy byta gorodskogo naseleniia SSSR*. Leningrad.

Turchaninova, S. I. 1975. "Trends in Women's Employment in the USSR." *International Labor Review*, 112 (October), pp. 253–64.

Turchenko, V. N. 1972. "O nekatorykh osobennostiakh truda zhenshchiny-uchitelia." In I. N. Lushchitskii et al. (eds.), *Proizvodstvennaia deiatel'nost' zhenshchin i sem'ia*. Minsk, pp. 141–5.

Velichkene, I. 1970. "Trud i zdorov'e zhenshchiky-rabotnitsy." In A. Gul'binskene (ed.), *Problemy byta braka i sem'i*. Vilnius, pp. 95–8.

Zdravomyslov, A. G., Rozhin, V. P., and Iadov, V. A. (eds.) 1967. *Chelovek i ego rabota*. Moscow.

# 7 Creditworthiness and balance-of-payments adjustment mechanisms of centrally planned economies

*Franklyn D. Holzman*

## I. Introduction

The level of world external indebtedness is rising and presently exceeds all previous historical levels. The external public debt of 84 developing nations amounted to approximately $174 billion in 1975 (IMF, 1977a, p. 177). As a result of the rise in raw materials prices, particularly of petroleum, many advanced Western industrial nations are rapidly liquidating external assets or are also going deeply into debt. At the end of 1975, Great Britain led the pack with a debt of about $45 billion, France was next with $20 billion[1] – an amount exceeded by Mexico and Brazil (*New York Times,* 1976). According to the same source, net foreign currency liabilities of Euromarket banks exceeded $275 billion. Finally, in tune for once with the capitalist world, the communist nations (referring here primarily to the USSR and the rest of Eastern Europe) have also been borrowing from abroad – and from the West at that – at unprecedented rates with debts, at the end of 1976, probably aggregating in excess of $40 billion[2] – and the end not in sight. This is surprising both because of the speed of the recent debt buildup and because until less than a decade ago, the Eastern nations followed policies largely designed to avoid any significant accumulation of external debt.

The issue with which we shall be concerned here is how to approach the question as to whether it is wise from an economic standpoint for the Western nations to continue to expand credits to the communist nations.

An early version of this paper was sponsored by the Bureau of East–West Trade, U.S. Department of Commerce. A later version was presented to the Fourth US–Hungarian Conference in Economics in Budapest in November 1978. I am indebted to members of that conference and to Rachel McCulloch, Steven Rosefielde, and Gordon Weil for helpful comments.

Such an assessment requires us to examine the criteria by which loans are made and creditworthiness is judged in general and then to determine whether these criteria are equally applicable to all nations, planned and unplanned alike. Such a study necessarily involves examining balance-of-payments adjustment mechanisms, and this is done for the centrally planned economies in the latter part of the paper.

The basic aim of the paper is methodological–theoretical: to establish a more satisfactory approach, especially for centrally planned economies, to the question of international creditworthiness. However, particularly in the latter half of the discussion, which deals with adjustment mechanisms, I have gone beyond this limited purpose and made judgments regarding the empirical magnitudes of some of the more important parameters in order to draw tentative policy conclusions. These empirical judgments, although, hopefully, "informed," are nevertheless admittedly "casual," and I trust that the reader, forewarned, will keep the distinction between these two aspects of the analysis in mind.

## II. The debt service/export ratio

It is typical in economic analysis to look for significant simple measures that provide criteria of performance. The criterion most widely used to measure creditworthiness of nations has been the debt service/export ratio (or, somewhat related to this, the total debt/export ratio). That is to say, a Western nation would be deemed creditworthy if current interest and amortization payments on its public and publicly guaranteed external debt[3] were less than a certain percentage (usually around 25 percent) of export earnings. This criterion is similar to the cash flow/liability ratio often applied to business enterprises.

How good a measure this is for enterprises will not concern us; as a measure of national creditworthiness, however, it is seriously deficient. This can be demonstrated empirically: Australia and Canada with ratios between 35 and 45 percent during the 1930s did not default, whereas various Latin American nations with ratios between 16 and 28 percent did default (Frank, cited in Portes, 1977). In recent years, Brazil with a ratio of 0.25 and Mexico with a ratio of 0.30 are still deemed creditworthy, Italy with only 0.10 is not, nor are Gambia and Mali with ratios below 0.10 because even so they are incapable of servicing their debts. There are several reasons why the debt service/export ratio (henceforth $ds/x$) is likely to be unreliable as a criterion of creditworthiness. First, it is a short-run cash flow concept. So a nation may have a 20 percent $ds/x$, which, depending on maturities and amortization rates, could represent a 5-year or alternatively a (say) 20-year annual burden. Obviously, the same ratio is less ominous in the former than in the latter case. In this sense, the

$ds/x$ is not unlike capital/output ratios, which abstract from the durability of the capital goods in question. Because the $ds/x$ is a short-run concept, it abstracts from a second long-run feature of creditworthiness: namely, the prospective ability of a nation to transform its economy in such a way as to improve the balance-of-payments situation and/or repay its debts. Two nations may have identical $ds/x$'s, but over a period of time one may go on to double it, the other to halve it, depending on policies, resources, potentialities for reducing imports and increasing exports (more on this below), and so forth. Third, the $ds/x$ takes no account whatsoever of the relative profitability of the debt from the standpoint of either the lenders or the borrowers. Given high rates of interest relative to alternative investments either at home or in third nations, lenders may be perfectly content to see $ds/x$'s rise still further. Similarly, given very high rates of return on investments financed by funds borrowed from abroad, a borrower may feel justified in further expansion, even with a high $ds/x$. Making this same point (with regard to the lenders) by analogy, Avramovic et al., 1964, p. 43, note that corporate investors do not look at cash flows but rather at potential growth, net earnings over time, diversification, and so forth.

Related to these points is another very important consideration: the question as to whether the excess of imports over exports results because a nation has to finance crucial consumption requirements and has large unexploited and profitable investment, *or* is simply overimporting because of an overvalued exchange rate.[4] This is not as serious an issue in the current era of greater exchange rate flexibility, but it has been in the past and still remains important. Although one can make a case for continuing to grant credit for urgent consumption and profitable investment needs, where the costs to lender and borrower are accurately reflected in relative prices under properly valued exchange rates, one cannot if exchange rates are out of equilibrium and deficits occur solely because buyers and sellers suffer from what amounts to a money illusion. Those who lend to nations with overvalued currencies in fact suffer a greater exchange rate risk.

Finally, even assuming that a borrowing nation's exchange rate is not overvalued and that debt-financed imports are invested profitably at home, it makes considerable difference whether the nation is investing adequately in exportables and import-competing products on the one hand, or in nontradeables on the other. The creditworthiness of the nation is greater in the former than in the latter case, of course.

### III. The transfer problem – an "elasticity-absorption" approach

Basically, then, $ds/x$ has to be rejected as an unambiguous indicator of creditworthiness of nations because it is exclusively a short-run measure and because it leaves out of account several important variables. This is not to deny that at times it may prove a useful warning signal. What alternative is there to the *ds/x?* In our opinion, there is no single measure that can be substituted. Creditworthiness must be judged with traditional balance-of-payments analysis tools, especially as these have been adapted to deal with problems relating to the transfer problem. For, essentially, what one wishes to know is whether the debtor nation can generate enough of a transferable surplus and earn enough foreign exchange to repay its debt within prescribed time limits. It is not proposed here to develop a quantifiable index but simply to try to spell out the differences between market and nonmarket economies in handling the transfer problem.

The international repayment of debt is then, like the transfer problem, a two-gap problem. The first gap is the savings–investment gap, or alternatively, the gap between income produced $Y$ and income absorbed $A$ ($A - Y$, where $A = C + I + G$ expenditures). That is, to repay a debt it is necessary, in the absence of past savings (reserves, stocks), for current savings to exceed current investment or for income produced to exceed income absorbed. If past savings do exist, they may be used to liquidate the debt even though current $I$ exceeds current $S$. In fact, even though the macro conditions (just noted) for repayment exist, repayment also requires that individual private debtors in a capitalist nation be in a sufficiently viable financial position to make the necessary payments. There are, of course, no private debtors in socialist nations.

The second gap is that between international current account payments and receipts, $M - X$ for short. In the absence of foreign exchange reserves, debt repayment requires that $X > M$ by the appropriate amount.

In the absence of past savings on any sort (stocks, foreign exchange reserves, etc.) the two gaps are equated:

$$S - I = X - M \quad \text{or} \quad Y - A = X - M$$

That is, at the macro level, foreign exchange can be earned to repay debts only by saving more than is invested or producing more than is absorbed.

The preceding analysis assumes that increasing $Y$ and/or reducing $A$ by the appropriate amount automatically results in an increase in $X - M$ which earns enough foreign exchange to service successfully the debt in question. This might be true for a small nation that faces perfectly elastic demands for its exports and can easily substitute domestically produced importables for its imports – but for many nations it is not. An improvement in the current balance may involve a loss in terms of trade either with or without a devaluation. In the case of a devaluation, of course, a given $X - M$ in domestic currency will exchange for less foreign currency than before and will be inadequate to service the debt denominated in foreign currency. This was termed, many decades ago, the secondary burden of a transfer and it is as relevant today as it was then. The common assumption is that a devaluation usually worsens the terms of trade because nations are usually more specialized as exporters than they are as importers; as a result, export prices are likely to fall (in foreign prices) to a greater extent than import prices are by efforts to improve the payments balance.

## IV. The $A - Y$ gap or savings gap

Before proceeding to discussions of the $A - Y$ and $M - X$ gaps, respectively, two additional preliminary comments are in order. First, in the discussion that follows we speak as though the current account consists exclusively of commodity trade and debt service. This is done primarily because there are so few data generally available on other invisibles; in fact, the debt service data presented below are all "estimated" by Western analysts. Second, the discussion proceeds on the assumption that the transfer problem facing a nation is the financing of the debt service. This ignores the fact that two nations with identical $ds/x$'s may have different current account balances. For example, given a $ds/x$ to begin with, three illustrative scenarios are:[5]

|     | (1)   | (2)   | (3)   |
|-----|-------|-------|-------|
| $X$  | $+50$ | $+50$ | $+50$ |
| $M$  | $-40$ | $-50$ | $-60$ |
| $ds$ | $-10$ | $-10$ | $-10$ |
| $K$  | $0$   | $+10$ | $+20$ |

Most centrally planned economies (CPEs) presently fall into classes (2) and (3), especially (3). The discussion that follows does not differentiate between these two classes. A major problem in including the deficit, over and above the debt service, is the fact that it can vary so much from year to year. In any event, because the primary purpose of this paper is methodological, this should not seriously limit the usefulness of the analysis.

The $A - Y$ gap of a nation is affected by at least two factors that are not totally systemic in nature: the intensity of its participation in trade or trade participation ratio (TPR $= X$/GNP or $M$/GNP[6]), and per capita income. As is well known, large and well-endowed nations such as the United States and the USSR trade a much smaller percentage of their GNPs than do smaller and less well-endowed nations. Ratios range from 6 percent for the USSR[7] and 7 to 8 for the United States to approximately 20 percent for the United Kingdom and West Germany and probably higher than 75 percent for many tiny nations and for nations such as Kuwait, whose production is confined almost exclusively to a single exportable. The debt service in any given $ds/x$ ratio will amount to a smaller percentage of GNP for a nation with a small than one with a large TPR. Hence, all other things equal, the nation with the small TPR will find it easier to achieve the required $Y - A$ or $S - I$ gap. So, for example, if we take two nations, each with a $ds/x$ ratio of 0.20, but with TPRs of 10 and 30 percent, respectively, the $ds/Y$ will amount to 2 percent in the former case and 6 percent in the latter. This is a very significant difference; hence equivalent debt-service problems, measured in the usual $ds/x$ fashion, can involve a much more serious internal strain to nations with large than with small trade participation ratios. Putting it another way, one could argue that this implies a serious shortcoming in the $ds/x$ as a measure of creditworthiness.[8]

There are two systemic factors that, when taken account of, tend to reduce the $A - Y$ gap problem of CPEs relatively to market economies. First, there is a tendency for CPEs to have lower TPRs than comparable market economies. This tendency has been documented by many scholars and need not be elaborated here (see, e.g., Hewett, 1976). Second, and of much greater practical importance, our concern with CPE debt problems has reference exclusively to the hard currency deficits of these nations.[9] Since hard currency trade varies from around 20 to about 50 percent of the total trade of the Council for Mutual Economic Assistance (CMEA) nations, the hard currency TPRs are considerably smaller than the aggregate TPRs. Correspondingly, any given hard currency $ds/x$ involves a much smaller $A - Y$ gap than in a comparable capitalist nation. These considerations suggest that the domestic financing of a given hard currency $ds/x$ requires a savings effort in a CPE that is usually much less than that of a comparable Western nation.

Some crude indications of the magnitudes involved in the East are presented in Table 1 (but see the caveats to Table 1). In column 3, we present the $X$/GNP ratios for 1973, where $X$ represents only Eastern *hard currency* exports. Compare the hard currency ratio for the USSR of 1.4 percent with that of the United States of 7 to 8 percent. Hungary has the highest ratio – 11.2 percent. The ratio of a comparable small Western nation would be upward of 25 percent. These small TPRs in hard currency translate into comparably small $ds$/GNP ratios, presented in column 5. These range from an insignificant 0.28 percent in the case of the USSR to, however, a moderately high 3.92 percent in the case of Hungary. The comparable figure for hypothetical small Western nations with TPRs of 0.25 to 0.50 and $ds/x$'s of 0.20 to 0.30 would be 5 to 15 percent. More than 5 percent of GNP would be a substantial drain on current output;[10] 0.2 to 3.9 percent much less so.[11] Further, as Table 1 shows (column 5), these low $ds$/GNP ratios were generated by fairly large $ds/x$ ratios, primarily much in excess of 0.20.

Table 1. *Hard currency trade and debt service/export ratio relationships, mid-1970s*

| | (1) Total X/GNP 1973 (%) | (2) %X to developed West, 1973 | (3) %X/GNP hard currency: (1) × (2) | (4) $ds/X: 1975 | (5) $ds/GNP: (3) × (4) | (6) Average annual ΔGNP, 1971–5 | (7) $ds/GNP ÷ %ΔGNP: (5) ÷ (6) |
|---|---|---|---|---|---|---|---|
| USSR | 6.0 | 23 | 1.4 | 20 | 0.28 | 2.9 | 9.7 |
| Bulgaria | 26.4 | 12 | 3.2 | 66 | 2.09 | 6.7 | 31.2 |
| Czechoslovakia | 30.9 | 21 | 6.5 | 22 | 1.43 | 3.6 | 39.7 |
| East Germany | 20.5 | 24.7 | 5.1 | 27 | 2.97 | 5.0 | 59.4 |
| Hungary | 45.7 | 24.5 | 11.2 | 35 | 3.92 | 3.8 | 103.2 |
| Poland | 12.1 | 32 | 3.9 | 43 | 1.68 | 5.8 | 28.9 |
| Romania | 6.4 | 32 | 2.1 | 42 | 0.86 | 7.8 | 11.0 |

*Caveat:* The data used and methodologies employed in constructing this table leave much to be desired. The table is presented for illustrative purposes only, with the hope and conviction that the resulting errors are of lesser magnitude than the effects described in the text. Some of the problems are as follows. In column 1, the Soviet figure was constructed by converting Soviet exports to domestic prices and dividing by official Soviet figures of net material product (NMP), also in domestic prices. The IBRD figures for Eastern Europe, however, use NMP in domestic prices in the denominator but incorrectly (perhaps for lack of better alternative) use for numerators exports in Western prices converted to local currencies at official exchange rates. These exchange rates, in many instances, may be pretty far off correct purchasing power parities. This may account for the very low Romanian (and perhaps Polish) X/GNPs. Column 2 is calculated in dollars and is subject to the qualification noted above in the source but, additionally, should be calculated in domestic prices to be consistent with column 1. Column 3, then, as a product of columns 1 and 2, is also a hybrid of inconsistent units, even for the USSR with its consistent column 1 figure. Column 4 is calculated in dollars and, for what it signifies, is satisfactory. Column 5, however, as a product of columns 3 and 4, is also a hybrid of inconsistent units; similarly with column 7.

*Sources:* Column 1: USSR: Treml, 1980; Eastern Europe: IBRD, 1977, p. 415. Column 2: Calculated from CIA, 1975, p. 158. No allowance was made for the fact that the price level in intra-CMEA trade is higher than in East–West trade. Column 4: USSR: JEC, 1976, p. 738; Eastern Europe: Zoeter, 1977, p. 1367. Column 6: CIA, 1976.

Another perspective on the primary burden of the $ds$/GNP is to compare it with the growth in GNP. In column 6 we present the average growth rates of GNP in the 1971–5 period, and in column 7, the ratio of $ds$/GNP to these growth rates. The percentage of an annual growth rate taken by the debt service ranges from 9.7 percent for the USSR to 103.2 percent for Hungary. Although the drains for nations such as Hungary and the GDR are large, it should be recognized that in terms of the growth of GNP, the resources devoted to a given amount of debt service take a once-and-for-all chunk. Assume a nation with a GNP of 100, annual growth of GNP of 6 percent, and annual debt service of 2. In the first year, although GNP would rise to 106, only 104 would be available domestically. In the subsequent year, domestically available GNP would rise by approximately 6 percent from 104 to 110.

In terms of GNP growth rates, $ds$/GNP ratios are perforce gradual and appear to be a small drain. Suppose, in the preceding example, that the debt service had risen from 2 to 2.5, an increase of 25 percent. Domestically available resources would rise from 104 to 109.5 instead of 110, an incremental loss of only $8\frac{1}{3}$ percent of the increase in GNP.

The conclusion one reaches from these calculations is that the $A - Y$ gaps (uncomplicated by possible terms of trade losses) are not of large magnitudes, with the possible exceptions of Hungary and East Germany.

Given an $A - Y$ gap of specific magnitude, how difficult is it for a CPE to close (or reverse) the gap. If one examines the experiences of the USSR in the 1930s and some of the Eastern European nations during the 1950s, one might be inclined to argue that most gaps would be easily within the reach of CPE planners. On the one hand, $Y$ was increasing rapidly in those periods, both through putting unemployed resources to work and getting closer to the production-possibilities frontiers; and through expanding the frontiers – the capacity to produce. On the other hand, the Eastern nations seemed to have had almost limitless power to reduce $A$, particularly by compressing standards of living. In the early 1930s, the USSR exported grain and other food products despite mass hunger. Under stress, in the early 1950s, some of the Eastern nations followed the Soviet example of the 1930s.

The possibilities of closing the gap appear to have lessened significantly in recent years. The goals of maximizing growth rates and achieving full employment (in practice over-full-employment planning) are pursued with such intensity under normal conditions that there is very little scope left for improvement either through growth or reducing unemployment. Further, the Soviet rate of growth has been in secular decline since the end of the 1950s. Eastern European rates of growth declined in the 1960s but have picked up again in the 1970s. However, no further increase appears probable in the near future.

The harsh measures once used to reduce $A$ are probably no longer politically possible nor are most Eastern governments even interested in taking such extreme measures. Widespread expectation of improved living standards – the so-called consumerism movement – is evidence of loss of flexibility with regard to downward manipulations of $A$ and $C$. Evidence: the USSR's huge grain imports since the early 1960s; inability of Poland to raise prices on foods and thereby eliminate enormous subsidies; the large food subsidies in most of the Eastern nations. The Soviet Union faces additional serious constraints on reducing $A$. Between the arms race with the United States and hostile relations with China, a reduction in military expenditures is unlikely. Further, the rate of investment appears to be creeping up slowly, probably in an atttempt to offset the secular rise in the capital/output ratio and decline in rate of growth of GNP.

It need also be mentioned that reducing $A$ in a manner that improves the balance of payments often involves diverting existing output from domestic use to export to the West and/or reducing imports from the West. Given taut planning, it is difficult to carry out such policies not only because of consumerism, already mentioned, but because in the short run at least, such policies could disrupt production. Actually, most products exported and imported are intermediate products, not final consumers' goods, and any reduction in availability of exportables or imports could have serious adverse effects on the plan and on GNP through the supply multiplier. In fact, a reduction in imports of intermediate products could even result in a reduction in exports to the extent that exports embody such imported goods.

Despite the loss in flexibility that the CPEs have experienced in the past decade or so in reducing absorption, it is worth noting that in 1975 and 1976, the growth in value of imports was substantially reduced in all of the Eastern nations, and in some cases absolutely reduced. It is also important to stress again the very small $ds$/GNP ratios vis-à-vis the West that these nations have.

## V. The $M - X$ gap: overall view

We have just demonstrated that the $A - Y$ gap should not present serious problems to most Eastern nations, representing as it does a very small percentage of either current output or of the annual increment to output. The smallness of the $A - Y$ gap is in fairly sharp contrast with the hard currency $M - X$ gap plus the $X - M$ surplus required to finance the debt service. The latter is indicated in column 4 of Table 1. Ratios range in 1975 from 22 to 28 percent for Czechoslovakia and the USSR, respectively, to ratios in excess of 40 percent in the cases of Romania, Poland, and Bulgaria (which has a high of 66 percent). Still higher figures for all nations were recorded in 1976 (same source). By ordinary standards, the Romanian, Polish, and Bulgarian debt service problems would appear to be serious – but as we indicated earlier, the $ds/x$ is not necessarily a good measure of debt service problems.

A major assumption of the discussion which follows is that the traditional CPE has to work through the market to increase its exports (i.e., by lowering prices) but can only adjust (reduce) imports by reducing import quotas. This is because, with the partial exception of Hungary, CPE exchange rates are not real prices, and devaluing the currency has no effect on exports or imports. Devaluation is, however, simulated on the export side by simply reducing prices. The analogous operation on the import side is obviously not a feasible policy. In the first part of this section we assume that reducing export prices is equivalent to a devaluation on the export side. In Section VII, we explore the special consequences of the fact that it is not.

The $M - X$ gap may be ameliorated even without changing the $A - Y$ gap by (1) diverting exports from Eastern to Western markets and imports from Western to Eastern markets. On the other hand, reversal of the $A - Y$ gap (ex ante), although necessary, may not be sufficient to reverse $M - X$ for two reasons: (2) the economy may have difficulty generating over the medium and long run more exportables and import-competing products; and (3) in the short run, the price elasticity of demand for exportables may be too low,[12] resulting in either no increase in foreign exchange or small increases because of the large adverse shift in terms of trade. (4) Finally, as a last resort, of course, the $M - X$ gap can be reduced by directly cutting back on $M$, as was done in 1975–6 in many CMEA nations. Let us discuss the first three of these issues in this order.

1. Diversion of exports from intrabloc to East–West trade faces the same obstacles as diverting output away from domestic markets. Taut planning and use of direct controls lead each CPE to be very dependent on planned imports of intermediate products from other CPEs. Consumerism also plays a constraining role here similar to that mentioned earlier. This is why the Russians import Western grain for domestic consumers *and* for *reexport* to Eastern Europe when their own crops fall short of commitments. It is worth noting, however, that the enormous increase in Western oil and gas prices after 1973 led the USSR to begin supplying a smaller percentage of Eastern Europe's needs of these products than had been the case!

The substitution of imports from the East or from other nondollar markets for imports from the West is also fraught with difficulty. Undoubtedly, attempts are made to implement such policies. Efforts along these lines would have the best chance of success in periods of Western recession during which Eastern hard currency balance-of-payments problems are widespread and are due to recession-induced declining exports to the West. Under these circumstances, both Eastern exporters and importers might be motivated to adopt the second best solution of trading with each other. There is undoubtedly a limit, however, to the substitutability of Eastern for desired Western imports, particularly of advanced machinery and equipment. It must be stressed that the shift of such imports from Western to Eastern sources undoubtedly involves a substantial reduction in gains from trade, a fact that creates resistance to change. It is, after all, the desire for Western products that creates the hard currency deficits in the first place. Data for 1976 show little or no shift in real terms to intra-CMEA trade, in aggregate, as a substitute for East–West trade.

2. The supply of exportables and import-competing products can be increased in the short-run by simply diverting output from the domestic market (as the USSR did with grain in the early 1930s) or, over the longer run, by transforming the structure of the economy (as the Polish government tried to do with its electrical golf carts). In the longer run, one might expect that part of Eastern imports from the West be allocated to try to improve the hard currency balance of payments.[13] We will not comment here on the short-run possibilities except to say that it seems highly probable – given the secular nature of Eastern deficits – that these possibilities have been by now largely exhausted.[14] Evidence regarding longer-run efforts is not plentiful, but what there is suggests that at least until 1975, new investment and imports were not concentrated as intensively as they might have been toward solving hard currency balance-of-payments problems. There is no question but that a substantial portion of CMEA imports are capital goods and designed to increase productivity.[15] However, according to one authority, these imports are more often designed to increase productivity in industries that service domestic and intra-CMEA markets than hard currency markets (Snell, 1974, pp. 688–9). If this is generally true, the long-run creditworthiness of the Communist nations achieved by expansionary means is seriously compromised.

The longer-run picture with regard to hard currency imports must be qualified as was the case with exportables. To quote: "[CMEA] import of Western technology has not led to an effective program of import substitution" (Crawford and Haberstroh, 1974, p. 38). According to the same source, not only have imports not been used to develop import-competing industries, but in fact many of the industries established on the basis of Western machinery imports require continual additional hard currency imports of high-quality inputs for their operation. Further, it turns out that the faster-growing industries in Eastern Europe typically require a faster growth in supporting imports from the West – in effect, a high output elasticity of demand for hard currency imports.

Whether Eastern investment policies have recently changed to address more directly hard currency balance-of-payments problems has not been investigated. Some efforts along these lines certainly have been made in Eastern Europe via industrial cooperation agreements. But the Eastern nations may have found the recession plus rising Western protectionism very discouraging to the adoption of rational balance-of-payments investment policies.

3. It is one thing to increase the supply of products to be marketed for hard currencies, and another to actually sell them. There are several constraints.

First, although some exports can undoubtedly be expanded without lowering prices (e.g., oil, gas, and other raw materials), others cannot. Lowering prices in order to compete, if successful, may lead to Western antidumping or anti-market-disruption actions. Inability of the CPEs to prove that they are not selling below cost or below domestic market price (because of the irrationality of domestic prices) makes it difficult for them to refute antidumping charges successfully – even when they are not, in fact, dumping.

Second, the antidumping problem is exacerbated by the fact that CPE prices cannot be lowered on world markets by currency devaluation.[16] As noted above, CMEA exchange rates are not real prices (Hungary is a partial exception).

Third, a significant percentage of Eastern exportables are manufactured products. For reasons discussed elsewhere,[17] these products have not found easy markets in the West. It might therefore be difficult to expand sales at all or at prices that do not involve a prohibitive decline in terms of trade.

Fourth, as noted earlier, a major part of the responsibility for the recent rise in the $ds/x$ has been the Western recession of the mid-1970s. Western imports fall below trend, partly because the rise in GNP is slowed or actually falls, and partly because under these conditions, nations have tended to increase protectionist curbs on imports (IMF, 1977b, p. 241). In periods like this, it becomes almost impossible to increase export earnings significantly. There is also some evidence that Western imports from the East decline more than Western imports from the West during recessions. That is to say, the East is viewed as the marginal supplier of imports.

## VI. The $M - X$ gap and terms of trade in light of static price elasticities

The first and third points just discussed can be illustrated using conventional analysis in terms of Figure 1. Let $TT$ be the domestic transformation curve between importables $M$ and exportables $X$ for any Eastern nation.

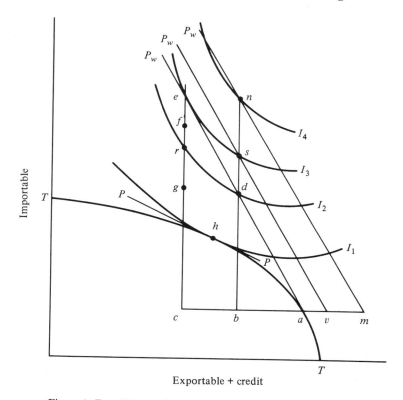

Figure 1. East–West trade of an Eastern nation ($E$).

Let $PP$ be the domestic rate of transformation and $h$ the autarky production point. Abstract from the possibility of intrabloc trade – simplifying the analysis but not changing its essence. (If intrabloc trade were included, we could have assumed that $PP$ was the intrabloc opportunity price.) Let $ae = mn$ represent the world price, $P_w$. The difference in slopes of $PP$ and $ae$ is large, reflecting the great profitability to the Eastern nation ($E$) of trade with the West. $E$ would like to produce at $a$, export $ac$ of $X$, and import $ce$ of $M$. Such a policy would put it at welfare point $e$ on $I_3$ as opposed to $h$ on $I_1$. In fact, it can only export $ab$ to finance $bd$ of $M$. Borrowing is resorted to secure additional imports. If $ce$ ($= bn$) of imports is necessary to the plan (consumption and/or investment), then $am$ ($= dn$) is borrowed and $E$ ends up at welfare level $n$ on $I_4$. If, on the other hand, $E$ just wishes to reach the equivalent of its original overall welfare target (but not its planned quantitative targets) of $I_3$, then $ds$ is imported by borrowing $av$. Or if $E$ does not wish to go further into debt, it will restrict imports to *bd*. In fact, *E* might well cut back *M* simultaneously with trying to increase *X* on the assumption, based on past experience, that $\Delta X$ will not bridge the gap. The trade data suggest that this happened in 1975–6.

We have posited that *E* cannot export more than *ab* at going prices. More might be exported if *E* were willing to accept poorer terms of trade – in this case, by a uniform lowering of export prices equivalent to devaluation on the export side. The losses involved in accepting poorer terms of trade would be, in effect, the secondary burden of the transfer problem mentioned earlier. If lowering export prices did not lead to antidumping action by the importing nations, then at least two sets of possibilities can be distinguished. First, if Western demand is sufficiently elastic, *E* could end up on a higher indifference curve (not shown) – passing through say point *f*. Because of the probable loss in terms of trade (from *ae* to *af*), that indifference curve (not shown) would be below $I_3$. Second, if demand is very inelastic, the terms of trade would drop to, say, *ag*, at which point *E* would be at a welfare level below $I_2$ – and the additional trade would not be worthwhile.[18] In my opinion, it is entirely conceivable that the Eastern nations face such a situation for a large number of manufactured products which they have attempted to market in the West. This is one reason why an expansionary solution to the deficit problem may not be promising (but see below).

It is illuminating to look at these issues using the conventional static price elasticity approach (see Kreinen and Heller, 1974). The elasticity of balance-of-payments formula is

$$b = k \; \frac{s_x(d_x - 1)}{s_x + d_x} + \frac{d_m(s_m + 1)}{s_m + d_m}$$

where given balanced trade to begin with, *b* is the percentage improvement in the balance of payments from a *k* percent devaluation, $d_m$ and $d_x$ are the price elasticities of demand for imports and for a nation's exports, and $s_m$ and $s_x$ are the corresponding supply elasticities.

An expansionary solution in this formulation requires that the price elasticity of foreign demand for a nation's exports, $d_x$, be greater than 1. This is because if $d_x < 1$, then the first (or export) term on the right side of the equality is 0 or negative. The preceding discussion, centered on Figure 1, argues that for many products which the CPEs are trying to sell to the West, $d_x$ may indeed be less than 1 and certainly less than that for a comparable market economy. As noted earlier, devaluation cannot be simulated on the import side (i.e., the CPEs have no mechanism or motivation for paying higher prices for imports). Import quotas are simply reduced, so the second term on the right is inoperative as a measure of market response. However, the magnitude of $d_m$ suggests whether it is easy (large $d_m$) or hard (small $d_m$) for the CPE to reduce imports, and this suggests the extent to which $M$ is cut back as a substitute for $\Delta X$. The magnitude of $s_m$ suggests whether the price of imports is likely to be much affected by the reduction in imports. Generally speaking, the likelihood is that $d_m$ (price elasticity of CPE demand for Western products) is low for several reasons: prevalence of taut planning, excess demand for Western products, consumerism, and the need to avoid (or remedy) bottlenecks (the so-called supply multiplier). On the other hand, $s_m$ – the price elasticity of supply of imports from the West – is undoubtedly very high simply because the CPEs are, for most imported products, a very small part of the market. So reducing imports probably has little or no effect on world prices (i.e., prices are not reduced by the loss of part of the CPE market).

These same elasticities can be used to gauge the change in terms of trade which probably would be experienced by a CPE *if* it could devalue. The terms of trade, $t$, improve after a devaluation if

$$d_m d_x > s_m s_x$$

There seems to be little doubt that $t$ would deteriorate if there could be a devaluation because both $d_m$ and $d_x$ are likely to be relatively very small, whereas, as we have seen, $s_m$ is probably very large. On a priori grounds it is difficult to assign a value to $s_x$. Tautness plus lack of responsiveness to market conditions suggests a smaller $s_x$ for some CPEs than for market economies. On the other hand, to the extent that the planners earmark existing output to foreign trade organizations (fto's) for additional exports or new investment to increase the supply of exportables, $s_x$ might be interpreted to be either elastic or inelastic: elastic if the products are offered at a given price with the quantity to be determined by demand; inelastic if the amount offered is fixed and price depends on what buyers are willing to pay. The latter case seems more realistic. But whatever the value of $s_x$, the large size of $s_m$ and the relatively small values attached to $d_x$ and $d_m$ would suggest a probable large drop in terms of trade if devaluation were possible, larger than that which would be experienced by a comparable market economy.

## VII. The CPE as price discriminator

In the real world, as we have noted, a CPE does not devalue to increase export earnings but simply reduces prices. What this means, in effect, is that the CPE is automatically put into the position of a price discriminator to the extent that it is dealing in markets in which the products are not homogeneous and/or markets can be effectively separated. As we are primarily discussing exports of manufactured products, the non-homogeneity condition holds and some separation of markets can be assumed possible. As a price discriminator, the CPE can drive a much

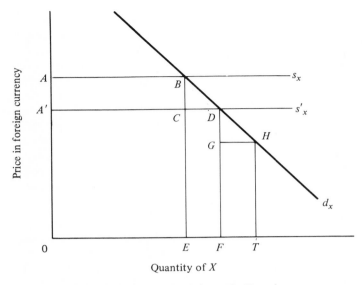

Figure 2. CPE as price discriminator in $X$ market.

better bargain for itself than the market economy devaluer.[19] This can be illustrated in terms of Figure 1.

Suppose that $P_w$ is not very elastic and at going terms of trade, $E$ can only sell $ab$ for $bd$ and is left with $bc$ of unsold exportables. If $E$ devalues from $ae$ to $ar$, it will be no better off than before because gains from the increased quantity of exports sold are just offset by the reduction in price of all goods due to devaluation. If, on the other hand, $E$ is able to continue to sell $ab$ at $ad$ prices, and then sell $bc$ additional exportables at a lower price, such as, say, $df$, which is parallel to $ar$, then the same drop in the prices of $bc$ exportables enables $E$ to come much closer to its target.

The point can also be made on a partial equilibrium diagram (Figure 2). Assume that $E$ is faced with a $d_x = 1$. If it devalues from $OA$ to $OA'$, it earns no additional foreign exchange because $CDEF$, the gain on additional exports, is just offset by the lower earnings $ABCA'$ on existing exports. If it successfully price discriminates, however, $CDFE + GHTF + $ etc. foreign exchange is earned without losses on previous markets. In fact, if discrimination were continuous rather than discrete, the supply curve would be continuous and negatively sloped (i.e., $ABDH$), thereby increasing foreign exchange earnings by $EBHT$. This process would stop when the real cost of foreign exchange, hence of imports, in terms of resources embodied in exports, becomes too high. (As noted earlier, the value of $d_m$ suggests when it may make sense to cut back imports rather than try to expand exports.) In effect, at some point along $ABDHD_x$, the supply curve turns positive. The $s_x$ might also turn positive if the foreign exchange target were exhausted. A negatively sloped $s_x$ must have characterized the USSR in the early 1930s when exports were increased sharply in the face of rapidly falling prices and terms of trade.

Whether a nation devalues or price discriminates makes a dramatic difference in the cost of earning additional foreign exchange through losses in terms of trade. Suppose that $E$ is a devaluer and desires to increase exports by 20 percent. If it faces a $d_x = \infty$ and has an $s_x = \infty$, it can do so without devaluing – just selling 20 percent more exportables. The burden of the transfer is just the 20 percent increase in exports. Suppose that it faces a $d_x = 2$. In this case, to increase the quantity of exports sold by 20 percent would require a 10 percent devaluation. Increasing the quantity of exports by 20 percent, would however, only increase the value of foreign exchange earned by approximately 10 percent because of the lower price now received on the previous volume of exports. In effect, $E$ has to export twice as many goods to earn the same amount of foreign exchange as before – the terms of trade cost of a 10 percent devaluation is 50 percent. The secondary burden of the transfer in this case is as large as the primary burden. If $d_x = 3$, a $6\frac{2}{3}$ percent devaluation is required to increase exports by 20 percent. In this case the terms of trade cost amounts to about 35 percent.

The price discriminating CPE fares much better. The cost of additional foreign exchange earnings through one-time price reductions in the preceding two cases are 10 and $6\frac{2}{3}$ percent, respectively. For the perfect discriminators, the losses would be one-half of these amounts, 5 and $3\frac{1}{3}$ percent. The secondary burden of transfer in these instances is obviously quite small.

The advantages accruing to the CPE price discriminators may be reduced by their relatively (to a comparable market economy) inelastic $d_m$. This could throw a larger burden of the balance-of-payments adjustment on increasing exports, where, as we have seen, the $d_x$ is also relatively inelastic. With so much of the adjustment required on the export side, prices are more likely to be pushed down to the very inelastic segments of $d_x$, even in the case of those products in which it was elastic to begin with.

The extent of CPE terms of trade losses and secondary transfer burdens depends very heavily on the extent to which the CPE is able to play the roles of devaluer and price discriminator, respectively, in East–West trade. The burden of achieving balanced payments for a CPE price discriminator may well be much less than that of a comparable market economy, despite the fact that it faces less favorable elasticities.

It might appear, at first glance, that the CPEs are in a superior economic position by virtue of not having real exchange rates that can function to equilibrate trade and thereby being put into the position of price discriminators. This is not necessarily true. In a well-functioning market system, a devaluation of the exchange rate efficiently eliminates marginal importers and induces entry of marginal exporters over the whole range of potential traders as well as serving to reduce purchases and increase sales in the cases of existing imports and exports. In the case of imports, the interests of individual enterprises and of the nation coincide. That is, the devalued exchange rate makes it unprofitable for some importers to continue buying from abroad. By maximizing profits under these conditions, they save the nation foreign exchange. In the case of exports, this coincidence of interests also exists when the price elasticity of demand is greater than unity: higher profits and increased foreign exchange earnings both result. National interests diverge from those of enterprises, however, when $d_x < 1$. Expansion of exports always leads to higher enterprise profits in local currency; on the other hand, these translate into smaller foreign exchange earnings at the new exchange rate when $d_x$ is inelastic. This is another aspect of the rationale for price discrimination, particularly in cases of low aggregate $d_x$.

The CPEs have no choice: they cannot obtain the benefits of a market exchange rate. The irrationality of domestic CPE prices and exchange rates plus the fact that convertible currencies are undervalued to them at world prices[20] (or why such convertible currency deficits?) makes it rational for them, as a second best strategy, to sell at varying amounts below world prices where necessary. This is particularly advisable in light of the low $d_x$'s they appear to face on many products. By price discriminating, they can make the best of a nonoptimal situation, but not achieve an optimal solution.

## VIII. The special case of Hungary

The People's Republic of Hungary is something of an exception to the foregoing generalizations. The basic difference is that Hungary has more market and less planning by direct controls than other CMEA nations. In terms of data presented in Table 1, Hungary's hard currency debt service appears to represent a substantially larger savings problem than those of the other CMEA nations. This is partly attributable to the fact that Hungary has the most "open" economy of the group – with a TPR of approximately 0.45. The openness is partly due, of course, to Hungary's small size and lack of diversified resources, but it may also be due to greater reliance on market mechanisms. Evidence suggests that the use of planning and direct controls reduces foreign trade below what it would be under market mechanisms (Hewett, 1976). If this is the case, then perhaps

Hungary's gains from greater trade provide some compensation for its more severe balance-of-payments problem.

With regard to price and exchange rate adjustments, it is not obvious to what extent internal Hungarian prices are rational market prices; nor is it obvious just what role the dollar and ruble exchange rates of the forint play in restoring balance-of-payments equilibrium (I suspect not very much). The question is: What is the optimum policy for a halfway house? In light of the preceding discussion, it seems reasonable to argue that if internal prices are rational, it would pay to take advantage of this fact by using market exchange rates and decentralizing foreign (as well as internal) trade. If, on the other hand, internal prices are not rational market prices, it would be second best to control trade centrally in order (1) to avoid purchases and sales based on improper price information as well as to encourage purchases and sales that are discouraged by improper price information and (2) to reap the benefits of price discrimination on exports.

## IX. Concluding remarks

The Eastern nations have large $ds/x$ ratios and, by traditional standards, some of them might be considered serious credit risks. The $ds/x$ is, however, a very poor measure of creditworthiness. Viewing creditworthiness as a transfer problem, it was concluded that, unlike the LDCs, the primary internal "savings" burden of the CPEs is not large relative to the size and growth of GNP. Converting these saved resources, particularly into exports but also into import replacements, thereby rectifying hard currency balances of payments and financing debt services, was deduced to be a much more difficult problem because of the assumption of relatively low values of the demand elasticities. By free-market standards, the CMEA nations might (1) find it extremely difficult to rectify their hard currency deficits and especially without (2) very large adverse shifts in terms of trade and resulting large secondary burdens of transfer. Sufficiently large secondary burdens of transfer could actually raise the savings burden ($ds/$GNP) for some of the CPEs (e.g., Hungary, East Germany) to levels more like those of the LDCs. It may not be appropriate to use free-market standards in judging the CPEs, however, because they are not devaluers but, in part, price discriminators. To the extent that they are price discriminators, they are in a position to reduce, substantially, their terms of trade losses.

## Notes

1 The debts of some other advanced industrial nations must be viewed with less concern than those of LDCs because the former are lenders as well as borrowers and own large external assets.

2 Forty billion dollars in external debt amounts to 4 to 5 percent of GNP, whereas the corresponding figure for the developing nations exceeds 15 percent.

3 All CPE debt is publicly guaranteed, so ratios in the West are usually relatively understated in comparison with CPEs as measures of total debt service, public plus private.

4 This point has been made by Brainard (1975).

5 $K$ stands for capital flows.

6 Although in theory $X$ and $M$ include goods and services, in this chapter we deal only with commodity trade because of the absence of reliable data on invisibles for the Eastern nations.

7 The 6 percent refers to $X$/GNP. The $M$/GNP ratio for the USSR is about twice as high (see Treml, 1980).

8 As noted above, the $ds/x$ ratio fails to indicate the magnitude of the $A - Y$ problem for still another nonsystemic reason, one that does not concern us here. Two nations with identical or similar ratios might have quite different per capita incomes. Consider the relative problems faced by two nations with vastly different per capita incomes, each of which has to reduce the level of absorption relative to income produced by the same percentage. Certainly, the problem would be simpler *ceteris paribus,* for a nation with a per capita income of $4,000 than one with a per capita income of $500. Eliminating the *ceteris paribus,* of course, might create a new ballgame. The ability of nations to collect taxes, reinvest profits, and so on, varies for many different reasons, political and social, as well as economic.

9 Since the 1973–4 price increases, many of the CMEA nations have developed deficits and debts with the USSR. Although these are not unimportant, we ignore them here.

10 This is not meant to imply necessarily that the gains from the imports financed by borrowing are not large enough to carry the debt service.

11 In a recent paper on LDC debt problems, Robert Solomon (1977) concerns himself almost exclusively with $A - Y$ problems to the neglect of the $M - X$ gap. This is probably largely because for the poor LDCs, the relatively large $ds/Y$ ratios represent serious resource drains.

12 Obviously, when demand curves are shifting to the left because of recessions – as in the West during 1974–5 – the relevance of price elasticities is sharply reduced.

13 To make an obvious point, it is not necessary for imports from the West to be directly usable in investments designed to improve the hard currency balance of payments; they can serve this function just as well by efficiently satisfying domestic requirements and thereby freeing up additional domestic resources for developing foreign trade industries. This qualification should be kept in mind in the discussion that follows.

14 Admittedly, the incentive to make short-run adjustments may have been blunted by the ready availability of relatively cheap hard currency credit.

15 However, on balance the percentage does not appear greater for the CMEA nations than it is for many Latin American and Asian middle-level developing nations (see Brainard, 1978).

16 On the other hand, since internal price inflation is not a serious problem – nor would it affect foreign trade if it was – the need for devaluation is much less acute in the CPEs.

17 See Holzman (1979a,b). Basically, the argument is that CMEA exports are hard to sell for nonprice reasons (quality, marketing, servicing, packaging, etc.), implying a low price elasticity of demand.

18 If the imports that would have to be foregone were intermediate products essential to domestic production, this conclusion might not follow so easily. The losses to the economy from a reduction in imports, in this case, could be much greater than the value of the foregone imports themselves. This effect could, of course, be included implicitly in the indifference curves.

19 By concentrating exports in products with a high $d_x$, in products not previously sold, in markets in which a product has not been previously offered, and in markets in which the $d_x$ is relatively higher. As a serious caveat to the argument of this section, one must question whether the foreign trade planners have sufficient flexibility in the market to successfully price-discriminate on a large scale.

20 One meaning of this statement is that CPEs are willing to export at very low prices if they estimate that the gains to them from imports, which otherwise could not be imported, are very high.

## References

Alton, T. 1974. "Economic Growth and Resource Allocation in Eastern Europe." In Joint Economic Committee, U.S. Congress, *Reorientation and Commercial Relations of the Economies of Eastern Europe.* Washington, D.C.

Avramovic, D., et al. 1964. *Economic Growth and External Debt.* John Hopkins Press, Baltimore, Md.

Brainard, L. 1975. "Criteria for Financing East–West Trade." In John Hardt (ed.), *Tariff, Legal and Credit Constraints on East-West Commercial Relations.* Carleton University, Ottawa.

Brainard, L. 1978. "Eastern Europe's Indebtedness Policy Choices for East and West." In C. T. Saunders (ed.), *Money and Finance in East and West.* Springer-Verlag, New York, pp. 79–98.

CIA. *Handbook of Economic Statistics, 1975.* Washington, D.C.

CIA. *Handbook of Economic Statistics, 1976.* Washington, D.C.

Crawford, J. and Haberstroh, J. 1974. "Survey of Economic Policy Issues in Eastern Europe: Technology, Trade and the Consumer." In Joint Economic Committee, U.S. Congress, *Reorientation and Commercial Relations of the Economies of Eastern Europe.* Washington, D.C.

Hewett, Edward. "A Gravity Model of CMEA Trade." In Josef Brada (ed.), *Quantitative and Analytical Studies on East–West Economic Relations.* 1976. Indiana University Press, Bloomington, Ind.

Holzman, Franklyn D. 1979a. "Some Theories of the Hard Currency Shortages of Centrally Planned Economies." In Joint Econ. Committee, U.S. Congress, *Soviet Economy in a Time of Change.* Washington, D.C.

Holzman, Franklyn D. 1979b. "Some Systemic Factors Contributing to the Convertible Currency Shortages of Centrally Planned Economies." *Proceedings of American Economic Association,* May.

International Bank for Reconstruction and Development. 1977. *World Tables,* Washington, D.C.

International Monetary Fund. 1977a. *Survey*, June 6.

International Monetary Fund. 1977b. *Survey*, August 1.

Joint Economic Committee, U.S. Congress, 1974. *Reorientation and Commercial Relations of the Economies of Eastern Europe*. Washington, D.C.

Joint Economic Committee, U.S. Congress. 1976. *The Soviet Economy in a New Perspective*. Washington, D.C.

Joint Economic Committee, U.S. Congress. 1977. *East European Economies Post-Helsinki*. Washington, D.C.

Kreinin, M. and Heller, H. R. 1974. "Adjustment Costs, Optimal Currency Areas, and International Reserve." In Willy Sellssekaerts (ed.), *International Trade and Finance* (*Essays in Honour of Jan Tinbergen*). International Arts and Sciences Press, White Plains, N.Y., pp. 127–40.

*New-York Times*. 1976. November 11, p. 60.

Portes, Richard. 1977. "East Europe's Debt to the West: Interdependence Is a Two-Way Street." *Foreign Affairs*, July.

Snell, E. 1974. "Eastern Europe's Trade and Payments with the Industrial West." In Joint Economic Committee, U.S. Congress, *Reorientation and Commercial Relations of the Economies of Eastern Europe*. Washington, D.C.

Solomon, R. 1977. "A Perspective on the Debt of Developing Countries." *Brookings Papers on Economic Activity 2*.

Treml, Vladimir. 1980. "Foreign Trade and the Soviet Economy: Changing Parameters and Interrelations." In E. Neuberger and L. Tyson (eds.), *The Impact of International Economic Disturbances on the Soviet Union and Eastern Europe: Transmission and Response*. Pergamon Press, New York, pp. 184–207.

Zoeter, J. 1977. "Eastern Europe: The Growing Hard Currency Debt." In Joint Economic Committee, U.S. Congress, *East European Economies Post-Helsinki*. Washington, D.C.

## 8  Comparative advantage and the evolving pattern of Soviet international commodity specialization 1950–1973

*Steven Rosefielde*

## I. Introduction

Western specialists hold sharply divergent views on whether Soviet international trade is economically rational.[1] This chapter attempts to advance the position developed in my previous studies that comparative advantage explains the pattern of Soviet foreign trade better than alternative hypotheses.[2] Acknowledging all the bureaucratic impediments that constrain Soviet foreign trade planning, acknowledging that Soviet prices are not general equilibrium prices and that efficiency indices do not substantially remedy their deficiencies, it is nonetheless argued that Soviet foreign trade is determined by its "fundamental comparative advantage." The term "fundamental comparative advantage" implies that comparative advantage holds in a delimited sense. It suggests that for a set of basic industries at a high level of aggregation, production costs are sufficiently differentiated to permit various sectors to be grouped into high and low domestic cost categories, which can be utilized to compute gains or losses from foreign trade.

Fundamental comparative advantage does *not* imply that individual commodities within any particular sector will be properly valued or exchanged according to the norms of general equilibrium. Similarly, fundamental comparative advantage does *not* imply that composite goods will

This paper has benefited from the suggestions of a great many people, but most especially J. M. Montias, Paul Marer, Alan Brown, Franklyn Holzman, Abram Bergson, Gregory Grossman, Knox Lovell, and Edward Hewett.

185

be traded in optimal volumes and proportions. All that it stipulates is that low-cost goods for the basic aggregates will be exported and high-cost goods imported, and that when opportunity costs change, the pattern of tradeables will adjust appropriately.

This amounts to the assertion that the first-order partial derivatives of aggregate sectoral tradeables with respect to price are positive and the second-order partials are negative, as theory requires, without further presumption as to global properties or full general equilibrium optimality. Such a formulation, of course, has affinities with the more conventional viewpoint. It recognizes the limitations of Soviet planning and the arbitrary elements of bureaucratic practice. It differs from the conventional interpretation, however, by treating these obstacles as constraints, restricting but not overwhelming the principle of sectoral comparative advantage. Thus, although our description of Soviet foreign trade behavior will be familiar, the theory developed here is linked to opportunity cost, allowing predictive verification in a causal sense that is often lacking in alternative conceptions. This enables Soviet practice to be embedded squarely in the framework of traditional international trade theory, which not only obviates the need for unfamiliar terminology, but strengthens our confidence in the correctness of our causal specification.

Before proceeding with our analysis, one more introductory remark is in order. The economic conditions determining the structure of international comparative advantage during the postwar period were drastically altered by the Arab oil embargo of 1973. Not only was the world plagued by double-digit inflation and economic stagnation, but changes in relative prices and expectations profoundly affected the terms of international trade. Although the Soviet Union managed to insulate itself tolerably well from the macroeconomic consequences of these disruptive events,[3] changes in the terms of international trade had a significant effect on the composition of Soviet trade. A thorough analysis of these events and the changes they have wrought unfortunately constitutes an undertaking of substantial proportions and cannot be attempted within the confines of this essay. For this reason the present study is confined to the period 1950–73.

## II. Calculating exchange advantage under central planning

Until quite recently, the mechanics of Soviet foreign trade decision making have been shrouded in secrecy. This reticence has spawned considerable speculation concerning the principles employed in determining foreign trade commodity specialization and has prompted some to conclude that expediency is the ruling criterion. This judgment is predicated partly on the politicized nature of the foreign trade decision-making process, partly on the cumbersomeness of material balance planning, and partly on the contention that Soviet prices do not reflect scarcities and therefore are not utilized in practice as an operational criterion for establishing the observed pattern of trade.[4]

Soviet practitioners however strongly reject this characterization. According to Vladimir Bezrukov and Andrei Chursin, respectively Deputy Chief, and Sub-Department Chief for Foreign Trade of the Main Computer Center, USSR State Planning Committee, Soviet planners systematically strive to maximize gains from trade, evaluated with prevailing average cost production prices and ancillary efficiency criteria.[5] They assert that Gosplan, in conjunction with the general priorities established by the Council of Economic Ministers, taking into consideration available information on long-term trade contracts, comparative price advantage, and special market exigencies, compiles a basic foreign trade plan that is built into the material balances. Before 1968, comparative price advantage was computed in official prices; thereafter, efficiency indices based on modified enterprise wholesale prices were employed. Once completed, the foreign trade plan is sent to the Ministry of Foreign Trade for implementation. Within the general outline of this Gosplan directive, the Ministry then decides the precise assortment of traded goods subject to the distributional constraints imposed by the plan, long-term commodity contracts, promotional goals, credit conditions, and relative international prices.[6]

Although some latitude exists in interpreting distributional constraints, implementing long-term contracts, and extending promotional discounts to achieve market penetration, the domain of effective ministerial decision making really becomes significant in the choice of the specific mixes and volumes of goods exchanged with individual blocs and countries that fulfill the divisional targets established by the plan. These decisions are made on the basis of computed budgetary effectiveness, where official accounting prices rather than adjusted efficiency prices are used to measure alternative exchange benefits. Since budgetary measures of foreign trade effectiveness cannot by themselves determine the volumes in which individual goods are traded, it may be inferred that a two-phase simulation of the automatic market mechanism is in operation.

In the first phase, average domestic production cost prices appear to be employed as a sorting device for distinguishing the relative dearness or cheapness of all domestic goods compared with the ruble acquisition cost of analogous foreign commodities. Goods whose foreign exchange acquisition costs exceed domestic production costs are designated as exportables, goods that are less expensive domestically as importables. Within each of these categories tradeables are further identified according to function using the standard Soviet industrial nomenclature. Some commodity groups, such as industrial consumer goods, fall predominantly in the importable category, whereas others, such as petroleum products, most often appear as exportables. Moreover, regardless of the precise distribution of commodity groups between importables and exportables, individual commodity groups are ranked according to their mean domestic cost, making it possible to distinguish those groups that afford the greatest exchange advantages.

In the second phase, having established the general structure of trading opportunities, the planners are required to determine how much of each good within every commodity group should be produced domestically or imported. Although theory makes it clear that the rule to be followed here is to equate marginal costs with prices reflecting marginal rates of consumer product substitution, lack of reliable information on costs and consumer utilities compels planners to employ discretionary methods. At the highest administrative level of planning where broad policy decisions regarding funded composite goods are made, material balances in conjunction with both budgetary and efficiency measures of price effectiveness computed in the first phase codetermine the overall pattern of trade, subject of course to the usual political considerations. The actual implementation of the foreign trade plan, after the basic proportions have been established, however, depends on the actions of the foreign trade organizations guided by budgetary effectiveness indicators, long-term contractual obligations, credit conditions, and the willingness of individual ministries to supply and receive specific items to and from the foreign trade sector.

The range of discretion in these matters is very extensive, too extensive to assert with any conviction that the administrative simulation of the automatic market adjustment mechanism bears a close relationship to some ideal general equilibrium solution. Nonetheless, the two-phase approach to foreign trade decision making allows administrators not only to employ prices as indicators of relative advantage in both stages, it enables them to simulate the automatic market price adjustment mechanism, albeit in an ad hoc way by bringing a wide range of supplementary information to bear on the crucial problem of determining the volumes in which specific goods in each commodity classification are to be traded.

Several independent sources appear to confirm the plausibility of this characterization. Holzman, for example, has pointed out that although Soviet commodity trade is reported and payments balanced in world prices, the difference between their export and import values in domestic prices, which is almost always positive, is added to the gross national product as an imputation for value added attributed to exchange.[7] Because the contribution of the Ministry of Foreign Trade to the gross national product will necessarily be maximized by minimizing the cost of the export bill and maximizing the domestic value of imports (including turn-over taxes on final retail sales), it is easy to imagine that these criteria weigh heavily in the actual choice of traded goods.[8] Indeed, Stanislav Zakharov, a well-known international trade expert at Gosplan, has explicitly stated that budgetary profit is a basic determinant of commodity specialization for the Ministry of Foreign Trade and the foreign trade organizations, whereas more sophisticated efficiency indices derived from adjusted accounting prices are utilized primarily by Gosplan.[9]

In this regard, it should be noted that minimizing nominal export cost and maximizing nominal import value are highly operational indicators for bureaucratic decision making. From the viewpoint of managerial control, indices of budgetary effectiveness not only serve as an objective and defensible standard of choice, they are easily verified and coincide with the success criteria employed throughout the rest of the production system. This point was emphasized to me in an extremely instructive way by a Soviet colleague, who explained that optimal programming shadow prices (not adjusted accounting prices) computed by the State Committee on Science and Technology were *not* implemented by the Ministry of Foreign Trade primarily because in superseding official accounting prices they conflicted with prevailing measures of profitability, imposing accounting losses on both the ministry and the firms supplying them with exportables. Of course, had the government really been willing to force such a reform, these objections might have been overcome. This little episode does suggest, however, that accounting profitability is a basic indicator for the Ministry of Foreign Trade, which conforms with standard bureaucratic practice and therefore facilitates the vital process of consistent administrative control.

A more specific instance of the role prices play in the determination of commodity specialization involves the crucial issue of capital durables. According to Bezrukov and Chursin it is standard operating procedure to import representative units of technologically advanced Western machinery and equipment, build prototypes, compute projected unit costs, estimate anticipated revenue streams, and apply the Typical Method to calculate the expected internal rate of return. The results of these computations are next compared with the average domestic accounting cost of exports sold in order to acquire foreign exchange for the purchase of foreign durables. The decision to import or import substitute is then made on the basis of the implied comparative rates of return.[10] The entire computation is handled by Gosplan with a standard computer algorithm that has been in use since 1966.

What is most striking in all this is not so much that the Soviets have adopted sophisticated methods to improve foreign trade decision making, but the consistent application of domestic accounting prices in either pure or adjusted form for decisions that involve both domestic investment and foreign trade. It appears that although the Soviets are generally aware of the limitations of their average direct-plus-indirect labor accounting prices compared with optimal scarcity prices, they have been willing to rely on some form of accounting cost prices as basic economic decision criteria in the absence of a dependable alternative because they are comprehensive, ostensibly objective, and facilitate managerial control. Although a mounting effort to introduce efficiency indices at the foreign trade organization level in progress since 1968 has necessarily modified established practice, the fundamental rationale of Soviet price planning is unlikely to have been affected in a drastic way. Efficiency indices employed by Gosplan are based on official prices modified for omitted scarcity charges, credit costs, and so on. Unlike shadow prices, which are extremely sensitive to the specification of any particular linear program, *relative* efficiency prices are unlikely to deviate drastically from official prices, except where credit constitutes a significant component of total price.

It appears, then, that whether accounting prices or efficiency indices are in force, the composition of Soviet foreign trade does not depend on *arbitrary* quantitative directives, as some Western scholars suppose. Rather, within the broad quantitative framework established by Gosplan, taking price and nonprice factors into consideration, the Ministry of Foreign Trade determines the commodity composition of traded goods with a sharp eye for nominal comparative advantage (measured in accounting or efficiency terms), which serves simultaneously as a criterion of choice and a standard of bureaucratic justification.

### III. Price trends and the changing composition of Soviet foreign trade

Empirical evidence supporting this interpretation takes three forms. First, it can be shown that the geographical distribution of Soviet international trade is sensitive to changes in the structure of world prices; second, that the commodity composition of Soviet imports and exports are responsive to prices and factor productivities; and third, that the Soviets export domestically cheap goods and import products that are comparatively dear. Complete confirmation of these assertions is a complex matter that is elaborated systematically in the ensuing sections. A prima facia case substantiating the first proposition, however, can be easily developed by comparing trends in Soviet terms of trade with changes in the geographical distribution of Soviet imports and exports.

Table 1 provides the relevant data for assessing geographic trends. It reveals that the steady comparative deterioration in bilateral Soviet terms of trade with the CMEA (Council for Mutual Economic Assistance), fall-

Table 1. *Soviet bilateral terms of trade and real trade volume growth with the CMEA and the West, 1960–73*

| | Terms of trade, CMEA/West | Volume | |
| --- | --- | --- | --- |
| | | CMEA | West |
| 1960 | 100 | 100 | 100 |
| 1965 | 88.6 | 155 | 155 |
| 1970 | 72.5 | 225 | 243 |
| 1973 | 63.1 | 271 | 386 |
| Compound annual rate of growth (%) | | | |
| 1960–73 | | 8 | 11 |
| 1960–5 | | 9.1 | 9.1 |
| 1965–70 | | 7.7 | 9.4 |
| 1970–3 | | 6.4 | 16.7 |

*Note:* CMEA denotes Soviet bloc nations that are members of the Council for Mutual Economic Assistance. West denotes the category "developed industrial capitalist countries" found in the official Soviet handbook *Vneshniaia torgovlia.*
*Sources: Column 1.* Paul Marer, *Postwar Pricing and Price Patterns in Socialist Foreign Trade (1946–1971)*, International Development Research Center, Indiana University, Bloomington, Ind., 1972, Table 8, p. 31. The entry for 1973 was computed by the author from data on real and nominal imports and exports found in various editions of *Vneshniaia torgovlia, SSSR,* Statistika, Moscow, Tables III and VIII. *Column 2. Vneshniaia torgovlia,* various issues, Tables III and VIII. Entries for 1960–9 are valued in 1960 prices; 1970 prices are employed thereafter. *Column 3. Vneshniaia torgovlia,* various issues, Tables III and VIII. Soviet statistics on the growth of real foreign trade turnover pertain to all capitalist countries. To estimate volume growth with the developed capitalist nations (West), the ratio of real to nominal volume growth for all capitalist countries was computed and applied to the nominal growth of trade volume with the West on the assumption that price changes in the traded goods of less developed capitalist countries were similar to those in the more developed nations of the West.

ing from 100 in 1960 to 63.1 in 1973, is associated not only with a slow rate of real volume growth compared to Soviet trade with the West (developed industrial capitalist countries), but decelerates at the same time that Soviet trade with the West is accelerating. For the entire period 1960–73, trade with the West increases 11 percent annually compared to 8 percent with the CMEA, accelerating from 9.1 percent in 1960–5 to 16.7 percent in 1970–3, whereas trade with the CMEA continuously decelerates from 9.1 percent in 1960–5 to 6.4 percent in 1970–3. These correspondences vividly demonstrate that the changing geographical pattern of Soviet foreign trade is consistent with the incentives established by changes in the structure of world prices.

The correlation between commodity price-trends and the composition of Soviet foreign trade, however, is more ambiguous. Table 2 indicates that the terms of Soviet trade with the CMEA deteriorated more or less proportionally for machinery, natural resources (CTU, 2, 3, 5) and food in the period 1960–5, diverging thereafter. The terms of trade fell sharply

Table 2. *Comparative Soviet foreign trade prices with CMEA and the world for various sectors (1960 = 100)*

| Commodity group | CTN | CMEA export prices[a]/world prices[b] | | CMEA import prices[c]/world prices | | CMEA export prices[a]/CMEA import prices | |
|---|---|---|---|---|---|---|---|
| | | 1965 | 1970 | 1965 | 1970 | 1965 | 1970 |
| Machinery | 1 | 93 | 81 | 101 | 91 | 92 | 89 |
| Minerals | 2 | 89 | 75 | 95 | 92 | 93 | 82 |
| Chemicals | 3 | n.a. | n.a. | n.a. | n.a. | n.a. | n.a. |
| Nonfood agricultural raw materials | 5 | 103 | 101 | 120 | 161 | .85 | 62 |
| Food | 6–8 | 83 | 90 | 98 | 92 | .90 | 98 |
| Industrial consumer goods and building materials | 4, 9 | n.a. | n.a. | 103 | 101 | n.a. | n.a. |

*Note:* n.a., not available.

[a] Computed as the unweighted average of all bilateral Soviet exports from individual CMEA states. See Edward A. Hewett, *Foreign Trade Prices in the Council for Mutual Economic Assistance*, Cambridge University Press, 1974, pp. 71–2.

[b] World prices do not refer to prices either paid or charged by the Soviets in interbloc exchange. The same world prices therefore appear in the denominators of both the import and export indices reported above. See Paul Marer, *Postwar Pricing and Price Patterns in Socialist Foreign Trade (1946–1971)*, International Development Research Center, Indiana University, Bloomington, Ind., 1972, p. 89.

[c] Computed as the unweighted average of all Soviet bilateral imports from individual CMEA states. See Hewett, *Foreign Trade Prices*, pp. 71–2.

Table 3. *Net proportioned exports in Soviet–CMEA trade, 1955–73*
*(foreign trade ruble prices)*

| Year | Machinery | Natural resources | Agriculture plus food | Light industry |
|------|-----------|-------------------|-----------------------|----------------|
| 1955 | −0.28 | 0.12 | 0.84 | −0.03 |
| 1960 | −0.31 | 0.33 | 0.97 | −0.16 |
| 1965 | −0.28 | 0.41 | −0.02 | −0.17 |
| 1970 | −0.24 | 0.43 | −0.02 | −0.19 |
| 1973 | −0.20 | 0.42 | −0.04 | −0.17 |

*Sources:* Paul Marer, *Soviet and East European Foreign Trade, 1946–1969: Statistical Compendium and Guide,* Indiana University Press, Bloomington, Ind., 1972, and subsequent computer updates. Marer's data are taken from official Soviet statistics. The figures above represent the export share of each commodity aggregate less the correlative import share. The CTN commodity groups underlying the aggregates above are machinery (CTN 1), natural resources (CTN 2, 3, 5), agriculture (CTN 6, 7, 8), industrial consumer goods (CTN 9). The residual group of unallocated commodities has been omitted from the table. Note that the term "natural resources" subsumes fuels, metals, metal semifabricates, chemicals, fertilizer, rubber, and nonfood agricultural raw materials and timber.
    Net proportioned exports represent the difference between the export and import commodity shares. This procedure is used to eliminate the distortive effect of absolute export or import imbalances.

during the period 1965–70 in natural resources, rose in the food sector, and remained relatively constant in the machinery industry. Other things equal, it should therefore be anticipated that the trade pattern for the first half of the 1960s would have continued past trends, followed by a decrease in net machinery and food imports and a decline in net natural resource exports. Table 3 reveals, however, that only the machine sector follows the predicted pattern for 1965–70. The growth of net natural resource exports decelerates but is not reversed, whereas the growth of net food imports remains unchanged. These results do not necessarily contradict the hypothesis that the commodity composition of Soviet foreign trade is sensitive to comparative advantage, but they do not confirm the hypothesis either. To ascertain whether the behavior exhibited in Table 3 is truly consistent or is inconsistent with the logic of comparative advantage, the changing pattern of domestic opportunity costs must be taken explicitly into consideration.

## IV. Capital–labor substitution and the changing structure of opportunity costs in Soviet domestic production

Diverse methods exist for computing relative production costs at the margin of managerial choice. These range from simple input–output computations of direct-plus-indirect factor utilization to dynamic convex programming models. The input–output approach is limited, among other things, by its restrictive assumptions regarding factor substitution, which stipulate that all sectors can be adequately characterized by zero elasticities of factor substitution. Elaborate programming models also have their drawbacks, particularly in their sensitivity to the specification of the constraint system, boundary values, and the objective function.

A middle course, although one subject to well-known debilities of its own, lies in production function analysis.[11] The strategy here is to use nonlinear multiple regression techniques to estimate parameters of abstract technology by correlating outputs and inputs according to alternative algebraic specifications, each having its own explicit economic meaning. The relative merit of competing specifications can then be assessed using conventional statistical tests, in conjunction with consistency checks on the plausibility of the economic behavior implied by the fully estimated model.

In recent years, mounting evidence has suggested that the constant elasticity of factor substitution specification (CES) best explains the postwar Soviet experience.[12] Because the more familiar Cobb–Douglas form as well as the Leontief fixed-input expression are both subsumed as special CES cases, all three specifications can be conveniently explored within the CES framework. An elaborate econometric CES production function study was therefore carried out using Soviet sectoral data on inputs and outputs. The results showed conclusively that the Cobb–Douglas and Leontief fixed-input forms were statistically and behaviorally inferior to other CES alternatives.[13] Among the diverse specificational forms that the general CES expression permits, the Hicks neutral variant, assuming disembodied, variable technological progress with constant returns to scale, proved best.

$$Y(t) = \gamma \exp(\lambda t + \beta t^2)[\delta K(t)^{-\rho} + (1 - \delta)L(t)^{-\rho}]^{-1/\rho} \qquad (1)$$

The Hicks neutral CES form expressed in equation (1) specifies output in any particular year $Y(t)$ to be a nonlinear function of two variables, capital $(K)$ and labor $(L)$. The five parameters in the specification measure the efficiency of prevailing technology $(\gamma)$, relative factor utilization intensities $(\delta$ and $1 - \delta)$, the elasticity of factor substitution $(\sigma = 1/1 + \rho)$, and technical progress expressed both by a constant $(\lambda)$, and a variable term $(\beta)$.

Although all variables and parameters are integral to CES specification, $\sigma$ (the elasticity of substitution) is especially important because it determines relative factor productivities whenever primary inputs grow at differential rates. More precisely, should $\sigma$, the relative ease of substituting capital for labor, be less than unity, the marginal productivity of the more rapidly growing factor must fall in the familiar one-sector case.[14] *Ceteris paribus* this implies that the implicit or shadow price of the fast-growing

Table 4. *Estimates of abstract CES technology (direct inputs)*

| Sector | $\gamma$ | $\delta$ | $\sigma^a$ | $\lambda$ | $\beta$ | $R^2$ |
|--------|------|------|------|------|------|------|
| Fuels | 0.9815 | 0.3206 | 0.9998 | 0.0292 | $-0.0002$ | 0.9982 |
| | (74.83) | (1.18) | (0.0001) | (1.79) | $(-0.31)$ | |
| Metals | 1.002 | 0.6000 | 0.1536 | 0.0417 | $-0.0002$ | 0.9993 |
| | (113.80) | (7.77) | (3.62) | (5.55) | $(-0.81)$ | |
| Construction materials | 0.9994 | 0.4360 | 0.3874 | 0.0287 | $-0.1 \times 10^{-7}$ | 0.9966 |
| | (63.2) | (1.30) | (1.54) | (1.26) | $(-0.00002)$ | |
| Chemicals | 1.019 | 0.4473 | 0.1012 | 0.0356 | $-5 \times 10^{-5}$ | 0.9951 |
| | (33.5) | (0.89) | (0.51) | (2.0) | $(-0.001)$ | |
| Machinery | 1.018 | 0.4971 | 1.0000 | 0.0381 | $-0.0011$ | 0.9926 |
| | (33.87) | (0.66) | ($0.13 \times 10^{-4}$) | (1.94) | $(-2.03)$ | |
| Light industry | 1.036 | 0.8541 | 0.0728 | 0.0279 | $-0.7 \times 10^{-4}$ | 0.9870 |
| | (31.91) | (2.90) | (1.12) | (1.74) | $(-0.14)$ | |
| Food | 1.008 | 0.8716 | 0.1147 | 0.0267 | $-0.1 \times 10^{-5}$ | 0.9975 |
| | (74.85) | (9.07) | (4.44) | (2.73) | $(-0.003)$ | |
| Industry | 1.013 | 0.5030 | 0.2027 | 0.0308 | $-0.1 \times 10^{-7}$ | 0.9974 |
| | (55.58) | (3.27) | (1.23) | (1.78) | $(-0.2 \times 10^{-4})$ | |
| 12% AFC[b] | 1.021 | 0.5103 | 0.1669 | 0.0294 | $-0.8 \times 10^{-5}$ | 0.9969 |
| | (54.8) | (3.26) | (1.12) | (2.25) | $(-0.02)$ | |

*Note:* $T$ tests for all parameters are reported in Section C of the Appendix.
[a] Standard deviations reported for $\sigma$ refer to $\rho$ from which $\sigma$ was derived, $\sigma = 1/1 + \rho$.
[b] 12% AFC signifies that adjusted factor cost weights, assuming a 12% rate of return on capital, were used to aggregate total industrial production.

factor must decline relative to other inputs.[15] With some qualification, a similar result can be expected as well in the multisectoral case, where commodity substitution can affect relative factor prices.[16]

This, of course, is directly relevant to the changing structure of opportunity costs in the USSR and by straightforward extension to comparative advantage as well. Table 4 provides the necessary statistical information needed to evaluate these issues. It presents CES estimates [equation (1)] of the parameters of abstract technology for the postwar years 1950–73.[17] The underlying data series are described in Section A of the Appendix. As is easily observed, $\sigma$ is significantly less than one for five of the seven sectors. Given the growing scarcity of Soviet labor, this implies that the relatively labor-intensive sectors, such as food, light industry, and construction materials, have become increasingly costly at the margin compared with fuels, metals, chemicals, and machinery. As a corollary, if we assume constant foreign trade exchange prices, Soviet comparative advantage has increased in fuels, metals, chemicals, machines, and decreased in food, light industry, and construction materials.[18]

Strictly speaking, this argument presumes that the value of the marginal products of labor and capital are the same in all sectors. Under Soviet

Table 5. *Soviet industrial opportunity cost in 1960 and 1973*

|  | $-dY_i/dY_l$ | |
| --- | --- | --- |
| Sector | 1960 | 1973 |
| Machinery | 1.51 | 2.00 |
| Chemicals | 1.07 | 1.65 |
| Fuels | 1.19 | 1.58 |
| Metals | 1.01 | 1.33 |
| Construction materials | 1.21 | 1.27 |
| Light industry | 1.06 | 1.05 |
| Food | 1.00 | 1.00 |

conditions where factors are administratively allocated, such an assumption is likely to be unwarranted. To assess whether differential sectoral marginal productivities invalidate our inferences drawn from equilibrium theory, marginal capital and labor productivities were computed sector by sector and utilized together with other information to calculate the marginal output generated from unit capital and labor inputs in 1973. This was accomplished by computing the total derivative for each sector:

$$dY = \frac{\partial Y}{\partial K}\, dK + \frac{\partial Y}{\partial L}\, dL \tag{2}$$

on the assumption that the increments $dK$ and $dL$ would be added according to the proportions prevailing on average in the light industrial sector. The marginal products of capital,

$$\partial Y/\partial K = \delta\gamma^{-\rho} \exp\left[-\rho(\lambda t + \beta t^2)\right](Y/K)^{1/\sigma} \tag{3}$$

and labor,

$$\partial Y/\partial L = (1 - \delta)\gamma^{-\rho} \exp\left[-\rho(\lambda t + \beta t^2)\right](Y/L)^{1/\sigma} \tag{4}$$

were calculated from the parameters of abstract technology reported in Table 5 and the underlying output and factor series.[19]

Opportunity costs were then estimated by forming ratios of total output derivatives,

$$\Omega = -dY_i/dY_l \tag{5}$$

where the subscripts refer to the $i$th and $l$th (light industry) sector, respectively. These ratios express marginal rates of sectoral transformation as the amount of incremental output that can be obtained if a unit bundle of inputs in the light industrial sector were released and transferred to the production of the $i$th industry.[20]

Table 5 presents opportunity cost ratios estimated in this way. The rank order for 1973 demonstrates that our calculated opportunity cost structure

Table 6. *Soviet industrial opportunity cost rankings, sample years*

| | Sector | | |
|---|---|---|---|
| Rank | 1950 | 1960 | 1973 |
| 1 | Machinery | Machinery | Machinery |
| 2 | Construction materials | Construction materials | Chemicals |
| 3 | Fuels | Fuels | Fuels |
| 4 | Food | Chemicals | Metals |
| 5 | Metals | Food | Construction materials |
| 6 | Light industry | Metals | Light industry |
| 7 | Chemicals | Light industry | Food |

*Note:* Ranks 1–3 can be considered exportables; ranks 5–7, importables.

corresponds with those inferred from pure theory. More output per input bundle is obtained in machinery, chemicals, fuels, and metals than in construction materials, light industry, and food. Starting with machinery and proceeding through chemicals, fuels, and metals, the opportunity costs of domestic Soviet production indicate that capital-intensive activities are relatively cheap and labor-intensive activities relatively dear, confirming our previous assertions about the existence of a fundamental pattern of Soviet comparative cost advantage. *Ceteris paribus,* therefore, the Soviets should be able to increase domestic output by shifting factors into sectors with relatively high marginal products.[21]

The fundamental pattern of Soviet comparative advantage displayed in Table 5, of course, should not be seen as immutable. Not only may our findings be sensitive to the form of the production function chosen for this study, they can be expected to vary over time. Table 6, which compares opportunity cost for 1973 with rankings for 1950 and 1960, demonstrates that in the early postwar period construction materials and food were more apt to be exportables and chemicals were more apt to be importables than is the case now. This evolutionary pattern not only seems reasonable in terms of the structural development of the Soviet economy, but can also be inferred from the changing pattern of Soviet factor availability. In the early years when labor was abundant, the opportunity costs of labor-intensive activities could be expected to be comparatively low. As this situation changed, theory suggests and our empirical calculations confirm that the opportunity cost of labor-intensive industries should have increased. It can thus be concluded, subject to further empirical analysis, that opportunity costs in the Soviet Union during the postwar period have made it increasingly profitable to export chemicals, machinery, fuels, and metals and to import construction materials, food, and light industrial products.

This finding illuminates the puzzling trends observed in Soviet–CMEA commodity trade in the late 1960s detected in the preceding section. Table 6 indicates that although the terms of Soviet natural resource trade deteriorated with CMEA during the period 1960–70, factor productivity in the chemical–fuels–metals group rose in a compensatory manner. Similarly, although the terms of food trade improved during the period 1965–70, this effect was offset by a decline in the relative factor productivity of the food sector. The correlation between the changing pattern of Soviet commodity trade with the CMEA and changes in the structure of single-factorial terms of trade thus appears to be broadly compatible with the dictates of comparative advantage.

## V. Purchasing power parity, domestic opportunity costs, and the fundamental structure of Soviet comparative advantage

This conclusion implies that two of the three criteria specified to appraise whether Soviet foreign trade behavior is consistent with comparative advantage have been substantially satisfied. All that remains to be demonstrated is that the prevailing structure of Soviet commodity trade, as distinct from changes in the pattern of trade, favors the export of low-cost products and the import of high-domestic cost goods. This can be accomplished by comparing the price of high and low domestic opportunity cost goods with their foreign counterparts, supplemented with data on the relationship between adjusted factor cost prices and Soviet enterprise wholesale prices. In principle, the first phase of this demonstration should be based on a purchasing power parity calculation of all Soviet tradeable goods. If Zakharov, Bezrukov, and Chursin are to be believed, purchasing power parity calculations of precisely this type are routinely carried out by Gosplan, the Ministry of Foreign Trade, and the foreign trade organizations. Lacking access to this material, however, a less comprehensive but reliable alternative can be found in Franklyn Holzman's extensive purchasing power parity study of traded Soviet goods, based on price data taken directly from Soviet price handbooks.[22] Although the latest year for which Holzman provides purchasing power parity estimates is 1956, the trend in single-factorial terms of trade suggests that 1956 can be accepted as a representative year, a surmise supported by the close correlation of Holzman's figures with analogous estimates computed by Treml for 1959 and 1966.[23] Moreover, the minor disadvantage imposed by the use of this early date is more than compensated by the fact that the ratio of domestic import prices is reported in both enterprise wholesale and purchasers' prices, the former providing a much more accurate measure of domestic production cost.

Holzman divides the commodities in his study into two groups, producer goods and consumer goods, which correspond broadly with our high and low domestic Soviet opportunity cost sectoral classification. Producer goods include coal, coke, petroleum products, ferrous and nonferrous metal products, chemicals, varnish, paints, machinery, cement, lumber, and grain. Except for the last three items, this inventory encompasses our low-opportunity-cost sectors: fuels, metals, chemicals, and machinery. Consumer goods include food and industrial goods, both previously identified as high-opportunity-cost sectors. Only construction materials are omitted from this category, appearing insofar as they are represented under producer goods.

For each of these groups, as well as for their weighted sum, Holzman computes the ratio of the domestic price of imports and exports to their unit values measured in foreign trade rubles. These purchasing power parity ratios will provide support for the hypothesis that the static structure of Soviet foreign trade is consistent with comparative advantage if they reveal that the domestic cost of imported goods in every commodity group is higher than the domestic cost of exported goods in the same group, if the domestic cost of the Soviets' principal exports exceeds the domestic cost of its principal imports, and if it is further assumed (as seems reasonable) that full factor price equalization has not been achieved between the Soviet Union and its diverse trading partners.

Holzman's findings are summarized in Table 7. They demonstrate two important points. First, regardless of the valuation standard, Soviet export prices for producer and consumer goods are below their respective import prices for commodities classified in the same category. This indicates that from the standpoint of nominal gains from trade, the Soviets should benefit from international exchange because, other things being equal, they appear to be exporting goods in all categories for which they have a comparative cost advantage and importing goods in which they possess a comparative cost disadvantage. Second, and perhaps more revealing, Soviet imports are concentrated in consumer goods where they have the greatest comparative disadvantage, and Soviet exports are concentrated in producer goods where they have the greatest comparative advantage. Using the mean purchasing power parity value for all traded goods, 3.37 (line 3b, column 2), computed from the consumer import figure 4.84 (line 3a, column 3) and the producer export figure < 1.90 (line 3c, column 1), both valued in enterprise wholesale prices, Holzman's data indicate that the domestic cost of Soviet producer goods exports (line 5, column 1) is 44 percent below the cost of foreign substitutes, whereas the domestic cost of consumer goods imports exceeds foreign costs in like proportion (line 5, column 3). Computed in purchasers' prices, the dispar-

Table 7. *Soviet foreign trade purchasing power parity ratios for 1956*

| | Producer goods[a] | Weighted total | Consumer goods[b] |
|---|---|---|---|
| 1. Imports | | | |
|   a. Including turnover tax | 3.24 | 4.85 | 9.68 |
|   b. Excluding turnover tax | 3.24 | 3.63 | 4.84 |
| 2. Exports | | | |
|   a. Including turnover tax | 1.90 | 3.12 | 9.16 |
|   b. Excluding turnover tax | <1.90 | 2.47 | 4.58 |
| 3. Combined: variant I | | | |
|   a. Imports excluding turnover tax | — | — | 4.84 |
|   b. Export–import mean[c] excluding turnover tax | — | 3.37 | — |
|   c. Exports excluding turnover tax | <1.90 | — | — |
| 4. Equal world and domestic[d] relative prices (variant I) | 3.37 | 3.37 | 3.37 |
| 5. Deviation of domestic[e] from the world price (variant I) | −44% | — | +44% |
| 6. Combined: variant II | | | |
|   a. Imports including turnover tax | — | — | 9.68 |
|   b. Export–import mean including turnover tax | — | 5.79 | — |
|   c. Exports including turnover tax | 1.90 | — | — |
| 7. Equal world and domestic[f] relative prices (variant II) | 5.79 | 5.79 | 5.79 |
| 8. Deviation of domestic[f] from the world price (variant II) | −67% | — | +67% |

[a] Producer goods include coal, coke, petroleum products, ferrous metal products and alloys, nonferrous metals and products, chemicals, paints, varnish, cement, lumber and lumber products, and grain.
[b] Consumer goods include food, cigarettes, and industrial goods.
[c] This mean establishes the average ratio of domestic to world prices for producer good exports and consumer good imports. Producer goods are the predominant Soviet export, consumer goods the dominant Soviet import. If we were concerned with establishing the degree to which the ruble were overvalued however, the export ratio for producer goods, 1.90, should be used to approximate the ratio where domestic goods become competitive in the world market.
[d] If relative domestic prices equaled relative world prices, the only difference between domestic and world prices would be different unit measures for domestic and world prices, 3.37.
[e] The deviations reported here reflect the average difference in domestic Soviet relative prices for consumer good imports and producer good exports compared with world price relatives.
[f] Same as variant I, but computed in purchasers' prices, including turnover tax.
*Source:* Franklyn D. Holzman, "The Ruble Exchange Rate and Soviet Foreign Trade Pricing Policies, 1929–1961," in Holzman, *Foreign Trade under Central Planning,* Harvard University Press, Cambridge, Mass., 1974, pp. 248–50.

ity between the domestic cost and foreign cost of tradables increases to 67 percent; the purchasing power parity ratio for producer goods exports in this instance, 1.90, lies 67 percent below the mean value for all traded goods, 5.79 (line 6b, column 2), and the purchasing power parity ratio for consumer goods imports, 9.68 (line 6a, column 3), lies 67 percent above the mean.

These behavioral regularities, moreover, are not restricted to the broad commodity aggregates reported in Table 7. They are also displayed by the subaggregates that comprise the principal types of Soviet producer goods exports and consumer goods imports. This can be easily verified by consulting Holzman's original tables, which reveal that the purchasing power parity ratios of coke, coal, petroleum products, metals, machinery, and chemicals all fall below the minimum consumer good export parity, 4.58. Thus, nominal Soviet comparative advantage corresponds very closely with the pattern of domestic opportunity costs prevailing in 1960 (see Table 6).[24] Fuels, machinery, chemicals, and construction materials are nominal exportables; food, metals, and industrial consumer goods are nominal importables. The only group falling in a category inconsistent with computed opportunity costs is metals. This anomaly, however, was short-lived. By 1973, our opportunity-cost calculations show that metals had become exportables.

The significance of these correspondences, interesting as they are, however, is mitigated by the fact that our purchasing power parity calculations measure only nominal comparative advantage. Soviet prices determined according to diverse accounting formulas may misrepresent the real costs of production. The possibility cannot be overlooked that purchasing power parity relatives calculated with prices reflecting the forces of supply and demand might imply a different pattern of comparative advantage. Although this contingency needs to be borne in mind, two factors make it highly unlikely that the ratio of consumer to producer good prices is higher than the rate implied by domestic Soviet opportunity costs. First, as will be discussed in greater depth shortly, Soviet enterprise wholesale prices are tied directly to relative average production costs in Soviet industry. Second, although some disparity should be expected between our computed opportunity costs and Soviet enterprise wholesale prices, for a reversal in the direction of comparative advantage implied by the purchasing power parity ratios to occur, industrial wholesale prices would have to understate the opportunity cost of producer goods, and overstate the opportunity cost of consumer goods by 44 percent, the adjustment that would just bring domestic price relatives into line with world price relatives. If purchasers' prices including turnover tax are considered, domestic prices would have to *overstate* consumer goods prices by 67 percent.

Overstatements of consumer goods and understatements of producer goods prices of these magnitudes seem extremely implausible. In a comprehensive input–output study of the effect that adjusted factor cost pricing had on the relative value of producer and consumer good values measured in enterprise wholesale prices, it was determined that accounting prices did understate producer good costs and overstate consumer good costs. But the disparity even under the most extreme assumptions, where the rate of return on capital was set at 18 percent, was still under 1 percent.[25] The disparity for individual subsectors, such as fuel, metals, chemicals, machinery, construction materials, food, and light industry, is somewhat greater but in no case in excess of 20 percent.[26]

It can be concluded, therefore, on the basis of all the foregoing analysis that there is a wide dispersion in opportunity costs between producer and consumer goods in the Soviet Union, that accounting prices broadly reflect this discrepancy, and if adjusted factor costs validly establish the limits in which opportunity costs diverge from enterprise wholesale prices for the aggregate goods under discussion, then the observed pattern of Soviet foreign trade is consistent with the imperative of comparative advantage. More specifically, in both intra- and interbloc trade the Soviet Union enjoys a fundamental comparative advantage in fuels, metals, machinery, and chemicals, which should be considered as basic Soviet exportables, in contrast with food and light industrial products, which are comparatively disadvantageous and best classified as basic Soviet importables.

This characterization, although it appears persuasively consistent with the facts as they have been ascertained, requires two qualifications. First, it needs to be recognized that without direct knowledge of domestic opportunity costs prevailing in each CMEA member state, we cannot be sure that the structure of Soviet comparative advantage is as rational as it appears. For example, if production function analysis were to show that the East Europeans were lower-cost machinery producers and higher-cost light industrial manufacturers than the Soviets, natural resources aside, bilateral comparative advantage within the CMEA customs union would be the reverse of what it appears to be, measured in official CMEA foreign trade prices. In this particular hypothetical case, were the Soviets to differentiate their pattern of specialization according to noncompeting blocs, they would export light industrial goods to CMEA and import them from the West, following the reverse course with machinery. A highly complex multiregional trade pattern would then arise, necessitating an analysis far more subtle than has been the standard in the past.[27] Although this is an intriguing possibility, the very complexity of the problem makes it difficult to evaluate without unwarranted speculation until the necessary production function studies for Eastern Europe have been completed.

Another and related issue concerning the fundamental character of Soviet importables and exportables involves quality. The CES regression reported in Section IV treats the machinery sector as if it were a homogeneous entity. This, of course, glosses over qualitative differences of considerable importance. In particular, it is widely accepted that Western machinery is often technologically superior to Soviet machinery. The same assertion has also been advanced for Czechoslovakia and East German equipment. If it should turn out, as is likely, that the opportunity cost of sophisticated machinery is substantially lower in the West, in Czechoslovakia, and in East Germany than in the Soviet Union, then the fundamental Soviet comparative advantage in machine tools would seem to apply not to machinery in general but to relatively simple equipment amenable to the mass production techniques favored by the Soviets. In this case it should be anticipated that the Soviets might both import and export large volumes of machinery without actually infringing the logic of comparative advantage. Even a cursory glance at Table 11, which shows the trend in Soviet machinery trade with Eastern Europe expressed as the difference between the machinery share of exports and imports, demonstrates that the Soviets had been exporting a growing volume of machinery to Eastern Europe, moving toward a point where machinery exports and imports will be balanced. An investigation of the nomenclature of traded Soviet machinery revealed, moreover, that the Soviets import and export very different types of mechanical equipment, lending further support to our surmise that qualitative differences play an important part in determining the composition of Soviet machinery imports and exports.

What, then, can be said in sum about Soviet comparative advantage? First and foremost, changes in the structure of Soviet opportunity costs, although mitigating the deterioration in Soviet–CMEA trade terms, provide an incentive for trade diversion to the West. Second, taking both world and CMEA prices as a referent, domestic Soviet production costs make machinery and natural resources appear to be fundamental exportables and food and light industrial consumer goods fundamental importables. Finally, and more speculatively, although the Soviets probably do have a comparative advantage in many types of machinery, this is not likely to be the case for sophisticated technology-intensive equipment, which should be classified as a fundamental importable rather than as an exportable.

## VI. Official accounting prices, domestic opportunity costs, and comparative advantage

In Section V it was demonstrated that in all probability both nominal and real comparative advantage dictated that the Soviets export fuels, metals, machinery, and chemicals in exchange for food and light industrial goods. As we shall see shortly, the Soviet response to the basic structure of exchange opportunities confronting them was the appropriate one. But how could this have been achieved? Did they carry out an elaborate series of CES production function regressions? Did they rely on material balances or, as our discussion of administrative price planning suggests, were they somehow able to utilize official accounting prices to discern the changing pattern of comparative exchange advantage?

Part of the answer to this question has already been provided. Our analysis of Holzman's purchasing power parity estimates makes it perfectly clear that Soviet official accounting prices could have been used administratively to establish a pattern of trade consistent with comparative advantage. But foreign prices and domestic opportunity costs changed between 1956 and 1973. Although our single-factorial terms of trade analysis indicated that they largely offset each other, unless domestic prices were somehow tied to opportunity costs, planners would not be able to properly evaluate prevailing exchange opportunities. Could official accounting prices serve in this additional capacity as an effective indicator of changing opportunity costs?

To answer this question, let us briefly consider the principles upon which Soviet prices are formed. Official accounting prices are computed by taking average branch production costs, which include labor, depreciation, intermediate inputs, overhead, and profit; allocating them among all the outputs produced in the branch; and dividing the cost of each product by the number of units produced. Product prices therefore reflect both labor and capital costs, the former through the wage bill, the latter via depreciation, with both costs measured directly on own production and indirectly on intermediate inputs.[28] Although this approach does not take account of relative marginal capital and labor productivities, it does directly tie input volumes to output values, making relative prices in each sector inversely proportional to average productivity. Stated in this manner it is easily seen that sectors with relatively slow rates of productivity growth will experience increasing relative average costs compared with the more dynamic branches of the economy. As a consequence, when prices are periodically revised, infrequently as this may be, they will express the changing structure of average branch costs.[29]

Evidence of the inverse relationship between productivity and prices can be found in the official Soviet enterprise wholesale price series reported in Table 8. Two distinct periods need to be discerned, 1950–65 and 1967–73. During both intervals prices declined in the fuel, metal, chemical, machinery, and construction material sectors while increasing in the food industry. Light industrial prices fell in 1950–65 and rose in the latter period. In all cases the prices of the group identified earlier as basic exportables declined at least as rapidly as any of the sectors producing basic importables. Although the trend is most marked before 1967, when the average price of the sectors specializing in exportables declined 27 percent (2.1 percent per annum), compared with an increase of 11 percent (0.7 percent per annum) in basic importables, a similar pattern prevailed during 1967–73.

Table 8. *Wholesale prices for the basic branches of
Soviet industry* (1950 = 100)

|  | 1955 | 1965 | 1967 | 1973 |
|---|---|---|---|---|
| *Enterprise* (*excluding turnover tax*) | | | | |
| Fuels[a] | 80 | 75 | 115 | 114 |
| Metals | 85 | 85 | 126 | 125 |
| Chemicals | 80 | 79 | 79 | 76 |
| Machinery | 68 | 54 | 53 | 45 |
| Construction Material[b] | 83 | 92 | 111 | 110 |
| Light industry | 88 | 89 | 92 | 102 |
| Food | 100 | 151 | 153 | 158 |
| *Industrial* (*including turnover tax*) | | | | |
| Fuels[a] | 81 | 77 | 88 | 88 |
| Metals | 85 | 85 | 125 | 124 |
| Chemicals | 80 | 80 | 75 | 72 |
| Machinery | 68 | 58 | 56 | 47 |
| Construction material[b] | 72 | 72 | 86 | 86 |
| Light industry | 81 | 77 | 74 | 81 |
| Food | 71 | 76 | 74 | 75 |

[a] Fuels were computed by aggregating the electricity, petroleum, and coal price indices with weights derived from the 1966 Soviet input–output table.
[b] Construction materials were computed by aggregating the price indices of timber, paper, and construction materials, each component weighted equally.
*Source: Narodnoe khoziaistvo SSSR*, 1974, Statistika, Moscow, 1975, pp. 211–2. Both tables were normalized to a 1950 price base.

The regularity of these intraperiod price trends is, however, obscured if proper account is not taken of the major price reform of 1967. Reversing a long-standing policy of undervaluing natural resources production costs through the use of subsidies and other devices, the Soviets substantially increased the prices of metals and fuels in 1967. The price of coal rose 8 percent, ferrous metallurgy 50 percent, petroleum 38 percent, and electricity 33 percent. Although it is impossible to ascertain the precise basis on which these increases were determined, several factors having little to do with annual productivity trends clearly contributed to the rise in natural resource prices, including removal of subsidies and the implicit establishment of high rents for low-cost fuels through the equalization of energy prices per Btu.[30] If proper allowance is made for these extraordinary price adjustments, it seems probable that the trends which prevailed during 1950–65 and 1967–73 would characterize the entire period 1950–73, supporting our deduction that Soviet average factor cost prices are sensitive to the changing structure of sectoral factor productivity.[31]

From the standpoint of foreign trade decision making and the hypothesis that prices play a crucial role in determining the pattern of Soviet foreign trade, validation of the connection between average cost prices and sectoral productivity would be little comfort if the price reform of 1967 reversed the direction of comparative advantage. The evidence at hand, however, suggests that this probably was not the case. According to Treml's calculations in 1966, the ratio of domestic prices to the foreign price of Soviet exports was 1.25 for heavy industrial goods (metals, fuels, machinery, chemical, and construction materials) and 1.89 for light industrial products (textiles and food).[32] Simple extrapolation of these purchasing power parity ratios to 1967 using an unweighted average of increased producer good and consumer good prices shown in Table 8 (27 and 2 percent, respectively) brings these ratios to 1.59 and 1.93. If it is remembered that the enterprise wholesale price of consumer good imports is undoubtedly greater than consumer good exports, the disparity between producer and consumer good purchasing power parity ratios remains significant.

Additional evidence supporting the view that the 1967 price reform did not alter the nominal structure of comparative advantage is provided by Franklyn Holzman. His data for 1956 reveal that the turnover-tax-adjusted domestic import purchasing power parity for consumer goods (food, cigarettes, and light industrial products) was 4.84 compared with 2.11 for natural resources (coal, coke, petroleum products, iron, manganese ores, and ferrous and nonferrous metal products) valued in export prices.[33] The natural resource figure, an unweighted average, is somewhat inflated because it includes turnover tax on petroleum products. Nonetheless, if 1956 domestic Soviet natural resource parity is adjusted to 1973 with the official price series (ignoring changes in world prices), the resulting figure is only 3.07, substantially smaller than either the 1956 consumer good parity (4.84) or the adjusted 1973 figure (6.81), both based on enterprise wholesale prices.

Thus, it can be concluded with some confidence that whereas the 1967 price reform changed the structure of prices, the relationship of natural resource prices to consumer goods prices differed little in 1973 from those prevailing in 1956, and as a consequence official prices continued to indicate a steady Soviet comparative advantage in natural resources and a growing comparative advantage in chemicals and metals. However, and this is a crucial point, the relative domestic price of natural resources did rise substantially compared with other exportables. Although chemicals and metals remained exportables, if planners were sensitive to comparative price advantage, as we have maintained, it should be anticipated that the natural resource component of exports should have declined. Table 10 suggests that this is indeed the case, although the decline was of modest proportions. In this regard, however, it should be noted that after the price reform of 1967, the Soviets made it abundantly clear that as a quid pro quo for maintaining natural resource exports to CMEA, in the face of their revised estimates of natural resource costs, they wanted additional compensation in the form of financing for the exploration, exploitation, and transportation of fuels and other mineral raw material. Therefore, it seems fair to conclude that the 1967 reform in natural resource prices was an exception that proved the rule. Natural resource prices rose not because of a sudden fall in productivity, but because of a change in the price formation standard. Once the new basis was established, prices continued to change slowly along the lines indicated by changing opportunity costs, and after the once-and-for-all natural resource price standard adjustment, foreign trade planners moved to alter the composition of exportables in the appropriate way.

Needless to say, the foregoing discussion does not resolve the entire price issue. In addition to the question of the completeness of foreign trade price data, many problems remain. For example, whereas Zakharov informs us that Gosplan uses adjusted enterprise wholesale prices as the basis for deciding the commodity composition of trade, the foreign trade organizations use enterprise wholesale price for exports only, pricing imports at domestic purchaser's prices. There is a remote possibility that more than one price standard is employed to decide which goods should be considered importables and exportables. If this were the case, the price relationship reported above might not be appropriate and a further inquiry would be in order. It should also be borne in mind that the official machinery price index might exaggerate the actual fall in Soviet machinery export prices because of the way the Soviets treat new goods in their official machine price series.[34] It seems unlikely, however, that these problems or related issues, such as agricultural subsidies, would on further analysis significantly modify either the fundamental structure of comparative advantage already indicated by official prices or the link between sectoral productivity and average cost prices that connects our production function results with the price structure employed by planners in the determination of the composition of Soviet foreign trade. Thus, although it could hardly be argued that Soviet prices are optimal, they may serve to avoid gross irrationalities and may well be causally responsible for the overall sensibleness of Soviet intra- and interbloc commodity specialization.[35]

## VII. Comparative advantage and the evolving pattern of Soviet international commodity specialization

To establish that the postwar pattern of Soviet foreign trade has been shaped by comparative advantage, we have investigated changes in Soviet terms of trade, calculated domestic opportunity costs, computed

Table 9. *Postwar Soviet trade with CMEA and the West [compound annual rates of real volume growth (percent)]*

| | CMEA | | West | |
|---|---|---|---|---|
| Year | Imports | Exports | Imports | Exports |
| 1960–73 | 7.8 | 8.2 | 12.4 | 9.6 |
| 1970–3 | 8 | 4.5 | 21 | 12.7 |

*Source: Vneshniaia torgovlia,* various issues, Tables III and VIII. Estimates of real volume growth for the developed capitalist countries (West) are computed in two steps. Price inflation for all capitalist countries is calculated by forming the ratio of nominal to real import and export growth. These coefficients are then utilized to deflate nominal import and export growth of the developed capitalist countries reported in Table III.

single-factorial terms of trade, identified basic groups of exportables and importables, demonstrated a systematic connection between accounting prices and sectoral production costs, and elaborated a two-phase administrative procedure that explains how official prices are employed for the purpose of foreign trade decision making. All that remains now is to assemble and recapitulate the empirical evidence demonstrating that postwar trends in Soviet commodity specialization correspond with the imperatives of comparative advantage. Because estimates of domestic opportunity cost for individual CMEA states are unavailable, our analysis will be restricted to two issues, trade diversion and commodity structure, leaving the analysis of intra-CMEA bilateral relations for another study.[36]

Table 9 restates the evidence on trade diversion introduced earlier. It shows that trade exhibited a noticeable relative increase with the West compared to CMEA, accelerating markedly during 1971–3, both in imports and exports. This behavior is consistent with the deterioration in the Soviet–CMEA terms of trade reported in Table 2.

The data on the commodity structure of Soviet foreign trade are also consonant with the imperatives of comparative advantage, especially if proper weight is accorded to trends as well as the precise composition of importables and exportables. Notice, however, that this was not always so. Table 10 reveals that in 1955, at the inception of the post-Stalin era, the Soviets were net importers of machinery and net exporters of consumer goods to CMEA, at a time when Holzman's purchasing power parity estimates indicate that the opposite pattern should have prevailed.[37] Differences in machinery quality may have explained part of this anomaly but cannot be considered the whole explanation. By 1960, perhaps as a delayed response to the new economic order, the anomalous pattern existing in 1955 disappeared. Consumer goods became net imports and producer

Table 10. *Import and export trends in Soviet machinery, natural resource, food, and light industrial goods, 1955–73, with the CMEA (shares of total imports or exports in foreign trade rubles)*

| | Imports | | | | Exports | | | |
|---|---|---|---|---|---|---|---|---|
| Year | Machinery | Natural resources | Agriculture plus food | Light | Machinery | Natural resources | Agriculture plus food | Light |
| 1955 | 44.3 | 27.4 | 6.8 | 4.6 | 16.7 | 27.3 | 15.2 | 1.5 |
| 1960 | 43.2 | 15.9 | 6.5 | 18.3 | 12.7 | 39.7 | 16.2 | 2.4 |
| 1965 | 45.0 | 11.6 | 8.2 | 18.9 | 17.3 | 43.1 | 8.0 | 1.6 |
| 1970 | 45.2 | 7.1 | 8.8 | 20.3 | 20.8 | 40.7 | 6.7 | 1.7 |
| 1973 | 47.1 | 6.3 | 7.4 | 19.0 | 26.9 | 41.3 | 3.8 | 1.9 |
| 1973/1955 | +6% | −77% | +8% | +31% | +61% | +51% | −75% | +26% |

*Sources:* Paul Marer, *Soviet and East European Foreign Trade 1946–1969: Statistical Compendium and Guide,* Indiana University Press, Bloomington, Ind., 1972, and subsequent computer updates. The figures reported omit the unassigned residual in the commodity breakdown of foreign trade. It is widely believed that this category is composed primarily of weapons. Because of the uncertainty surrounding this question and the large impact that the residual might have on individual components of total trade, they have been omitted. For an alternative handling of this matter, see J. M. Montias, "The Structure of Comecon Trade and the Prospects for East–West Exchanges," in Joint Economic Committee, U.S. Congress, *Reorientation and Commercial Relations of the Economies of Eastern Europe,* Washington, D.C., 1974, pp. 662–81, and Barry Kostinsky, "Description and Analysis of Soviet Foreign Trade Statistics," Foreign Demographic Analysis Division, Bureau of Economic Analysis, Social and Economic Statistics Administration, U.S. Department of Commerce, Washington, D.C., 1974.

Table 11. *Net proportional exports in Soviet–CMEA trade, 1955–73 (valued in adjusted factor cost prices, assuming a 12% rate of interest)*

| Year | Machinery | Natural resources | Agriculture plus food | Light industry |
|---|---|---|---|---|
| 1955 | − 20.1 | − 0.1 | 8.3 | − 8.0 |
| 1960 | − 18.1 | 29.5 | 9.3 | − 33.8 |
| 1965 | − 16.3 | 39.5 | 0.8 | − 37.5 |
| 1970 | − 13.2 | 41.6 | − 0.7 | − 40.4 |
| 1973 | − 11.2 | 43.5 | − 2.4 | − 38.2 |

*Note:* Analyzing foreign trade structure is as much an art as a science. The concept of net proportioned exports measures the difference between the export share of a particular commodity and the equivalent import share. This formulation allows us to assess the pattern of trade without having to worry about bilateral trade imbalances. Where such imbalances are of concern for their own sake, absolute ruble values should be used. Note also that unassigned commodities usually classified as the residual are omitted from the commodity groups.
*Source:* See Table 2. See Steven Rosefielde, "Soviet Postwar Foreign Trade Policy: Stability and Metamorphosis," in J. Shapiro and P. Potichnyj, *From the Cold War to Detente,* Praeger, New York, 1976, pp. 122–43.

goods dominant net exports. In 1973, the new structure already apparent in 1960 had been significantly extended. Machinery had become an important export item, together with fuels, metals, and chemicals (included under natural resources), and consumer good exports had dwindled to a marginal level. On the import side, food and light industrial goods loomed large, together with machinery, whereas natural resources contracted to minor proportions.

Looking at the trend during 1955–70 we find that the natural resource import share fell 77 percent and the light industrial share rose 31 percent. Similarly, the export share of machinery increased 61 percent and natural resources 51 percent, whereas food declined 75 percent. The impression created by these figures is corroborated by the time trend of net proportional exports (the difference between the export and import share of each commodity) displayed in Table 11, which shows that the Soviets have intensified their specialization in natural resources and consumer goods and reduced their import dependence on foreign machinery, just as the empirical evidence suggests that they should have done. Interestingly, food and agriculture have switched from net exports to net imports.

It should be noted, however, that the net export proportions reported above do not correspond with Table 10. This is because Table 11 is valued in adjusted factor cost prices computed with a hypothetical 12 percent rate of return to capital.[38] These prices more nearly approximate domestic Soviet *purchasers'* prices than CMEA foreign trade rubles and thus better reveal how Soviet foreign trade decision makers perceive specialization at internal values.[39] As can be readily seen, light industrial consumer goods have a far more important place in Soviet trade valued in domestic opportunity cost prices than they do at world prices. Thus, if as has been asserted here, the Soviets are sensitive to comparative advantage, as evidenced by accounting costs, their internal measures of commodity specialization conform all the better with the theoretical implications of our calculated opportunity cost prices.

Taken together with the evidence on the overall composition of Soviet imports and exports and remembering that the bulk of Soviet machinery imports come from East Germany and Czechoslovakia, which both probably have a comparative advantage in sophisticated equipment, these trends indicate that the pattern of Soviet trade with CMEA has grown steadily more consistent with the fundamental pattern of Soviet comparative advantage. It appears that as economic factors came to play a more decisive role in Soviet foreign trade decision making, and as changing opportunity costs refracted through changes in domestic prices continued to justify the restructuring of Soviet trade in accord with the imperatives of comparative advantage, Soviet foreign trade planners embarked on an evolutionary program to rationalize their foreign trade behavior.

But what about the commodity composition of Soviet trade with the developed West? Are these bilateral exchanges also compatible with comparative advantage? Yes, although this is less obvious than one might have supposed. Paul Marer has shown using Western data that two-thirds of Soviet exports are regularly concentrated in nonfood agricultural raw materials and natural resources (SITC 2-4), whereas three-fourths of Soviet imports fall into the machinery and other manufactured-products group (SITC 6, 7, 8).[40] This ostensibly corroborates the fundamental pattern of Soviet comparative advantage, if as can hardly be doubted, the West is a relatively low cost producer of technology-intensive machinery.

However, Table 12, compiled from Soviet sources, presents an import series that conflicts with the straightforward picture drawn by Marer. Natural resources, for example (CTN 2-5), bulk surprisingly large in total Soviet imports and increase their share over time. The machinery import share starts out large as anticipated, but the trend unexpectedly declines. Can it be that the Soviets really believe that their true comparative advantage lies in importing natural resources? This would indeed be perverse because the Soviets overwhelmingly export natural resources to the West. Fortunately, this riddle has an easy solution. The Soviets only appear to be importing raw materials. Actually, they are importing sophisticated metal products and chemicals which are subsumed under the resource classification. For example, large-diameter petroleum transmission pipes

Table 12. *Import shares of machinery, natural resources, food, and industrial consumer goods in Soviet trade with the West, 1964–73*

| Year | Machinery | Natural resources | Food | Industrial consumer goods |
|------|-----------|-------------------|------|---------------------------|
| 1964 | 47.2 | 29.9 | 15.3 | 2.4 |
| 1965 | 38.4 | 44.1 | 9.4 | 4.7 |
| 1966 | 41.8 | 37.5 | 8.3 | 7.1 |
| 1967 | 40.0 | 38.8 | 2.5 | 12.6 |
| 1968 | 48.1 | 31.5 | 1.4 | 12.8 |
| 1969 | 47.5 | 29.4 | 1.2 | 11.1 |
| 1970 | 41.6 | 36.9 | 1.7 | 11.6 |
| 1971 | 36.2 | 39.7 | 2.9 | 10.6 |
| 1972 | 34.9 | 31.5 | 16.4 | 8.0 |
| 1973 | 32.1 | 28.0 | 24.6 | 4.6 |

*Note:* West here is defined as the United Kingdom, West Germany, Italy, France, Finland, Japan, and the United States.
*Source: Vneshniaia Torgovlia,* various issues 1964 through 1973.

are classified logically enough under metals, but for analytical purposes it would be misleading to interpret this product as unfabricated raw material.

When the distortion introduced by high-technology goods of an unconventional sort concealed in raw materials and semifabricates is removed, Marer is vindicated and the Soviets once again appear to behave sanely according to the logic of comparative advantage. The pattern of Soviet specialization in commodity trade viewed as a totality takes on a highly coherent form in which basic comparative advantage governs both intra- and interbloc exchange. As has been previously pointed out, this does not imply that a global equilibrium has been attained. Pressure for diverting trade away from CMEA is real and has manifested itself in increased Soviet commerce with the West, financed in significant part by exports of natural resources that would otherwise have been sold to CMEA. This pressure may also be intensified by the similarity of CMEA domestic production structures that may limit the gains from intrabloc trade. But this is merely conjecture. On its resolution, however, depends any ultimate judgment of the overall rationality of Soviet foreign trade behavior.

## VIII. Conclusion

Western appraisals of Soviet foreign trade are often cast in a disparaging light. McMillan and Gardner have claimed, for example, that the Soviets actually lose more from foreign trade than they gain.[41] Hewett describes the Soviet foreign trade model as primitive and autarkic. These may be extreme views, but they accurately reflect a widely held presumption that the Soviets do not align their trade with the dictates of comparative advantage.

Since 1973, however, when it was demonstrated using Leontief input–output factor proportions that Soviet bilateral exchange conformed surprisingly well with the strictures of Heckscher–Ohlin theory, the appropriateness of characterizing Soviet foreign trade behavior as primitive and autarkic has been increasingly called into question. The analysis carried out in this chapter extends and confirms my earlier findings. It demonstrates that the Soviets are not only capable of administratively calculating comparative advantage with the prices at their disposal, but that they arranged their pattern of trade accordingly during the period 1955–73.

### Appendix

*A. Data*

The data used in this chapter come from the SRI data bank and were compiled by Donald Green. The capital series is an updated version of Stanley Cohn's study, "The Economic Burden of Soviet Defense Outlays," in JEC, *Economic Performance and the Military Burden in the Soviet Union,* Washington, D.C., 1970, pp. 166–88. The labor series, which measures average annual employment, was developed by Stephen Rapawy and is published in Murray Feshbach and Stephen Rapawy, "Soviet Population and Manpower Trends and Policies," in JEC, *Soviet Economy in a New Perspective,* Washington, D.C., October 14, 1976, p. 137. Employment in adjusted worker-hours was also compiled by Rapawy. Donald Green, who worked very closely with these data, considered them unreliable, however. The use of adjusted worker-hours also poses a ticklish problem in evaluating productivity, because as Denison has shown, a reduction in the workday usually causes an increase in productivity per worker-hour. Nonetheless, both labor series were employed for estimating Soviet production functions. The results were sufficiently similar so that only those based on average annual employment are reported in Table 5. The sectoral output series was constructed by Rush Greenslade and Phyllis Wallace, "Industrial Production in the USSR," in JEC, *Dimensions of Soviet Economic Power,* Washington, D.C., 1962, pp. 115–36, and subsequently updated by Greenslade, "Industry Production Statistics in the USSR," in Vladimir Treml and John Hardt, eds., *Soviet Economic Statistics,* Duke University Press, Durham, N.C., 1972, pp. 155–94; Rush Greenslade and Wade Robertson, "Industrial Production in the USSR,"

Table A.1

| Sector | $\gamma$ | $\delta$ | $\rho$ | $\lambda$ | $\beta$ |
|--------|------|------|------|------|------|
| Fuels | 48.78 | 0.98 | 0.32 | 1.46 | $-0.2 \times 10^{-5}$ |
| Metals | 113.80 | 7.77 | 3.62 | 5.55 | $-0.81$ |
| Construction materials | 63.20 | 1.30 | 1.54 | 1.26 | $-0.2 \times 10^{-4}$ |
| Chemicals | 33.5 | 0.89 | 0.51 | 2.0 | $-1 \times 10^{-2}$ |
| Machinery | 33.89 | 0.67 | $0.1 \times 10^{-5}$ | 1.94 | $-2.04$ |
| Light | 31.91 | 2.90 | 1.12 | 1.74 | $-0.14$ |
| Food | 74.85 | 9.01 | 4.44 | 2.7 | $-0.3 \times 10^{-2}$ |

*Note:* With 23 degrees of freedom, the $t$ value for both tails at the 95% confidence interval is 2.069; for the 90% confidence interval, 1.645.

in JEC, *Soviet Economic Prospects for the Seventies,* Washington, D.C., June 27, 1973, pp. 270ff; and Rush Greenslade, "The Real Gross National Product of the USSR, 1950–75," in JEC, *Soviet Economy in a New Perspective,* Washington, D.C., October 14, 1976, pp. 269–300.

The choice of these data were determined by a desire to make the present study compatible with the SRI modeling project. To test the sensitivity of our opportunity cost calculations, official Soviet output data were substituted for the Greenslade–Wallace series. They make very little difference. One caveat is in order, however. In a recent CIA publication, "Estimated Soviet Defense Spending in Rubles 1970–1975," SR76-10121U, May 1976, it was revealed that Western estimates of Soviet military production were understated by several hundred percent. There is a real possibility that this error may affect the evaluation of both Western and official Soviet GNP series. Until this matter is resolved, no final judgment on the merit of our calculations or the comparative virtue of official versus Western output series can be made.

*B. Nomenclature*

The sectors employed in this study include the following activities:

1  Fuels: coal, oil, gas, and electric power
2  Metals: ferrous and nonferrous metals and metal semifabricates
3  Construction materials: forest products, paper and paper products, and construction materials
4  Machinery: civilian machinery and metalworking
5  Chemicals: organic and inorganic chemistry
6  Light industry: textiles, apparel, other light industrial goods
7  Food: processed vegetable and animal products

Omitted from consideration are construction, agriculture, transportation, communications, trade, and services.

## C. T Statistics

The $T$ statistics for the parameters estimated in Table 4 are presented in Table A.1. Kumar and Gapinski have demonstrated, however, that the parameters of the CES production function may not have a normal distribution. For this reason $T$ statistics, or more correctly pseudo $T$ statistics, are often referred to as "tongue-in-cheek" statistical tests.

## Notes

1 Abram Bergson, "The Geometry of Comecon Trade," *European Economic Review,* 14, 1980, 291–306.
2 Steven Rosefielde, *Soviet International Trade in Heckscher–Ohlin Perspective,* D. C. Heath, Lexington, Mass., 1973; Rosefielde, "Factor Proportions and Economic Rationality in Soviet International Trade 1955–1968," *American Economic Review,* 64, September 1974, 670–81; Rosefielde, "The Embodied Factor Content of Soviet International Trade: Problems of Theory, Measurement and Interpretation," *Association of Comparative Economic Systems Bulletin,* December 1973, 3–12; Rosefielde, "Foreign Trade Ruble Prices and the Heckscher–Ohlin Interpretation of Soviet Foreign Trade," *Association of Comparative Economic Systems Bulletin,* Fall 1976; C. H. McMillan, "Factor Proportions and the Structure of Soviet Foreign Trade," *Association of Comparative Economic Systems Bulletin,* Spring 1973, 57–82; C. H. McMillan, "More on the Factor Content of Soviet Trade," *Association of Comparative Economic Systems Bulletin,* Spring 1974, 56–58.
3 Steven Rosefielde, "Was the Soviet Union Affected by the International Economic Disturbances of the 1970s?" in Egon Neuberger and Laura Tyson, (eds.), *Transmission and Response: Impact of International Economic Disturbances on the Soviet Union and Eastern Europe,* Pergamon Press, New York, 1980.
4 See, for example, Edward A. Hewett, *Foreign Trade Prices in the Council for Mutual Economic Assistance,* Cambridge University Press, Cambridge, 1974, pp. 116–56. Hewett's interpretation is strongly influenced by his desire to differentiate the primitive Soviet material balance approach from the sophisticated, semioptimal, shadow price methods adopted in Poland and Hungary. The dichotomy is achieved, however, by exaggerating the efficacy of programming and understating the usefulness of accounting prices in an administrative price decision-making framework. Those interested in a more thorough discussion of material balances and programming methods as they bear on Soviet foreign trade planning should consult John Michael Montias, *Central Planning in Poland,* Yale University Press, New Haven, Conn., 1962, chap. 1; Montias, "Planning with Material Balances in Soviet-Type Economies," *American Economic Review,* 49, December 1959, 963–85; Montias, "On the Consistency and Efficiency of Central Plans," *Review of Economic Studies,* 29, October 1962. Also see Herbert Levine, "Input–Output Analysis and Soviet Planning," *American Economic Review,* 52, May 1962; and

Michael Ellman, *Soviet Planning Today: Proposals for an Optimally Functioning System,* Cambridge University Press, Cambridge, 1971, pp. 60–94; see esp. pp. 70–88.

5 Bezrukov and Chursin explicated their views at a conference on information systems held in Denver under the auspices of the National Bureau of Economic Research and the National Science Foundation in the summer of 1976.

6 Promotional goals refer to any and all strategies for achieving export market penetration abroad, including substantial price discounts from industrial wholesale prices.

7 Holzman points out that there are two interpretations of this phenomenon, the first (UN) attributing it to differences in domestic and foreign prices, which he calls "account of price differences," the second (Ivanov) ascribed to changes in real national product, "gross output of foreign trade." See Franklyn Holzman, "Foreign Trade in the GNP Accounts under Central Planning," in Franklyn D. Holzman, *Foreign Trade under Central Planning* Harvard University Press, Cambridge, Mass., 1974, pp. 319–21.

8 Holzman expresses serious reservations on this score.

> It seems pertinent to remark that if relative prices provide even a rough indication of domestic rates of substitution or transformation, then it would be highly irrational for the CPE's to export anything but producer goods, and import anything but consumer goods, thereby maximizing the gross output of foreign trade. Their failure to do just that suggests some recognition on their part that the relative values of consumer goods are overstated at retail prices. [Ibid., p. 328]

Although Holzman's reservations are well taken, the Soviets can avoid concentrating their imports and exports in consumer and producer goods by applying the two-phase administrative technique for simulating a market price adjustment process discussed above. See also Holzman, "Foreign Trade GNP Accounting Methodology in Centrally Planned and Capitalist Economies," in *Foreign Trade under Central Planning,* pp. 338–9.

9 Stanislav N Zakharov, *Raschyoty effektivnosti vneshne-ekonomicheskikh svyazei,* Ekonomika, Moscow, 1975, p. 31. Also on the related problem of efficiency indices, see S. Zakharov and V. Sulyagin, "Sistema ASOP-vneshtorg: tseli, zadachi, struktura," *Planovoe khozyaistvo,* no. 12, 1974, pp. 39–47. For a discussion of these issues in English, see Lawrence J. Brainard, "Soviet Foreign Trade Planning," in Joint Economic Committee, U.S. Congress, *Soviet Economy in a New Perspective,* Washington, D.C., October 1976, pp. 695–708.

10 On the Typical Method, see "Standard Methodology for Determining the Economic Effectiveness of Capital Investments," translated in the *ASTE Bulletin,* 13, Fall 1971, 25–36. For a discussion of the method, see Abram Bergson, *The Economics of Soviet Planning,* Yale University Press, New Haven, Conn., 1964, chap. 11; Alan Abouchar, "The New Soviet Standard Methodology for Investment Allocation," *Soviet Studies,* 24, January 1973, 402–410; and Phillip Bryson, *Scarcity and Control in Socialism,* Lexington Books, Lexington, Mass., 1976, pp. 105–110.

11 For a discussion of the application of production function analysis to Soviet data, see Rosefielde, *East–West Trade and Postwar Soviet Economic Growth: A Sector Production Function Approach,* SRI, Washington, D.C., 1976.

12 See ibid., chap. 3. Some basic articles in this literature include Martin Weitzman, "Soviet Postwar Economic Growth and Capital Labor Substitu-

tion," *American Economic Review,* 60, September 1970, 676–92; T. Kumar and E. Asher, "Soviet Postwar Economic Growth and Capital Labor Substitution: Comment," *American Economic Review,* 64, March 1974, 210–42; Rosefielde and Knox Lovell, "The Impact of Adjusted Factor Valuation on the CES Interpretation of Postwar Soviet Economic Growth," *Economica,* 44, November 1977, 381–92; Stanislaw Gomulka, "Soviet Postwar Industrial Growth, Capital Labor Substitution and Technical Changes: A Re-examination," In Zbigniew Fallenbuchl, *Economic Development in the Soviet Union and Eastern Europe,* vol. 2, Praeger, New York, 1976, pp. 1–47; and Padma Desai, "The Production Function and Technical Change in Postwar Soviet Industry: A Re-examination," *American Economic Review,* 66, June 1976, 372–81.

13  Rosefielde, *East–West Trade,* chap. 3.
14  Murray Brown, *On the Theory and Measurement of Technological Change,* Cambridge University Press, Cambridge, 1968, pp. 17–20.
15  Shadow prices of course are assumed to be directly proportional to marginal costs.
16  The issue of the relationship between factor prices and differential rates of factor growth in a multisector model was brought to my attention by J. M. Montias. The effect of commodity substitution on marginal factor productivities can be demonstrated graphically in the familiar Edgeworth–Bowley diagram, representing the situation before substitution begins but after the annual factor increments have been employed. The sides of the box represent

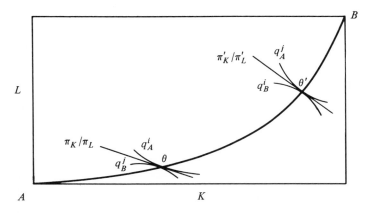

available factor supplies. The contract curve $AB$ is a locus of all efficiently produced combinations of goods manufactured in industries $A$ and $B$. Initially, the capital-intensive good $A$ is produced in relatively small amounts at point $\theta$, where the relative price of capital, the rapidly growing factor, is low. If, however, planners decided to increase output in the $A$ sector, the production point could slide along the production possibility frontier (contract curve) from $\theta$ to $\theta'$. Under these new conditions, even though the marginal productivity of capital had initially fallen due to the effect of factor growth, this decline might be offset by an increase in marginal capital productivity attributable to the substitution effect indicated in the diagram by the increased price of capital $(\pi'_K/\pi'_L > \pi_K/\pi_L)$.

Without detailed knowledge of the parameters of abstract technology prevailing in each sector, it is impossible to determine whether the rate of change in sectoral factor products will bias growth in any particular direction. To see this, one need only examine the second partial derivative of output with respect to either factor, which in addition to factor proportions and factor substitution elasticities depends on factor intensity parameters that may vary from sector to sector. Taking the simplest example,

$$Y = [\delta K^{-\rho} + (1 - \delta)L^{-\rho}]^{-1/\rho}$$

$$\partial Y/\partial K = (\cdot)^{-1/\rho-1}\delta K^{-\rho-1} > 0$$

$$\partial^2 Y/\partial K^2 = (1 + \rho)(\delta K^{-\rho-1})^2(\cdot)^{-1/\rho-2} + (\cdot)^{-1/\rho-1}(-\rho - 1)\delta K^{-\rho-2}$$

$$= [(1 + \rho)\delta K^{-\rho-2}(\cdot)^{-1/\rho-1}][\delta K^{-\rho}(\cdot)^{-1} - 1]$$

$$= [(1 + \rho)\delta K^{-\rho-2}(\cdot)^{-1/\rho-1}(\cdot)^{-1}][\delta K^{-\rho}(\cdot)^{-1}(\cdot)^1 - (\cdot)^1]$$

$$= [(1 + \rho)\delta K^{-\rho-2}(\cdot)^{-1/\rho-2}][\delta K^{-\rho} - \delta K^{-\rho} - (1 - \delta)L^{-\rho}]$$

$$= \frac{-\delta(1 - \delta)}{\sigma} L^{-\rho}K^{-\rho-2}[K^{-\rho} + (1 - \delta)L^{-\rho}]^{-1/\rho-2} < 0$$

17  Rosefielde, *East–West Trade,* pp. 50–60, and Rosefielde, "Production Functions and the Estimation of Opportunity Costs in Centrally Planned Economies," unpublished manuscript, 1979.

18  For a discussion of the conceptual and statistical problems involved in evaluating the meaning and reliability of CES parameters derived from nonlinear multivariate regressions, especially their nonnormal properties, see Rosefielde, *East–West Trade,* pp. 25–44.

19      $$Y = \gamma \exp(\lambda t + \beta t^2)[\delta K^{-\rho} + (1 - \delta)L^{-\rho}]^{-1/\rho}$$

$$\partial Y/\partial K = -1/\rho\gamma \exp(\lambda t + \beta t^2)(\cdot)^{-1/\rho-1}(-\rho\delta K^{-\rho-1})$$

As

$(\cdot)^{-1} = \gamma^{-\rho} \exp[-\rho(\lambda t + \beta t^2)]Y^\rho$     (derived by raising the original production function to the $\rho$th power)

then

$$\partial Y/\partial K = \delta\gamma^{-\rho} \exp[-\rho(\lambda t + \beta t^2)]Y^{1+\rho}K^{-(1+\rho)}$$
$$= \delta\gamma^{-\rho} \exp[-\rho(\lambda t + \beta t^2)](Y/K)^{1+\rho}$$

and given that $1/\sigma = 1 + \rho$,

$$\partial Y/\partial K = \delta\gamma^{-\rho} \exp[-\rho(\lambda t + \beta t^2)](Y/K)^{1/\sigma}$$

20  For a detailed discussion of the meaning of opportunity costs computed in this way, see Rosefielde, "Production Functions."

21  The exact pattern of opportunity costs varies with the assumptions made about input proportions. Alternative results are reported in Rosefielde, ibid. By and large they are remarkably consistent, but the reader interested in assessing their implications for comparative advantage in greater detail is directed to this source.

22  Franklyn Holzman, "The Ruble Exchange Rate and Soviet Foreign Trade Pricing Policies, 1929–1961," in Holzman, *Foreign Trade under Central Planning,* pp. 243–68. In my article, "International Trade Theory and Practice under Socialism," *Journal of Comparative Economics,* 1, Spring 1977, I suggested that the figures in this study might have been at variance with input–output data published subsequently. After a lengthy exchange with Vladimir Treml and Holzman, I am now convinced that the discrepancies which exist can all be attributable to intractable problems involved in allocating residual

goods in Soviet foreign trade statistics. In view of this it should be noted that the conclusions drawn from Holzman's data will be roughly compatible with the data presented by Treml in *The Structure of the Soviet Economy*, Praeger, New York, 1972, pp. 159–66, and "Conversion of Soviet Input–Output Tables to Producers' Prices: The 1966 Reconstructed Table," *Foreign Economic Reports*, No. 1, U.S. Department of Commerce, BEA, Washington, D.C., 1973, p. 115.

23  Treml, "Conversion of Soviet Input–Output Tables." The ratio of consumer good/ producer good prices for imports and exports calculated by Holzman for 1956 are 2.98 and 2.41; Treml's estimates for 1966 are 2.31 and 1.50, respectively. His range of estimates for 1959 are 1.03 to 2.27 and 1.69 to 2.85 (personal correspondence). In all cases these figures refer to purchasing power parity ratios using industrial wholesale prices to value domestic exports and purchasers' prices for imports.

24  Holzman, "Ruble Exchange Rate," pp. 248–50.

25  See Steven Rosefielde, "The Effect of Adjusted Factor Cost Valuation on the Interindustry Structure of Soviet National Product," unpublished manuscript, p. 11.

26  Ibid., p. 13. Incidentally, it is interesting to note that fuels and metals were the two most undervalued sectors. This is compatible with the aforementioned increase in fuel and metal prices in the 1967 reform.

27  Behavior of this sort is consistent with Holzman's interpretation of CMEA as a Soviet bloc customs union. See Holzman, "Soviet Foreign Trade Pricing and the Question of Discrimination," in Holzman, *Foreign Trade under Central Planning*, pp. 269–91.

28  Joseph Berliner has pointed out that capital charges introduced after 1965 are treated as a deduction from profits and therefore may not systematically alter the structure of pre-reform prices. See Berliner, *The Innovation Decision in Soviet Industry*, MIT Press, Cambridge, Mass., 1976, p. 243.

29  For a full discussion of Soviet price formation practice, see ibid., pp. 240–5. Regarding the frequency of price changes, Berliner writes:

> In the periods between general price revisions, specific groups of prices may be revised from time to time. Such partial revisions may occur when a great many new products have been introduced since the last general price revision, or when a general review of quality standards has taken place. It may also be called for by changes in cost conditions in some industries which cause earned profits to fall far below or above planned profit rates. [P. 245]

All these causes are legitimately related to sectorial productivity.

30  *Ibid.*, pp. 242–4, 307.

31  In the last few years a great deal has been written about hidden inflation caused by the fictitious introduction of new products especially in the machinery sector. The extent of the distortion caused by fictitious innovation is highly conjectural. It should be noted, however, that even if the machinery price trend is understated, the observed price movements are still in the right direction from the standpoint of our productivity hypothesis. For a fuller discussion of these issues, see Berliner, ibid., pp. 235–296; Abraham Becker, "The Price Level of Soviet Machinery in the 1960's," *Soviet Studies*, 26 July 1974, 363–79; David H. Howard, "A Note on Hidden Inflation in the Soviet Union," *Soviet Studies*, October 1976, 599–608; Steven Rosefielde, "A Comment on David Howard's Estimation of Hidden Inflation in the Soviet

Retail Sales Sector," *Soviet Studies,* 32, July 1980, 423–7; and Rosefielde, "Are Soviet Industrial Production Statistics Significantly Distorted by Hidden Inflation?" *Journal of Comparative Economics,* July 1981.

32  Treml, "Conversion of Soviet Input–Output Tables," p. 115.

33  Holzman, "Ruble Exchange Rate," pp. 248–50.

34  See note 31.

35  It should be clearly understood that the foregoing discussion neither implies that the bill of goods and services is even roughly socially desirable, nor that the underlying wage rates correspond with the marginal social products of labor. All that is being asserted is that Soviet accounting cost prices are rank-correlated with CES shadow prices. Those concerned with the deep welfare issues raised here are directed to Abram Bergson's *Essays in Normative Economics,* Harvard University Press, Belknap Press, Cambridge, Mass., 1966, esp. pp. 3–26.

   Similarly although the evidence provided above supports the contention that prices are linked to sectoral productivities, it does not preclude the possibility that the same results might have been obtained through material balances or other alternative techniques. However, for the record, I doubt that alternative techniques were actually utilized.

36  Some important suggestive evidence on the economic rationality of bilateral Soviet commodity specialization can, however, be found in Rosefielde, "Factor Proportions."

37  It should be noted regarding the composition of traded goods in 1956 that Holzman's detailed price-ratio-variance computations demonstrated that there was no correlation between purchasing power parity ratios for individual commodities and the quantities in which goods were traded. If our analysis is correct, a counterpart study for the current mix of traded goods would exhibit a positive correlation for importables and an inverse correlation for exportables. See Holzman, "Ruble Exchange Rate," pp. 260–7.

38  Rosefielde, *The Transformation of the 1966 Soviet Input–Output Table from Producers to Adjusted Factor Cost Values,* G. E. Tempo, Washington, D.C., 1975, GE75TMP-47; and Rosefielde, "Soviet Postwar Foreign Trade Policy: Stability and Metamorphosis," in J. Shapiro and P. Potichnyj, *From the Cold War to Detente,* Praeger, New York, 1976, pp. 122–43.

39  For an analysis of the relationship between adjusted factor cost and producers' and purchasers' prices, see Steven Rosefielde, "Effect of Adjusted Factor Cost Valuation."

40  See Paul Marer, *Postwar Pricing and Price Patterns in Socialist Foreign Trade (1946–1971),* International Development Research Center, Indiana University, Bloomington, Ind., 1972.

41  McMillan, "Factor Proportions." Hewett arrived at a similar conclusion in "Prices and Resource Allocation in Intra-CMEA Trade," in Alan Abouchar (ed.), *The Socialist Price Mechanism,* Duke University Press, Durham, N.C., 1977, pp. 95–128. H. Stephen Gardner synthesizes their work in "The Factor Content of Soviet Foreign Trade: A Synthesis," *Association for Comparative Economic Studies Bulletin,* 21, Summer 1979, 1–16. McMillan's results were obtained by valuing imports and exports in foreign prices that do not reflect domestic opportunity costs and therefore misstate gains and losses from trade. Hewett converts capital into labor equivalents and works with what is in effect a one-factor Marxian labor model. For a detailed discussion of the deficiencies of these calculations, see Steven Rosefielde, "Is the Embodied Factor Content of Soviet Foreign Trade Hyper-irrational?" *Association for Comparative Economic Studies Bulletin.* 21, Summer 1979, 19–51.

# Part II

**Economic Welfare**

# 9  Bergsonian welfare economics

*Paul A. Samuelson*

As I write, the new welfare economics is just over four decades old. This subject, in its essentials as we know it today, was born when the 24-year-old Abram Bergson – then still a Harvard graduate student – wrote his classic 1938 *Quarterly Journal of Economics* article. To one like myself, who before 1938 knew *all* the relevant literature on welfare economics and just could not make coherent sense of it, Bergson's work came like a flash of lightning, describable only in the words of the pontifical poet:

> Nature and Nature's laws lay hid in night:
> God said, Let Newton be! and all was light.

King Alphonse claimed that if he had been in on the Creation, he could have done a better job. By sheer good luck, as a fellow graduate student and comrade at arms, I *was* in on Bergson's creation: but time has shown that I have not been able to do a better job of it; nor, I believe, has anyone else[1] – and this despite the quite confused rumors that Kenneth Arrow's Impossibility Theorem rendered Bergson's "social welfare function" somehow nonexistent or self-contradictory.

Here I hope to set the record straight as only a living witness and participant can. After a few introductory sections that sketch the historical setting of modern welfare economics, I provide under the heading "Existence and Property of a Bergsonian Social Welfare Function" an analytical exposition of some of the fundamentals of the Bergsonian welfare economics.

## Conception and gestation

Mine was the best spectator's seat for Bergson's creative travail. I was the coarse stone against which he honed his sharp axe – the semiabsorbing, semireflecting surface against which he bounced off his ideas.

I owe thanks to the National Science Foundation for financial aid, and to Aase Huggins and Kate Crowley for editorial assistance.

223

"What can Pareto mean by this 1898 use of the French singular when he speaks of 'the social optimum'?" Bergson would ask himself and me. In the end the innovator demonstrated the wisdom of what Gertrude Stein was to declare on her deathbed: "What is the question?" points the way to what is the answer.

From 1930 to 1938 a host of writers were rediscovering in an unsystematic way the finding of John Stuart Mill, Edgeworth, Pareto, and other earlier writers – that those who lose from various deviations from ideal free-trade situations can bribe or buy off those who gain, so that there does exist a movement from the status quo which by unanimity *could* make *everyone* better off. Prominent among such rediscoverers of "compensationism" were Abba Lerner, Harold Hotelling, Jacob Viner, Nicholas Kaldor, R. F. Harrod, John Hicks, myself, and many others. The *necessary condition(s)* for an optimum, that such a *universal* improvement *not* be possible, Ian Little came in 1950 to call "Pareto optimality," a felicitous and useful coinage. But just what accomplishment this necessary condition was necessary for, that question was not clarified until 1938 when Bergson defined and clarified the concept of an *individualistic social welfare function* – which ethically orders the various states of the world and which lets "individual tastes 'count,'" in the sense of agreeing with individuals' orderings *when those orderings are unanimous* and *resolving them ethically* when they are not unanimous."

The skeleton key to understanding provided by Bergson in 1938 was logically what mathematicians call a "weakly separable function." Thus, for (bread$^1$, wine$^1$) and (bread$^2$, wine$^2$) the "private goods" consumed respectively by two nonenvying and nonsympathizing people, Person$^1$ and Person$^2$, the Bergson (individualistic and ordinal) Social Welfare Function (BISWF), could be described by the separable indicator function

$$W = w[U^1(\text{bread}^1, \text{wine}^1), U^2(\text{bread}^2, \text{wine}^2)]$$
$$w[A^1, A^2] \geq w[B^1, B^2] \quad \text{if } A_1 \geq B_1, A_2 \geq B_2$$
$$U^i(a_1^i, a_2^i) \geq U^i(b_1^i, b_2^i) \quad \text{if } a_1^i \geq b_1^i, a_2^i \geq b_2^i \quad (i = 1, 2) \quad (1)$$

As I shall explicate, any one cardinal indicator of ethical preferences such as that above can be replaced by an infinity of different renumberings or stretchings of the $w[\cdot]$ and $U^i(\cdot)$ functions. (Indeed, to underline the completely *ordinal* nature of the BISWF, my analytical account shows that it can be given solely in *indifference-contour and marginal-rate-of-substitution* form; and it is also expressed in terms of a "complete ordering" symbolism à la Debreu.)

This concept of the social welfare function enabled one to understand for the first time the germ of truth in Adam Smith's paradigm of the Invisible Hand: namely, that when conditions of returns and tastes, nonexternalities, and nonmonopolies are right, the algorithm of Walrasian competition can be combined with the device of ideal lump-sum transfers to achieve the maximum of a prescribed well-behaved individualistic social welfare function.

It took more than a decade after 1938 for the Bergsonian message to be understood within the profession. For a long time scholars confused two versions of the New Welfare Economics:

1. The narrow version that emphasized and stopped short at "compensation payments" made by gainers to losers (or determined to be *capable* of being made, *even if not actually made*) – an approach that when stripped of its pretensions was revealed to merely catch up to the concept of Pareto optimality.

2. Bergson's synthesis of the Old Welfare Economics of the additive-hedonistic type with the more general notion of a Social Welfare Function that introduces, from outside positivistic economic science, ethical norming of alternative states of the world. Within this broad genus, interest attaches to those species that involve ethics of *individualistic* type rather than of *paternalistic* type. Benthamite hedonism is only one of many varieties within the individualistic species. Bergson not only clarified the relationship of this general New Welfare Economics to the previous Old Welfare Economics; but, as well, his 1938 analysis enabled scholars to understand how the narrow "New Welfare Economics" of Hicks, Kaldor, Scitovsky, and a dozen others reached only the state of necessary conditions rather than that of necessary-and-sufficient conditions. By means of Bergson's analysis, the practioners of the narrow welfare economics could not only apprehend the crucial distinction between necessary condition(s) and sufficient condition(s) – but he also provided them with an understanding of for what the sufficient conditions may suffice.

## Prior history

The Old Welfare Economics flourished in the nineteenth century. Bentham, Sidgwick, and the general run of neoclassical economists – Edgeworth, Marshall, Wicksell, Böhm-Bawerk, Walras, Carver, and Pigou – believed that cardinal utility was a scientifically definable magnitude for each person. With appropriate interpersonal constants these intrapersonal utilities could be added to form Total Social Utility, a magnitude that manifestly ought to be maximized.

Most neoclassical economists remained confused on what this all implied for laissez-faire. Many vulgarly believed that this mandated laissez-faire. Bastiat, L. von Mises, and lesser lights are examples. Some – Wicksell is a good example – realized that only *after* the initial distribution of endowments of dollar-voting power were *ethically proper* would that which perfect competition accomplished be a desirable accomplishment.[2] Still others were confused.[3]

I have recorded somewhere in print how in the year 1935 as a puzzled student I could not get satisfactory answers anywhere in the Harvard Yard or the University of Chicago quadrangle to the simple question: "Exactly why is it *right* for price to equal marginal cost?" Jacob Viner, Frank Knight, Joseph Schumpeter, Wassily Leontief, Paul Sweezy, and other leading economists of the time had written material with a bearing upon this question. But none could give me a clear understanding. Lest it be thought that my own experience was singular, recall that several years later Ragnar Frisch could engage in a public controversy with Harold Hotelling concerning the cogency of what Hotelling had alleged in this regard. When Thomas Kuhn comes to amplify his taxonomy of *The Structure of Scientific Revolutions,* he will find that in addition to the division between scholars who believe in conflicting paradigms, there is always a normal state of science in which confusion and ambiguity play a role.

This unsatisfactory state of the Old Welfare Economics reached a climax with the 1932 publication of Lionel Robbins's *An Essay on the Nature and Significance of Economic Science.* This well-written and brief work fit in with the postivistic strain of modern times. Darwin and Biblical criticism contributed to the decay of Victorian religious orthodoxy. By the end of the century, positivism is well represented in the passionate writings of Vilfredo Pareto. The time was overripe within the Anglo-Saxon tradition for nihilistic questioning of the inherited Bentham–Edgeworth hedonistic utilitarianism. When Robbins sang out that the emperor had no clothes – that you could not prove or test by any empirical observations of objective science the normative validity of comparisons between different persons' utilities – suddenly all his generation of economists felt themselves to be naked in a cold world. Most of them had come into economics seeking the good. To learn in midlife that theirs was only the craft of a plumber, dentist, or cost accountant was a sad shock.

It was to salvage something from the ruins that the narrow new welfare economists worked toward the concept of production efficiency and consumption efficiency. Actually, as we now know, these various concepts of Pareto optimality were not only already in Pareto's post-1894 writings, but in fact with care we can detect in the works of J. S. Mill, Ricardo, and other early writers explicit glimpses of the notion that interferences with competition bring gains to those who benefit which are less in an objective sense than the losses brought to those who suffer. That this may be so is the germ of truth not quite isolated by Adam Smith when enunciating his doctrine of the Invisible Hand.

The Invisible Hand doctrine cannot cogently be used to deduce the optimality of laissez-faire, although many have fallen into this confusion. What is saying the same thing, the Pareto-optimality property of competitive equilibrium is no theoretical argument for laissez-faire, and is in many situations no cogent practical argument for favoring the use of competition. After Bergson laid the foundations for modern welfare economics in 1938, all these issues could be properly sorted out.

I do not think it is interesting at this point to review the pretentious claims made for the narrow version of compensationist economics and the retreats that subsequently had to be made. Nor is it useful to go into the various tests proposed by Hicks and Kaldor, Scitovsky, and myself to determine whether a particular policy change is or is not a good thing.

Although the matter is not clearly thought out, what gives some lasting relevance to this muddled literature was its tacit dependence upon a vague asymptotic theorem of the following sort.

> *Heuristic theorem.* Most technical changes or policy choices directly help some people and hurt others. For some changes, it is possible for the winners to buy off the losers so that everyone could conceivably end up better off than in the prior status quo. Suppose that no such compensatory bribes or side payments are made, but assume that we are dealing with numerous inventions and policy decisions that are quasi-independent. Even if for each single change it is hard to know in advance who will be helped and who will be hurt, in the absence of known "bias" in the whole sequence of changes, there is some vague presumption that a hazy version of the law of large numbers will obtain: so as the number of quasi-independent events becomes larger and larger, the chances improve that any random person will be on balance benefited by a social compact that lets events take place that push out society's utility possibility frontier, even though any one of the events may push some people along the new frontier in a direction less favorable than the status quo.

My language and logic have purposely been left fuzzy to model the actual thought processes economists muddled through some four decades back.

### Dissemination of Bergsonian welfare economics

One of the first to follow Bergson's road was Oskar Lange in his 1942 *Econometrica* article, "Foundations of Welfare Economics." This unnecessarily stressed *additive* hedonism of the BSWF, what the mathematician calls "strong separability" rather than "weak separability." Evidently, Lange had not yet freed himself from his mid-1930s misconception that cardinal measurement of utility was intrinsically necessary for welfare economics.

My *Foundations of Economic Analysis* treatment of welfare economics in Chapter 8 still reads as a convenient summary of the Bergsonian *Weltanschauung*. Jan van de Graaf's *Theoretical Welfare Economics* (1957) provides an elegant and useful treatment of the same subject. Bergson's own 1966 *Essays in Normative Economics* not only reproduces his 1938 classic but also contains valuable extensions and further developments.

In my writing on the subject, here and elsewhere, the reader will notice that I have not shown much interest in the process by which particular social welfare functions arise and are deemed to be of interest or relevance. I have been satisfied to consider it not to be the task of economics as such to pass judgments on whether this social welfare function is in some sense more important than that social welfare function. Abram Bergson's writings show that he has been interested in exploring the topics that I have been content to turn over to disciplines other than my own.

In completing this general introduction to the analytical discussion that follows, I should not ignore an important misunderstanding of welfare economics and of Bergsonian welfare economics. In 1951, Kenneth Arrow published his classic, *Social Choice and Individual Values*. This founded an important branch of mathematical politics and has spawned some hundreds of papers on social choice. In particular, Arrow proved the impossibility of existence of a well-behaved "Constitutional Function," one that was supposed to provide an answer in the way of decision to any ballots given as inputs by $K$ individuals who are permitted to vote according to *any and all possibilities of the rankings of various states of the world*. This Impossibility Theorem is a landmark in the history of ideas. It ends for all time our hope that there exists some ideal form of democracy, one that has eluded us up to this time but can be found in the future if only we continue an intelligent search for it. Arrow has earned a Nobel Prize at least twice over – once for his important breakthroughs in the economics of risk bearing, and once for this Impossibility Theorem in the theory of social choice.

Unfortunately, what I and Bergson and Ian Little have called a "Constitutional Function" – other and perhaps better names could be given to it – Arrow happened to call a "social welfare function." He used the same name for his unicorn that Bergson and other writers had used for their existent animals. So it is not particularly surprising that Arrow's readers, learning that he had proved the impossibility of a "social welfare function," should have formed the mistaken inference that there cannot exist a reasonable and well-behaved Bergsonian social welfare function.

By now this has all been sorted out in the advanced literature. But plenty of signs still abound that the misunderstanding lives on. All I can do is call attention once again to this spurious matter of confusion.[4] The rest of this chapter analyzes the content of Bergsonian welfare economics.

### Existence and property of a Bergson social welfare function

1. To be brief, I start with the case of $j = 1, 2, \ldots, J$ "private" goods, each to be split up among $k = 1, 2, \ldots, K$ men. Man $k$ has the consumption vector $(x_1^k, \ldots, x_J^k) = \mathbf{x}^k$. A *state of the world* is given by $\mathbf{x} = (\mathbf{x}^1; \mathbf{x}^2; \ldots; \mathbf{x}^K) = (x_1^1, \ldots, x_J^1; x_1^2, \ldots, x_J^2; \ldots; x_1^K, \ldots, x_J^K) = (x_j^k)$

A *Bergsonian social welfare function* (BSWF) is a *complete order* that ethically orders all the states of the world. Thus, if there are many states of x, given by a, b, c, ..., between every pair of states, we have a relationship "at least as good ethically as," written as $\succeq$, which is transitive. With standard technicalities understood, we have a *complete binary ordering* that obeys *transitivity*.

$\alpha$ For *any* pair, say a and b, just one of the three cases holds:

$\quad$ $\mathbf{a} \succeq \mathbf{b}$ and $\mathbf{b} \succeq \mathbf{a}$: "indifference" ($\mathbf{a} \sim \mathbf{b}$, $\mathbf{b} \sim \mathbf{a}$)

$\quad$ $\mathbf{a} \succeq \mathbf{b}$ and not $\mathbf{b} \succeq \mathbf{a}$: "strong preference" ($a > b$)

$\quad$ $\mathbf{b} > \mathbf{a}$ and not $\mathbf{a} \succeq \mathbf{b}$: "strong preference" ($b > a$)

$\quad$ (Thus, $\mathbf{a} \sim \mathbf{a}$; etc.)

$\beta$ For any three states,

$\quad$ $\mathbf{a} \succeq \mathbf{b}$ and $\mathbf{b} \succeq \mathbf{c}$ implies that $\mathbf{a} \succeq \mathbf{c}$

$\quad$ ($\mathbf{a} \succeq \mathbf{b}$ and $\mathbf{b} > \mathbf{c}$ implies that $\mathbf{a} > \mathbf{c}$; $\mathbf{a} > \mathbf{b}$ and $\mathbf{b} \succeq \mathbf{c}$ implies that $\mathbf{a} > \mathbf{c}$; etc.)

There need not exist a scalar function $z(\mathbf{x})$ with the property that $\mathbf{a} \sim \mathbf{b}$ if and only if $z(\mathbf{a}) = z(\mathbf{b})$. However, if the sets that satisfy $\mathbf{x} \succeq \mathbf{a}$ and $\mathbf{a} \succeq \mathbf{x}$ have specified simple topological properties, there will always exist an infinity of such $z(\mathbf{x})$ functions, each such "cardinal welfare indicator" being a monotone stretching of any other – as with $Z(\mathbf{x}) = f[z(\mathbf{x})]$, $f'[z] > 0$.

For us it will do if *each* state x can be found to be ethically indifferent to a state in which *every person gets the same scalar number of units, z, of every good*. Thus, we posit a root for $z$ of the relation

$$(x_1^1, \ldots, x_J^1; \ldots; x_1^K, \ldots, x_J^K) \sim (z, \ldots, z; \ldots; z, \ldots, z)$$
$$(1.1)$$

This then defines a ("nonsubjective") "scalar indicator" of ethical welfare, $z(x_1^1, \ldots, x_J^1; \ldots; x_1^K, \ldots, x_J^K)$. For brevity, assume that $z(\cdot)$ is a smooth twice-differentiable function of its $KJ$ arguments, with partial derivatives $\partial z / \partial x_j^k$:

$$\text{grad } z \quad = \nabla z(\mathbf{x}) = [z_j(\mathbf{x})] \tag{1.2}$$
$$\text{Hessian } z = \nabla^2 z(\mathbf{x}) = [z_{ij}(\mathbf{x})] \tag{1.3}$$

*Remark.* Since units of goods are arbitrary, so is this $z$ metric. But any choice of units – tons rather than loaves of bread, drops rather than quarts of wine, . . . . – will serve indifferently. (If some subsets of goods had been irreplaceable for life, a $z$ root would not always have had to exist. I also ignore lexigraphic orderings and other well-known complications.) Until later sections I have no need for the $z(\cdot)$ function.

2. Now we focus down from the general BSWF to the narrow *individualistic* BISWF. Let the men first be *atoms – sans* envy or altruism. Man $k$ has "tastes" that depend only on his $\mathbf{x}^k$ and not on others' $\mathbf{x}^s$ when $s \neq k$. He has "his" complete ordering of states of the world, written as $\overset{k}{\geq}$. This has the properties $\alpha$ and $\beta$ above (but of course generally does not give the *same* decisions about points as the ethical ordering $\geq$ did). Being atomistic, he has

if
$$(\mathbf{b}^1; \mathbf{b}^2; \ldots; \mathbf{b}^k; \ldots; \mathbf{b}^K) \overset{k}{\geq} (\mathbf{a}^1; \mathbf{a}^2; \ldots; \mathbf{a}^k; \ldots; \mathbf{a}^K)$$

$$(\mathbf{c}^1; \ldots; \mathbf{c}^{k-1}; \mathbf{b}^k; \mathbf{c}^{k+1}; \ldots; \mathbf{c}^K) \overset{k}{\geq} (\mathbf{c}^1; \ldots; \mathbf{c}^{k-1}; \mathbf{a}^k; \mathbf{c}^{k+1}; \mathbf{c}^K)$$

for *any* $(\mathbf{c}^1; \mathbf{c}^2; \ldots; \mathbf{c}^{k-1}; \mathbf{c}^{k+1}; \ldots; \mathbf{c}^K)$. So to speak, for man $k$, there is essential relevance only for "his own" $J$-dimensional subspace, $(x_1^k, \ldots, x_J^k)$, out of the $KJ$-dimensional full space, $(x_1^1, \ldots, x_J^1; \ldots; x_1^k \ldots; \ldots x_J^k)$. This means that we can record *all* intraperson information about the $K$ atoms by knowledge of their separate respective complete orders over (their own) $J$ private-goods spaces: $\mathbf{a}^k \overset{k}{\geq} \mathbf{b}^k$, $\mathbf{c}^k \overset{k}{\geq} \mathbf{b}^k$, and so on $(k = 1, \ldots, K)$.

*Remark.* Later we can make use for each man of a scalar function that is a "cardinal utility indicator" of *his* well-being: we assume that one can *always* solve for the *scalar* root, $z^k$, . . . , each person's indifference relation:

$$(z^k, \ldots, z^k) \overset{k}{\sim} (x_1^k, \ldots, x_J^k) = \mathbf{x}^k$$

$$z^k = z^k(\mathbf{x}^k) \qquad (k = 1, \ldots, K) \tag{2.1}$$

$$\nabla z^k(\mathbf{x}^k) = [z_j^k(\mathbf{x}^k)] = [\partial z^k(x_1^k, \ldots, x_J^k)/\partial x_j^k] \tag{2.2}$$

$$\nabla^2 z^k(\mathbf{x}^k) = [z_{ij}^k(\mathbf{x}^k)] = [\partial z^k(x_1^k, \ldots, x_J^k)/\partial x_i^k \, \partial x_j^k] \tag{2.3}$$

3. Now we must explicate the implications of the individualistic dogma that the "individuals' tastes are to count when they are unanimous and to be ethically resolved when they are not." This means that the ethical $\geq$ is constrained to agree with the separate $\overset{k}{\geq}$'s when they *all* happen to agree about two states of the world.

$\gamma$   If for *all* $k$, $\mathbf{a}^k \overset{k}{\sim} \mathbf{b}^k$ $(k = 1, \ldots, K)$, then necessarily

$$\mathbf{a} = (\mathbf{a}^1; \ldots; \mathbf{a}^k; \ldots; \mathbf{a}^K) \sim \mathbf{b} = (\mathbf{b}^1; \ldots; \mathbf{b}^k; \ldots; \mathbf{b}^K)$$

This forces the BISWF to be "weakly separable" in the men's tastes. When I come to use the $z(x)$ and $z^k(x^k)$ functions, it will be seen that weak-separability implies that $z(x)$ can be written in the form

$$z(x_1^1, \ldots, x_J^1; \ldots; x_1^K, \ldots, x_J^K)$$
$$\equiv z[z^1(x_1^1, \ldots, x_J^1), \ldots, z^K(x_1^K, \ldots, x_J^K)] \quad (3.1)$$

where $z[z^1, \ldots, z^K]$ is a function of $K$ scalar variables that records *all* the ethical information needed for interpersonal comparisons and judgments.

Specifically, we can infer by repeated substitutions of indifference that the only *independent* interpersonal ethical judgments that we need record about the BISWF are those involving states in which, for each man $k$, the goods he consumes are in the same scalar quantity, $z^k$. I use the symbol $(\gtrsim)$ for $\geq$ as applied to such special states.

This means that we need only define $(\gtrsim)$ over the $K$-dimensional space of $\hat{z} = (z^1, z^2, \ldots, z^K)$, where a vector of these scalars adequately stands for

$$\hat{\mathbf{a}} = (a^1, a^1, \ldots, a^1; a^2, \ldots, a^2; \ldots; a^K, \ldots, a^K)$$
$$= (a^1, a^2, \ldots, a^K)$$
$$\hat{\mathbf{b}} = (b^1, b^1, \ldots, b^1; b^2, \ldots, b^2; \ldots; b^K, \ldots, b^K)$$
$$= (b^1, b^2, \ldots, b^K) \quad \text{etc.}$$

Since $K \ll KJ$, the economy in mustering ethical judgments is significant. It is this same weak-separability economy that permits *decentralized* market algorithms to function optimally and that lets optimal interpersonal redistributions be made solely in terms of a single good or in terms solely of abstract purchasing power.

Let me sketch how any two arbitrary states of the world can be decided upon once we know the $K \overset{k}{\geq}$ orderings and the ethical $(\gtrsim)$ ordering in the $(z^1, \ldots, z^K)$ reduced space of $K$ dimensions. For general $\mathbf{a}$ and $\mathbf{b}$, solve for respective $K$ scalars

$$\hat{a} = (a^1, a^2, \ldots, a^K) \quad \text{and} \quad \hat{b} = (b^1, b^2, \ldots, b^K)$$
$$(a^k, a^k, \ldots, a^k) \overset{k}{\sim} (a_1^k, \ldots, a_J^k) = \mathbf{a}^k \quad (k = 1, \ldots, J)$$
$$(b^k, b^k, \ldots, b^k) \overset{k}{\sim} (b_1^k, \ldots, b_J^k) = \mathbf{b}^k$$

Then find out how $(a^1, \ldots, a^K) = \hat{\mathbf{a}}$ and $(b^1, \ldots, b^K) = \hat{\mathbf{b}}$ are ethically ordered by $(\gtrsim)$. The answer found for $(\gtrsim)$ judgments then provides the needed answer for $\geq$ as applied to the original $\mathbf{a}$ and $\mathbf{b}$!

Although Bergson did not in 1937 use the Debreu–Arrow notation and symbolism about complete orders, the foregoing discussion fairly describes his 1938 thought in that language. Before relaxing the *atomistic* simplifications, I sketch his 1938 thought in terms of observable marginal-rates-of-(ethical)-substitution functions.

**4.** It will be useful sometimes to renumber the $KJ$ variables in $(x_1^1, \ldots;$ $\ldots; \ldots; \ldots, x_J^K) = \mathbf{x}$ and write this vector as $\mathbf{x} = (y_1, \ldots, y_Q) = \mathbf{y}$, where $Q = KJ$. Then, under standard regularity conditions, such as (2.1)–(2.3) and (1.1)–(1.3), we can replace $\gtreqqless$ by an equivalent symbolism that uses only marginal-rates-of-substitution functions denoting slope elements of ethical indifference. Any good may be taken as reference *numéraire* – say $x_1^1 = y_1$. Then we write, for a general BSWF, its marginal rates of substitution as

$$-\partial x_1^1/\partial x_j^k = R^{jk}(x_1^1, \ldots; \ldots; \ldots, x_J^K)$$
$$= R^{jk}(\mathbf{x}) = R^{jk}(\mathbf{x}^1; \ldots; \mathbf{x}^K) \qquad (4.1)$$

What is just the same in easier notation is

$$-\partial y_1/\partial y_i = R^i(y_1, \ldots, y_Q) = R^i(\mathbf{y}) \qquad (i = 2, \ldots, Q = KJ) \quad (4.2)$$

In order that the BSWF have "integrable" contours of indifference in $KJ$ space, the foregoing MRS functions must satisfy well-known standard Antonelli–Allen integrability conditions, $\frac{1}{2}(Q - 1)(Q - 2)$, in independent number:

$$R_j^i(\mathbf{y}) - R^j(\mathbf{y})R_1^i(\mathbf{y}) = R_i^j(\mathbf{y}) - R^i(\mathbf{y})R_1^j(\mathbf{y})$$
$$(i, j = 2, \ldots, Q; \; i \neq j) \quad (4.3)$$

Recall that

$$R_j^i(\mathbf{y}) = \partial R^i(y_1, \ldots, y_Q)/\partial y_j; \quad \text{etc.}$$

We know from the standard theory of Pfaffian differentials that with (4.3) assured, the following expression admits of an "integrating factor," $\gamma(\mathbf{y})$, that defines an "exact differential" of an existent "cardinal BSWF indicator":

$$dy_1 + \sum_{j=2}^{Q} R^j(\mathbf{y}) \, dy_j = \gamma(y_1, \ldots, y_Q)^{-1} \, dZ(y_1, \ldots, y_Q) \quad (4.4)$$

Indeed, we can pin down from the infinity of existent $\gamma(\mathbf{y})$ factors and $Z(\mathbf{y})$ indicator functions a unique $z(\mathbf{y})$ function if we require that (4.2) be equivalent to the ratio of $z(\mathbf{y})$'s "marginal social utilities" and satisfy the arbitrary *boundary conditions* of (4.5b), along loci where each person consumes the same number of units of one good as of any other, namely:

$$-\partial y_1/\partial y_i = R^i(\mathbf{y}) = [\partial z(\mathbf{y})/\partial y_i]/[\partial z(\mathbf{y})/\partial y_i] \qquad (i = 2, \ldots, Q) \quad (4.5a)$$

$$z(y, y, \ldots, y; y, \ldots, y; \ldots; y, \ldots, y) \equiv y \qquad (4.5b)$$

**5.** How does this simplify when Bergson narrows the BSWF to being a BISWF? Now we have the atomistic (individualistic) property of the men, respected by the ethical judge:

$$R^{ik}(\mathbf{x})/R^{1k}(\mathbf{x}) = {}^kR^i(\mathbf{x}^k) \quad \text{independently of } \mathbf{x}^s, \; s \neq k \quad (5.1)$$

where $R^{11}(\mathbf{x}) \equiv 1$.

All this involves $(K - 1)J$ weak-separability conditions

$$\partial[R^{ik}(\mathbf{x})/R^{1k}(\mathbf{x})]/\partial x_j^s \equiv 0 \qquad \text{if } s \neq k \tag{5.2}$$

In the presence of these weak-separability conditions holding, it can be shown that many less than the $\frac{1}{2}(KJ - 1)(KJ - 2)$ integrability conditions of (4.3) are now *independently* needed. We can parallel for each man what was done for the whole $KJ$ social space in (4.3), (4.4), and (4.5). Briefly, for each man we have $\frac{1}{2}(J - 1)(J - 2)$ integrability conditions

$$^kR_j^i(\mathbf{x}^k) - {}^kR^j(\mathbf{x}^k){}^kR_1^i(\mathbf{x}^k) = {}^kR_i^j(\mathbf{x}^k) - {}^kR^i(\mathbf{x}^k){}^kR_1^j(\mathbf{x}^k)$$
$$(i, j = 2, \ldots, J; k = 1, \ldots, K) \tag{5.3}$$

These being satisfied, we have defined existing exact differentials of existent $z^k(\mathbf{x}^k)$ functions

$$[dz^k(\mathbf{x}^k)]/\gamma^k(\mathbf{x}^k) = dx_1^k + \sum_2^J {}^kR^j(\mathbf{x}^k)\, dx_j^k \qquad (k = 1, \ldots, k) \tag{5.4}$$

$$z^k(z, \ldots, z) \equiv z \tag{5.5}$$

**6.** Now, as in Section 4, we need only observe interpersonal ethical judgments in the $K$-dimensional space of $(\hat{a}, \hat{b}, \hat{c}, \ldots)$, which adequately denote the $(\mathbf{a}, \mathbf{b}, \mathbf{c}, \ldots)$ points of the full space. Thus, in terms of the scalars $(z^1, \ldots, z^K)$, which stand for $(\hat{z}_1, \ldots, \hat{z}_K)$ but omit for brevity the circumflexes, we have interpersonal-ethical integrable MRS functions:

$$-\partial z^1/\partial z^k = E^k(z^1, \ldots, z^K) = E^k(\mathbf{z}) \qquad (k = 2, \ldots, K) \tag{6.1}$$

These need satisfy only $\frac{1}{2}(K - 1)(K - 2)$ integrability conditions:

$$E_s^k(\mathbf{z}) - E^s(\mathbf{z})E_1^k(\mathbf{z}) = E_k^s(\mathbf{z}) - E^k(\mathbf{z})E_1^s(\mathbf{z})$$
$$(k, s = 2, \ldots, K; k \neq s) \tag{6.2}$$

These guarantee the existence of an exact differential

$$dz^1 + \sum_{k=2}^K E^k(\mathbf{z})\, dz^k = dz[z^1, \ldots, z^K]/\hat{\gamma}(z^1, \ldots, z^K) \tag{6.3}$$

Subject to the boundary condition

$$z[z, \ldots, z] \equiv z \tag{6.4}$$

the $z[z^1, \ldots, z^K]$ function is uniquely defined.

Thus, we have finally arrived at *a nonsubjective cardinal indicator of ethical social welfare that is individualistically weakly separable,* as in (3.1):

$$z = z[z^1(x_1^1, \ldots, x_J^K), z^2(x_1^2, \ldots, x_J^2), \ldots, z^K(x_1^K, \ldots, x_J^K)]$$
$$= z[z^1, \ldots, z^K] = z(\mathbf{x}) \tag{6.5}$$

*Remark.* A general BSWF in $Q = KJ$ variables must have its $Q - 1$ marginal-rate-of-substitution functions, $R^{1+i}(\mathbf{y})$, satisfy $\frac{1}{2}(KJ - 1)$ $\cdot (KJ - 2)$ integrability conditions. If it is also an atomistic BISWF, it satisfies $K(J - 1)(K - 1)J$ weak-separability conditions. The sum of these, $\frac{1}{2}(KJ - 1)(KJ - 2) + K(J - 1)(K - 1)J$, represents many more conditions than are truly an *independent* set. Actually, as has been indicated above and as I hope to write up for publication, only $\frac{1}{2}(K - 1)(K - 2) + \frac{1}{2}(J - 1)(J - 2)$ integrability conditions can be *independently* specified in addition to the $K(J - 1)(K - 1)J$ weak-separability conditions. For $K$ and $J$ large, this saves us virtually 100 percent of the drudgery of verifying the integrability conditions. Furthermore, the (6.2) conditions need hold only for a limited set of points and then with (5.3) they guarantee that (4.3) holds *everywhere* in the space of $Q$ dimensions!

7. Geometry may help a reader understand the power of the individualistic weak-separability axiom. To stay in three-dimensional space that one can visualize, I assume two persons only, $K = 2$: he and she. Person 1, he, consumes (bread[1], wine[1]) = $(x_1^1, x_2^1)$ and lacks envy or altruism. Person 2, she, is a teetotaler consuming only (bread[1]) = $x_1^2$; she is an atom sans envy and altruism. Individuals' tastes are to "count" ethically.

Use the lower corner on the floor of a cubical room as your origin. Use the two sides of the floor emerging from that origin-corner as your axes to measure *his* consumptions $(x_1^1, x_2^1)$. Use the vertical line above the origin-corner as your third axis for her bread consumption $x_1^2$. Then Bergson's *general* BSWF provides indifference contours (i.e., surfaces) that fill the space like nested soup bowls with their bottoms faced toward the origin.

But now assume that each person's tastes are ethically to "count." A tremendous economy of ethical specification immediately applies. Now draw on the floor, for the space of (bread[1], wine[1]) or $(x_1^1, x_2^1)$, *his* personal indifference curves dictated by his atomistic tastes. Each such Person 1 indifference curve can be given a number equal to its ordinary distance from the origin-corner as measured along the diagonal drawn on the floor between the origin-corner and its opposite corner. For *her,* the loci of personal indifference are given by all points that are the same bread[2] height above the floor. These loci of hers can be numbered by that $x_1^2$ coordinate.

The Ethical Observer's power to arbitrarily specify shapes of ethical-indifference contours is seriously reduced by the individualistic axiom. Thus, erect a thin glass wall that rises vertically above the floor's diagonal (splitting the cubical room into two geometrically equal prismatic volumes). The interpersonal judgments required for the BISWF from the ethical preceptor consist of no more and no less than the ethical-interpersonal indifference curves chalked in on the thin glass partition. Each such curve specifies how much must be her increased bread[2] to compensate ethically for balanced reductions in his (bread[1] = wine[1]). There is no avoiding such interpersonal judgments if we are to be provided with a complete ethical ordering of all the states of the world. But once they are made in this small (glass-partition) part of the vast three-dimensional space, *all the rest* of the interpersonal judgments are already implied!

Mathematically, the weak-separability conditions on the slope elements of ethical indifference – slope elements that fill the interior of the room like myriad thumbtacks oriented at each interior point – are partial differential equations that have solution functions uniquely determined once the values of those functions are specified along the boundary conditions (the agreement on the floor with *his* autonomous indifference curves; the agreement on the glass partition with the interpersonal ethical-indifference curves). Twist a set of wires into the shape of each one of the floor's indifference curves. Raise any such wire vertically evenly above its profile on the floor: any such lifting will provide a locus of points ethically indifferent. So the whole space is filled with such twisted wires. Can these one-dimensional wires be "integrated" to form two-dimensional indifference *surfaces of ethical indifference?* The answer is necessarily, Yes.

*Note.* For $Q = 3$, *generally* one integrability condition would have to be imposed. But when the BSWF is a BISWF, we had no need to specify *any* integrability condition – since neither the floor's two-dimensional indifference curves nor the glass wall's two-dimensional indifference curves need any such reciprocity conditions. Weak separability has done the work for us!

8. Now a Bergson Individualistic Social Welfare Function has been carefully devised (1) in terms of *ordinal* ethical ordering, (2) honoring people's autonomous tastes when those lead to unanimity, and (3) providing the irreducibly required *inter*personal ethical orderings. We have arrived at a position to dispose of a misunderstanding concerning whether a certain odd Axiom of Neutrality makes any sense as a requirement; and concerning whether, whatever its foolishness, it was actually implied in the earlier writings of such Bergsonians as Samuelson (1947) or Bergson (1938). [See Samuelson (1977) for a rebuttal of Kemp and Ng (1976, 1977).] If it were not that a number of writers in the social choice vineyard (Kemp and Ng, Parks, Hammond, Pollak, . . .) attach disproportionate importance to this issue, I would be even briefer in disposing of it here.

Note that my BISWF is *not* formulated in terms of "an ethical *ranking*" determined as an output of a function whose input variables are individual *rankings*. It is not the case, and not intended to be the case, that sign $\{z(x) - z(y)\}$ for the BISWF is always determinable from knowledge alone of

$$[\text{sign}\{z^1(x) - z^1(y)\}, \text{ sign } \{z^2(x) - z^2(y)\}, \ldots, [\text{sign}\{z^k(x) - z^k(y)\}]$$

Why should it be? To call such a requirement an Axiom of Neutrality is to dignify it beyond its merits in the present context.

In axiomatics more than almost anywhere else must the watchword be: By their fruits shall you know assumptions. *Caveat emptor.* The poisoned apple borne by the axiom above (when combined with some harmless regularity conditions) is that some *one* single person's tastes must rule *dictatorially*. It tells us something about the state of present-day "social choice" writing that such an axiom would be considered even momentarily as applying to Bergsonian welfare economics or to the Old Welfare Economics.

Consider the simplest case of two persons, between whom a fixed total of a single private good is to be allocated.

$$x_1^1 + x_1^2 = x \qquad x_1^k \geq 0$$

Suppose that they are deemed ethically "alike" and that Jesus, long before Abram Bergson was born, considers the *bonum bonorum* to be at the maximum of a symmetric, strictly quasi-concave (ordinal!) function of their respective consumptions. Then Jesus's BISWF will judge it better to go from $y = (x, 0)$ to $y = (\frac{1}{2}x, \frac{1}{2}x)$. We know that there is no self-contradiction in this *final* decision; and many would say, no absurdity in this ethos. Also, Jesus has let the individuals' tastes "count," in the sense of not judging more of $x_1^k$ bad for a person. No paternalism or merit wants here. (And, actually, coming together in a Rawlsian convention under a veil of ignorance, risk-averse individuals might all by *unanimous* vote always opt for such completely egalitarian taxes.)

Now how do the lobbyists for the Axiom of Neutrality view all this? They say,

Since $[\text{sign}(\frac{1}{2}x - x), \text{sign}(\frac{1}{2}x - 0)] = [-, +]$, and
since $[\text{sign}(0 - x), \text{sign}(x - 0)] = [-, +]$,
Jesus has committed himself to giving *everything* to Man![1]

Jesus's amused answer, and mine, is this: Neither Bergson, nor Lange, nor Samuelson, nor Little, nor de Graaf – nor Buddha, nor Father Divine, nor the Wizard of Oz, Pareto, Bentham, Edgeworth – expected an *ordinal* social welfare function of individualistic type (that respects people's tastes when they are unanimous) to obey such an odd axiom-on-signs.

*Moral:* I blow on my soup to cool it off and, *without contradiction,* I blow on my hands to warm them up.

**9.** It is inhuman to be an atom, sans envy and altruism. It is also unrealistic. What happens to the *individualistic* social welfare function when people are more human?

We can still define a BISWF, as a species of the genus BSWF. Now each person's $\geq^k$ ordering involves *all* the goods, $x_j^s$ items as well as $x_j^k$ items. Now we write the cardinal indicator of man $k$'s preferences in a general form lacking any separability properties:

$$z^k = z^k(\mathbf{x}^1, \ldots, \mathbf{x}^k, \ldots \mathbf{x}^K) = z^k(\mathbf{x}) \tag{9.1}$$

$$y \equiv z^k(y, \ldots, y; y, \ldots, y; \ldots; y, \ldots, y) \tag{9.2}$$

Each of these is *formally* indistinguishable from a general BSWF. As long as we stay with a BSWF, and not a BISWF, there is *no* necessary relation between any of (9.1) and the BSWF of (1.1):

$$z = z(\mathbf{x}^1, \ldots, \mathbf{x}^K) \tag{9.3}$$

$$y = z(y, \ldots, y; \ldots; y, \ldots, y) \tag{9.4}$$

What if the ethical observer still wishes to be individualistic in the sense that persons' tastes are to "count" when they are unanimous and to be ethically resolved when they are not? Then (9.3) takes the form like that in (3.1), but with each $z^k(\mathbf{x})$ function there now involving $\mathbf{x}^s$ as well as $\mathbf{x}^k$ items:

$$z = z[z^1(\mathbf{x}); \ldots; z^K(\mathbf{x})] \tag{9.5}$$

$$y = z[y; \ldots; y] \tag{9.6}$$

In *general*, the BISWF of (9.5) written for nonatomistic people is mathematically indistinguishable from the BSWF of (1.1)–(1.3). This is a fairly devastating observation from the standpoint of economists enamored of the market. In general, when there are *no* weak separability properties, there is no useful role for *decentralized* pricing mechanisms[5] – either à la von Mises and Schumpeter or à la Lerner and Lange.

An all-powerful ethical mind could use its perfect computer to select the best state of the world. Pareto-optimal states can still be identified. But most states of the world might well be trivially Pareto optimal. And, in any case, the perfect computer will not only screen out all non-Pareto-optimal points but as well must do the job itself of picking out of those that remain the one that is ethically best. There are, in general, no lump-sum algebraic transfers of goods or of dollars that can be given to people in the justified confidence that men can be counted on to harness their self-interest to achieve the Ethical Observer's orchestrated maximum.

Alas, for much of conventional political economy.

**10.** Fortunately for the vanity of economists, the presence of *some* externalities in preferences and values does not render useless the atomic private-good model that can utilize decentralized market pricing. Thus, if there are only trace elements of "paternalism" – or, to use a less pejorative language, of "merit wants" – one might still hope to get a tolerable approximation to the optimum by a system of markets-cum-lump-sum transfers plus a few adjustments to take account of the externality complications.

One man's trace element is another man's mountain. So there may well be problems in deciding when the remarks of this section are of relevance.

**11.** Economists have studied some special patterns of *external* interdependences. My 1954 "Pure Theory of Public Expenditure" represents a logical culmination of the "voluntary theory of public exchange" doctrines associated historically with Erik Lindahl (1919), Knut Wicksell (1896), and other writers in the Austrian and Italian utility literature.[6]

I sketch a few of its properties as they relate to Bergsonian welfare economics and Pareto optimality. Now, in addition to the $J$ private goods of Sections 2 and 3 and relation (3.1), namely $(x_1^k, \ldots, x_J^k)$, I introduce a category of $M$ "public goods":

$$(x_{J+1}, \ldots, x_{J+M}) \equiv (x_{J+1}^k, \ldots, x_{J+M}^k) \qquad (k = 1, \ldots, K) \qquad (11.1)$$

The essence of any such public good, $x_{J+m}$, is that it enters into the indifference curves of more than one person.

Each person's tastes are summarizable by

$$z^k = z^k(x_1^k, \ldots, x_J^k; x_{J+1}, \ldots, x_{J+M}) = z^k(\mathbf{x}^k; \bar{\mathbf{x}}) \qquad (11.2)$$

$$y = z^k(y, \ldots, y; y, \ldots, y) \qquad (11.3)$$

If the BSWF is to be "individualistic" and respect tastes, so that it is to be a BISWF, then it becomes

$$z = z(z^1[\mathbf{x}^k; \bar{\mathbf{x}}], \ldots, z^K[\mathbf{x}^K; \bar{\mathbf{x}}]) \qquad (11.4)$$

$$y = z(y, \ldots, y) \qquad (11.5)$$

Although it is hard to find a decentralized price–tax mechanism that will motivate people to reveal their preferences[7] and help achieve the ethical optimum, it is easy to write down in the 1954 fashion the conditions of the optimum. For brevity, I make some overly strong assumptions.

Assume that $z[z^1(\ ), \ldots] \equiv z(\mathbf{x})$ and that all $z^k(\mathbf{x}^k, \bar{\mathbf{x}})$ functions are strictly monotone-increasing, smooth, strictly quasi-concave functions of their positive arguments, and that every good is *essential* to every person. Also, assume there is a smooth *concave* production-possibility frontier technologically connecting the *totals* of the $J + M$ goods

$$\sum_1^K x_1^k = T\left(\sum_1^K x_2^k, \ldots, \sum_1^K x_J^k, x_{J+1}, \ldots, x_{J+M}\right) \qquad (11.6)$$

$$T_q(a_2, \ldots, a_{J+M}) = \partial T(a_2, \ldots, a_{J+M})/\partial a_q < 0$$
$$(q = 2, \ldots, J + M)$$

Then it is a necessary and sufficient condition for the ethical maximization of $z(x; \bar{x})$ in (11.4) that the following 1954 relations be satisfied:

$$\frac{z_j^k(x^k; \bar{x})}{z_1^k(x^k; \bar{x})} = -T_j\left(\sum_1^K x_2^k, \ldots, \sum_1^K x_J^k, x_{J+1}, \ldots, x_{J+m}\right)$$
$$(j = 2, \ldots, J; k = 1, \ldots, K) \qquad (11.7)$$

$$\sum_1^K \frac{z_{J+m}^k(x^k; \bar{x})}{z_1^k(x^k; \bar{x})} = -T_{J+m}\left(\sum_1^K x_2^k, \ldots; \ldots, x_{J+m}\right)$$
$$(m = 1, \ldots, M) \qquad (11.8)$$

$$\frac{z_k[z^1(\mathbf{x}^1;\bar{\mathbf{x}});\ \dots\ ;z^K(\mathbf{x}^K;\bar{\mathbf{x}})]z_1^k(\mathbf{x}^k;\bar{\mathbf{x}})}{z_1[z^1(\mathbf{x}^1;\bar{\mathbf{x}});\ \dots\ ;z^K(\mathbf{x}^K;\bar{\mathbf{x}})]z_1^1(\mathbf{x}^1;\bar{\mathbf{x}})} = 1$$

$$(k = 2,\ \dots\ ,K) \quad (11.9)$$

The relations (11.6)–(11.8) alone do not define a unique state of the world. They define only the Pareto-optimality utility-possibility frontier involving a $(K - 1)$-fold infinity of Pareto-optimal possibilities. The final interpersonal relations (11.9) render the interpersonal ethical judgments to select out of this infinity the single best state of the world (best according to this specified BISWF, of course).

12. Where there are no public goods and only private goods, with $M = 0$, (11.8) would be vacuous and market pricing can be used to achieve the ethical optimum when we assume (a) the atomistic case of an individualistic social welfare function, a BISWF free of envy and altruism; and (b) that the laws of technical returns are those most favorable to viable competition – constant returns to scale, convex technology, and so forth – and each person's indifference contours are strictly convex and involve every good as an essential item; and where we introduce an optimal set of lump-sum transfers to ensure that dollar votes are ethically commensurable.

I make some (overstrong) assumptions about the various slopes and curvatures. The people's tastes are given by strictly quasi-concave functions

$$z^k = z^k(x_1^k,\ \dots\ ,x_J^k;x_{J+1},\ \dots\ ,x_{J+M}) = z^k(\mathbf{x}^k;\bar{\mathbf{x}}) \quad (12.1)$$
$$z_q^k(\mathbf{x}^k;\bar{\mathbf{x}}) > 0 \quad (q = 1,\ \dots\ ,J, J + 1,\ \dots\ ,J + M)$$
$$\lim_{x_q^k \to 0} \frac{z_q^k(\mathbf{x}^k;\bar{\mathbf{x}})}{z_q^{k\prime}(\mathbf{x}^k;\bar{\mathbf{x}})} = \infty, \qquad \lim_{x_q^k \to \infty} \frac{z_q^k(\mathbf{x}^k;\bar{\mathbf{x}})}{z_q^k(\mathbf{x}^k;\bar{\mathbf{x}})} = 0$$

$$(q \neq q';q, q' = 1,\ \dots\ ,J,\ \dots\ ,J + M)$$

The weakly separable BISWF also satisfies similar properties: $z[z^1, \dots, z^K]$ is strictly quasi-concave, with positive partials and obeys limit relations like the last set.

Finally, $T(x_2, \dots,)$ is a strictly concave function with negative partial derivatives; and so on.

Set $p_1 \equiv 1$ as *numéraire* and let $(p_2, \dots, p_J)$ be market prices for the remaining $J - 1$ private goods. Each person $k$, given his lump-sum payment $L^k$, expressed in terms of the first, *numéraire* good, acts to maximize $z^k(\mathbf{x}^k)$:

$$\text{subject to } x_1^k + \sum_2^J p_j^k x_j^k = L^k \quad (k = 1,\ \dots\ ,K) \quad (12.2)$$

$$\max_{x_j^k} z^k(\mathbf{x}^k) = z^k(X^k[L^k;1,p_2,\ \dots\ ,p_J]) \quad (12.3)$$

where the $k$th person's single-valued demand functions each depend on the parameters

$$[L^k; 1, p_2, \ldots, p_J] \equiv [L^k; p]:$$
$$x_j^k = X_j^k[L^k; 1, p_2, \ldots, p_J] = x^k[L^k; \mathbf{p}]$$
$$(j = 1, \ldots, J; \quad k = 1, \ldots, K) \quad (12.4)$$

Whatever the values that $[L^k]$ take in (12.1) and (12.2), the consumers' demand maximizations will assure that the following hold:

$$\frac{z_j^k(\mathbf{x}^k)}{z_1^k(\mathbf{x}^k)} = p_j \quad (j = 2, \ldots, J; \quad k = 1, \ldots, K) \quad (12.5)$$

If the technological return conditions in (11.6) are suitable for perfect competition, then the market mechanism can be used to assure equality of $p_j$ to marginal (social) cost. Or this may result from Pareto–Barone or Lerner–Lange bureaucratic planning. In any case, we have

$$p_j = -T_j \left( \sum_1^K x_2^k, \ldots \right) \quad (j = 2, \ldots, J) \quad (12.6)$$

To ensure that all goods produced are consumed, the ethical planners must make the $(L^1, \ldots, L^K)$ vector satisfy

$$\sum_1^K X_1^k[L^k; \mathbf{p}] = T \left( \sum_1^K X_2^k[L^k; \mathbf{p}], \ldots, \sum_1^K X_J^k[L^k; \mathbf{p}] \right) \quad (12.7)$$

Under my strong assumptions on convexity (which are stronger than those spelled out by early writers such as Pareto), we are guaranteed that the pricing model's relations (12.1)–(12.7) will define an equilibrium for this system of atomistic individuals as a result of a proper (unique) choice of $(L^1, \ldots, L^K)$; and one of these competitive equilibria does achieve the desired ethical maximum of $z(\mathbf{x})$.

As will be discussed later, Pareto sensed correctly that each such competitive solution is Pareto optimal[8] (and, what is exactly the same thing, *could* represent the *optimum optimorum* of *some* existent BISWF). Also – as Pareto at least vaguely realized, Lerner clearly realized, and Arrow proved in our time – the *optimum optimorum* called for by *any* given specified BISWF is capable (under my *strong* assumptions!) of being effectuated by a competitive equilibrium achievable through an appropriate choice of $(L^K)$.

Of course, a BSWF that is *not* a BISWF need not be achievable by pricing in decentralized competitive markets.

**13.** Now restore the condition that $M$ be positive and there be at least one public good. This "externality" kills off any simple use of the pricing system.

Lindahl (1919) naively believed something like the following:

    a  In (12.3) we are to replace $(\mathbf{x}^k)$ by $(\mathbf{x}^k; \bar{\mathbf{x}})$ and write $z^k(\mathbf{x}^k; \bar{\mathbf{x}})$. (There can be no objection to that.)

b For the $M$ public goods and for each $k$th person, let us define respective "pseudo-tax-prices," $(p^k_{J+1}, \ldots , p^k_{J+M})$. (The name is mine and is meant to sound a warning.)

c Adjoin to (12.2) and (12.3) relations that *pretend* each person can buy as much or little of any public good at its pseudo-tax-price to him:

$$x^k_1 + \sum_2^J p_j x^k_j + \sum_1^M p^k_{J+M} x_{J+M} = L^k \qquad (k = 1, \ldots , K) \qquad (13.1)$$

$$\frac{z^k_{J+M^k}(\mathbf{x}^k; \bar{\mathbf{x}})}{z^k_1(\mathbf{x}^k; \bar{\mathbf{x}})} = p^k_{J+m} \qquad (m = 1, \ldots , M; \quad k = 1, \ldots , K)$$

$$(13.2)$$

$$\frac{z^k_j(\mathbf{x}^k; \bar{\mathbf{x}})}{z^k_1(\mathbf{x}^k; \bar{\mathbf{x}})} = p_j \qquad (j = 1, \ldots , J) \qquad (13.3)$$

Equations (13.1), (13.2), and (13.3) generate $J + M$ pseudo-demand functions for each man $k$:

$$x^k_q = X^k_q[L^k; 1, p_2, \ldots , p_J; p^k_{J+1}, \ldots , p^k_{J+M}]$$
$$= X^k_q[L^k; \mathbf{p}; \bar{\mathbf{p}}^k] \qquad (k = 1, \ldots , K;$$
$$q = 1, \ldots , J, \ldots , J + M) \qquad (13.4)$$

d Equate to each public good's marginal cost the *sum* of its pseudo-tax-price taken over all the people: that is, adjoin to (12.6):

$$P^1_{J+m} + \cdots + p^K_{J+m}$$

$$= -T_{J+m} \left( \sum_1^K x^k_2, \ldots , \sum_1^K x^k_J, x_{J+1}, \ldots , x_{J+M} \right)$$
$$(m = 1, \ldots , M) \qquad (13.5)$$

$$p_j = -T_j \left( \sum_1^K x^k_2, \ldots , \sum_1^K x^k_J, x_{J+1}, \ldots , x_{J+M} \right) \qquad (13.6)$$

e The total pseudodemand of each public good given in (13.4) must equal that public good's common value:

$$X^k_{J+m}[L^k; 1, \mathbf{p}; \bar{\mathbf{p}}^k] = x_{J+m}$$
$$(k = 1, \ldots , K; \quad m = 1, \ldots , M) \qquad (13.7)$$

f Finally, there must be a *feasible* choice of $(L^1, \ldots , L^K)$, a vector picked to assure that all which is produced and supplied must be demanded and consumed.

$$\sum_1^K X^k_1[L^k; \mathbf{p}, \mathbf{p}^{-k}]$$

$$= T \left( \sum_1^K X^k_2[L^k; \mathbf{p}, \mathbf{p}^{-k}], \ldots , x_{J+1}, \ldots , x_{J+M} \right) \qquad (13.8)$$

These Lindahl pseudo-tax-price functions, (13.1)–(13.8), do define a solution for each feasible choice of $L^k$'s under my strong assumptions. Every one of these $(K - 1)$-infinity-fold of Lindahl solutions can be shown to define a point of Pareto optimality – and, under my strong assumptions, *all* Pareto-optimal points can be generated by the Lindahl equations for proper choice of $(L^k)$. And, of course, the ethical maximum of the specified BISWF will be achievable formally by the one best selection of the $(L^k)$ lump-sum transfers.

However, what Lindahl never sufficiently realized, people will not be motivated to act in accordance with the "Lindahl" relations (13.2) if they are smart enough to realize that (13.5) is to hold! It pays you to *hide* your true tastes for a public good, not to reveal them as you are selfishly motivated to do with regard to a private good.

**14.** There is another pattern of altruism or envy that economists have found interesting to analyze. In it, I am not an atom. The private bread and wine I eat affect me. The private bread and wine you eat also affect me.

But my altruism and envy are themselves "individualistic." If *you* (privately) feel as well off with (4 of your bread, 2 of your wine) and (3 of your bread, 3 of your wine), then *I* feel equally well off (on your account) in these alternative situations.

To avoid infinite regress, economists sometimes postulate in this situation a "first-order level of atomic tastes": prior to my envy or altruism concerning your $x^s$, I as man $k$ have a *first-order* utility indicator function $^{(1)}z^k(x^k)$, like that in (2.1):

$$^{(1)}z^k = {}^{(1)}z^k(x^k) \qquad (k = 1, \ldots, K) \tag{14.1}$$
$$y \quad \equiv {}^{(1)}z^k(y, \ldots, y)$$

To introduce empathy and make your $x^s$ matter to me, I define for me (or any person $k$) a *second-order* utility indicator function, $^{(2)}z^k(x)$, *that is weakly separable* in my own first-order tastes and every other person's first-order tastes:

$$^{(2)}z^k = {}^{(2)}z^k[^{(1)}z^1(x^1); {}^{(1)}z(x^2), \ldots, {}^{(1)}z(x^K)] \qquad (k = 1, \ldots, K) \tag{14.2}$$
$$y \quad \equiv {}^{(2)}z^k[y; \ldots; y]$$

One could even envisage a countable infinity of higher-order values or tastes, each dependent on the next lower-order taste function:

$$^{(h+1)}z^k = {}^{(h+1)}z^k\{^{(h)}z^1[\cdot], \ldots, {}^{(h)}z^K[\cdot]\}$$
$$= {}^{(h+1)}z[^{(1)}z^1(x^1), \ldots, {}^{(1)}z^K(x^K)]$$
$$(h = 1, 2, \ldots; k = 1, \ldots, K) \tag{14.3}$$

Note that, by induction, we can verify that each of these higher-order functions is weakly separable in terms of the *same* first-order functions of people's atomic tastes. So each is weakly separable in a meaningful sense.

There might even be a limit set of functions:

$$\lim_{h \to \infty} {}^{(h)}\bar{z}[^{(1)}z^1(x^1), \ldots, {}^{(1)}z^k(x^k)]$$
$$= \bar{z}^k[^{(1)}z^1(x^1), \ldots, {}^{(1)}z^K(x^K)] \qquad (k = 1, \ldots, K) \tag{14.4}$$

A good reference for this hierarchy of utility functions is that of Tintner (1946). Just as nothing very interesting seemed to come from speaking of "the probability of a (person's subjective) probability," so cascading higher-order utilities has not seemed to lead to anything very novel or interesting. So I shall couch my exposition here in terms of $h$ equal to 2, or equal to *any* integer, or equal to infinity as in (14.4). Notationally, I shall omit the superscript in $^{(1)}z(\mathbf{x}^k)$ and the $h$ superscript in $^{(h)}\bar{z}[\quad]$ (whatever be the relevant final $h$).

As far as individuals' tastes and values are concerned, we have arrived at a special kind of nonatomic people, those who are "quasi-atomic" in the sense of having for *their* personal indifference contours the *same* weakly separable structure – the same "atoms" in their "molecules":

$$\bar{z}^k = \bar{z}^k[z^1(\mathbf{x}^1), \ldots, z^k(\mathbf{x}^k)] \qquad (k = 1, \ldots, K) \qquad (14.5)$$
$$y = \bar{z}^k[y, \ldots, y]$$

What individualistic BISWF does this imply for the ethical observer? Clearly, the BISWF must *also* have the common weakly separable structure, the same atoms as building blocks but of course with its own molecular composition:

$$z = z[z^1(\mathbf{x}^1), \ldots, z^K(\mathbf{x}^K)]$$
$$y = z[y, \ldots, y]$$

Remember that no superscript, $(k = 1, \ldots, K)$, means that the utility function is a *social* welfare function of some ethical norming system.

What makes this common-atomic case interesting is that, despite its "externalities," it may still lend itself to use of decentralized pricing mechanisms.

15. The quasi-atomistic structures of the preceding section can involve either benevolent sympathy [in which my $\bar{z}^k$ rises when your $z^s(\mathbf{x}^s)$ rises], or envy [in which my $\bar{z}^k$ falls when your $z^s(\mathbf{x}^s)$ rises], or elements of both. The case most clearly seen to be favorable to the use of competitive pricing in decentralized markets is that of positive sympathy or altruism.

For, in this case, the final BISWF has *all* the properties of the atomic BISWF case. Indistinguishable from (3.1) will be the present

$$z = z[z^1(\mathbf{x}^1), \ldots, z^K(\mathbf{x}^K)] \qquad (15.1)$$
$$\partial z[\cdot]/\partial z^k > 0, \qquad \partial z^k(x_1^k, \ldots, x_J^k)/\partial x_j^k > 0$$

The market demand functions generated by giving each man $k$ the money to spend at given market prices, $(1, p_2, \ldots, p_J)$, are *strictly atomic* even though the person's "values" are quasi-atomic. Let me explain. Because $\bar{z}^k[\ldots, z^k(\mathbf{x}^k), \ldots, z^s(\mathbf{x}^s), \ldots]$ has the indicated weak-separability property, maximizing it, for given income of $k$, given prices, and *given quantities* for others, means that his maximizing his *private* (first-order) tastes will do the trick (of course with some implied harmless "simultaneity"). Man $k$ solves

$$\max_{x^k} z^k(\mathbf{x}^k) \text{ subject to } \sum_1^J p_j x_j^k = L^k = z^k(\mathbf{X}^k[L^k; 1, p_2, \ldots, p_J]) \quad (15.2)$$

where his demand functions are roots of the atomic equations

$$\sum_1^J p_j x_j^k = L^k; \quad \frac{z_j^k(\mathbf{x}^k)}{z_1^k(\mathbf{x}^k)} = p_j \quad (j = 2, \ldots, J) \quad (15.3)$$

*Reminder:* Weak separability makes $z^k(\mathbf{x}^k)$ independent of $x_j^s$, $s \neq k!$

There will always exist one choice of $(L^1, L^2, \ldots, L^K)$ that will achieve the maximum of (15.1)'s $z[\bar{z}^1(\mathbf{x}^1), \ldots, \bar{z}^K(\mathbf{x})]$ by assuring that the interpersonal equity relations hold:

$$\frac{z_k[z^1, \ldots]z_1^k(\mathbf{x}^k)}{z_1[z^1, \ldots]z_1^1(x^1)} = 1 \quad (k = 2, \ldots, K) \quad (15.4)$$

*Remark.* The set of points that are Pareto optimal vis-à-vis the quasi-atomic vector of functions $\{\bar{z}^k[z^1(\mathbf{x}^1), \ldots, z^K(\mathbf{x}^K)]\}$ will have *shrunk* relative to the set of points that are Pareto optimal vis-à-vis the atomic vector of functions $\{z^1(\mathbf{x}^1), \ldots, z^K(\mathbf{x}^K)\}$. Why? Because altruistic people may well *voluntarily* give up some of their own $(L^k)$ to others – for that's what makes them "selfishly" happy.[9]

**16.** An extreme case is that of Perfect Consensus. Everyone then has the *exact same* $\bar{z}^k[\mathbf{x}]$ function. So the BISWF must exactly agree with this common values function. So the set of Pareto-optimal points shrinks to the *single* "best state of the world," to the maximum of the agreed-on BISWF.

Theological zealots argue that this is the way the world should be. In Samuelson (1956), I gave a fanciful example of family consensus that generates a peaceful collective utility function with weakly separable demands for pappa, mamma, brother, and sister. What I regarded as a fanciful polar case, I understand Gary Becker has proposed as a serious sociological archetype.

**17.** Suppose that we reverse altruism, replacing it by envy? Then $\partial \bar{z}^k / \partial x_j^s < 0$ for $s \neq k$. Just as positive empathy shrinks the set of Pareto-optimal states of the world, sadism and envy widen the set. A limiting case is that of a zero-sum game: pure *power* rather than welfare prevails. It does not matter how few or many chapeaux I have – as long as I have many more than you!

In the zero-sum case, *every* state of the world is Pareto optimal. Despite any formal difference between a BSWF and a BISWF, they are in substance exactly the same thing.

Use of decentralized pricing would be hopeless in seeking the best state of the world if the BISWF shared these malevolence properties and delighted in inequalities and resentments. Direct computation or selection would be needed to arrive at such an odd best state of the world.

**18.** Despite the widening of the Pareto-optimal set brought by envy, the pricing system could still be used in the quasi-atomic model provided that the degree of intraperson envy is not too large and that $\partial z [. . . , z^k, . . .] / \partial z^k > 0$. The Ethical Observer need work only in the $K$-dimensional space of $\{z^1, . . . , z^K\}$, where $z^k = z^k(x^k)$. By choice of the $(L^k)$ set, He or She can swing the system into any and every such point. The best state of the world will be found along the *atomic* Pareto-optimality set.

What only seemingly complicates matters are cases where too much for one man is so resented by the rest that the individualistic Ethical Observer is virtually forced into resenting it: this means that some $\partial z/\partial x^k$ become negative; and then $\partial z/\partial \bar{z}^k$ must be negative in such regions.

If you plot the ethical (interpersonal) indifference curves in the $(z^1, z^2)$ space, where $K = 2$, those curves bend back and have positive slopes in some regions. However, just as atoms avoid consuming too many chocolates if that makes them sick, the Ethical Observer faced with choice along a negatively inclined $(z^1, z^2)$ trade-off locus of feasibility will then most assuredly avoid oversatiated branches of the indifference curve with positive slope.

**19.** This section explains what has been mentioned in note 1, the resurrection for ethics of *additive* hedonism by John Harsanyi (1955) through a consideration of rational *stochastic* choice axioms. Harsanyi advances persuasive reasons why the weakly separable BISWF of (3.1) or (15.1), call it $z [z^1(\mathbf{x})], . . . , z^K(\mathbf{x})]$, should have a monotone stretching that makes it *linear:*

$$V(x) = Z\{z[z^1(\mathbf{x}), . . . , z^K(\mathbf{x})]\}, \qquad Z'\{z\} > 0 \gtreqqless Z''\{z\}$$

$$\equiv \sum_1^K \lambda^k V^k(\mathbf{x}), \qquad \lambda^k > 0 \tag{19.1}$$

In case the individuals are atoms, without envy or altruism and consuming only private goods, then of course $z^k(\mathbf{x})$ and $V^k(\mathbf{x})$ can be replaced by $z^k(\mathbf{x}^k)$ and $V^k(\mathbf{x}^k) \equiv Z^k\{z^k(\mathbf{x}^k)\}$, where $Z^k\{\cdot\}$ is a strictly monotone-increasing stretching that is allowed to be of any curvature.

Recall some fundamentals about individual stochastic decision making. You face alternative states of the world $(\mathbf{a}, \mathbf{b}, . . . )$, and you believe that each obtains with respective (subjective, personal) probabilities of $p(\mathbf{a})$, $p(\mathbf{b}), . . . $, where $p(\mathbf{a}) + p(\mathbf{b}) + \cdots = 1$ because some one of the mutually exclusive, exhaustive set of possible states of the world must "occur." You are able to order consistently, according to which you "like better'' all such "prospects." Your "stochastic ordering," designated by $\gtrsim$, obeys certain natural rules: It is transitive, not self-contradictory; you prefer 2 chocolates with certainty to 1 chocolate with certainty . . . ; you prefer a 50–50 chance of either 2 or 3 chocolates to a certainty of 1 chocolate . . . ; and so on. Finally, in accordance with Frank Ramsey (1931), Jacob Marschak (1950), L. J. Savage (1954), and other writers in the tradition that goes from 1738 (Daniel Bernoulli) to 1944 (von Neumann and Morgenstern), you choose to obey a natural "independence axiom": If you prefer prospect $A$ to prospect $B$, then you will prefer a 50–50 chance of $A$ or $C$ to a 50–50 chance of $B$ or $C$ (it being understood that $C$ never occurs except when neither $A$ nor $B$ occurs).

It follows that you *must* react in your stochastic decision making so as to maximize the "Expected (or "mean") value" of your (existent) utility function defined for each state of the world. You act to maximize

$$\text{Exp } V^k = p(a)V^k(\mathbf{a}) + p(b)V^k(\mathbf{b}) + \cdots \tag{19.2}$$

where $V^k(\cdot)$ is a well-defined metric (up to an arbitrary scaling and origin constant, $\alpha V^k + \beta, \alpha > 0$).

So far, "you" have been one of our individuals. But let us suppose that the Ethical Observer is no less "rational" or "consistent" than is any one fallible human being. The Ethical Observer then also has a utility metric, $[V(\mathbf{a}), V(\mathbf{b}), \ldots]$, written without a superscript. The BSWF then must, in stochastic situations, be expressible in the form

$$\text{Exp } V = p(\mathbf{a})V(\mathbf{a}) + p(\mathbf{b})V(\mathbf{b}) + \cdots \tag{19.3}$$

where

$$V(\mathbf{x}) = Z\{z(\mathbf{x})\}, \quad Z'\{\cdot\} > 0 \gtreqless Z''\{\cdot\} \tag{19.4}$$

So far I have been talking about any general BSWF. Now let me concentrate on an individualistic BISWF, in which individuals' tastes are to rule when individuals are unanimous (and where, we have seen, weak separability is implied). Harsanyi in effect argues:

If your individualistic ethic respects people's tastes in non-stochastic situations, the same logic suggests you will want to respect people's tastes in stochastic situations. Thus, just as you don't second guess individuals when they say they prefer beans to caviar, when consenting adults want not to gamble you respect their (ex ante, probabilistic) preferences.

This persuasive reasoning leads to the following axiom system:

$\alpha$  Individuals behave consistently in stochastic situations so as to become maximizers of their *Expected* utilities.

$\beta$  The Ethical Observer similarly behaves consistently and maximizes Expected social utility.

$\gamma$  In the individualistic case, weak separability is imposed so that individual's tastes rule when they are unanimous on nonstochastic situations (and, when they are not, are ethically resolved).

δ In the individualistic case, where stochastic elements can occur, weak separability in individuals' Expected utilities is imposed on the BISWF Expected utility function, so that whenever all say "We prefer the stochastic prospect $A$ to $B$," the ethical judgment must be rendered, "$A$ is ethically preferred to $B$."

Harsanyi's new element is to adjoin γ to the earlier axioms. This requires the following functional equation, weakly separable in the expected values:

$$\text{Exp } V = \phi[\text{Exp } V^1, \ldots, \text{Exp } V^K] \tag{19.5}$$

where $\phi$ is a strictly monotone-increasing function of its arguments. This is a strong – not unreasonable! – requirement.

To understand how $\phi[\cdot]$ relates to $z[\cdot]$ and to derive the implications of (19.5), consider the case where, with 50–50 odds, the $K$ persons get their personal utilities respectively of

$$[\alpha^1, \alpha^2, \ldots, \alpha^K] \quad \text{or} \quad [\beta^1, \beta^2, \ldots, \beta^K]$$

where

$$\alpha^k = V^k(\mathbf{a}) = Z^k\{z^k(\mathbf{a})\}$$
$$\beta^k = V^k(\mathbf{b}) = Z^k\{z^k(\mathbf{b})\}$$
$$p(\mathbf{a}) = \tfrac{1}{2} = p(\mathbf{b}) \qquad (k = 1, \ldots, K)$$

Then (19.5) becomes

$$\tfrac{1}{2}V[\alpha^1, \ldots, \alpha^K] + \tfrac{1}{2}V[\beta^1, \ldots, \beta^K]$$
$$\equiv \phi[\tfrac{1}{2}\alpha^1 + \tfrac{1}{2}\beta^1, \ldots, \tfrac{1}{2}\alpha^K + \tfrac{1}{2}\beta^K] \tag{19.6}$$

The functional equation (19.6), after we impose the overstrong condition that it be twice differentiable, implies that $V[y^1, \ldots, y^K]$ and $\phi[y^1, \ldots, y^K]$ be *linear* and be the *same* function:

$$V[y^1, \ldots, y^K] \equiv \lambda^0 + \lambda^1 y^1 + \cdots + \lambda^K y^K$$
$$\equiv \phi[y^1, \ldots, y^K] \tag{19.7}$$

To prove that (19.6) implies (19.7), differentiate (19.6) with respect to $\alpha^s$ and $\beta^k$; equating both sides then requires that $\phi[\cdot]$ have all vanishing second derivatives and be linear. Q.E.D.

Thus, we have proved the Harsanyi contention that the (stochastic) BISWF must be of the form

$$z[z^1(\mathbf{x}), \ldots, z^K(\mathbf{x})] = \text{a monotone-increasing function of}$$
$$\lambda^1 V^1(\mathbf{x}) + \cdots + \lambda^K V^K(\mathbf{x}) = V(\mathbf{x}) \tag{19.8}$$

where $V(\mathbf{x})$ is the utility whose Expected value is to be ethically maximized, and where $V^k(\mathbf{x})$ is a monotone-increasing stretching of $z^k(\mathbf{x})$.

**20.** John Chipman (1976) has given a magisterial review of Pareto's attempts to relate competitive equilibrium to welfare optimality. What was later to be called Pareto optimality was definitely glimpsed by Pareto in the years after 1894 [as it had been in Edgeworth (1881) in connection with the "contract" curve there]. Pareto's attempts at mathematical proof are, to put it kindly, obscure. Why does this matter? For one thing, if you do not manage to get your proof of a theorem right, you are not able to understand the theorem's precise limitation of application.

I have reread for the present essay the English translations of Pareto. This confirms my view of 45 years ago – that a fresh treatment of welfare economics was still needed. After, and only after, you have worked out a clear understanding of this subject are you able to recognize the bits of the puzzle that Pareto had already discerned. Nor will this surprise historians of science such as Robert Merton (1973) or Thomas Kuhn (1962): they have learned to expect multiple discoverers and rediscoverers of important scientific phenomena and theories. Thus, no less than 12 scientists can be said to be discoverers of the law of the conservation of energy. The fact that some of their writings were known to others in the group does not preclude legitimate claims to independent discovery if, as is often the case with early pioneers, the expositions are unclear and even defective in spots.

Let it be agreed at the beginning that Pareto was remarkably ahead of his time.

**21.** Pareto (1894) deals with optimal production conditions. Although I shall skip that topic here, it is worth mentioning that Pareto in this article discovers much of marginal productivity theory that is important in Wicksteed's famous *Essay on the Coordination of the Laws of Distribution*. Pareto's work seems to antedate that of Barone, his disciple; so Walras' 1896 third edition treatment, which Walras seemed to owe in large measure to Barone, essentially traces back to Pareto. Thus, my ordered list of discoverers of the general equilibrium theory of marginal productivity would include J. B. Clark, V. Pareto and P. H. Wicksteed, Barone and Walras, Wicksell, . . . .

Pareto (1903) represents his matured thought, with a fair sample of its obscurity. My notation will resemble that of Chipman (1976) in an understandable way. It is enough to consider Pareto's simplest case of competitive exchange with fixed production endowments of private goods by the persons: $(a_j^k)$, a $K$ by $J$ nonnegative matrix, with row sums and column sums that are positive.

I begin by making the strong assumptions on slopes and curvatures made in (12.1): smoothness, nonsatiation, and strict quasi-concavity for every atomic person and for the BISWF; every good a private good and an essential item in the sense of (12.1)'s limit relations. We moderns know that these assumptions suffice to guarantee the existence of a competitive solution (with positive prices). There may well be multiple solutions.

Pareto is correct to assert at the turn of the century:

Any observed competitive solution is Pareto optimal.

I am also correct to assert after mid-century:

Every *Pareto*-optimal point, under our strong curvature and nonexternality assumptions, can be achieved by a competitive equilibrium provided the laissez-faire "endowments" of income are altered by suitable algebraic lump-sum transfers, $(\lambda^1, \lambda^2, \ldots, \lambda^K = -\lambda^1 - \lambda^2 - \cdots - \lambda^{K-1})$, where

$$\sum_1^J p_j x_j^k - \sum_1^J p_j a_j^k = \lambda^k \qquad (k = 1, \ldots, K) \tag{21.1}$$

To prove this, all Pareto had to do was note that competitive equilibrium must fall on Edgeworth's contract locus, the locus of points of mutual tangency so that from each such point no mutually beneficial move is possible. And note that any finite movement from a contract-curve point must harm *at least one* person (and *possibly* all persons).

For a mathematical proof that the first-order conditions for Pareto optimality are implied by the first-order conditions effectuated under perfect competition, Pareto had need only to describe the following procedure.

The equations necessary for competitive equilibrium are now

$$x_1^k + \cdots + p_j K_j^k - a_1^k - \cdots - p_j a_j^k = \lambda^k \qquad (k = 1, \ldots, K) \tag{21.2}$$

$$\frac{z_j^k(\mathbf{x}^k)}{z_1^k(\mathbf{x}^k)} = p_j \qquad (j = 2, \ldots, J; \quad k = 1, \ldots, K) \tag{21.3}$$

$$\sum_1^K x_j^k = \sum_1^K a_j^k \qquad (j = 1, 2, \ldots, J) \tag{21.4}$$

$$\Lambda = \lambda^1 + \lambda^2 + \cdots + \lambda^K = 0 \tag{21.5}$$

*Remark.* The first equation in (21.4) follows redundantly from all the other equations and could be omitted in any listing of *independent* relations. For arbitrary choices of $(\lambda^2, \ldots, \lambda^K)$ not too large in absolute value, one (or more) solution(s) are determined: $(\bar{x}_j^k; \bar{p}_j)$.

For a feasible $(\bar{x}_j^k)$ to be Pareto optimal, it is necessary (and, under my strong assumptions, sufficient) that the tangencies be realized

$$\frac{z_j^k(\mathbf{x}^k)}{z_1^k(\mathbf{x}^k)} = \frac{z_j^1(\mathbf{x}^1)}{z_1^1(\mathbf{x}^1)} \qquad (j = 2, \ldots, J; \quad k = 2, \ldots, K) \tag{21.6}$$

All Pareto had to say, in the *Cours, Manual,* or 1903 polemic, is that the competitive relations (21.3) do imply the needed (21.6) welfare optimality conditions.

Mind you, a proper proof requires discussion of *second*-derivative conditions as well as *first*-derivative conditions. (In other words, *my* repeated assertions that quasi-concavity turns necessary conditions into sufficiency conditions needs explicit proof, something not hard to give in our times but quite beyond Pareto's knowledge of *un*bordered determinants.) Pareto never adequately dealt with secondary curvature conditions, for which I do not fault him in this review. It is his obscurities on *basics* that I here concentrate on. And I do that because these confusions clouded his pre-1913 expositions of what a SWF is all about.

**22.** Instead of simply identifying the (21.6) relations contained in (21.3), Pareto stubbornly worked with a hybrid sum (or its differential)

$$\Pi(\mathbf{x}) = \frac{z^1(\mathbf{x}^1)}{z_1^1(\bar{\mathbf{x}}^1)} + \frac{z^2(\mathbf{x}^2)}{z_1^2(\bar{\mathbf{x}}^2)} + \cdots + \frac{z^K(\mathbf{x}^K)}{z_1^K(\bar{\mathbf{x}}^K)} \tag{22.1}$$

Here, $\Pi(\mathbf{x})$ is my shorthand for $\Pi(\mathbf{x}, \bar{\mathbf{x}})$ and $z_1^k(\mathbf{x}) \equiv \partial z^k(\mathbf{x})/\partial x_1^k$.

For a positivist $\Pi(\mathbf{x})$ smacks of being a Benthamistic Social Welfare Function. It adds together what Pareto might be expected to regard as cheese and chalk – the weighted utility of man $k$ to the weighted utility of man $s$. And Pareto squeamishly avoids ever writing down the sum $\Pi(\mathbf{x})$ or the sum of differentials that total up to $d\Pi(\mathbf{x})$. Such forebearance cannot, however, succeed in exorcising the devil.

But actually that does not seem to be what Pareto is aiming at. His total differential

$$d\Pi(\mathbf{x}) = \sum_1^K \frac{dz^k(\mathbf{x}^k)}{z_1^k(\bar{\mathbf{x}}^k)}$$
$$= \sum_1^K \frac{\Sigma_1^J z_j^k(x_1^k, \ldots, x_j^k)\, dx_j^k}{z_1^k(\bar{x}_1^k, \ldots, \bar{x}_j^k)} \tag{22.2}$$

is intended solely to help him prove the Pareto-optimality property. It is an artifice that I would compare with a Lagrangean multiplier expression so beloved by advanced calculus texts in their dealings with constrained maxima problems. (Strangely, Pareto seems not to employ the Lagrangean multiplier technique, albeit one would suppose that he was familiar with this standard procedure that seems made to order for his kind of problem.)

At the equilibrium point itself, where Pareto equates $\mathbf{x}$ to $\bar{\mathbf{x}}$ and *there* evaluates (22.1)'s expression, he finds that $d\Pi(\mathbf{x})$ (which has the dimensionality of the *numéraire* good itself, of $dx_1$) *vanishes;*

$$d\Pi(\mathbf{x})|_{x=\bar{x}} \equiv d\Pi(\mathbf{x}, \bar{\mathbf{x}})|_{x=\bar{x}}$$
$$= \sum_1^J \sum_1^K \frac{z_j^k(\bar{\mathbf{x}}^k)}{z_1^k(\bar{\mathbf{x}}^k)}\, dx_j^k \tag{22.3}$$
$$= \sum_1^J \bar{p}_j \sum_1^K dx_j^k \qquad \text{by (21.3)} \tag{22.4}$$

$$d\,\Pi(\mathbf{x})|_{x=\bar{x}} = \sum_{1}^{J} \bar{p}_j \, d\left(\sum_{1}^{K} x_j^k\right) = \sum_{1}^{J} \bar{p}_j \cdot (0) \qquad \text{by (21.4)} \qquad (22.5)$$

$$= 0 \qquad\qquad\qquad (22.6)$$

Note that the $z_j^k/z_1^k$ ratios have common values of $\bar{p}_j$ in competitive equilibrium. And if the total endowment of a good is given, the feasible variation in its *total* consumption must vanish by virtue of

$$\sum_{1}^{K} x_j^k = \sum_{1}^{K} a_j^k, \qquad d\left(\sum_{1}^{K} x_j^k\right) = d\left(\sum_{1}^{K} a_j^k\right)$$

$$\equiv 0 \qquad (j = 1, \ldots, J) \quad (22.7)$$

Why is it important to prove that $d\Pi(x, \bar{x}) = 0$ at $x = \bar{x}$? And why important to prove – if only Pareto had been able to do so! – that $d^2\Pi(x) = d^2\Pi(x, \bar{x}) <$ at $x = \bar{x}$? Remember that $\Pi(x)$ is a positively weighted sum of the people's individual (allegedly cardinal) utilities. If such a sum genuinely reaches its maximum at the competitive equilibrium, then manifestly there exists *no* movement away from the equilibrium along which *every* $z^k$ $(x^k)$ grows! So $(\bar{x}_j^k)$ is then indeed a Pareto-optimal point.

**23.** Let me motivate a defense for Pareto's trucking with the devil of *adding inter* personal utilities. It involves only mathematical artifice and no philosophical capitulation. It is, however, defective in its unnecessary dependence on *concavity* of *cardinal* utility instead of properly relying only on *quasi-concavity* of any *ordinal* indicator of people's utility.

Actually, if $z^k(x^k)$ is strictly quasi-concave, in a finite neighborhood of $\bar{x}^k$ there exists an (infinity of) stretchings of $z^k(x^k)$ which will yield a *strictly concave* $Z^k(x^k)$ in that neighborhood. If we and Pareto agree to use such strictly concave individual utilities, one way of tracing out the utility-possibility frontier of points near $\bar{x}$ is to vary the positive weights, $(\omega^1, \omega^2, \ldots, \omega^K)$, and maximize for each choice of the $\omega$'s the positive sum

$$\max_{x} \; \Phi(x) = \max_{x_j^k} \sum_{1}^{k} \omega^k Z^k(x^k) \qquad (23.1)$$

subject to

$$\sum_{1}^{K} x_j^k = \sum_{1}^{K} a_j^k \qquad (j = 1, \ldots, J)$$

One choice of $\omega$ weights is $[\omega^k] = [1/Z_1^k(\bar{x}^k)]$ and for it, we and Pareto can verify that $(x^k) = (\bar{x}^k)$ is indeed a solution of the implied first-order extremal conditions:

$$\frac{Z_j^k(x^k)}{Z_1^k(x^k)} = \frac{Z_j^1(x^1)}{Z_1^1(x^1)} \qquad (j = 2, \ldots, J; \quad k = 2, \ldots, K) \quad (23.2)$$

$$\sum_{1}^{K} x_j^k = \sum_{1}^{K} a_j^k \qquad (j = 1, \ldots, J; \quad k = 1, \ldots, K) \quad (23.3)$$

By using Pareto's $[1/Z_1^k(x^k)]$ coefficients as our $\omega$'s, we've selected for $\Phi(x)$ precisely $\Pi(x) = \Pi(x, \bar{x})$ as defined in (22.1).

What is good about this version of Pareto's proof of the Pareto-optimality property of competitive exchange is that it enables us not only to derive Pareto's first-order conditions properly; it also can provide a rigorous proof that the critical point represents a *local* true maximum. The critical point, one realizes, is actually a *global* maximum, but it would be a delicate task to ensure that quasi-concave $z^k(x^k)$ can be globally stretched into a single concave $Z^k(x^k)$ (or into an appropriate sequence of such).

I have lingered on Pareto's $\Sigma_1^K \, dz^k(x^k)/z^k(\bar{x}^k)$ discussions not because they are very appealing in their own right but to help clarify the mysteries of discussions by Pareto and by Barone (1908).

**24.** There is a still better approach to a proof of competitive equilibrium's being Pareto optimal that stays in the spirit of Pareto's several skirmishes with the problem. Instead of $\Pi(x, \bar{x})$, it works with a related $\Lambda(x, \bar{x})$ function. I offer it not for its own sake, since my Section 21 has already provided straightforward proof, but rather to help in the interpretation of Pareto's historic writings.

Let me begin with a fresh start. Consider Pareto's observed competitive-equilibrium point, $(\bar{x}_j^k)$. It was achieved within the initial endowments $(\Sigma_1^K \, a_j^k) = (a_j)$. If it was a laissez-faire point, as most of the writings of Pareto and neoclassical economists concentrate on, it is a solution to the following equations when $(\lambda^1, \lambda^2, \ldots, \lambda^K) = (0, 0, \ldots, 0)$.

$$0 = x_1^k + \sum_2^J p_j x_j^k - \left( a_1^k + \sum_2^J p_j a_j^k \right) \\ - \lambda^k \qquad (k = 1, \ldots, k) \quad (24.1)$$

$$\frac{z_j^k(x^k)}{z_1^k(x^k)} = p_j \qquad (j = 2, \ldots, J) \quad (24.2)$$

$$0 = \sum_1^K x_j^k - \sum_1^K a_j^k \qquad (j = 1, 2, \ldots, J) \quad (24.3)$$

$$-\Lambda = \lambda^1 + \lambda^2 + \cdots + \lambda^K = 0 \quad (24.4)$$

A laissez-faire solution may be called $(\bar{x}_j^k)$ to distinguish it from the infinity of *interventionist* competitive solutions, $(\bar{x}_j^k)$, which are achieved with choices of $(\lambda^2, \ldots, \lambda^K)$ not all equal to zero. For Pareto or Smith to prove that the laissez-faire solution is Pareto optimal is not to prove much about it. *That* does not warrant the Bastiat–Mises–Friedman inference that $(\bar{x}_j^k)$ is "a good thing." There are infinities of non-Pareto-optimal points that are "ethically better" than the laissez-faire point in the view of "almost all" ethical systems – even those of "individualistic type."

Mathematically, this is a precise statement:

Given *any* $z[z^1(\mathbf{x}^1), \ldots, z^K(\mathbf{x}^K)]$ with well-behaved properties, for *almost all* $(a_j^k)$ endowment points, no laissez-faire solution can provide the feasible maximum to $z[\cdot]$.

So let us in 1980 widen Pareto's focus. We consider not only $(\bar{x}^k)$ laissez-faire points but also $(\bar{x}^k)$ points that are the competitive solution for some choice of $(L^2, \ldots, L^K)$ in (24.1) and (24.4). Scorza and Cassel are dead wrong to doubt that each such point is Pareto optimal. Here help will be given to explicate Pareto's purported proof of this by use of his $\Lambda$ function. [*Reminder:* To prove that a $(\bar{x}_j^k)$ is a Pareto-optimal point does not mean "it is a good thing." Unless the $(L^k)$ intervention that generated it was at the singular level(s) needed to maximize the BISWF in question, there will exist infinities of x points for which $z[\cdot]$ is greater than at this $\bar{x}$!]

Pareto (1894) in effect makes this observation pertinent to our present problem. "Unless $(\bar{x}_j^k)$ is Pareto Optimal, society will be able to provide it with *less* of total endowment of the *numéraire* good and the same total endowments for all the other goods." So write the saving achieved on the total endowment of the first good as $\Lambda$:

$$\Lambda = a_1 - \sum_1^K x_1^k$$
$$= \sum_1^K (a_1^k - x_1^k) \tag{24.5}$$

Let us now maximize this saving achievable while we achieve the levels of well-being $[z^k(\bar{x}^k)]$ for every person and stay within the endowment totals of the non-*numéraire* goods.

We solve the new maximum problem,

$$\max_{x_j^k} \Lambda(x) = \max_{x_j^k} \sum_1^K (a_1^k - x_1^k) \tag{24.6}$$

subject to

$$z^k(\mathbf{x}^k) \geq z^k(\mathbf{x}^k) \qquad (k = 1, \ldots, K) \tag{24.6'}$$

$$\sum_1^K x_j^k \leq \sum_1^K a_j^k = a_j \qquad (j = 2, \ldots, J) \tag{24.6''}$$

If the competitive equilibrium is Pareto optimal, and only then, will max $\Lambda$ equal zero and be achieved at $(x_j^k) = (\bar{x}_j^k)$. For if there were any positive saving possible, competitive equilibrium could be improved upon for every individual by giving each some of the achievable saving.

Under my overstrong curvature and satiation conditions on the contours of $z^k(\mathbf{x}^k)$, this last maximum problem is solved for x*, the root of the following equations for the critical point of the Lagrangean expression.

$$L(\mathbf{x}; \boldsymbol{\alpha}, \boldsymbol{\beta}) = \sum_1^K (a_1^k - x_1^k) + \sum_1^K \alpha^k[z^k(\mathbf{x}^k) - z^k(\bar{\mathbf{x}}^k)]$$

$$+ \sum_2^J \beta_j \sum_1^K (a_j^k - x_j^k) \tag{24.7}$$

At $L(\cdot)$'s critical point,

$$\partial L/\partial x_1^k = 0 = -1 + \alpha^k z_1^k(\mathbf{x}^k) \qquad (k = 1, \ldots, K)$$
$$\partial L/\partial x_j^k = 0 = \alpha^k z_j^k(\mathbf{x}^k) - \beta_j \qquad (k = 1, \ldots, K; \; j = 2, \ldots, J)$$
$$\partial L/\partial \alpha^k = 0 = z_K^k(\mathbf{x}^k) - z^k(\bar{\mathbf{x}}^k) \qquad (k = 1, \ldots, K) \tag{24.8}$$
$$\partial L/\partial \beta_j = 0 = \sum_1^K a_j^k - \sum_1^k x_j^k \qquad (j = 2, \ldots, J)$$

Eliminating $(\alpha^k, \beta_j)$ from the first two sets of (24.8) leaves us with the last two sets and with

$$\frac{z_j^k(\mathbf{x}^k)}{z_1^k(\mathbf{x}^k)} = \frac{z_j^1(\mathbf{x}^1)}{z_1^1(\mathbf{x}^1)} \qquad (j = 2, \ldots, J; \; k = 2, \ldots, K) \tag{24.9}$$

Any $\mathbf{x}^*$ root is, under my strong conditions, unique. So these necessary conditions are also sufficient (since the maximum patently exists and is an interior one). From the nature of $(\bar{x}_j^k)$ as a competitive solution, we recognize at sight that $\mathbf{x}^* = \bar{\mathbf{x}}$ is indeed a solution of (24.8)–(24.9). And for it $\Lambda$ is indeed zero.

There remains only to show that the $\Lambda$ saving magnitude is the sum (with sign reversed to keep our problem a maximum rather than minimum formulation) of the lump-sum transfers $(\lambda^1, \lambda^2, \ldots, \lambda^K)$ in (24.1).

$$-\Lambda = \lambda^1 + \lambda^2 + \cdots + \lambda^K \tag{24.10}$$

To verify this, multiply each endowment relation of (24.3) respectively by $p_j$; then from their sum subtract the sum of the $k$ relations in (24.1) and observe that you will be left with (24.4)'s right-hand side.

Just as $\partial \Pi(x)/\partial x_1^k$ equals unity at $x = \bar{x}$, so does $-\partial \Lambda(\mathbf{x})/\partial x_1^k$ equal unity at $x = \bar{x}$ (it being understood that all other $x_1$'s are held constant in this variation). Thus, even though the degrees of freedom of $x$ in $\Pi(\mathbf{x})$ and in $-\Lambda(x)$ are not the same, these two Paretian functions are closely related up to the first order.

**25.** In his forties Pareto began to emancipate himself from *cardinal* (as opposed to *ordinal*) utility: to concentrate on the indifference contours' curvatures and to ignore the noninvariant utility metric. He never quite integrated his new thinking, never quite purged from his mind his old thinking. In part this was because he lacked mathematical knowledge of bordered quadratic forms relevant for constrained extrema – a lack he shared with most mathematicians of his day.

Rather than belabor these invariant-curvature niceties, let me show why they matter. Suppose that a million people have (well-behaved) rectangular hyperbola for atomic indifference curves in their private goods $(x_1^k, x_2^k)$. Suppose that a single person has for his indifference curves quarter circles, an *admissible* case of *nonconvex* indifference contours in his $(x_1^K, x_2^K)$ space ($K = 1,000,001$).

*Now competitive equilibrium fails utterly.* For given endowments $(a_j^k)$, there is no market-clearing intersection of supply and demand to determine an equilibrium $p_2$. But Pareto optimality is still well defined no matter what $K$ is!

Thus, with $K = 2$ and $(a_1, a_2) = (4, 4)$, the point $(x_1^1, x_2^1; x_1^2, x_2^2) = (1, 1; 3, 3)$ is Pareto optimal. It is also Bergson optimal for a BISWF of the form

$$V = [x_1^1 x_2^1]^{1/4} + \sqrt{3[\tfrac{1}{2}(x_1^2)^2)^2 + \tfrac{1}{2}(x_2^2)^2]^{1/4}}$$

What went wrong? Pareto never correctly stated the curvature conditions necessary and sufficient for Pareto optimality, distinguishing them from the curvature conditions necessary and sufficient for competitive equilibrium. And modern textbook writers, aware that Arrow and Debreu have provided conditions under which Pareto-optimal and competitive points can be interrelated, usually neglect to reproduce the fine print in which certain assumptions of the argument are specified.

Ironically, in Pareto's somewhat confused extensions of the theory of production to handle increasing returns to scale, he had already sensed some similar formal difficulties that mar the use of (Lerner–Lange) *competitive role playing* by the socialist bureaucrats.

**26.** To complete this brief survey of Pareto's pre-Bergson contribution to welfare economics, I call attention to the notice in Chipman (1976) of Pareto (1913). Here Pareto finally does consider the genuine sum of utilities across persons, at least as part of "sociology" (which is Pareto's catchall for that which is not rational economics). It is not clear that Pareto is returning to a Benthamite or Old Welfare Economics social welfare function. Rather he is doing at least two things.

1. As in my Sections 14–18 discussion of quasi-atomic higher-order individual tastes, Pareto considers how "do-gooders and humanitarians" want to act in accordance with (what is in my notation)

$$\alpha^{1k} V^1(\mathbf{x}^1) + \alpha^{2k} V^2(\mathbf{x}^2) + \cdots + \alpha^{Kk}(\mathbf{x}^K) \qquad (k = 1, \ldots, K) \qquad (26.1)$$

2. But, since some people $k$ are do-gooders and some people $s$ are (like Pareto) less altruistic, these different $\alpha$ weights are discordant between people. Pareto envisages a "government" that second-guesses and compromises between them, applying *its* superweights $[\alpha^{1G}, \alpha^{2G}, \ldots, \alpha^{kG}, \ldots, \alpha^{KG}]$ to form

$$\alpha^{1G} \sum_1^K \alpha^{k1} V^k(\mathbf{x}^k) + \cdots + \alpha^{KG} \sum_1^K \alpha^{kK} V^k(\mathbf{x}^k)$$

$$= \left( \sum_s \alpha^{SG} \alpha^{ST} \right) V^1(\mathbf{x}^1) + \cdots + \left( \sum_s \alpha^{SG} \alpha^{SK} \right) V^K(\mathbf{x}^K)$$

$$= \sum_1^K \beta^k V(\mathbf{x}^k)$$

Rather than this resultant Social Function being a social *welfare* function (of ethical-norming nature), for Pareto this may simply have been a positivistic function to account for the behavior of quasi-democratic government – in Chipman's felicitous phrase merely "an expression of the revealed preferences of a centrally organized society, as exhibited by its observed behavior."[10]

To sum up what Pareto had accomplished in 1913, 25 years before Bergson's 1938 formulation, let me say:

1. Pareto may or may not have given in 1913 an Old Welfare Economics social welfare function of Bentham's additive-hedonistic form.
2. Or Pareto may have tried to account for the behavior resulting from group and governmental interactions by collective utility and indifference fields.

In all likelihood, Pareto never had to make up his mind on just what he was hoping to accomplish.

**27.** I mention a new topic. Abba Lerner (1944), and other writers, have tried to argue in this vein:

Our knowledge of people's actual and proper $\lambda$'s in Benthamite expressions $\Sigma_1^K \lambda^k V^k(\mathbf{x}^k)$ is (necessarily) imperfect. But in the absence of any knowledge or presumption that people's initial endowments are correlated with their $\lambda^k$ deservingnesses, it is valid to infer, "An *egalitarian* division of a given (conserved) total output, $x = x^1 + \cdots + x^k$, is in a defendable probability sense best."

In my 1964 salutation to Lerner's sixtieth birthday, I used pre-Rawlsian arguments to buttress this insight. [Later, Kenneth Arrow reminded me that the pre-Rawlsian argument of Samuelson (1964) had already appeared in Vickery (1945)!] Here is how the argument goes.

I am any person $k$. What tax charter will each of us want for society if, under the Rawlsian veil of ignorance, we suppose that the probability distribution determining *my* initial endowment $a^k$ and others' endowments $a^s$ is *symmetric* in $(k, s = 1, \ldots, K)$? If each of us is risk averse with concave $V^k(\mathbf{x}^k)$, I and everyone will then opt for egalitarian progressive taxation.[11] Q.E.D. [This holds even if our $V^k(x^k)$ functions are all different, and known only to be concave.]

Rawls, Sen, Varian, and others have extended such arguments to include questions such as this:

What if I don't know whether I'll be a man, woman, cockroach, or teetotaler. Gathered together under the veil of ignorance to form a social contract, we each selfishly may be able to arrive at unanimous agreement on what is "fair" and an ethically best state of the world or generator of best future states.

28. The argument I presented to Lerner was not quite the one he had originally desired. Perhaps it can be given a valid formulation in its own right, along the following lines. [For brevity, I shall assume that all $V^k(\cdot)$ functions are the *same* unknown concave function, $V(\cdot)$; and shall assume that $J = 1$, so there is a single scalar good to divide up. The simplifications are inessential.]

Without redistributive taxes, the BISWF would take on the value

$$\lambda^1 V(a^1) + \cdots + \lambda^K V(a^K) \tag{28.1}$$

Suppose that you as Legislator do not know what the values of $(\lambda^k, a^k)$ are but know only that the $\lambda$'s and $a$'s obey *independent* probability distributions.

$$\text{Prob}\{a^1 < \alpha^1, \ldots, a^K < \alpha^K, \lambda^1 < \beta^1, \ldots, \lambda^K < \beta^K\}$$
$$= P(a^1, a^2, \ldots, a^K)Q(\lambda^1, \ldots, \lambda^K) \tag{28.2}$$

and where $P(\cdot)$ is *symmetric* in its arguments.

You as Legislator want to vote on the degree of tax progression, $t$, which moves every person with initial $a^k$ toward the mean, $\Sigma_1^K a^k/K = \mu$, by the fraction $t$ of that distance.

If $t = 0$, we have laissez faire. If $t = 1$, we have complete egalitarian taxation. For every $t$, we assume no deadweight loss, with $\Sigma_1^K a^k = \Sigma_1^K x^k$.

The Expected value of social utility becomes a function of the parameter $t$ alone once the probability distributions $P(\cdot)$ and $Q(\cdot)$ are given. We have for this Expected social utility:

$$v(t) = \text{Exp} \sum_1^K \lambda^k V(x^k)$$
$$= \int \cdots \int \sum_1^K \lambda^k V([1 - t]a^k + t\mu) \, d[P(a^1, \ldots)Q(\lambda^1, \ldots)] \tag{28.3}$$

It is easy to show that $v(t)$ is concave and that $v(t)$ achieves its minimum at $t = 1$, where

$$v'(1) = V'(\mu) \sum_1^K [\int \cdots \int \lambda^k \, dQ(\lambda^1, \ldots)][\int \cdots \int (a^k - \mu) \, dP(a^1, \ldots)]$$
$$= V'(\mu) \sum_1^K [\text{Exp}(\lambda^k)] \cdot 0 = 0 > v''(1) \tag{28.4}$$

What confidence we should have in the axiom of $P(a^1, \ldots)Q(\lambda^1, \ldots)$ *probabilistic independence* is not a question of deductive logic.

29. My final topic reiterates the warning against confusing (a) Arrow's proof that a Constitutional Function with certain desirable properties does

not exist, with (b) a belief that well-behaved Bergson Social Welfare Functions do not exist. In the spirit of Samuelson (1967), I make one more try.

Consider two people: He and She. Consider three states of the world: $A$, $B$, and $C$. Preference orderings on these states will, for simplicity, permit no ties of indifference. Always $A > B$ or $B > A$, with $A \sim B$ never encountered.

First, contemplate the BISWF problem. He has his preference ordering $>^k$, for $k = 1$. She has hers, for $k = 2$. Either can have any *one* of the six possible orderings of $(A, B, C)$. I write these six possibilities as $ABC$, $ACB$, $BAC$, $BCA$, $CAB$, $CBA$. If He has any one of six, and She has any one of six, between them there are 36 different pairs of orderings that could be the actual one that confronts the Ethical Observer. Whichever *one* of the 36 the Ethical Observer is confronted with – and it will be one precise one – the Observer must come up with a BISWF ordering that (a) agrees with theirs whenever they are unanimous and (b) resolves the choice ethically when they disagree.

Does such a BISWF exist? Yes. I can write down, for any pair of specified individuals' orderings, a well-behaved BISWF. Indeed, more than one admissible BISWF exists for most pairs of individuals' preferences, and it is not for me to appraise the relative merits of alternative admissible BISWFs.

I shall now display the *existent* BISWFs and shall do so in the context where Arrow's Impossibility Theorem does apply (apply to show there is no Arrow Constitutional Function, even though there do exist BISWFs in abundance).

Rather than go through 36 different specifications, I can deal with six only. Since labels are arbitrary, I can by relabeling make His ordering always be $(ABC)$. So the one case confronting the Ethical Observer must be one of the six cases corresponding to Her six alternative possible orderings: $ABC$, $ACB$, $BAC$, $BCA$, $CAB$, *and* $CBA$. I examine each in turn and write out the existent BISWFs for each:

$ABC$: Here they are unanimous on $(ABC)^k$, $k = 1, 2$. So the social ordering or BISWF, written without a superscript, must be the sole choice of $(ABC)$. *Conclusion:* In this first of six cases, yes, a BISWF does exist.

$ACB$: I propose for the reader's testing that the following two BISWFs do exist: $(ABC)$ and $(ACB)$. *Note:* Since the individuals are unanimous that $A$ is better than $B$, and that $A$ is better than $C$, the BISWF is required to agree to that. But since the individuals disagree on the merits of $B$ versus $C$, the Ethical Observer can resolve their difference in either of two ways: decreeing *B* better ethically than *C,* or vice versa. *Conclusion:* Again the existence of a BISWF has been affirmed; actually the above two exist.

*BAC:* This is like the previous case. He and She are unanimous that *B* is better than *C* and that *A* is better than *C.* They have one disagreement on whether *A* is better than *B,* or vice versa. *Conclusion:* A BISWF does exist in this case; actually two of them, (*ABC*) and (*BCA*).

*BCA:* Now there are two disagreements between Him and Her. They only agree unanimously that *B* is better than *C.* The Ethical Observer can go in favor of either person in each of the two disagreements. So you might think there are four existent BISWFs. Actually, though, we must not forget transitivity, which will rule out one of the four contingencies as self-contradictory,[12] leaving us with the three existent BISWFs: (*ABC*), (*BCA*), and (*BAC*).

*CAB:* As with the previous case there are here two disagreements between Him and Her. They only agree unanimously that *A* is better than *B.* They disagree on whether *C* is better than *A* or better than *B,* and the ethical resolution of the discordance can go in favor of either one of each of these pair comparisons. Again, insisting on transitivity of the resulting BISWF, we find that there do indeed exist three alternative BISWFs: (*ABC*), (*CAB*), and (*ACB*).

*CBA:* This is the case where She and He perversely differ in every respect. So every state of the world must be Pareto optimal. The Ethical Observer is free to pick any of the six possible transitive orderings in order to resolve the ethical normings. Hence, in this last case, as in all of our previous cases, there do exist well-behaved BISWFs: (*ABC*), (*ACB*), (*BAC*), (*BCA*), (*CAB*), and (*CBA*).

*Summary.* I have now shown constructively that well-behaved Bergson social welfare functions do exist, exactly as Bergson and Samuelson have always defined them.

**30.** I have now proved that a BISWF always exists in a two-person three-state universe. Does an Arrow Constitutional Function, an ACF, with well-behaved properties exist for that universe? After I describe how such an ACF is defined, we will see why none can exist with Arrow's postulated good properties.

A BISWF is defined for *only one* of the six alternative taste patterns prevailing. An ACF is defined so that *no matter which of the six* orderings

She fills out for Her voting ballot, the Constitutional Function or Vote-Scoring Machine must come out with its answer – its social ordering, which, remember, must then be a selection of one of the six possible orderings *ABC, ACB, BAC, BCA, CAB,* or *CBA.*

Arrow posits the following axioms as a well-behaved ACF.

1.   For every possible pattern of votes or orderings on the part of the *K* ( =2 in our example) that people put into the ACF as inputs, it must be wired to come out with a definite social ordering as output – a social ordering that is *transitive.*
2.   When the people are *unanimous* on any choice among a pair of states of the world, the ACF must agree with them. When some differ, it must resolve their difference in *its* chosen way.
3.   In making its above choice among a pair of states, say among *A* or *B,* the preferences involving other states – *B* or *C, A* or *C,* and the actual feasible occurrence of such other states – cannot have any relevance.
4.   The ACF must not be "dictatorial" in the sense of *always* giving one of the *k* persons the deciding choice.

Still other axioms could be added, or different combinations and permutations of these and other axioms could be posited. But it will suffice to show that there exists no ACF satisfying these four axioms of (1) unlimited domain, (2) Pareto unanimity principle, (3) independence of irrelevant alternatives, and (4) nondictatorship.

An ACF must be a selection of one each from the following six input orderings and their possible output orderings as given in the previous section on BISWF:

| Her input | ABC | ACB | BAC | BCA | CAB | CBA |
|---|---|---|---|---|---|---|
| Possible BISWFs | ABC | ABC | ABC | ABC | ABC | ABC |
| | | ACB | BAC | BCA | CAB | CBA |
| | | | | BAC | ACB | ACB |
| | | | | | | BAC |
| | | | | | | BCA |
| | | | | | | CAB |

There are plenty of Constitutional Functions we can select from the table, but none will be "well behaved" in the Arrow sense.

How many possible CFs are there? There are $1 \times 2 \times 2 \times 3 \times 3 \times 6$ or 216 in all, representing all possible independent choices of one each from the elements in the six columns of the table. But each one of the 216 is found to violate one or more of the reasonable axioms.

Let us sample to verify this. Suppose that we pick the *ABC* element from the top of every column and define our CF by that set of choices.

Clearly, this CF gives Him his way every time. He is a dictator. So that CF is no ACF.

Let us try again. To avoid dictatorship, each person must be given the decisive choice in at least one case where the two differ in ordering a pair of states. Since our example involves only three pairs of states – $A$ versus $B$, $A$ versus $C$, $B$ versus $C$ – our ACF must resolve differences in favor of one of the people twice and in favor of the other person once. Since the gender label is arbitrary, in mock chivalry let us give Her the decisive role in two pairs and Him that role in one.

Thus, let Him prevail only when there is discordance over $A$ and $B$. This defines our CF, and we must examine it to see whether it is an ACF. Here is its decision in the cases of the six possible ballots for Her (and, it is understood, for His constant ABC ballot):

| Her input | ABC | ACB | BAC | BCA | CAB | CBA |
|---|---|---|---|---|---|---|
| CF output | ABC | ACB | ABC | Null | CAB | CAB |

Corresponding to $BCA$ there is no possible social ordering that is transitive and agrees with our stipulated rules; He to prevail on the $A$ versus $B$ choice; She to prevail on the rest. For, applying these rules to the $BCA$ ballot gives us: $A$ socially better than $B$ (to please Him); $B$ socially better than $C$ (to please Her); $C$ better than $A$ (to please Her) – but this is a contradiction to social transitivity (how can $C$ be better than $A$ when $A$ is better than $B$, which is better than $C!$).

Symbolically, the fifth item is null because our rules produce the following contradiction to transitivity:

$$A > B > C > A \quad \text{or} \quad ABCA, \qquad \text{a contradiction} \qquad (30.1)$$

Lest the reader thinks the above contradiction comes from giving Him dominance only on his choice between his very best and next best, let us derive a similar contradiction from the cases where He prevails on his choice between $B$ or $C$. Now the table is similarly uncompletable:

| Her input | ABC | ACB | BAC | BCA | CAB | CBA |
|---|---|---|---|---|---|---|
| CF output | ABC | ABC | BAC | BCA | null | null |

Finally, and this exhausts the possible essentially different cases, consider the case where He gets his way only on the choice between $A$ or $C$ (between his actual most preferred and least preferred states). This uncompletable table obtains:

| Her input | ABC | ACB | BAC | BCA | CAB | CBA |
|---|---|---|---|---|---|---|
| CF output | ABC | ACB | BAC | BAC | ACB | null |

Thus, without bothering to enumerate all 216 cases, we have shown that in *no* possible case will there exist a definable Arrow Constitutional Function satisfying the four plausible axioms.[13] And, despite this, a BISWF does exist to ethically norm the states of the world while respecting the actual (one out of the six possible) individuals' orderings that do obtain.

**31.** My task is done. Space did not permit me to address topics of only secondary importance. Thus, I have not dealt with "consume*r's* surplus," which is only a subspecies in the "revealed preference" zoo. I have not dealt with "consume*rs'* surplus" either and must refer the reader to a more general treatment of how to make inferences from aggregate data on $\Sigma_1^K x_j^k$ in Samuelson (1950). Samuelson and Swamy (1973) sum up the easier problem of interpreting index numbers based on one person's $(\mathbf{p}, x_j^k)$ observations. Frank Ramsey's theory of the "second best" (or, better, of the feasible "first best" when a person can be subjected only to excise taxes on goods and services), as in Ramsey (1927), takes simplest form in a one-person society, or in "a good society," where initial endowments have been rectified in the background. These and many other topics, such as the existence of "cheat-proof" algorithms in game situations, would take me too far afield.

Enough has been said to honor the magnificent edifice of Bergsonian welfare economics.

### Notes

1 A possible qualification to this comes from what I have called the quantum jump of progress in modern welfare economics due to John Harsanyi (1955). He showed there that *individualistic* ethics applied to *stochastic* (i.e., probabilistic) states can lead back naturally to the *additive* hedonism of Bentham, Edgeworth, and the "old" welfare economists (Pigou, Marshall, Wicksell, etc.). In terms of the notation in my later equation (1), the BISWF there can then be written in terms of *strongly* separable functions, namely as $\lambda_1 U^1(\text{bread}^1, \text{wine}^1) + \lambda_2 U^2(\text{bread}^2, \text{wine}^2)$, where the *only* remaining judgment required of the ethical judge is the ratio of the $\lambda$'s once the metrics of the $U$'s have been specified.

2 Marshall's 1890 *Principles of Economics* noted, but did not emphasize, that the existence of *multiple* solutions to a microsystem would cast doubt that all such (quite different) solutions could *simultaneously* each be ethically optimal. So why should a system with a unique competitive equilibrium have accorded to that equilibrium social optimality?

3 Thus, Walras, and Frank Knight in my time, sometimes believed that perfect competition "maximized each person's utility subject to the constraints on everybody of being a price-taking competitor." That this is a confusion and irrelevancy is simplest seen in the case where competitive equilibrium is unique: Its outcome then is the *only* possible outcome, as much the *worst* feasible state of the world as the *best*. What Knight had in the back of his mind was that, somehow, a one-price competitive regime involves some im-

portant personal freedom. Walras seems to have had a related fuzzy notion about "commutative justice" independently of "distributive justice." As a rich man I ought ethically to give to poor men, but it is ethically right for me not to do so and to use *my* private property as I wish.

4 Relevant to this are Bergson (1954, chap. 2), Little (1952), and Samuelson (1967).

5 A competitive equilibrium may exist under lighter conditions than my assumptions. Externalities aside, it can be proved to be Pareto optimal. However, a socialist's desired Bergson optimum, which will of course be a Pareto-optimal point, need not be realizable as a competitive solution when (a) laws of returns are not appropriate, and (b) when some people's indifference contours violate quasi-concavity. I return to this later.

6 Richard Musgrave (1959) and Leif Johansen (1965) are standard references on the public goods model.

7 Vickery (1961), Groves and Ledyard (1975), Tideman and Tulloch (1976), and others in our time have tried to work out alternatives to the Lindahl solution that will motivate people not to try to be "free riders" in their use of and rates for public goods. My exposition here parallels Samuelson (1954, 1956, 1964) and overlaps with Johansen (1965).

8 Perhaps Pareto's *literary* exposition is, for once, better than his mathematical. Thus his *Manual* (chap. 6, §33–8) adequately recaptures tangencies of indifference contours along the "contract curves [of Pareto optimality]" in Edgeworth's 1881 *Mathematical Psychics*.

9 Some ideologically conservative people seriously propose that redistribution of income and wealth should be limited to what people *want* to give in *private* charity.

10 We should not expect too much from a paper as short as this 1913 fragment of Pareto. But, on reflection, we realize that no integrable social preference field is likely to emerge from the game-theoretic interactions of group politics. Samuelson (1956) shows by the concept of "a good society" how strict are the requirements (in the way of optimizing lump-sum transfers) if family or group demand behavior of weakly separable members is to satisfy the Slutsky–Antonelli reciprocity conditions of transitive preferences. In particular, as Pareto the cynic knew, observations from political compromises are unlikely to be Pareto optimal and hence could not have been generated by any quasi-individualistic social function of the type Pareto here attributes to "government."

11 Redistribution of $\Sigma_1^K a^k$ may involve deadweight transfer loss as $\Sigma_1^K x^k$ is lowered. This realistic fact will cause each of us to opt for less than complete egalitarianism, unless each and every one of us is a Maxaminer in the Rawls (1971) manner. See my contribution to the Vickery *Festschrift* (1976), where I analyze what Arthur Okun was to call the "leaky bucket experiment"; and where it is shown that following Rawls's Maxaminer dogma would force all parties to the social compact into more egalitarianism than any of them would want.

12 Thus, suppose that He is given his way on the $A$ and $B$ disagreement and She is given her way on the $A$ and $C$ disagreement. This would lead to "$C$ better than $A$, $A$ better than $B$, and $B$ better than $C$," a contradiction to transitivity of the BISWF.

13 Some had hoped to get around the Impossibility Theorem by invoking a *cardinal* intensity for each individual's private ordering. Samuelson (1967) has

argued that a new Impossibility Theorem will be found to obtain in the realm of intensity orderings. So there is no escape from the Arrow nullity in that direction.

## References

Arrow, Kenneth. 1951. *Social Choice and Individual Values,* 2d ed. New York: Wiley, 1963.

Barone, Enrico. 1908. "Il ministerio della produzione nello stato colletivista," *Giornale degli Economisti,* pp. 267–93, 391–414. Translated in F. A. Hayek (ed.), *Collectivist Economic Planning.* London: Routledge and Kegan Paul, 1935.

Bastiat, F. 1850. *Economic Harmonies.*

Bentham, J. 1789. *An Introduction to the Principles of Morals and Legislation.* Payne; also Clarendon Press, Oxford, 1907.

Bergson, Abram. 1938. "A Reformulation of Certain Aspects of Welfare Economics," *Quarterly Journal of Economics* 52, 310–34.

Bergson, Abram. 1954. "On the Concept of Social Welfare," *Quarterly Journal of Economics* 68, 233–52.

Bergson, Abram. 1966. *Essays in Normative Economics.* Cambridge, Mass.: Harvard University Press.

Bernoulli, Daniel. 1738. "Specimen theoriae novae de mensura sortis." English translation: "Exposition of a New Theory on the Measurement of Risk," *Econometrica* 22, 23–6 (1954).

Chipman, John. 1976. "The Paretian Heritage," *Revue Europeene des Sciences Sociales et Cahiers Vilfredo Pareto* 14, 65–171.

Debreu, Gerard. 1959. *Theory of Value.* New York: Wiley.

Edgeworth, F. Y. 1881. *Mathematical Psychics.* London: C. Keagan Paul.

Graaf, Jan van de. 1957. *Theoretical Welfare Economics.* Cambridge: Cambridge University Press.

Groves, T., and J. Ledyard. 1975. "Optimal Allocation of Public Goods: A Solution to the 'Free Rider'." Discussion paper 144, Center for Mathematical Studies, Economics and Management Science, Northwestern University, Evanston, Ill.

Harrod, R. F. 1938. "Scope and Methods of Economics," *Economic Journal* 48, 383–412.

Harsanyi, John. 1955. "Cardinal Welfare, Individualistic Ethics, and Interpersonal Comparisons of Utility," *Journal of Political Economy* 63, 309–21.

Hicks, J. R. 1939. "The Foundations of Welfare Economics," *Economic Journal* 49, 696–712.

Hotelling, H. 1938. "The General Welfare in Relation to Problems of Taxation and of Railway and Utility Rates," *Econometrica* 6, 242–69.

Johansen, L. 1965. *Public Economics.* Chicago: Rand McNally.

Kaldor, Nicholas. 1939. "Welfare Propositions of Economics and Interpersonal Comparisons of Utility," *Economic Journal* 49, 549–52.

Kemp, M. C., and Y.-K. Ng. 1976. "On the Existence of Social Welfare Functions, Social Orderings and Social Decision Functions," *Economica* 43, 59–66.

Kemp, M. C., and Y. K. Ng. 1977. "More on Social Welfare Functions: The Incompatibility of Individualism and Ordinalism," *Economica* 44, 89–90.

Kuhn, Thomas. 1962. *The Structure of Scientific Revolutions.* Chicago: University of Chicago Press.

Lange, O. 1942. "The Foundations of Welfare Economics," *Econometrica* 10, 215–28.

Lerner, A. P. 1934a. "Concept of Monopoly and the Measurement of Monopoly Power," *Review of Economic Studies* 1, 157–75.

Lerner, A. P. 1934b. "Economic Theory and Socialist Economy," *Review of Economic Studies* 2, 51–61.

Lerner, A. P. 1944. *Economics of Control.* New York: Macmillan.

Lindahl, Erik. 1919. *Die Gerechtigkeit der Besteuerung, eine Analyse der Steuer Prinzipen auf Grundlage der Grenznutzentheorie.* Lund.

Little, Ian. 1950. *A Critique of Welfare Economics.* Oxford: Clarendon Press.

Little, Ian. 1952. "Social Choice and Individual Values," *Journal of Political Economy* 60, 422–32.

Marschak, Jacob. 1950. "Rational Behavior, Uncertain Prospects and Measurable Utility," *Econometrica* 18, 111–41.

Marshall, A. 1890. *Principles of Economics.* London: Macmillan.

Merton, Robert K. 1973. *The Sociology of Science.* Chicago: University of Chicago Press.

Mises, Ludwig von. 1920. "Die Wirtschaftsrechnung im sozialistischen Gemeinwesen," *Archiv fur Sozialwissenschaften,* pp. 86–121. Translated in F. A. Hayek (ed.), *Collectivist Economic Planning.* London: Routledge & Kegan Paul, 1935.

Musgrave, Richard. 1959. *The Theory of Public Finance.* New York: McGraw-Hill.

Neumann, J. von, and O. Morgenstern. 1944. *Theory of Games and Economic Behavior.* Princeton, N.J.: Princeton University Press.

Pareto, Vilfredo. 1894. "Il massimo di utilita data dalla libera concorrenza," *Giornale degli Economisti* 2, 9, 48–66.

Pareto, Vilfredo. 1896, 1897. *Cours d'économie politique,* vols. 1 and 2. Lausanne: F. Rouge.

Pareto, Vilfredo. 1903. "A proposito del massimo di ofelimita," *Giornale degli Economisti* 2, 26, 177–8.

Pareto, Vilfredo. 1909. *Manuel d'économie politique.* Paris: M. Giard et E. Brière. English translation: *Manual of Political Economy.* New York: Augustus Kelly, 1971.

Pareto, Vilfredo. 1913. "Il massimo di utilita per una colletivita in sociologia," *Giornale degli Economisti* 3, 46, 337–41.

Pigou, A. C. 1932. *Economics of Welfare.* London: Macmillan.

Pollak, Robert A. 1979. "Bergson–Samuelson Social Welfare Functions and the Theory of Social Choice," *Quarterly Journal of Economics* 93, 73–92.

Ramsey, Frank. 1927. "A Contribution to the Theory of Taxation," *Economic Journal* 37, 47–61.

Rawls, John. 1971. *A Theory of Justice.* Cambridge, Mass.: Harvard University Press.

Robbins, Lionel. 1932. *An Essay on the Nature and Significance of Economic Science.* London: George Allen & Unwin.

Samuelson, Paul A. 1938. "Welfare Economics and International Trade," *American Economic Review* 38, 261–66; reprinted in Joseph E. Stiglitz (ed.), *The Collected Scientific Papers of Paul A. Samuelson,* vol. 2. Cambridge, Mass.: MIT Press, 1966, chap. 60.

Samuelson, Paul A. 1947. *Foundations of Economic Analysis*. Cambridge, Mass.: Harvard University Press.

Samuelson, Paul A. 1950. "The Evaluation of Real National Income," *Oxford Economic Papers* (N.S.) 2, 1, 1–29; reprinted in *CSP*, vol. 2, chap. 77.

Samuelson, Paul A. 1954. "The Pure Theory of Public Expenditure," *Review of Economics and Statistics* 36, 4, 387–9; reprinted in *CSP*, vol. 2, chap. 92.

Samuelson, Paul A. 1956. "Social Indifference Curves," *Quarterly Journal of Economics* 70, 1–22; reprinted in *CSP*, vol. 2, chap. 78.

Samuelson, Paul A. 1964. "A. P. Lerner at Sixty," *Review of Economics and Statistics* 31, 169–78; reprinted in Robert C. Merton (ed.), *The Collected Scientific Papers of Paul A. Samuelson*, vol. 3. Cambridge, Mass.: MIT Press, 1972, chap. 183.

Samuelson, Paul A. 1967. "Arrow's Mathematical Politics," in S. Hook (ed.), *Human Values and Economic Policy*. New York: New York University Press. Reprinted in *CSP*, vol. 3, chap. 167.

Samuelson, Paul A. 1973. "Invariant Economic Index Numbers and Canonical Duality: Survey and Synthesis" (with S. Swamy), *American Economic Review* 64, 566–93. Reprinted in Hiroaki Nagatani and Kate Crowley (eds.), *The Collected Scientific Papers of Paul A. Samuelson*, vol. 4. Cambridge, Mass.: MIT Press, 1977, Chap. 209.

Samuelson, Paul A. 1976. "Optimal Compacts for Redistribution," in R. E. Grieson (ed.), *Public and Urban Economics*. Lexington, Mass.: Lexington Books (D. C. Heath). Reprinted in *CSP*, vol. 4, chap. 257.

Samuelson, Paul A. 1977. "Reaffirming the Existence of 'Reasonable' Bergson-Samuelson Social Welfare Function," *Economica* 44, 81–8.

Savage, L. J. 1954. *Foundations of Statistics*. New York: Wiley.

Scitovsky, Tibor. 1941. "A Note on Welfare Propositions in Economics," *Review of Economic Studies* 9, 77–88.

Scorza, Gaetano. 1903. "A proposito del massimo di ofelimita data dalla libera concorrenza," *Giornale degli Economisti* 2, 41–62.

Sen, Amartya. 1971. *Collective Choice and Social Welfare*. San Francisco: Holden-Day.

Tideman, T. N., and G. Tullock, 1976. "A New and Superior Process for Making Social Choices," *Journal of Political Economy* 84, 1145–59.

Tintner, G. 1946. "A Note on Welfare Economics," *Econometrica* 14, 69–78.

Vickery, W. 1945. "Measuring Marginal Utility by Reactions to Risk," *Econometrica* 13, 319–33.

Vickery, W. 1961. "Counterspeculation, Auctions, and Competitive Sealed Tenders," *Journal of Finance* 16, 8–37.

Viner, Jacob. 1937. *Studies in the Theory of International Trade*. New York: Harper & Bros.

Wicksell, Knut. 1896. *Finanztheorestische Unterschungen*.

Wicksell, Knut. 1934. *Lectures on Political Economy*. Translated by E. Classen from the 3rd edition published in Swedish; edited by Lionel Robbins. London: Routledge & Kegan Paul.

Wicksteed, P. H. 1894. *An Essay on the Coordination of the Laws of Distribution*. London: Macmillan.

# 10 Optimal and voluntary income distribution

*Kenneth J. Arrow*

## 0. Introduction and summary

The concept of the social welfare function was introduced by Bergson in his classic paper (1938) to express preferences over resource allocations to all individuals in society. Just as the commodity bundles of an individual are supposed to be compared by his or her individual preference ordering, so the alternative allocations of commodity bundles to all individuals can be ordered by a social welfare ordering over this entire space. As with any ordering satisfying certain regularity properties, the social welfare ordering can be represented by a real-valued function, the social welfare function. Its significance is essentially ordinal, but under additional conditions of separability the function representing an ordering can be chosen to be additive in an appropriate choice of variables.[1]

The optimization of a social welfare function should determine the entire allocation of resources among individuals and therefore includes the normative problems of income distribution. To concentrate on this topic, I will confine attention to the special case where there is only one commodity in the economic system. A resource allocation is then simply a vector with a (nonnegative) component for every individual in the economy.

To combine attention to the simplest normative aspects, I will further abstract from incentive questions. It will simply be assumed that the total available of the one commodity is given and is not diminished by any transfers.

When we speak of an individual utility function or preference ordering, we usually mean *both* that it is an ordering over the possible commodity bundles for that individual *and* that it is a characteristic of the individual. A social welfare function orders social resource allocations (income distributions in the present limited analysis); but of whom is it a characteristic? One point of view, inherent in the theory of social choice, is that a social ordering is a social construct. In this chapter, I will follow Bergson in his view that a social welfare function is characteristic of an individual. Each individual is supposed to have a social conscience, an ordering over income distributions.[2] The social welfare function for a given individual determines the answers he or she would give to the following hypothetical questions: For all pairs of income distributions, which would I choose if I were dictator?[3]

If social welfare functions differ from individual to individual, how shall the normative question be posed? We can give one answer by using the criterion of Pareto optimality. We can at least ask for the class of income distributions which are not dominated in the sense that another income distribution will be superior according to everyone's social welfare function. We are thus led into the field of Pareto-optimal income redistribution, which has been the object of considerable study in the last decade; leading papers are those of Kolm (1969) (unfortunately little noticed, possibly because of the extremely careless printing of the English version), Winter (1969), Hochman and Rodgers (1969), and Archibald and Davidson (1976).

I will not review these papers in detail. Considerable attention is paid in them to Pareto efficiency in the distribution of specific goods, a problem from which I am abstracting. I follow particularly Kolm and Archibald and Davidson in a symmetric formulation of interdependence of utilities.

Since each individual has his or her own social welfare function, we can incorporate in it any selfish tendencies. It is presupposed that, in a clearly defined sense, an individual will prefer own income to income for others. However, this preference is limited, so that a sufficiently wealthy individual will prefer to give an extra dollar to a sufficiently poor one rather than retain it. Hence, the Pareto-optimality concept includes both regard for others and for self. I make some specific separability assumptions about social welfare preferences; they amount to saying that if redistributions over a limited set of individuals only are permitted, preference by any individual over those distributions is independent of the income levels of the remainder of society. It is further assumed that any individual regards all other individuals symmetrically and that judgments about redistribution among others are the same for all individuals, the product perhaps of a code of ethics.

Under these conditions, there is a preferred additive representation of the social welfare function, as shown in Section 1. Let $x_i$ be the income of individual $i$, $n$ the number of individuals, and $W_i(x_1, \ldots, x_n)$ the social welfare function. Then in Section 1 it is shown that, under the assumptions made, there exists an altruistic utility function of income, $U$, and, for each individual, an egoistic utility function, $U_i$, such that

$$W_i(x_1, \ldots, x_n) = U_i(x_i) + \sum_{j \neq i} U(x_j)$$

The hypothesis of selfish preference takes the form

$$U_i'(x) > U'(x) \qquad \text{for all } i \text{ and all } x$$

That is, starting from an equal distribution between individual $i$ and some other individual, $i$ would prefer to shift some income to himself.

In Section 2, a characterization is given of the conditions for Pareto-optimal income distributions with these social welfare functions. From this, the following is shown in Section 3: *If the number of members of the economy, $n$, grows indefinitely with mean income remaining constant, then the Pareto optimal income distributions converge to the egalitarian.*

If the social welfare function is an expression of individual preference, then an individual cannot merely express opinions but he or she can act on them in the form of giving to others. There has been surprisingly little discussion of the economics of charity, the most extensive being that of Ireland and Johnson (1970). In this chapter, I formalize the concept of charity as a noncooperative game. Each individual starts with a given income, which can be given away to others. At the end of the game, any individual's income will equal the original income plus all gifts to him or her less all gifts by him or her. The $i$th individual seeks to maximize $W_i$. The equilibrium point of the game is completely characterized. The conditions for it to be Pareto optimal are determined. If the equilibrium is nontrivial, in the sense that some gifts occur, then it is never Pareto optimal unless there is exactly one giver and all others receive the same final income.

## 1. Assumptions on the social welfare functions of individuals

In a given society, an *income allocation* is an assignment of income to the members of the society. If the society is denoted by $S$, then an income allocation is a specification of $x_i$ for all $i \in S$. For convenience, the notation $x_S$ will stand for an income allocation over $S$.

Each individual $i$ is supposed to have a preference ordering for income allocations over any society $S$, whether or not $i \in S$. We can certainly imagine a situation in which an individual has some say in allocating income in a society but is not allowed to affect his or her own income.

A "sure thing" principle will be postulated. That is, a preference ordering for income allocations over some society $S$ will not be affected by incomes outside $S$, which cannot be reallocated, or even by the existence of individuals outside $S$.

*Assumption 1.* If $S \subset T$, let $x_T$ and $x_T'$ be two income allocations over $T$ that differ only on $S$ (i.e., $x_{T \sim S} = x_{T \sim S}'$). Then $x_T$ is preferred to $x_T'$ by individual $i$ if and only if $x_S$ is preferred to $x_S'$ in $i$'s ordering of income allocations over $S$.

Here $T \sim S$ is the set of individuals in $T$ but not in $S$; $x_S$ and $x_S'$ are, respectively, the parts of the income allocations $x_T$ and $x_T'$ for individuals in $S$.

A second assumption is that each individual regards all other individuals alike as far as income allocations are concerned.

*Assumption 2.* Let $x_S$ and $x_S'$ be two income allocations over $S$, where $x_j' = x_{\sigma(j)}$ for all $j \in S$, for $\sigma$ a permutation of the members of $S$. Any individual $i$ not belonging to $S$ regards $x_S$ and $x_S'$ as indifferent.

A stronger assumption is that preferences about income allocations among others are socially formed; specifically, such preferences are the same no matter which individual holds them.

*Assumption 3.* If neither $i$ nor $j$ belong to $S$, then they have the same preferences over income allocations in $S$.

The next assumption states the concept of selfishness; in any redistribution between one individual and another, the first will prefer some degree of inequality in his or her favor to equality.

*Assumption 4.* If $S$ consists of two individuals, $i$ and $j$, then at any allocations in which $x_i = x_j$, the marginal rate of substitution of $i$'s income for $j$'s according to $i$ is greater than 1.

Finally, the usual concavity assumptions are imposed.

*Assumption 5.* For any individual $i$ and any society $S$, if $x_S$ is preferred or indifferent to $x_S'$ according to $i$, then $(1 - t)x_S + tx_S'$ is preferred to $x_S'$ for any $t$, $0 < t < 1$.

## 2. Characterization of the social welfare function

Following the standard theorems on separable utility (see Debreu, 1960), Assumption 1 implies immediately that we can choose an additive utility indicator, $W_i^S$, for individual $i$'s ordering over income distributions over a society $S$,

$$W_i^S(x_S) = \underset{j \in S}{W_{ij}(x_j)} \tag{1}$$

Note that because the society $S$ is variable and the preferences are independent not only of the incomes outside $S$ but even of the existence of individuals outside $S$, the functions $W_{ij}$ are independent of the set $S$.

The symmetry condition for others, Assumption 2, implies immediately that $W_{ij}$ is the same function for all individuals $j \neq i$. Let $V_i = W_{ij}$ for $j \neq i$. Consider any two individuals, $i$ and $j$, and any set of individuals $S$, to which neither belong. Then, from (1), the preferences of $i$ and $j$, respectively, over income allocations in $S$ are determined by the utility indicators,

$$W_i^S(x_S) = \sum_{k \in S} V_i(x_k)$$

$$W_j^S(x_S) = \sum_{k \in S} V_i(x_k)$$

But from Assumption 3, these two utility indicators must represent the same ordering over $x_S$'s. Since they are additive, one must be a positive linear transformation of the other; without loss of generality, they must be the same, which implies that $V_i = V_j$. Since $i$ and $j$ were arbitrary, we can write, $V_i = U$ for all $i$.

Then, for any set of individuals $S$ and any $i \in S$,

$$W_i^S(x_S) = W_{ii}(x_i) + \sum_{j \in S \sim \{i\}} W_{ij}(x_j) = W_{ii}(x_i) + \sum_{j \in S \sim \{i\}} V_i(x_j)$$

$$= U_i(x_i) + \sum_{j \in S \sim \{i\}} U(x_j) \tag{2}$$

where we have written $U_i$ for $W_{ii}$.

Consider in particular the case where $S$ contains two members, $i$ and $j$. Then

$$W_i^S(x_i, x_j) = U_i(x_i) + U(x_j)$$

The marginal rate of substitution of $x_i$ for $x_j$ is $U_i'(x_i)/U'(x_j)$ in individual $i$'s preference. If $x_i = x_j = x$, then, from Assumption 4, $U_i'(x)/U'(x) > 1$. Finally, Assumption 5 implies that the functions $U_i$ and $U$ are concave.

*Theorem 1.* Under Assumptions 1 through 5, the preferences of individual $i$ among income allocations over a set of individuals $S$ containing $i$ have as a utility indicator

$$W_i^S(x_S) = U_i(x_i) + \sum_{j \in S \sim \{i\}} U(x_j) \tag{3}$$

where

$$U_i'(x) > U'(x), \quad \text{all } x \tag{4}$$

and the functions $U_i$ and $U$ are strictly concave.

To illustrate the implications of the social welfare function (3), we consider the allocations that would be made by an individual $i$ who has dictatorial powers. As the size of the economy grows, the number of terms concerned with the welfare of others grows. One might mistakenly infer that individual $i$ would pay less and less attention to his or her own welfare. In fact, as the economy grows with the same mean income, individual $i$ would allocate more income to himself or herself, although not unboundedly more.

To see this, maximize (3) subject to the constraint on total income,

$$\sum_{j \in S} x_j \leqq (\#S)\bar{x} \tag{5}$$

where

$$\bar{x} \quad = \text{mean income} \tag{6}$$

$$\#S = \text{number of members of } S \tag{7}$$

Then, if we let $p$ be the Lagrange parameter associated with the constraint (5),

$$U_i'(x_i) \leqq p; \quad \text{if } U_i'(x_i) < p, \quad \text{then} \quad x_i = 0 \tag{8}$$

for each $j \in S$, $j \neq i$, $U'(x_j) \leqq p;$     if $U'(x_j) < p$,     then     $x_j = 0$ (9)

Suppose that $U_i'(x_i) < p$. Since constraint (5) is clearly binding, for some $j \neq i, x_j > 0$, so that $U'(x_j) = p > U_i'(x_i) = U_i'(0) > U'(0)$ from (4), which contradicts the concavity of $U$. Hence,

$$U_i'(x_i) = p$$

Suppose that for some $j \in S \sim \{i\}$, $U'(x_j) = p$, while for another member, $k$, of $S \sim \{i\}$, $U'(x_k) < p$. Then $U'(x_j) = p > U'(x_k) = U'(0)$, again a contradiction to the concavity of $U$. Hence, either

$$x_j = 0 \quad \text{for all } j \in S \sim \{i\}$$

or

$$U'(x_j) = p \quad \text{for all } j \in S \sim \{i\}$$

In either case, for some $x'$,

$$x_j = x' \quad \text{for all } j \in S \sim \{i\} \tag{10}$$

In the first case, $x_i = (\#S)\bar{x}$ from (5), (8), and (9).

$$U_i'((\#S)\bar{x}) = p \geqq U'(0) \tag{11}$$

In the second case,

$$U_i'(x_i) = U'(x') \tag{12}$$

Now define, for both present and future reference,

$$U_i'[\xi_i(x)] = U'(x) \tag{13}$$

Since $U_i'$ and $U'$ are both decreasing functions, $\xi_i(x)$ is an increasing function of $x$. It might not be defined for all $x$. From (4), $\lim_{x \to \infty} U_i'(x) \geqq \lim_{x \to \infty} U'(x)$. If the equality holds, then $\xi_i$ will be defined for all $x$. However, if the strict equality holds, then $\xi_i$ is defined only for $0 \leqq x < \bar{x}$, where $U'(\bar{x}) = \lim_{x \to \infty} U_i'(x)$.

It follows immediately from (4) and the concavity of $U_i$ and $U$ that

$$\xi_i(x) > x, \quad \text{for all } x \tag{14}$$

From (11), $x' = 0$ and $x_i = (\#S)\bar{x}$ if

$$(\#S)\bar{x} \leqq \xi_i(0) \tag{15}$$

On the other hand, when $x' > 0$,
$$x_i = \xi_i(x') \tag{16}$$

If $\bar{x} > \xi_i(0)$, then (15) cannot hold even if $S$ contains just the one member, $i$. Otherwise, (15) will hold for $\#S$ sufficiently small.

From (10) and the resource constraint (5),
$$x_i + (\#S - 1)x' = (\#S)\bar{x} \tag{17}$$

From (15)–(17), $x_i$ and $x'$ will depend only on the number of elements of $S$ for given $i$. We wish to show that $x_i$ will increase with $\#S$.

For simplicity of notation, let $\#S = n$: we will exhibit $x_i$ and $x'$ as functions of $n$. There are three possible cases: (a) $(n + 1)\bar{x} \leq \xi_i(0)$; (b) $n\bar{x} \leq \xi_i(0) < (n + 1)\bar{x}$; and (c) $\xi_i(0) < n\bar{x}$. If (a) holds, then also $n\bar{x} \leq \xi_i(0)$. Then, from (15), $x' = 0$, both when $\#S = n$ and when $\#S = n + 1$; $x_i(n + 1) = (n + 1)\bar{x} > n\bar{x} = x_i(n)$. If (b) holds, then $x_i(n) = n\bar{x}$, by (15), and from (16) and the fact that $\xi_i$ is an increasing function, $x_i(n + 1) = \xi_i[x'(n + 1)] > \xi_i(0) \geq n\bar{x} = x_i(n)$. In both cases, $x_i(n + 1) > x_i(n)$.

Now suppose that (c) holds. From (17) with $\#S = n$, $n + 1$, respectively, we have
$$x_i(n) + (n - 1)x'(n) = n\bar{x}$$
$$x_i(n + 1) + nx'(n + 1) = (n + 1)\bar{x}$$

Multiply the first equation by $(n + 1)$ and the second by $n$, and then subtract the first from the second. Simplification implies that
$$n[x_i(n + 1) - x_i(n)] + n^2[x'(n + 1) - x'(n)] = x_i(n) - x'(n) \tag{18}$$

From (14) and (16),
$$x_i(n) = \xi_i[x'(n)] > x'(n) \tag{19}$$

so that the right-hand side of (18) is positive and the left-hand side must be. But in case (c), (16) holds both for $\#S = n$ and for $\#S = n + 1$. Since $\xi_i$ is increasing, $x_i(n + 1) - x_i(n)$ has the same sign as $x'(n + 1) - x'(n)$; hence, both must be positive.

From (17) and (19), $x'(n) < \bar{x}$ if $\xi_i(0) < n\bar{x}$; the inequality holds trivially in the opposite case, since then $x'(n) = 0$. Hence, $x_i(n) = \xi_i(x') \leq \xi_i(\bar{x})$ from (16), if applicable, or else (15). Therefore, $x_i(n)$ increases with $n$ but has an upper bound. If we divide through by $\#S = n$ in (17), it follows that $x'(n)$ approaches $\bar{x}$, and therefore $x_i(n)$ approaches $\xi_i(\bar{x})$ as $n$ grows large.

*Corollary 1.* If individual $i$ is a dictator with respect to choice of income allocation, then for given mean income $\bar{x}$, his or her income depends only on the individual's own characteristics and the number of individuals in the economy and is an increasing function of that number. The income of each other individual is also an increasing function of the size of the economy, the same for all such. The income of $i$ is bounded above by $\xi_i(\bar{x})$, the solution of the equation, $U_i'(x) = U'(\bar{x})$, and converges to that limit as the size of the economy grows; the income of each other individual approaches $\bar{x}$.

This corollary shows that an increase of the size of the economy increases the selfish implications of the welfare function in absolute terms but decreases it relatively to the size of the economy.

## 3. Characterization of Pareto-optimal income allocations

The allocation determined by setting any individual as a dictator is Pareto optimal, by definition. However, there are many other Pareto-optimal allocations.

I shall assume that Pareto optimality for any economy is defined relative to the members of that economy only and not other individuals.

*Definition 1.* For a given economy $S$, the allocation $x'_S$ *dominates* the allocation $x_S$ if, for every $i \in S$, $W_i^S(x'_S) \geqq W_i^S(x_S)$, with the strict inequality holding for at least on $i \in S$. An allocation $x_S$ is *Pareto optimal* in $S$ if there is no other allocation over the members of $S$ that dominates $x_S$ and whose total income is the same.

As all the functions involved are concave, we have the obvious equivalence,

$x_S^*$ is Pareto optimal in $S$ if and only if there exist $\lambda_i \geqq 0$ for all $i$ in $S$, $\lambda_j > 0$, some $j \in S$, such that $x_S^*$ maximizes $\Sigma_{i \in S}$ $\lambda_i W_i^S(x_S)$ subject to $\Sigma_{i \in S} x_i$ given

If we substitute for $W_i^S$ from Theorem 1 (3), we see that Pareto-optimal allocations are characterized as maximizing,

$$\sum_{i \in S} \lambda_i \left[ U_i(x_i) + \sum_{j \in S \sim \{i\}} U(x_j) \right]$$

for given $\Sigma_{i \in S} x_i$. But

$$\sum_{i \in S} \lambda_i \sum_{j \in S \sim \{i\}} U(x_j) = \sum_{j \in S} \lambda_j \sum_{i \in S \sim \{j\}} U(x_i)$$

$$= \sum_{i \in S} \sum_{j \in S \sim \{i\}} \lambda_j U(x_i) = \sum_{i \in S} \left( \sum_{j \in S \sim \{i\}} \lambda_j \right) U(x_i)$$

$$= \sum_{i \in S} (\lambda - \lambda_i) U(x_i)$$

where $\lambda = \Sigma_{j \in S} \lambda_j$. Hence, Pareto-optimal allocations maximize

$$\sum_{i \in S} [\lambda_i U_i(x_i) + (\lambda - \lambda_i) U(x_i)]$$

subject to $\Sigma_{i \in S} x_i$ given. Let $p$ be the Lagrange parameter corresponding to the last constraint. Then a Pareto-optimal allocation satisfies the conditions

$$\lambda_i U_i'(x_i) + (\lambda - \lambda_i) U'(x_i) \leqq p, \qquad \text{all } i \tag{20}$$

with equality if $x_i > 0$. As these conditions are homogeneous of degree 1, we can let $p = 1$ without loss of generality (clearly, $p > 0$). Hence, by a slight rewriting of (20), $x_S$ is Pareto optimal (compared with other allocations with the same total) if and only if there exist $\lambda_i \geqq 0$, with strict inequality for at least one $i \in S$, such that

$$\lambda_i [U_i'(x_i) - U'(x_i)] + \lambda U'(x_i) \leqq 1 \tag{21}$$

with equality for such $i$ that $x_i > 0$.

We will eliminate the Lagrange parameters to derive a criterion for Pareto optimality in terms of the proposed allocation $x_S$ alone. From Theorem 1 (4), $U_i'(x_i) - U'(x_i) > 0$. Let

$$\alpha_i = [U_i'(x_i) - U'(x_i)]^{-1} > 0, \qquad \beta_i = U'(x_i) \tag{22}$$

Multiplying through in (21) by $\alpha_i$ yields

$$\lambda_i + \lambda \alpha_i \beta_i \leqq \alpha_i \qquad \text{for all } i \tag{23a}$$

$$\lambda_i + \lambda \alpha_i \beta_i = \alpha_i \qquad \text{if } x_i > 0 \tag{23b}$$

From (23a), the condition $\lambda_i \geqq 0$ implies that $\alpha_i \geqq \lambda \alpha_i \beta_i$, or

$$\beta_i \lambda \leqq 1, \qquad \text{all } i$$

If we define

$$\bar{\beta} = \max \beta_i \tag{24}$$

the last condition can be written

$$\bar{\beta} \lambda \leqq 1 \tag{25}$$

Suppose that there exists a solution to (23a–b) with $\lambda_i \geqq 0$, all $i$; in particular, (25) holds for $\lambda = \Sigma_{i \in S} \lambda_i$. I will show that there exists a solution in which it is required that $\lambda_i = 0$ for all $i$ for which $x_i = 0$; in other words, any individual who gets zero income can, without loss of generality, be assigned zero social weight.

Let $\Sigma^0$, $\Sigma^+$ denote sums for values of $i$ for which $x_i = 0$, $x_i > 0$, respectively, and let $\lambda^0 = \Sigma^0 \lambda_i$. Then

$$\Sigma^+ \lambda_i = \lambda - \lambda^0$$

Sum (23b) over all $i$ for which $x_i > 0$.

$$\lambda - \lambda^0 + \lambda \Sigma^+ \alpha_i \beta_i = \Sigma^+ \alpha_i$$

Solve for $\lambda$:

$$\lambda = (\lambda^0 + \Sigma^+ \alpha_i)/(1 + \Sigma^+ \alpha_i \beta_i)$$

Now try a new solution $\lambda_i' (i \in S)$, as follows: Let

$$\lambda' = (\Sigma^+ \alpha_i)/(1 + \Sigma^+ \alpha_i \beta_i) \tag{26a}$$

$$\lambda_i' = \begin{cases} \alpha_i(1 - \beta_i \lambda') & \text{if } x_i > 0 \tag{26b} \\ 0 & \text{if } x_i = 0 \tag{26c} \end{cases}$$

Clearly, $\lambda' \leqq \lambda$. Hence, from (25), $\bar{\beta}\lambda' \leqq 1$, so that $\beta_i\lambda' \leqq 1$ for all $i$, and therefore, $\lambda'_i \geqq 0$ if $x_i > 0$; $\lambda'_i = 0$ and therefore $\lambda'_i \geqq 0$, if $x_i = 0$, so that $\lambda'_i \geqq 0$, all $i \in S$. Also,

$$\sum_{i \in S} \lambda'_i = \Sigma^+ \lambda'_i = \Sigma^+ \alpha_i - \lambda'\Sigma^+ \alpha_i\beta_i = \lambda'$$

Hence, $\lambda'_i$ $(i \in S)$ is a solution to (23a–b), with $\lambda'_i = 0$ when $x_i = 0$.

If we take a solution with $\lambda_i = 0$ when $x_i = 0$, we must have (26a–c). If the primes are dropped, condition (25) becomes

$$\bar{\beta}\Sigma^+ \alpha_i \leqq 1 + \Sigma^+ \alpha_i\beta_i \tag{27}$$

If this condition is satisfied, then from (26), the equations (23) are satisfied, and the allocation is therefore Pareto optimal.

Let $x = \min_i x_i$, the lowest income in the allocation. Then, since $U'$ is decreasing, it follows from (22) and (24) that $\bar{\beta} = U'(x)$. If $x = 0$, then (27) can be written

$$\sum_{x_i > x} (\bar{\beta} - \beta_i)\alpha_i \leqq 1 \tag{28}$$

If $x > 0$, then $\Sigma^+$ is a summation over all $i$. Sum separately over those $i$ for whom $x_i = x$ and those for whom $x_i > x$; note that for the former $\beta_i = \bar{\beta}$. Then (27) becomes

$$\bar{\beta} \sum_{x_i = x} \alpha_i + \bar{\beta} \sum_{x_i > x} \alpha_i \leqq 1 + \bar{\beta} \sum_{x_i = x} \alpha_i + \sum_{x_i > x} \alpha_i\beta_i$$

which again simplifies to (28).

*Theorem 2.* Let $x_S$ be an income allocation for the economy $S$. Let

$$\alpha_i = [U'_i(x_i) - U'(x_i)]^{-1}, \qquad \beta_i = U'(x_i)$$
$$x = \min_i x_i, \qquad \bar{\beta} = U'(x)$$

then $x_S$ is Pareto optimal if and only if

$$\sum_{x_i > x} (\bar{\beta} - \beta_i)\alpha_i \leqq 1$$

If $x_i > x$, then $\beta_i < \bar{\beta}$, so that each term, $(\bar{\beta} - \beta_i)\alpha_i > 0$. It follows that for any subset of the individuals who receive above minimum income, the inequality in the optimality criterion is strengthened.

*Corollary 2.* Let $x_S$ be a Pareto-optimal income allocation for the economy $S$, and $T$ be any set of individuals for whom $x_i > x$. Then

$$\sum_{i \in T} (\bar{\beta} - \beta_i)\alpha_i \leqq 1$$

To illustrate the applicability of the optimal criterion, it will be shown that the upper bound on the income of any individuals found for the

dictatorial case in Corollary 1 remains valid for all Pareto-optimal allocations. Consider any individual $i$. If $x_i = x$, then, by (14), $x_i < \xi_i(x)$. If
$x_i > x$, then choose $T$ in Corollary 2 to consist of the individual $i$ alone, so
that $(\bar{\beta} - \beta_i)\alpha_i \le 1$. This implies that $\bar{\beta} \le \beta_i + \alpha_i^{-1}$. From the definitions, $U'(x) \le U_i'(x_i)$; as $U_i'$ is decreasing, the definition (13) of $\xi_i$ then
implies

*Corollary 3.* If $x_S$ is any Pareto-optimal income allocation for any
economy $S$, then $x_i \le \xi_i(x) \le \xi_i(\bar{x})$ for all individuals $i$, where $x$ is the
minimum income in the allocation.

## 4. Pareto-optimal income allocations in large economies

It will now be shown that for large economies, Pareto-optimal income
allocations are approximately egalitarian, provided that the potential
members of the successively larger economies are not too different (more
precisely, not arbitrarily selfish). The meaning of the approximation needs
a little clarification. Clearly, a dictatorial allocation, as characterized in
Corollary 1, is always Pareto optimal; hence, we cannot say of any such
allocation that all individuals have incomes that are close to each other.
What is true is that the number of individuals whose income is above the
minimum by any given amount is relatively negligible in large economies.

By the income distribution corresponding to any given income allocation, we mean the proportion of individuals who receive any given income. Then it will be shown that if we take a sequence of economies of
increasing size but the same mean income and select from each any
Pareto-optimal income allocation, the corresponding sequence of income
distributions converges to an egalitarian distribution. Specifically, for any
$\varepsilon > 0$, the proportion of individuals with incomes more than $\varepsilon$ above the
minimum approaches zero.

Indeed, a stronger statement is true. For any given mean income and
any $\varepsilon > 0$, there is a number $N$ such that the number of individuals with
incomes more than $\varepsilon$ above the minimum never exceeds $N$, no matter how
large the economy and no matter who belongs to it.

To state precisely the notion of a large economy, let us introduce the
concept of a *population P* of individuals. Any given economy is a subset of
members of $P$. The population $P$ will be taken to be infinite.

*Assumption 6.* For any $x > 0$, the marginal rate of substitution of
$i$'s income for $j$'s according to $i$ when both have income $x$ is bounded
above as $i$ and $j$ range over all possible members of the population $P$.

Unbounded selfishness is thus ruled out.

For $j \neq i$, the marginal rate of substitution is $U_i'(x)/U'(x)$. Since $U'(x)$ is the same for all individuals, Assumption 6 is equivalent to the following statement:

For any given $x$, $U_i'(x)$ is bounded above as $i$ varies over $P$     (29)

Let $S$ be any economy, with mean income $\bar{x}$. For any given $\varepsilon > 0$ and any given Pareto optimal allocations, $x_S$, define

$$S' = \{i \in S \mid x_i > \mathbf{x} + \varepsilon\} \tag{30}$$

By Corollary 2,

$$\sum_{i \in S'} (\bar{\beta} - \beta_i)\alpha_i \leq 1 \tag{31}$$

Consider the function $U'(x) - U'(x + \varepsilon)$, as $x$ varies over the interval $0 \leq x \leq \bar{x}$. It is everywhere positive. Also, it is continuous everywhere, except possibly at $x = 0$; but if it is not continuous there, it approaches $+\infty$. Hence, $U'(x) - U'(x + \varepsilon)$ is bounded away from 0 on the interval. That is, there exists $\delta > 0$, depending only on $\varepsilon$ and $\bar{x}$, such that $U'(x) - U'(x + \varepsilon) \geq \delta$ for $0 \leq x \leq \bar{x}$. If $x' \geq x + \varepsilon$, $U'(x) - U'(x') \geq U'(x) - U'(x + \varepsilon) \geq \delta$. In particular, $\mathbf{x} \leq \bar{x}$, $x_i > \mathbf{x} + \varepsilon$ for $i \in S'$, so that

$$\bar{\beta} - \beta_i \geq \delta \qquad \text{for all } i \in S' \tag{32}$$

Also, $\alpha_i^{-1} = U_i'(x_i) - U'(x_i) \leq U_i'(x_i) < U_i'(\varepsilon)$ for $i \in S'$, since $x_i > \mathbf{x} + \varepsilon \geq \varepsilon$. From Assumption 6, in the form (29), $U_i'(\varepsilon)$ is bounded above as $i$ varies, the bound depending only on $\varepsilon$. Hence, $\alpha_i$ is bounded below.

$\alpha_i \geq \boldsymbol{\alpha}$ for all $i \in S'$, where $\boldsymbol{\alpha}$ depends only on $\varepsilon$.

Then, from (31) and (32),

$$1 \geq \delta\boldsymbol{\alpha}(\#S')$$

so that $\#S'$ is bounded above by a quantity depending only on $\varepsilon$ and $\bar{x}$.

*Theorem 3.* For any $\varepsilon > 0$ and any mean income $\bar{x}$, there is a number $N$ such that for all economies $S$ and all Pareto-optimal income allocations over $S$ with mean income $\bar{x}$,

$$\#\{i \in S \mid x_i > \mathbf{x} + \varepsilon\} \leq N$$

where x is the minimum income in that allocation.

*Corollary 4.* For any $\varepsilon > 0$, any $\delta > 0$, and any mean income $\bar{x}$, there is a number $N'$ such that the proportion of individuals whose income exceeds the minimum by more than $\varepsilon$ in a Pareto-optimal allocation is less than $\delta$ whenever the economy has more than $N'$ members.

Although Corollary 4 establishes that the income distribution converges in a certain sense to the egalitarian, it does not satisfy all the conditions that are implied by the usual definition of convergence in distribution.

What we really want to prove is that the proportion of individuals whose incomes differ by more than a preassigned value, $\varepsilon$, from the mean income approaches zero. This statement does not follow from Corollary 4. The difficulty is that Assumption 6 does not exclude the possibility that the total income going to individuals whose incomes are above the minimum by $\varepsilon$ may remain a nontrivial part of total community income. This can happen only if their mean income approaches infinity. In that case, it is possible that the minimum income will converge to a limit below the mean income, $\bar{x}$, and in fact that the proportion of individuals at or near the minimum may not converge to zero.

We now present two examples. The first shows that Assumption 6 is necessary to the conclusions thus far. The second shows that it is not sufficient to imply convergence in distribution and that an additional assumption is needed.

In both examples, it is assumed that the population is a sequence of individuals. In both, it is assumed that $U(x)$, the altruistic utility function, is any strictly concave increasing function.

For the first example, choose two income levels, $0 < x < x'$, and let $\bar{x} = (x + x')/2$. Let $\bar{\beta} = U'(x)$, $\beta = U'(x')$. Suppose that the sequence of individuals have egoistic utility functions $U_i$ satisfying the conditions

$$\sum_{i=1}^{\infty} [U_i'(x') - \beta]^{-1} < \infty, \qquad U_i'(x') > \beta \tag{33}$$

for example, $U_i'(x') = 2^i + \beta$. Note that if (33) is to hold, we must have that $[U_i'(x') - \beta]^{-1}$ approaches zero, and therefore that $U_i'(x')$ approaches infinity as $i$ approaches infinity, in contradiction to Assumption 6. Also note that (33) restricts $U_i'$ at only one point for each $i$. Let $S_n$ consist of the first $2n$ individuals in the sequence; let $x^n$ be the allocation over $S_n$ defined by

$$x_i^n = \begin{cases} x, & i = 1, \ldots, n \\ x', & i = n + 1, \ldots, 2n \end{cases}$$

Clearly, the mean income is $\bar{x}$, so this allocation is feasible. Also, the income distribution does not converge to the egalitarian, even in the limited sense of Corollary 4, since half the population has income $x'$, which does not get arbitrarily close to $\bar{x}$. We now show that $x^n$ is Pareto optimal. When $x_i > x$, $x_i = x'$, $U'(x_i) = \beta_i = \beta$, and $\alpha_i = [U_i'(x') - \beta]^{-1}$. The optimality condition of Theorem 2 becomes

$$(\bar{\beta} - \beta) \sum_{i=n+1}^{2n} [U_i'(x') - \beta]^{-1} \leq 1 \tag{34a}$$

But from (33), it must be that

$$\lim_{n \to \infty} \sum_{i=n+1}^{\infty} [U_i'(x') - \beta]^{-1} = 0$$

and therefore certainly

$$\lim_{n \to \infty} \sum_{i=n+1}^{2n} [U_i'(x') - \beta]^{-1} = 0$$

Hence, certainly (34) holds for $n$ sufficiently large. Thus, if Assumption 6 is violated, there is no convergence to a distribution concentrated near the minimum.

A second example will satisfy Assumption 6 and therefore Theorem 3 and Corollary 4 but will not converge in distribution to the egalitarian. Choose two numbers, x and $\bar{x}$, $0 < x < \bar{x}$. Let the $i$th individual have an egoistic utility function $U_i$ such that

$$U_i'[n\bar{x} - (n - 1)x] = U'(x) \tag{34b}$$

Note, again, that this simply restricts $U_i'$ at one point, for each $i$. This condition is compatible with Assumption 6. Since the functions, $U_i'$ are decreasing, it is clear that if Assumption 6 is satisfied at any point $x_0$, it is satisfied for all $x > x_0$. In particular, then, let $U_i'(x) = V(x)$, all $i$, in the interval $(0, x)$. Also, assume that $U_i'(x) > U'(x)$ in that interval. There is no difficulty, then, in constructing for each $i$, the function $U_i'$ for $x > x$ so as to satisfy the conditions that it be decreasing, that $U_i'(x) > U'(x)$, and that (34b) hold.

Under these conditions, let $S_n$ consist of the first $n$ individuals in the sequence, and let $x^n$ be the dictatorial allocation defined by

$$x_i^n = \begin{cases} x, & i = 1, \ldots, n - 1 \\ n\bar{x} - (n - 1)x & i = n \end{cases}$$

This allocation is feasible if the mean income is $\bar{x}$. Since $x_i^n > x$ only for $i = n$, it is easy to verify that $x^n$ is a Pareto-optimal allocation for $S_n$, for all $n$. Whereas the number of individuals for which $x_i^n > x$ is 1 for all allocations, so that Theorem 3 certainly holds, all other individuals have incomes that are x and therefore remain bounded away from $\bar{x}$. Hence, the distribution does not converge to the egalitarian one concentrated at $\bar{x}$; although in each economy the chosen distribution has only one individual whose income is above the minimum, that income is rising indefinitely above the others'.

To obviate this possibility, we need another assumption, which reflects the hypothesis of bounded selfishness in a different way.

*Assumption 7.* For every $x > 0$, there is an income $x' > 0$ such that, for all individuals $i$ in the population $P$, $i$'s marginal rate of substitution of $i$'s income for $j$'s is less than or equal to 1 when $x_i = x'$, $x_j = x$.

Where Assumption 6 measured selfishness by the benefit to others required per dollar of loss starting from equal incomes, Assumption 7 measures selfishness by the number of dollars of income needed to bring Ego to the point of being indifferent between an additional dollar to self or to Other.

Under Assumption 7, $\xi_i(x)$ is bounded above uniformly in $i$ for fixed $x$. In particular,

$$\xi_i(\bar{x}) \leqq \bar{\xi} \qquad \text{for all } i$$

From Corollary 3, $x_i \leqq \bar{\xi}$ for all $i$ in a Pareto-optimal allocation. Divide the members of $S$ into the members of $S'$, as defined by (30), and the others. For those not in $S'$, $x_i \leqq x + \varepsilon$, by definition; for those in $S'$, $x_i \leqq \bar{\xi}$, as just argued. Therefore, feasibility implies that

$$(\#S)\bar{x} \leqq (\#S - \#S')(x + \varepsilon) + (\#S')\bar{\xi}$$

or, equivalently,

$$x > \bar{x} - \varepsilon - \{(\#S')/[(\#S) - (\#S')]\}(\bar{\xi} - \bar{x})$$

By Theorem 3, $\#S'$ is bounded above for fixed $\varepsilon$; hence, for $\#S$ sufficiently large, the last term can be made less than $\varepsilon$, so that $x > \bar{x} - 2\varepsilon$ for $\#S$ sufficiently large. Thus the number of individuals with income a given amount below $\bar{x}$ can be made zero for $\#S$ sufficiently large.

*Theorem 4.* Under Assumptions 1 through 7, for any $\varepsilon > 0$ and any mean income $\bar{x}$, the minimum income in any Pareto-optimal income allocation exceeds $\bar{x} - \varepsilon$ in all economies with sufficiently large numbers of members. Therefore, the number of individuals with incomes differing from $\bar{x}$ by more than $\varepsilon$ in any Pareto-optimal allocation is bounded above uniformly in the economy.

*Corollary 5.* Under Assumptions 1 through 7, the proportion of individuals with incomes that differ from the mean income by more than $\varepsilon$ in a Pareto-optimal allocation approaches zero as the size of the economy increases.

*Remark.* It is easy to see that Assumptions 6 and 7 are independent. The egoistic utility functions of the first example, which violate Assumption 6, could be made to satisfy Assumption 7, whereas that of the second example was chosen to satisfy Assumption 6 but not Assumption 7.

## 5. The charity game

Consider a set of individuals $S$ with preferences for income allocations satisfying Assumptions 1 through 5. Suppose that they could make no cooperative agreements for income redistribution, through the government or any other way. However, each one starts with a given income, $x_i^0$, and each is permitted to give any amount away to any other individual.

Let $x_{ij}$ be the amount given by individual $i$ to individual $j$, $j \neq i$. The aim of each individual is to maximize his or her welfare.

This is a noncooperative game; the strategies of individual $i$ are the gifts, $x_{ij}$, constrained to nonnegative; it is permitted to give but not to demand from others. An equilibrium point of the game is one in which individual $i$ is choosing his or her strategy so as to maximize $W_i^S$, given all gifts of all other individuals.

The final income of individual $i$, after all gifts have been given and received, is

$$x_i = x_i^0 + \sum_{k \neq i} x_{ki} - \sum_{k \neq i} x_{ik} \qquad (35)$$

Note that $W_i^S$ depends only on the final incomes. Hence, the effect of a given gift, $x_{ij}$, works only through those final incomes. Clearly,

$$\partial x_i / \partial x_{ij} = -1, \qquad \partial x_j / \partial x_{ij} = 1 \qquad (36)$$

The requirement that individual $i$ be optimizing for given values of others' strategies can be written (in view of the concavity of $W_i^S$ in the $x_{ij}$'s)

$$\partial W_i^S / \partial x_{ij} \leq 0, \quad \text{all } j \neq i; \qquad \partial W_i^S / \partial x_{ij} = 0 \quad \text{if } x_{ij} > 0$$

From Theorem 1 and (36), the following statement follows immediately.

*Lemma 1.* The gifts, $x_{ij}$, $i \neq j$, are an equilibrium of the charity game if and only if they satisfy the conditions

$$U_i'(x_i) \geq U'(x_j) \qquad \text{for all } i, j, \quad \text{with } i \neq j \qquad (a)$$
$$U_i'(x_i) = U'(x_j) \qquad \text{if } x_{ij} > 0 \qquad (b)$$

*Remark.* We have not asserted at this stage that the charity game has an equilibrium. The existence does not follow from general theorems, because the domain of the $x_{ij}$'s may not be compact. Lemma 1 does characterize the equilibrium if it exists; its existence will be argued later.

Suppose that, at equilibrium, there were an individual, $j$, who both received a gift and gave one (i.e., for some $i$ and $k$, $x_{ij} > 0$ and $x_{jk} > 0$). Remember that, from Theorem 1 (4), $U_j'(x_j) > U'(x_j)$. Then, from Lemma 1 (b) applied to the pairs, $(i, j)$ and $(j, k)$, it follows that

$$U_i'(x_i) = U'(x_j) < U_j'(x_j) = U'(x_k)$$

in contradiction to Lemma 1 (a) for the pair $(i, k)$.

Let $G$ be the set of individuals who give some positive gift, and $R$ the set of individuals who receive at least one gift:

$$G = \{i \mid x_{ij} > 0 \quad \text{for some } j\}$$
$$R = \{i \mid x_{ji} > 0 \quad \text{for some } j\}$$

It has just been shown that $G$ and $R$ are disjoint.

Let $j$ be any member of $R$, $i$ an individual for whom $x_{ij} > 0$, and $k$ any member of $S$. Then, from Lemma 1 (b) and (a),

$$U'(x_j) = U_i'(x_i) \geq U'(x_k)$$

so that $x_j \leq x_k$. Since $k$ was any member of $S$, $x_j = \min_k x_k = x$.

$$x_i = x = \min_k x_k \qquad \text{for all } i \in R \tag{37}$$

That is, all receivers at equilibrium have the same final income, which is minimal among all individuals' final incomes.

If $i \in G$, then $x_{ij} > 0$ for some $j \in R$. From (37) and Lemma 1 (b), $U_i'(x_i) = U'(x)$, or

$$x_i = \xi_i(x) \qquad \text{for } i \in G \tag{38}$$

From Lemma 1 (a) and the definition of x,

$$x \leq x_i \leq \xi_i(x) \qquad \text{for all } i \tag{39}$$

We will use these facts to characterize the equilibrium in terms of the single parameter x and exhibit an equation for determining x. We first have to allow for the case where the equilibrium requires no transfers, so the final and original incomes coincide. A necessary condition for this trivial equilibrium is that (39) hold with $x_i = x_i^0$. But if (39) holds, then Lemma 1 (a) holds for all $i$ and $j$, whereas Lemma 1 (b) is inapplicable. The part of (39) which requires that $x_i^0 \geq x^0$ is, of course, a tautology.

*Lemma 2.* The charity game has the trivial equilibrium $x_i = x_i^0$ (and $x_{ij} = 0$, all $i$ and $j$) if and only if $\xi_i(x^0) \geq x_i^0$, all $i$.

In a trivial equilibrium $G$ and $R$ are empty sets; otherwise, they are not. Clearly, if one is nonempty, so is the other.

For simplicity of notation, let

$$G_i = \sum_{k \neq i} x_{ik}, \qquad R_i = \sum_{k \neq i} x_{ki} \tag{40}$$

so that, by (35),

$$x_i = x_i^0 - G_i + R_i \tag{41}$$

If $i \in G$, $R_i = 0$, $0 < G_i = x_i^0 - x_i$, and $x_i^0 > \xi_i(x)$, by (38). If $i \notin G$, then $G_i = 0$, and $x_i^0 \leq x_i \leq \xi_i(x)$, by (39). Hence, $G$ is characterized in terms of original incomes and x:

$$i \in G \quad \text{if and only if} \quad x_i^0 > \xi_i(x) \tag{42}$$

Also,

$$G_i = \begin{cases} x_i^0 - \xi_i(x) & \text{if } x_i^0 - \xi_i(x) > 0 \\ 0 & \text{otherwise} \end{cases}$$

Introduce the notation

$$x^+ = \begin{cases} x & \text{if } x > 0 \\ 0 & \text{if } x \leq 0 \end{cases} \tag{43}$$

Then

$$G_i = [x_i^0 - \xi_i(\mathbf{x})]^+ \qquad \text{for all } i \tag{44}$$

If $i \in R$, then $G_i = 0$, $0 < R_i = x_i - x_i^0$ and $\mathbf{x} > x_i^0$ by (37). If $i \notin R$, then $R_i = 0$, $x_i^0 \geqq x_i \geqq \mathbf{x}$, by (39).

$$i \in R \quad \text{if and only if} \quad \mathbf{x} > x_i^0 \tag{45}$$

$$R_i = (\mathbf{x} - x_i^0)^+ \qquad \text{for all } i \tag{46}$$

Conditions (42)–(46) define the income allocation completely if $\mathbf{x}$ is known. From the definitions (40), it is clear that

$$\sum_i G_i - \sum_i R_i = 0$$

Then, from (44) and (46), we see that $\mathbf{x}$ is a root of the equation, $F(x) = 0$, where

$$F(x) = \sum_i [x_i^0 - \xi_i(x)]^+ - \sum_i (x - x_i^0)^+ \tag{47}$$

Since $\xi_i$ is an increasing function and also $x^+$ is a (monotone) increasing function, $[x_i^0 - \xi_i(x)]^+$ is a monotone-decreasing function of $x$. Similarly, $-(x - x_i^0)$ is a monotone-decreasing function of $x$. Therefore,

$$F \text{ is monotone decreasing} \tag{48}$$

since it is a sum of monotone-decreasing functions. Further, if $x > x_i^0$, then $-(x - x_i^0)^+ = -(x - x_i^0)$ is a strictly decreasing function of $x$. Hence, if $x > x_i^0$ for at least one $i$, then $F$ is strictly decreasing.

$$F \text{ is strictly decreasing for } x > \mathbf{x}^0 \tag{49}$$

If $x = \mathbf{x}^0$, then $x - x_i^0 \leqq 0$ for all $i$, so that $-(x - x_i^0)^+ = 0$ for all $i$. Hence, $F(\mathbf{x}^0) \geqq 0$. Now choose any $x' > \max x_i^0$. Then

$$x_i^0 < x' < \xi_i(x') \qquad \text{for all } i$$

so that $[x_i^0 - \xi_i(x')]^+ = 0$ for all $i$. Also, $-(x' - x_i^0)^+ = -(x' - x_i^0) < 0$ for all $i$, so that $F(x') < 0$. Since $F(\mathbf{x}^0) \geqq 0$, $F(x') < 0$, the equation $F(x) = 0$ has a root. Consider two cases, according as $F(\mathbf{x}^0) > 0$ or $F(\mathbf{x}^0) = 0$. In the first case, from (48) and (49), the root $\mathbf{x}$ is unique, and $\mathbf{x} > \mathbf{x}^0$. Then there is at least one $i$ for which $\mathbf{x} > x_i^0$, so that $R$ and therefore $G$ are nonempty, a nontrivial equilibrium. Given the value of $\mathbf{x}$, the equilibrium is then defined by (42)–(46). The actual flows, who gives to whom, are not unique, since only the totals given by members of $G$ and received by members of $R$ are specified, but this nonuniqueness is not very interesting.

If $F(\mathbf{x}^0) = 0$, then, from (49), it cannot be that $F(x) = 0$ for any larger value of $x$. In this case, $G$ and $R$ are empty. Indeed, consider the condition that $F(\mathbf{x}^0) = 0$. As already argued, $-(\mathbf{x}^0 - x_i^0)^+ = 0$ for all $i$. Hence, from (47), the condition $F(\mathbf{x}^0) = 0$ requires that

$$\sum_i [x_i^0 - \xi_i(\mathbf{x}^0)]^+ = 0$$

For a sum of nonnegative terms to equal zero, it is necessary that each one be zero, so that $[x_i^0 - \xi_i(\mathbf{x}^0)]^+ = 0$ for all $i$, or $x_i^0 \leq \xi_i(\mathbf{x}^0)$ for all $i$, precisely the condition of Lemma 2 for the existence of a trivial equilibrium.

*Theorem 5.* The charity game always has a unique equilibrium. If the original income of individual $i$ is $x_i^0$ and $\mathbf{x}^0 = \min_i x_i^0$, then the equilibrium is trivial if $x_i^0 \leq \xi_i(\mathbf{x}^0)$ for all $i$. (If $x_i$ is the equilibrium income for individual $i$, the equilibrium is trivial if $x_i = x_i^0$ for all $i$.) If $x_i^0 - \xi_i(\mathbf{x}^0) > 0$ for some $i$, then the unique equilibrium is nontrivial. In that case, the minimum equilibrium income, $\mathbf{x} = \min_i x_i$, is the unique solution of the equation

$$\sum_i [x_i^0 - \xi_i(\mathbf{x})]^+ - \sum_i (\mathbf{x} - x_i^0)^+ = 0$$

The givers are precisely those individuals for whom $x_i^0 > \xi_i(\mathbf{x})$, and the total gifts of a giver are $x_i^0 - \xi_i(\mathbf{x})$. The receivers are precisely those individuals for whom $\mathbf{x} > x_i^0$, and the total gifts received by a receiver equal $\mathbf{x} - x_i^0$.

Is the equilibrium point of a charity game Pareto optimal? Suppose first that the equilibrium is nontrivial. For any $i \in G$, $x_i = \xi_i(\mathbf{x}) > \mathbf{x}$. Since

$$U_i'(x_i) = U'(\mathbf{x}), \qquad U_i'(x_i) - U'(x_i) = U'(\mathbf{x}) - U'(x_i)$$

from which it follows immediately that

$$(\bar{\beta} - \beta_i)\alpha_i = 1 \qquad \text{for } i \in G$$

However,

$$\sum_{x_i > \mathbf{x}} (\bar{\beta} - \beta_i)\alpha_i \leq 1$$

for a Pareto-optimal allocation, so the equilibrium allocation can be Pareto optimal only if there is exactly one member of $G$ and no other individual whose equilibrium income is above the minimum.

This is a condition on the equilibrium allocation of final incomes. It is useful to restate it as a condition on original incomes. Suppose that individual 1 is the sole member of $G$. Then $x_i^0 \leq x_i = \mathbf{x}$ for all $i > 1$. Clearly, $x_1^0 > \xi_i(\mathbf{x}) > \mathbf{x} \geq x_i^0$ for $i > 1$, so that individual 1 must in fact have the largest original income. Label all the individuals now in decreasing order of income, so that $x_2^0$ is the second-highest original income. Since $x_2^0 \leq \mathbf{x}$ and $F(\mathbf{x}) = 0$, it must be that $F(x_2^0) \geq 0$, since $F$ is decreasing by (48). Clearly, this condition is also sufficient that individual 1 be the sole member of $G$ and the sole individual whose equilibrium income exceeds $\mathbf{x}$.

Since $x_1^0 > \xi_1(\mathbf{x}) \geq \xi_1(x_2^0)$, $[x_1^0 - \xi_1(x_2^0)]^+ = x_1^0 - \xi_1(x_2^0)$. For $i > 1$, $x_i^0 \leq x_2^0 < \xi_i(x_2^0)$, so that $[x_i^0 - \xi_i(x_2^0)]^+ = 0$ for $i > 1$. For $i = 1, 2, x_2^0 - x_i^0 \leq 0$, so that $(x_2^0 - x_i^0)^+ = 0$. For $i > 2, x_2^0 - x_i^0 \geq 0$, so that $(x_2^0 - x_i^0)^+ = x_2^0 - x_i^0$. Hence, from (47),

$$0 \leq F(x_2^0) = x_1^0 - \xi_1(x_2^0) - \sum_{i>2} (x_2^0 - x_i^0)$$

or

$$x_1^0 \geq \xi_1(x_2^0) + \sum_{i>2} (x_2^0 - x_i^0)$$

The highest original income must be so high that if the holder brings every one else up to the second-highest income, he or she would be at least indifferent to giving up further income to the others.

*Theorem 6.* A nontrivial equilibrium of a charity game is Pareto optimal if and only if the final income allocation has exactly one individual above the minimum income or, equivalently, if and only if the original incomes satisfy the condition

$$x_1^0 \geq \xi_1(x_2^0) + \sum_{i>2} (x_2^0 - x_i^0)$$

where individuals 1 and 2 have the highest and next-highest original incomes, respectively.

In the case of a trivial equilibrium, less can be said beyond the Pareto-optimality criterion itself. By Lemma 1 (a), $U_i'(x_i^0) \geq U'(\mathbf{x}^0)$, and therefore $U_i'(x_i^0) - U'(x_i^0) \geq U'(\mathbf{x}^0) - U'(x_i^0)$, from which it follows that

$$(\bar{\beta} - \beta_i^0)\alpha_i^0 \leq 1 \tag{50}$$

where the superscript means evaluation at original incomes. Further, for fixed $\mathbf{x}^0$, we can vary $x_i^0$ until equality holds in (50), for any $i$ for whom $x_i^0 > \mathbf{x}$. Also, for those $i$, $U'(x_i^0) < U'(\mathbf{x}^0)$, so that $\bar{\beta} - \beta_i^0 > 0$ and can be made arbitrarily small, and hence $(\bar{\beta} - \beta_i^0)\alpha_i^0 > 0$ and can be made arbitrarily small. If $x_i^0 > \mathbf{x}^0$ for no or one value of $i$, then clearly the Pareto-optimality criterion is satisfied. Otherwise, let

$$m = \#\{i \,|\, x_i^0 > \mathbf{x}^0\}$$

Then, by suitable choice of $x_i^0$, we can make

$$\sum_{x_i^0 > \mathbf{x}^0} (\bar{\beta} - \beta_i^0)\alpha_i^0 \tag{51}$$

vary from as close to zero as desired up to $m$, without changing the level of $\mathbf{x}^0$, the number of individuals for whom $x_i^0 > \mathbf{x}^0$, or the triviality of the equilibrium. But if $m > 1$, then (51) can be made to be below or above 1, and the income allocations may be Pareto optimal or they may not.

*Theorem 7.* Suppose that the distribution of original incomes satisfies the conditions for the existence of a trivial equilibrium in the charity game. If there is at most one individual whose original income is above the minimum, then the allocation is Pareto optimal. Otherwise, the allocation may or may not be Pareto optimal.

*Corollary 6.* Any equilibrium allocation of the charity game (trivial or not) for which at most one individual has above-minimum income is Pareto optimal.

The reason why the charity game so rarely leads to a Pareto-optimal allocation is that the income of others is a public good. If there are two or more givers, then each would benefit by the other's giving; but the charity game does not permit mutually advantageous arrangements. Even if there is one giver and one additional individual above the minimum, the benefit to the latter from the former's giving to those with minimum income is never given representation.

## Notes

1 This point was first made in the context of social welfare functions by Fleming (1953). The classic statement of conditions for additive utility functions is that of Debreu (1960).
2 This position is implicit in Bergson (1938) and has been made explicit in Bergson (1966; see esp. pp. 35–6). Pareto also considered social welfare judgments to be made by individuals in a little-known paper (1913).
3 Little (1952) attacked the nondictatorship condition in social choice theory on the grounds that social welfare judgments were made by individuals.

## References

Archibald, G. C., and D. Davidson. 1976. Non-paternalism and the Basic Theorems of Welfare Economics. *Canadian Journal of Economics* 9:492–507.

Bergson, A. 1938. A Reformulation of Certain Aspects of Welfare Economics. *Quarterly Journal of Economics* 52:310–34.

Bergson, A. 1966. *Essays in Normative Economics.* Cambridge, Mass.: Harvard University Press.

Debreu, G. 1960. Topological Methods in Cardinal Utility Theory. In K. J. Arrow, S. Karlin, and P. Suppes (eds.), *Mathematical Methods in the Social Sciences, 1959.* Stanford, Calif.: Stanford University Press, pp. 16–26.

Fleming, J. M. 1953. A Cardinal Concept of Welfare. *Quarterly Journal of Economics* 66:366–84.

Hochman, H. M., and J. D. Rodgers. 1969. Pareto Optimal Redistribution. *American Economic Review* 59:542–7.

Ireland, T. R., and D. B. Johnson. 1970. *The Economics of Charity,* Part 2 (by D. B. Johnson). Blacksburg, Va.: Center for Study in Public Choice.

Kolm, S. C. 1969. The Optimal Production of Social Justice. In J. Margolis and H. Guitton (eds.), *Public Economics.* New York: St. Martin's Press, pp. 145–200.

Little, I. M. D. 1952. Social Choice and Individual Values. *Journal of Political Economy* 60:422–32.

Pareto, V. 1913. Il massimo di utilità per una colletività in sociologia. *Giornale degli Economisti,* pp. 337–40.

Winter, S. G., Jr. 1969. A Simple Remark on the Second Optimality Theorem of Welfare Economics. *Journal of Economic Theory* 1:99–103.

# 11 A note on production structure and aggregate growth

*Simon Kuznets*

## 1. Introduction

The initial hypothesis that led to this chapter concerns the effects on aggregate growth of differences among production sectors in the potential rise in their productivity (per worker, or per unit of total input). Assume production sector I, which, for a variety of reasons (e.g., lesser role of recent technological innovations or greater institutional resistance to them), is assigned an expected lower rise in productivity over the next decade than production sector II. Then, if two economies differ in the proportions of sectors I and II in their product and inputs, economy 1, with a larger proportion of sector I and lower proportion of sector II, would tend to show a lower rise per worker (or per unit of total input) than economy 2; and this, under usual conditions, would also mean a lower rate of increase in per capita product (i.e., aggregate growth) in economy 1.

The general statement above can be made more meaningful by referring to identifiable major production sectors – $A$, agriculture and related activities, and the rest, $(I + S)$, or the sum of industry and services. We can also use the familiar ratios for the less developed (LDC) and developed (DC) market economies. The simple example presented in Table 1, using labor force as the only productive factor (our data on others are still quite scarce), and thus dealing with changes in product per worker, illustrates the initial hypothesis.

The illustration is unrealistic in several respects. It sets the absolute magnitudes of labor force, total product, and per worker product at the same levels for the less and more developed countries – a simplification that permits concentration on the rates of *relative* increase in sectoral or total product per worker. Furthermore, whereas we allow for growth in product per worker in the two cases, the shares of the $A$ and $(I + S)$ in the labor force are kept constant. Changes in these shares, reflecting struc-

Table 1. *Effects of different rates of rise in sectoral product per worker on aggregate growth (of total product per worker)*

|  | (1) | (2) | (3) | (4) | (5) | (6) | (7) |
|---|---|---|---|---|---|---|---|
|  |  |  | Product per worker | | GDP | | Growth in |
|  | Labor | Force | | | | | product per |
|  | $A$ | $(I + S)$ | $A$ | $(I + S)$ | $A$ | $(I + S)$ | worker (%) |
| *Initial structure* | | | | | | | |
| 1. LDC | 70 | 30 | 0.714 | 1.667 | 50 | 50 | — |
| 2. DC | 14 | 86 | 0.714 | 1.047 | 10 | 90 | — |
| *Case 1. Rise in product per worker of 20% in A sector and of 40% in (I + S) sector* | | | | | | | |
| 3. LDC | 70 | 30 | 0.857 | 2.334 | 60 | 70 | 30 |
| 4. DC | 14 | 86 | 0.857 | 1.466 | 12 | 126 | 38 |
| *Case 2. Rise in product per worker of 20% in A sector and of 40% in the (I + S) sector in LDCs; rise in product per worker of 40% in both sectors in DCs* | | | | | | | |
| 5. LDC | 70 | 30 | 0.857 | 2.334 | 60 | 70 | 30 |
| 6. DC | 14 | 86 | 1.000 | 2.334 | 14 | 126 | 40 |

tural shifts, are, of course, important in the growth process of an economy. So are adjustments in the process of growth to differing changes in productivity in the several sectors. But we are concerned here, and throughout the paper, with the effects of differences in potential growth in product per worker among the several sectors on the growth of total product per worker – differences that prevail over a period long enough to affect substantial growth rates (say, a decade or two), but not so long as to merge different phases of long-term growth in which the differential constraints are likely to be modified.

The conclusions suggested by Table 1 are obvious. First, if we assume (case 1) a lower growth rate of per worker product in the $A$ sector, in both LDCs and DCs, and equal growth rates in sectoral product per worker in both sets of economies, the aggregate growth rate in per worker product in LDCs will fall short of that in the DCs.

Second, if we were to assume (case 2) that no such differential in sectoral growth in product per worker is found in the DCs, whereas it is characteristic of LDCs, the addition to the disparities in aggregate growth in per worker product is small. This is clearly due to the low weight of the $A$ sector in the DCs. In other words, it is the initial assumption of lesser capacity of per worker product in the $A$ sector to grow in the *LDCs* that yields the wide disparity in aggregate growth per worker.

Third, if there is a close relation between growth of labor force and growth of population, differences in aggregate growth of product per worker will be translated into similar differences in growth of product per capita, aggregate growth.

Thus, the crucial question in the initial hypothesis is whether it is plausible to expect, in the LDCs, a lower growth rate in per worker product in the $A$ sector than in the $(I + S)$ sector. This expectation would, presumably, be affected by the rate of increase in the sectoral labor force and the absence or presence of a shift in labor force away from the $A$ sector. All of this also disregards capital, human and material, as a complementary factor in production, in addition to labor force measured in numbers and without regard to quality differentials. This is not the place, nor is it fully within my competence, to deal with what is clearly a complex and variable set of production relations.[1] I can only suggest some factors that would lead to the expectation just stated.

These factors lie in the difference between the $A$ and the $(I + S)$ sectors, taken broadly, in the ease with which the diffusion of modern technology from the DCs to the LDCs can be expected to occur. If it can be assumed that in the wide difference in per worker product between the $A$ and the $(I + S)$ sectors in the LDCs, suggested in the illustration and confirmed by empirical evidence, a major source lies in the greater weight of "modern" technology in the $(I + S)$ sector (in manufacturing, public utilities, mining, transport and communication, and some professional services), it can be argued that the importation and implantation of such modern technology in the LDCs is far easier in the $(I + S)$ than in the $A$ sector. The reason may lie partly in the wider difference in natural conditions that affect the $A$ sector in the LDCs as compared with those in DCs; the lesser control over the environmental factors in the $A$ sector even in the DCs, relative to their weather and other conditions – let alone in the LDCs, in which the $A$ sector operates in soil and climate conditions relatively unfamiliar to modern agricultural technology in the DCs. One may also stress that in market economies, the $A$ sector in the LDCs (much more so than in DCs) is dominated by a large number of small-scale firms in conditions which, because of high-risk, limited reserves, and a wide degree of dispersion, would not encourage rapid diffusion of modern technology, even if it were as fully available and as suitable as is the modern production technology in much of the $(I + S)$ sector.

This argument can be elaborated further by reference to the limited transport and communication framework in the countryside of LDCs, inhibiting rapid diffusion of new elements in technology; the greater concentration of political power and government in the urban centers of the LDCs, so that government policy directed at economic growth is likely to favor the $(I + S)$ sector more than the $A$ sector; and the conditions of pressure on natural resources so much greater in the $A$ sector of the LDCs. But the comments already advanced are, perhaps, sufficient to explain why the initial hypothesis was framed in terms of growth propensities of per worker product in the $A$ and other sectors, particularly in the

Table 2. *Gross domestic product (GDP) and labor force (LF), market economies in six major regions, 1960 and 1970*

| | (1)<br>East and<br>Southeast<br>Asia,<br>excluding<br>Japan | (2)<br>Africa<br>exclud-<br>ing<br>South<br>Africa | (3)<br><br>Asia–<br>Middle<br>East | (4)<br><br><br>Latin<br>America | (5)<br><br><br><br>Europe | (6)<br><br><br>North<br>America |
|---|---|---|---|---|---|---|
| *GDP, 1970 market prices, $US billion* | | | | | | |
| 1. 1960 | 78.5 | 35.9 | 22.1 | 91.6 | 494 | 712 |
| 2. 1970 | 123.5 | 58.4 | 46.7 | 159.6 | 758 | 1,064 |
| 3. % change | 57.4 | 62.8 | 111.1 | 74.2 | 53.5 | 49.5 |
| *Population, millions* | | | | | | |
| 4. 1960 | 804 | 256 | 79.7 | 216 | 328 | 199 |
| 5. 1970 | 1,031 | 327 | 105 | 283 | 356 | 226 |
| 6. % change | 28.2 | 27.7 | 31.7 | 31.0 | 8.5 | 13.6 |
| *GDP per capita, $US, 1970 market prices* | | | | | | |
| 7. 1960 | 97.6 | 140 | 277 | 424 | 1,506 | 3,578 |
| 8. 1970 | 120 | 179 | 445 | 564 | 2,129 | 4,708 |
| 9. % change | 23.0 | 27.9 | 60.6 | 33.0 | 41.4 | 31.6 |
| *LF, excluding women in A sector, millions* | | | | | | |
| 10. 1960 | 251 | 75.5 | 23.3 | 67.6 | 132.0 | 79.3 |
| 11. 1970 | 305 | 94.8 | 29.7 | 86.2 | 140.9 | 95.3 |
| 12. % change | 21.4 | 25.5 | 27.5 | 27.6 | 6.8 | 20.2 |
| *% LF, excluding women in A sector, to population* | | | | | | |
| 13. 1960 | 31.2 | 29.5 | 29.2 | 31.3 | 40.2 | 39.8 |
| 14. 1970 | 29.6 | 29.0 | 28.3 | 30.5 | 39.6 | 42.2 |
| *GDP per worker, $US, 1970 market prices* | | | | | | |
| 15. 1960 | 313 | 475 | 948 | 1,355 | 3,742 | 8,979 |
| 16. 1970 | 405 | 616 | 1,572 | 1,852 | 5,380 | 11,165 |
| 17. % change | 29.7 | 29.7 | 65.8 | 36.6 | 43.6 | 24.4 |

*Notes: Lines 1 and 2:* The data on GDP in 1970 are from United Nations, *Yearbook of National Accounts Statistics 1976*, vol. 2, *International Tables* (New York, 1977), Table 1A, pp. 3–9. The totals for 1960 were calculated by applying to the 1970 totals the growth rates for the decade 1960–2 to 1970–2 (shown in line 3). The latter were computed from ibid., Table 6B, pp. 255–63. This table shows annual index numbers, for 1960 to 1975, of GDP in 1970 market prices, originating in six production subsectors, and the 1970 weights (shares in total GDP) for each. This permitted us to calculate the weighted indexes for the three major sectors (*A, I,* and *S*) and combine them to total GDP; and to compute the growth rates for 1960–2 to 1970–2 for GDP, and for the *A, I,* and *S* sectors (the latter used in Tables 3 and 4).

*Lines 4 and 5 and 10 and 11:* The data on population and on labor force (the latter excluding women in the *A* sector) are directly from International Labour Office, *Labour Force Estimates 1950–1970 and Projections 1975–2000,* vol 5, *World Summary* (Geneva, 1977), Table 2 (on population and total labor force), pp. 6–39, and Table 3 (on labor force by sex and sector), pp. 40–8; and vol 1, *Asia* (Geneva, 1977), analogous Table 2 (pp. 7–50) and 3 (pp. 51–61).

The more detailed data on population and labor force available in the ILO source were used to fit them into regions comparable to those used for the GDP indexes and sectors in the UN source. For East and Southeast Asia, excluding Japan, we combined East South Asia and Middle South Asia, excluding Iran, with the data on South Korea and Hong Kong. For Africa, excluding South Africa, we combined the data on North, East, and Middle Africa. For Asia–Middle East we took the sum of Western South Asia and Iran. The totals for Latin America were of the same coverage in the two sources. For Europe we took the sum of Northern, Western, and Southern less developed market economies. This naturally determined the direction of whatever statistical probing was feasible, and we turn to the latter.

## 2. Statistical findings

To secure broad coverage of the production structure and growth rates of product (GDP, at constant prices), we exploited the UN estimates for market economies in several broad regions, developed and less developed; and to these we matched the ILO estimates of labor force, total and by three broad sectors (see the UN and ILO sources cited in the notes to Table 2). In a more intensive analysis, not feasible here, it would have been more illuminating to deal with single countries rather than congeries of them for wide regions. But the main limitation of the data, even for a simple task of relating output to labor force, lies in the brevity of the period covered. The UN indexes of GDP, total and by sector, are available only back to 1950, and for some regions only back to 1960; the ILO estimates of labor force, total and by sector, are given only for 1950, 1960, and 1970. We have therefore concentrated on the decade from 1960 to 1970, using GDP and LF estimates that distinguish three major sectors: $A$ – agriculture and related activities; $I$ – mining, manufacturing, power, light and fuel utilities, and construction; $S$ – transport and communication, trade, other services. We secured these estimates for the market economies grouped into six major regions – four in the less developed group and two in the developed.

Table 2 presents the major absolute magnitudes, in the aggregate, without distinguishing the production sectors, for 1960 and 1970. The technical comments, not only on the sources but also on the procedures and some tests of the results, are in the notes to the tables so as not to encumber the text. Here the only point to be noted is the exclusion of female labor force in the $A$ sector from the LF totals and sectoral shares. This is done largely because of the highly variable treatment of this component in the several regions, with obvious effects in unlikely discrepancies of the resulting ratios.[2]

Table 2 summarizes a wide variety of data; and we comment briefly on aspects that are of interest.

First, the six regions distinguished include most of the less developed

## Notes to Table 2 (cont.)

Europe (the latter without adjustment for inclusion of Albania). For North America, largely Canada and the United States, the coverage of the two regions is the same.

The closeness of the adjustment can be checked by comparing the population totals for 1970 from the ILO sources (line 5) with those derivable from Table 1A in the UN source used for line 2. The latter, for the regions in successive columns 1–6 are, in millions 1,029; 324; 104; 271; 334; 225. The agreement is close.

*Lines 3, 6, 9, 12–24, and 17:* By calculation from entries in the other lines.

and developed market economies of the world, and reveal relatively fully the international disparities in the distribution of population and in their per capita product. Since the UN estimates involve conversion to comparable dollars by use of "prevailing dollar exchange rates," the wide ranges in per capita product in lines 7 and 8 exaggerate purchasing power differentials; but the adjustment to approximate the latter would still leave a wide spread in the range between say Asia and North America; and leave the rough sequence in comparative levels relatively unaffected for regions as broad as these.[3]

Second, the ratios of labor force (excluding women in the A sector) to total population, although roughly similar, at about 30 percent, for the four less developed regions, are distinctly below those for the two developed regions (see lines 13 and 14). The difference is associated with that in the rate of natural increase of population, which largely determines the rate of population growth in line 6 and also the structure of population by age. A high rate of natural increase means a high proportion in the population of age groups under 15, for whom the labor force participation rates are naturally low. Hence, growth rates in population over the decade of close to 30 percent (line 6, columns 1–4) are associated with low ratios of labor force to population in line 14, columns 1–4; whereas the low rates of growth of population in the two developed regions are associated with high ratios of labor force in total population (columns 5 and 6, lines 6 and 14). There is also evidence of the wide swing in the rates of natural increase in North America, where high rates of increase peaking in the late 1950s produced a larger upswing in the labor force proportions by the end of the 1960s (see column 6, lines 6, 12, and 14).

Third, despite significant differences among the regions in proportions of labor force to population, and in the movements of labor force relative to population, the differences among regions in product per worker (lines 15 and 16) are similar to those in product per capita (lines 7 and 8); and differences in changes over the decade in product per worker (line 17) are similar to those in the decadal change in product per capita (line 9). One can assume, therefore, that over long periods, differences in growth of product per worker among regions will be associated with differences in growth in product per capita; and whatever effect production structure will have on the former will be translated into effects on the latter (i.e., on aggregate growth as reflected in per capita product).

Finally, one should note the marked differences among the regions in the decade's growth of product per capita or product per worker. Some elements in these differences may be associated with factors specific to the rather short period covered; others may be due to longer-term factors. Thus, the high growth rate in the Asia–Middle East region is probably associated with the petroleum boom that occurred even before the recent sharp rise in oil prices; whereas the high rate of growth in Europe was probably in compensation for the preceding decades of stagnation and war destruction that reached back to the late 1920s and that would find an even more striking illustration in the case of Japan. Elements of the oil boom may have affected the African region, as well as Latin America, but to a much lesser degree; and in the case of the latter there may have also been the recovery from the recession of the 1930s and the slowdown during the World War II years. Were our record to cover a longer historical span, some of these transitory elements would have been reduced; and the longer-term differences in growth rates would have emerged more clearly.

We turn now to the data that reveal the sectoral structure of both GDP and LF for 1960 and 1970, data needed to derive our measures of levels and growth of sectoral product per worker (Table 3). The regions are the same as in Table 1; and because of the nature of the ILO data, the sectoral division must be limited to three sectors. One should also note that the exclusion from GDP of the output in two subsectors of the S sector, banking, insurance, and real estate and income from ownership of dwellings, which involve directly little of the total labor force, could not be carried out. Consequently, there is an exaggeration of the product per worker in the $S$ (and hence also $I + S$) sector; but it is not likely to invalidate the major findings.

Of the variety of differentials, changes over time, and associations, summarized in Table 3, the most conspicuous general, and most relevant to our discussion, is the low product per worker in agriculture compared with the product per worker in the $(I + S)$ sector. The former, in the less developed regions, is between a half and a fourth of the latter, even with exclusion of women workers from the $A$ sector. To be sure, the $A$ to non-$A$ gap in product per worker may be partly due to inadequate adjustment for factor price differentials between the two groups and for the greater extent to which $A$ workers may engage part of their time in non-$A$ pursuits than would be the case of $(I + S)$ workers in their part-time engagement in the $A$ sector. But one may doubt that adjustment would reduce materially the range of the gap.

Next, one should note that the relative disparity between per worker product in the $(I + S)$ and the $A$ sectors differs significantly among the regions, either in 1960 or 1970 (see particularly lines 21 and 22). It ranges from a low of about 2 in the lowest-income ESE Asia region to a high of over 4 in the Asia–Middle East, and more significantly the Latin American region; then drops back to between 2.6 and 1.3 in the two developed regions, Europe and North America. Insofar as the $A - (I + S)$ differential in product per work is an element in the inequality of income measured or conjectured in the distribution of total product among the relevant recipients units, the differential must have made greater contribution

Table 3. *Sectoral structure of GDP and LF, market economies, six major regions, 1960 and 1970*

| | (1) East and Southeast Asia, excluding Japan | (2) Africa excluding South Africa | (3) Asia– Middle East | (4) Latin America | (5) Europe | (6) North America |
|---|---|---|---|---|---|---|
| *% shares of sectors in GDP* | | | | | | |
| *1960* | | | | | | |
| 1. A sector | 49.3 | 42.3 | 25.0 | 16.7 | 7.8 | 3.9 |
| 2. I sector | 17.7 | 20.7 | 35.1 | 32.0 | 42.6 | 34.6 |
| 3. S sector | 33.0 | 37.0 | 39.9 | 51.3 | 49.6 | 61.5 |
| *1970* | | | | | | |
| 4. A sector | 40.9 | 32.1 | 16.9 | 13.7 | 6.1 | 2.9 |
| 5. I sector | 22.8 | 28.0 | 40.7 | 35.0 | 45.6 | 34.9 |
| 6. S sector | 36.3 | 39.9 | 42.4 | 51.3 | 48.3 | 62.2 |
| *% shares of sectors in LF (excluding women in A sector)* | | | | | | |
| *1960* | | | | | | |
| 7. A sector | 65.7 | 70.9 | 57.8 | 45.2 | 18.0 | 6.5 |
| 8. I sector | 13.6 | 10.7 | 19.3 | 21.0 | 43.3 | 36.5 |
| 9. S sector | 20.7 | 18.4 | 22.9 | 33.8 | 38.7 | 57.0 |
| *1970* | | | | | | |
| 10. A sector | 59.2 | 65.0 | 48.6 | 38.7 | 11.3 | 3.7 |
| 11. I sector | 16.1 | 13.7 | 22.0 | 22.6 | 43.7 | 34.3 |
| 12. S sector | 24.7 | 21.3 | 29.4 | 38.7 | 45.0 | 62.0 |
| *Relative product per worker, by sector (regionwide relative = 1.00)* | | | | | | |
| *1960* | | | | | | |
| 13. A sector | 0.75 | 0.62 | 0.43 | 0.37 | 0.43 | 0.60 |
| 14. (I + S) sector | 1.48 | 1.98 | 1.78 | 1.52 | 1.12 | 1.03 |
| 15. I sector | 1.30 | 1.93 | 1.82 | 1.52 | 0.98 | 0.95 |
| 16. S sector | 1.59 | 2.01 | 1.74 | 1.52 | 1.28 | 1.08 |
| *1970* | | | | | | |
| 17. A sector | 0.69 | 0.49 | 0.35 | 0.35 | 0.54 | 0.78 |
| 18. (I + S) sector | 1.45 | 1.94 | 1.62 | 1.41 | 1.06 | 1.01 |
| 19. I sector | 1.42 | 2.04 | 1.85 | 1.55 | 1.05 | 1.02 |
| 20. S sector | 1.47 | 1.87 | 1.44 | 1.33 | 1.07 | 1.00 |
| *Intersectoral ratio in product per worker, (I + S)/A* | | | | | | |
| 21. 1960 | 2.0 | 3.2 | 4.1 | 4.1 | 2.6 | 1.7 |
| 22. 1970 | 2.1 | 4.0 | 4.6 | 4.0 | 2.0 | 1.3 |
| *Total disparity between sectoral shares in GDP and in LF (TDM)* | | | | | | |
| 23. 1960 | 32.8 | 57.2 | 65.6 | 57.0 | 21.8 | 9.0 |
| 24. 1970 | 36.6 | 65.8 | 63.4 | 50.0 | 10.4 | 1.6 |

*Notes:* The *A* sector covers agriculture and related industries (fisheries, forestry, and hunting). The *I* sector includes mining, manufacturing, power and light utilities, and construction. The *S* sector covers transport and communication, wholesale and retail trade, and other services. This division is governed by that followed in the ILO data on labor force.

*Lines 1–6:* The sectoral structure of GDP in 1970 is directly from the UN source, Table 6B, cited in the notes to lines 1–2 of Table 2. The sectoral shares in GDP for 1960 were obtained by calculating them for 1960–2 and 1970–2, and applying the differences to the shares in 1970.

For four of the six regions (excluding Africa and Asia–Middle East), an alternative procedure was in the higher-income less developed regions (such as Latin America) than either in such low-income less developed regions as ESE Asia or in the developed regions.

Finally, it is clear from lines 21 and 22 that the intersectoral ratio in product per worker, $(I + S)/A$, changed significantly between 1960 and 1970. In three of the regions, the ratio rose over the decade, indicating that in them – Asia, Africa, and Asia–Middle East – the growth in per worker product in the $A$ sector must have been lower over the decade than the total growth in per worker product in the $(I + S)$ sector. In Latin America but more conspicuously in the two developed regions, Europe and North America, the intersectoral ratio declined, indicating that the product per worker in the $A$ sector must have grown over the decade more than the product per worker in the $(I + S)$ sector. And these results are shown explicitly in the top panel of Table 4. The *weighted* measures of intersectoral disparities in product per worker, calculated for three rather than two sectors, show the same pattern and changes, but qualified by the decline in the total share of the $A$ sector (see lines 23 and 24).

Before turning to Table 4, one may note that the disparities in per worker product between the $I$ and $S$ sectors, although significant, are far narrower than those between the $A$ sector and either $(I + S)$ sector, or the $I$ and $S$ sectors taken separately. Hence, given the conventional classification of production sectors, large differentials will be observed only in the $A$ to non-$A$ division, even in the developed countries; and in the latter, the sharp drop in the share of the $A$ sector reduces the weight of the disparity to quantitatively insignificant dimension. One may argue that the sectoral classification of the non-$A$ division should focus more than it does now on the subsectors that are distinctive in the level of their per worker product and the propensity in their growth.

## Notes to Table 3 (*cont.*)

feasible, using the annual indexes for total GDP and subsectors (in 1963 factor costs) reaching back from 1968 to 1950 as well as the sectoral shares in 1963 [see United Nations, *Yearbook of National Accounts Statistics, 1969,* vol 2, *International Tables* (New York 1970), Table 6B, pp. 159–65]. These data made it possible to extend the annual indices of GDP total and by sectors, in 1970 market prices, to cover 1958–9; and, instead of 1960–2 and 1970–2 use quinquennial averages, 1958–62 and 1968–72, centered on 1960 and 1970, respectively. The sectoral shares in GDP yielded by these calculations differed only slightly from those shown in lines 1–6; and the same is true of the alternative percent changes in sectoral product per worker, when we compared them with those now shown in Table 4. The differences would affect the major findings but little; and there was no need to show the results of alternative sets of calculations.

*Lines 7–12:* Calculated from Table 3 of the ILO source cited for lines 10–11 of Table 2.

*Lines 13–20:* Obtained by division of the given sector's share in GDP by the same sector's share in LF. This yields the ratio of product per worker in the given sector to the aggregate product per worker in the region.

*Lines 21 and 22:* By division of the relative product for the $(I + S)$ sector by that for the $A$ sector.

*Lines 23 and 24:* Obtained by subtracting the three sectoral shares in GDP from the shares of the corresponding three sectoral shares in LF, and adding the deviations regardless of sign. This may be shown to equal the sum of deviations of the relative product of each sector from 1.00 (the regionwide average), each weighted by the shares of the sectors in LF – the deviations being taken regardless of sign.

Table 4. *Growth from 1960 to 1970 (%), GDP, LF, and product per worker, total and by sector, market economies in six major regions*

| | (1)<br>East and<br>Southeast<br>Asia,<br>excluding<br>Japan | (2)<br>Africa,<br>excluding<br>South<br>Africa | (3)<br>Asia–<br>Middle<br>East | (4)<br>Latin<br>America | (5)<br><br>Europe | (6)<br>North<br>America |
|---|---|---|---|---|---|---|
| *A. Growth from 1960 to 1970 (%)* | | | | | | |
| *Gross domestic product* | | | | | | |
| 1. Total | 57.4 | 62.8 | 111.1 | 74.2 | 53.5 | 49.5 |
| 2. A sector | 29.7 | 22.9 | 42.9 | 41.5 | 19.5 | 10.7 |
| 3. $(I + S)$ sector | 82.6 | 91.1 | 133.8 | 80.6 | 56.4 | 51.1 |
| 4. $I$ sector | 100.6 | 119.8 | 144.6 | 90.2 | 64.5 | 50.9 |
| 5. $S$ sector | 72.9 | 75.3 | 124.2 | 74.6 | 49.4 | 54.2 |
| *Labor force (excluding women in A sector)* | | | | | | |
| 6. Total | 21.4 | 25.5 | 27.5 | 27.6 | 6.8 | 20.2 |
| 7. A sector | 9.2 | 15.0 | 7.4 | 9.3 | −32.7 | −32.0 |
| 8. $(I + S)$ sector | 44.7 | 51.1 | 55.5 | 42.6 | 15.4 | 23.8 |
| 9. $I$ sector | 44.4 | 60.8 | 45.1 | 36.9 | 7.6 | 13.0 |
| 10. $S$ sector | 44.8 | 45.5 | 64.3 | 46.2 | 24.2 | 30.7 |
| *Product per worker* | | | | | | |
| 11. Total | 29.7 | 29.7 | 65.8 | 36.6 | 43.8 | 24.4 |
| 12. A sector | 18.8 | 6.9 | 33.1 | 29.5 | 77.5 | 62.8 |
| 13. $(I + S)$ sector | 26.2 | 26.5 | 50.4 | 26.7 | 35.5 | 22.0 |
| 14. $I$ sector | 38.9 | 36.7 | 68.6 | 36.9 | 53.0 | 33.5 |
| 15. $S$ sector | 19.4 | 20.6 | 36.5 | 19.4 | 20.3 | 15.7 |
| *B. Decomposition of growth in total product per worker (line 11)* | | | | | | |
| *Growth in sectoral product per worker, weighted* | | | | | | |
| 16. A sector | 9.3 | 2.9 | 8.3 | 4.9 | 6.0 | 2.4 |
| 17. $(I + S)$ sector | 13.3 | 15.2 | 37.8 | 22.2 | 32.7 | 21.1 |
| 18. Weighted total<br>(lines 16 + 17) | 22.6 | 18.1 | 46.1 | 27.1 | 38.7 | 23.5 |
| 19. Residual (due to<br>sectoral shift) | 5.8 | 9.8 | 13.5 | 7.5 | 3.7 | 0.73 |
| 20. Total shift (% points) | 6.5 | 5.9 | 9.2 | 6.5 | 6.7 | 2.8 |
| 21. First factor | 0.73 | 1.36 | 1.35 | 1.15 | 0.69 | 0.43 |
| 22. Second factor | 1.062 | 1.183 | 1.130 | 0.978 | 0.764 | 0.749 |
| 23. Combined factors<br>(line 21 × line 22) | 0.775 | 1.609 | 1.526 | 1.125 | 0.527 | 0.322 |
| 24. Contribution to<br>growth, % points<br>(line 20 × line 23) | 5.0 | 9.5 | 14.0 | 7.3 | 3.5 | 0.90 |

*Notes: Lines 1–15:* The percentage changes from 1960 to 1970, for GDP, LF, and product per worker, total and by sector, were calculated from the two sources used for Tables 2 and 3. Indeed, for the totals (lines 1, 6, and 11) the percentage changes are identical with those in lines 3, 12, and 15 for the corresponding regions in Table 2.

*Lines 16 and 17:* The growth in sectoral product per worker (in lines 12 and 13) was weighted by the shares of the two sectors in total GDP in 1960 (since the proper weights are the initial share in LF, weighted by the comparative level of product per worker at that date).

*Line 19:* The difference between line 18 and line 11, related to the entry in line 18 (the latter treated as

As already indicated, the top panel of Table 4 reveals a variety of implications of the sectoral shares in GDP and LF shown in Table 3. The commonly observed declines in Table 3 of the shares of the $A$ sector in GDP are translated in lines 2 and 3 of Table 4 into the commonly observed lower growth of GDP in the $A$ sector than in the $(I + S)$ sector; the commonly observed declines in Table 3 of the share of the $A$ sector in total LF are translated in lines 7 and 8 of Table 4 into a much lower growth (or actual decline) of labor force in the $A$ sector than of labor force in the $(I + S)$ sector. Finally, the different movements of the intersectoral ratio in per worker product $(I + S)/A$ observed in Table 3 are translated here in lower growth rates of per worker product in the $A$ than in the $(I + S)$ sector in ESE Asia, Africa, and Asia–Middle East, and in higher growth rates in per worker product in the $A$ sector in Latin America, Europe, and North America (lines 12 and 13). One should note particularly the very high rates of growth in per worker product in the $A$ sector in the two developed regions, in which the estimates of labor force in that sector show a marked relative decline. This may reflect an almost revolutionary change in the technology of the $A$ sector in the developed market economies following World War II, and induced by rapid spread to this sector of technological innovations that may have been held in abeyance over the preceding decades of depression and war, reaching perhaps as far back as the 1930s.

The distinction between the $I$ and $S$ sectors (lines 4 and 5, 9 and 10, and 14 and 15) reveals interesting differences in growth within the combined non-$A$ division. Except in North America, GDP originating in the $I$ sector grew more than that in the $S$ sector; but in most regions, labor force in the $I$ sector grew less than in the $S$ sector. In consequence, growth in product per worker in the $I$ sector was strikingly greater than that per worker product in the $S$ sector, in all regions. Indeed, if we except the untypical case of the Asia–Middle East region, the rise in per worker product in the $S$ sector was about the same in the remaining five regions, ranging from 16 to 21 percent (see line 15). There is a suggestion here of a limit on the growth rate of productivity for this sector, but for reasons unlike those

Notes to Table 4 (*cont.*)

a fraction and added to 1.0). For example, the 5.8 in column 1, line 19, is 29.7 − 22.6 = 7.1, the latter divided by 1.226. The residual multiplied by the weighted total (in line 18), used as a fraction and added to 1, yields the relative that, minus 1.0 and converted to percentages, would yield the entry in line 11.

*Line 20:* The shift from the $A$ to the $(I + S)$ sectors in their share in the labor force (derived by subtracting the percent share of the $A$ sector in total labor force in 1970 from that in 1960; see lines 7 and 10 of Table 3).

*Line 21:* The first factor is the difference between the relative product in the $(I + S)$ sector and that in the $A$ sector, in 1960 (derivable from lines 13 and 14 of Table 3).

*Line 22:* The second factor is the relative difference between the growth per worker product in the $(I + S)$ sector and in growth of per worker product in the $A$ sector. These are shown in lines 12 and 13 of this table; and the factor is derived by using the percentages as fractions, adding them to 1.0, and then dividing the result for the $(I + S)$ sector by that for the $A$ sector.

suggested for the *A* sector. They may lie partly in the difficulty of measuring productivity levels and changes for several important subsectors within the *S* sector, partly in the substantial in-migration of labor into the low-productivity subsectors.

In panel B we decompose the growth in aggregate product per worker in each region (line 11) into the contribution of growth in product per worker in the sectors, properly weighted; and the contribution of the shift of the labor force from the lower-product-per-worker sector, such as *A*, to sectors with higher product per worker. To simplify calculation and presentation, the analysis is carried through for two sectors, *A* and $(I + S)$, although it could have been done for three (and, in general, can be carried through for several sectors).

Lines 16–20 reveal that the weighted growth of the two sectors account for only a part of the aggregate growth of product per worker in line 11 – and this was to be expected as long as there was a shift in the structure of the labor force from lower- to higher-product-per-worker sectors. But the significant aspect of this finding is that the shortfall of the weighted growth of sector relative to aggregate growth in per worker product is significantly greater for the less developed regions than for the developed regions. Even excluding the untypical Asia–Middle East region, we find that the shortfall (observable by comparing lines 18 and 11) is about one-fourth of the aggregate growth rate in ESE Asia, about four-tenths in Africa, and over one-fourth in Latin America – compared with somewhat over one-tenth in Europe and insignificant in North America. In consequence, the weighted contribution of sectoral growth in product per worker in the LDC regions, if it were to have been observed with the sectoral structure of the labor force constant, would have yielded distinctly lower aggregate growth rates and their level relative to those in the DC regions would have been lower (compare the range in line 18 with that in line 11). To the extent that the lower growth rates in per worker product in the *A* sector in the LDC regions contributed to a lower level of the total in line 18, there was partial compensation in the intersectoral shift in the labor force of a magnitude that could not be easily matched in the DC regions.

Lines 20–2 attempt to approximate the contribution of the shift in labor force from the *A* to the $(I + S)$ sectors to the growth in aggregate product per worker in the region. The total shift, in percentage points of the shares of the sectors in total LF from 1960 to 1970, is weighted first by the initial difference in relative product per worker between the two sectors (line 21) and then by the relative difference in growth rates between the per worker product in the two sectors (line 22). The first factor ranges from a low in the lower-income LDCs to higher levels in the higher-income LDCs and then declines sharply for the DC regions; and a somewhat similar pattern is observed for the second factor, in line 22. The resulting approximations in line 24 differ somewhat from the residuals in line 19, owing partly to errors of rounding and partly to intercorrelation between the two sets of variables; but the differences are minor, within 1.0 percentage point.

## 3. Concluding comments

The findings, relating to the decade 1960–70 and the market economies in several major regions, can be briefly stated.

First, excepting the unusual case of the Asia–Middle East region, the major lower-income regions, ESE Asia and Africa (excluding South Africa) showed a lower growth of per worker product in the $A$ than in the $(I + S)$ sectors; the higher-income LDC region of Latin America showed a rise in per worker product in the $A$ sector about the same as in the $(I + S)$ sector; whereas in the two developed regions, the rise in per worker product in the $A$ sector far exceeded that in per worker product in the $(I + S)$ sector.

Second, the growth per worker in the $A$ sector in the three LDC regions, ranging between 30 and less than 10 percent for the decade, was clearly below the growth in the $A$ sector in the two developed regions. The growth rates per worker in the $(I + S)$ sector in the three LDC regions were about the same at about 27 percent for the decade, distinctly below that for Europe but somewhat higher than that for the North American region.

Third, weighted sectoral growth in per worker product in the LDC regions was substantially below the growth in aggregate product per worker, the difference contributed by the shift in labor force away from the $A$ to the $(I + S)$ sectors. The contribution of this intersectoral shift in labor force to the level of growth in aggregate product per worker was relatively greater in the three LDC regions than in the two developed regions.

There is thus a clear suggestion in the data of limiting constraints on growth of per worker productivity in the $A$ sector in the low-income LDCs, in which the share of the $A$ sector in total labor force and product are still high – as compared with the higher-income LDCs, in which these proportions of the $A$ sector have declined to moderate levels and as compared with the developed regions. There is also a suggestion of low-level constraints on the growth in per worker product in the $S$ sector, in both LDC and DC regions, in all of which (again excepting the Asia–Middle East region) growth over the 1960–70 decade was between 16 and 21 percent.

Although the statistical data here relate to a short period and to broad regions, two brief comments can be made to suggest broader empirical relevance and wider general significance of the findings.

One may reasonably surmise that occurrence of lower growth rates in product per worker in the $A$ sector than in the $(I + S)$ sector was fairly widespread. To illustrate (a full demonstration would require summary of a large literature on the subject), one may refer to the discussion of long-term trends in sectoral product per worker for a number of countries in the monograph cited in note 1 (pp. 289–302). This discussion, carried on largely in terms of the basic intersectoral ratio in product per worker, $(I + S)/A$, reveals that for the majority among the 13 currently developed countries, this ratio tended to rise over the decades, until World War II, thus indicating a lower growth rate in per worker product in sector $A$, with the decline in this ratio emerging largely after World War II. The discussion also suggests, although on the basis of a limited number of countries for 1950 to 1960, that "the basic sectoral inequality in product per worker did not respond to rising per capita (and presumably per worker) product in the less developed countries, but did so in the developed countries" (p. 301). Nor would it be difficult to suggest plausible factors that would account for lower growth rates in per worker product in the $A$ than in the $(I + S)$ sector even for developed countries in the earlier phases of their modern economic growth experience.

The more general comment is to reiterate the emphasis in the brief discussion here on the supply side of output and productivity – as distinct from the demand side, which may be more important in understanding differences in growth rates of sectoral output (rather than of productivity). The differences among production sectors in availability of innovational sources for increase in productivity, sources lying either in technological innovations, or in institutional innovations or resistance, are clearly important in that they are prevalent among production sectors, in different ways in countries at different levels of economic development and change over time. It is, therefore, likely that such differences in potential growth of productivity, due to supply side factors, influence the levels of aggregate growth rates, per worker or per capita, that can be attained. And their influence, combined with conditions that facilitate or impede the shift of resources from sectors of lower to those of higher product per worker (or per unit of total inputs), must be considered in explaining differences in aggregate growth rates among countries at different levels of economic development, and hence with different sectoral structure of production.

### Notes

1 See, however, a brief discussion of the factors underlying intersectoral inequality in product per worker, largely between $A$ and $(I + S)$ sectors, in my *Economic Growth of Nations: Total Output and Production Structure* (Cambridge, Mass.: Harvard University Press, Bethnap Press, 1971), pp. 236–48. The general bearing of that discussion was "to emphasize various aspects of

duality of structure in the less developed countries, and suggest that such duality, if present in the developed countries, plays a much less important role'' (p. 247). In this emphasis the earlier discussion supports the argument in the text relating to factors that might result in a lowered growth rate in product per worker in the $A$ than in the $(I + S)$ sectors in the less developed market economies.

2 Thus, the ILO source shows for Latin America a ratio of female to total workers in the $A$ sector of less than 10 percent in both 1960 and 1970. A similar ratio of Africa (total) was over 30 percent in both years; and somewhat higher for eastern south Asia and middle South Asia. (See Table 3 in the World Summary volume of the ILO source cited in the note to Table 1.) There are also differences among Moslem and non-Moslem subregions in the reporting of female labor in agriculture.

3 On this topic, see Irving B. Kravis, Zoltan Kenessey, Alan Heston, and Robert Summers, *A System of International Comparisons of Gross Product and Purchasing Power* (Baltimore, Md.: Johns Hopkins University Press, 1975); and by three of the four authors (excluding Zoltan Kenessey), *International Comparisons of Real Product and Purchasing Power* (Baltimore, Md.: Johns Hopkins University Press, 1978), and ''Real GDP *per Capita* for More than One Hundred Countries,'' *Economic Journal,* 88 (June 1978), 215–41.

The exchange rate deviation index (i.e., relative disparity between dollar exchange and purchasing power rates) ranges from somewhat over 3 for the low-income LDCs, such as India, to over 2 for the upper ranges of the LDCs (such as Brazil) to somewhat over 1.3 for the DCs in Europe. With these ratios for 1970, their application to per capita GDP in line 8 would reduce the range between columns 1 and 6, from almost 40 : 1 to 13 : 1; and that between columns 4 and 6 from somewhat over 8 : 1 to about 4 : 1. The adjustment applies also to the differences in GDP per worker in line 16.

# 12 Optimal education, occupation, and income distribution in a simplist model

*Jan Tinbergen*

## 1. Features of model

The model used in the present essay is extremely simple, and hence is called simplist. This will become clear from a list of its features.

1.  It is static and hence at most applicable to a sequence of slowly changing equilibria.[1]
2.  Three levels of education are distinguished: $i = 1, 2, 3$.
3.  Individual welfare $\omega_i$ is assumed to be dependent only on disposable income $x$, education $i$, and occupation $j$.
4.  The labor market is in equilibrium, meaning that everybody has the education level $i$ required by his or her occupation $j$; or $i = j$, with the consequence that $\omega$ needs only the index $i$.
5.  Social welfare $\Omega$ is welfarist[2] (i.e., depends on individual welfare only); moreover, it is assumed to be the unweighted sum of the $\omega_i$.
6.  The macro production function is a Cobb–Douglas function $F(\phi_1, \phi_2, \phi_3) = C_0\phi_1^{\lambda_1}\phi_2^{\lambda_2}\phi_3^{\lambda_3}$, where the impact of physical capital is, together with the size of total active population and units used, hidden in $C_0$, $\phi_i$ is the proportion of active population with education and occupation $i$, and $\Sigma \lambda_i = 0.8$, reflecting the fact that 20 percent of the national product constituted income from assets.

## 2. Aim and scope of exercise

In two previous publications on income distribution (Tinbergen, 1975; Pen and Tinbergen, 1977), a distinction between an equitable and an optimal income distribution was discussed. As an illustration, optimum distribu-

305

tions were calculated under two alternative restrictions. The first restriction was that the number of active population with education levels 1, 2, and 3 was assumed given for each level. The second restriction was that only the total of the three groups was given and shifts in education levels admitted. Education costs were not considered, however, and this omission was rightly criticized by R. H. Haveman (1977). The present essay constitutes a correction of the omission. It is offered as a modest tribute to Abram Bergson, whose pioneering work in the field of social welfare functions is one among many facets of his contributions to economic science.

To maintain comparability with previous approaches of mine, this essay concentrates on the case of the Netherlands in 1962. An application to other countries or years might not be too cumbersome but will be postponed until later.

## 3. Mathematical formulation of the optimum problem

The symbols used in the formulation developed below include:

| | |
|---|---|
| $i$ | level of education, $i = 1, 2, 3$ |
| $\phi_i$ | proportion of active population with eduction level $i$ |
| $x_i$ | disposable income per capita of active population with education level $i$ |
| $f_i$ | income correction reflecting (dis)utility of education and occupation $i$ |
| $\omega(x_i - f_i)$ | welfare of person with disposable income $x_i$ and education and occupation $i$ |
| $F(\phi_1, \phi_2, \phi_3) \equiv C_0 \phi_1^{\lambda_1} \phi_2^{\lambda_2} \phi_3^{\lambda_3}$ | production per capita function |
| $y$ | product per capita of active population |
| $T'$ | total tax revenue minus public and private expenditure for education |
| $\kappa_i$ | total annual cost of education per capita of stock of active population with education $i$ expressed as part of product per capita; for a more detailed description, see Section 4, where estimation is described |
| $\lambda, \pi, \rho$ | Lagrange multipliers |

Formulation of the optimum problem: Maximize the social welfare $\sum_i \phi_i \omega(x_i - f_i)$ with restrictions:

$$\Sigma \, \phi_i = 1 \quad \text{(balance equation)} \tag{A}$$
$$y = F(\phi_1, \phi_2, \phi_3) \quad \text{(production function)} \tag{B}$$
$$y = \Sigma \, \phi_i x_i + T' + y \, \Sigma \, \kappa_i \phi_i \quad \text{(destination of product)} \tag{C}$$

Using Lagrangian multipliers, we have to maximize

$$\Sigma\ \phi_i\omega(x_i - f_i) + \lambda(1 - \Sigma\ \phi_i) + \pi\{y - F(\phi_i)\}$$
$$+ \rho\{y - \Sigma\ \phi_i x_i - T' - y\ \Sigma\ \kappa_i\phi_i\} \quad (0)$$

In this expression the $f_i$, $T'$, and $\kappa_i$ are figures to be estimated, as are the $\lambda_i$ and $C$ of the production function. Differentiation of (0) with regard to the variables appearing in (0) yields

$$\omega(x_1 - f_1) - \lambda - \pi\ \partial F/\partial\phi_1 - \rho x_1 - \rho y \kappa_1 = 0 \quad (1)$$
$$\omega(x_2 - f_2) - \lambda - \pi\ \partial F/\partial\phi_2 - \rho x_2 - \rho y \kappa_2 = 0 \quad (2)$$
$$\omega(x_3 - f_3) - \lambda - \pi\ \partial F/\partial\phi_3 - \rho x_3 - \rho y \kappa_3 = 0 \quad (3)$$
$$\phi_1\omega'(x_1 - f_1) - \rho\phi_1 = 0 \quad (4)$$
$$\phi_2\omega'(x_2 - f_2) - \rho\phi_2 = 0 \quad (5)$$
$$\phi_3\omega'(x_3 - f_3) - \rho\phi_3 = 0 \quad (6)$$
$$\pi + \rho - \rho\ \Sigma\ \kappa_i\phi_i = 0 \quad (7)$$

The solution of our problem may start by reminding ourselves that the $\phi_i \neq 0$ and deriving from (4), (5), and (6):

$$x_1 - f_1 = x_2 - f_2 = x_3 - f_3 = g(\rho) \quad (8)$$

Substitution into (1)–(3) and using $\partial F/\partial\phi_i = (\lambda_i/\phi_i)y$ provides us with

$$h(\rho) - \lambda - \pi y \lambda_1/\phi_1 - \rho x_1 - \rho y \kappa_1 = 0 \quad (1')$$
$$h(\rho) - \lambda - \pi y \lambda_2/\phi_2 - \rho x_2 - \rho y \kappa_2 = 0 \quad (2')$$
$$h(\rho) - \lambda - \pi y \lambda_3/\phi_3 - \rho x_3 - \rho y \kappa_3 = 0 \quad (3')$$

Subtraction of (2') from (1') and of (3') from (2') yields

$$\pi y(\lambda_2/\phi_2 - \lambda_1/\phi_2) = -\rho(x_2 - x_1) - \rho y(\kappa_2 - \kappa_1) \quad (I)$$
$$\pi y(\lambda_3/\phi_3 - \lambda_2/\phi_2) = -\rho(x_3 - x_2) - \rho y(\kappa_3 - \kappa_2) \quad (II)$$

Equation (7) can be used to eliminate $\pi$ from (I) and (II) and rewrite them, using (8):

$$(L_1 =) \lambda_1/\phi_1 - \lambda_2/\phi_2 = \frac{-f_2 + f_1}{y(1 - \Sigma\ \kappa\phi)} - \frac{\kappa_2 - \kappa_1}{1 - \Sigma\ \kappa\phi} \quad (III)$$

$$(L_2 =) \lambda_2/\phi_2 - \lambda_3/\phi_3 = \frac{-f_3 + f_2}{y(1 - \Sigma\ \kappa\phi)} - \frac{\kappa_3 - \kappa_2}{1 - \Sigma\ \kappa\phi} \quad (IV)$$

Equations (A), (B), (III), and (IV) contain four variables – the three $\phi_i$ and $y$ – and can be solved numerically, as discussed in Section 5.

## 4. Data base used

In our model three sets of data (given coefficients) appear:

1  Those characterizing the production function, written $\lambda_i$ and $C$.
2  Those characterizing the welfare function, written $f_i$.
3  Those characterizing the costs of education, indicated by $\kappa_i$.

The coefficients $\lambda_i$ of the production function have been taken from the admittedly crude estimations shown in more detail in Tinbergen (1975); they are $\lambda_1 = 0.648$, $\lambda_2 = 0.088$ and $\lambda_3 = 0.064$. As is well known for a Cobb–Douglas function, these figures constitute the shares (in total income) of labor of levels 1, 2, and 3 of education. As stated in Section 1, they add to 0.8, supposed to have been the share of earnings in total income. With the units chosen for income (thousands of guilders per active person), this amounts to 9.123 for 1962. This implies a value of $C_0 = 15$.

The estimates of the compensations $f_i$ for net labor disutility have been derived from the same source, extremely crude indeed, and amount to $f_1 = 0.45$, $f_2 = 0.90$, and $f_3 = 1.35$.

The cost-of-education figures have been derived from the annual public expenditure per student at each of the three levels of education, since in the Netherlands private expenditures are almost negligible. They amount to hfl. 518, hfl. 1,508, and hfl. 10,167 for levels 1, 2, and 3, respectively (Central Bureau of Statistics, 1966). What we need in the model is not annual cost per student in the year observed, however, but annual cost per member of the labor force in a stationary situation. Assuming the number of schooling years to be six for each level, which is very close to reality in 1962, and further assuming an active life in production of 40 years, the figures have to be multiplied by $6/40 = 0.15$. To express them as a portion of $y$, as chosen in Section 3, we have to divide through 9.123 and accordingly obtain 0.009, 0.025, and 0.167, respectively.

Finally, the question must be answered whether the cost figures per student should not be raised by "income forgone" by students at the second and third levels, amounting to, respectively, the average earnings of the first and second levels, amounting, according to Tinbergen (1975), to 6.75 and 9.70. As in equation (C), indicating the destination of product, on the left-hand side we have actual production value, not including income forgone by students, we must not include income forgone on the right-hand side. The argument may be restated by rewriting the destination of product equation verbally as follows:

$$\begin{aligned}
\text{potential production} &= \text{production foregone} + \text{actual production} \\
&= \text{production available for private spending} \\
&\quad + \text{production available for government} \\
&\quad \text{spending (both for other purposes than} \\
&\quad \text{education)} + \text{total costs of education} \qquad \text{(C')}
\end{aligned}$$

Here, indeed, the last item constitutes the usual definition of costs. Since, however, on the left-hand side, we have production forgone, this term must be deducted if on the left-hand side, as in (C), we want to retain actual production.

Table 1. *Values of the expressions $L_1$ and $L_2$ around the solution values for $\phi_2$ and $\phi_3$, for $\kappa_i = 0$*

| $\phi_3$ | $\phi_2$ 0.10 | | $\phi_2$ 0.105 | | $\phi_2$ 0.11 | |
| --- | --- | --- | --- | --- | --- | --- |
| | $L_1$ | $L_2$ | $L_1$ | $L_2$ | $L_1$ | $L_2$ |
| 0.07 | −0.10 | −0.03 | −0.05 | −0.08 | −0.01 | −0.11 |
| 0.072 | −0.10 | −0.01 | −0.05 | −0.05 | −0.01 | −0.09 |
| 0.075 | −0.09 | +0.03 | −0.05 | −0.02 | −0.00 | −0.05 |
| 0.08 | −0.09 | +0.08 | −0.04 | +0.04 | 0.00 | 0.00 |

Table 2. *Values of the expressions $L_1$ and $L_2$ around the solution values for $\phi_2$ and $\phi_3$, for $\kappa_i = 0.009, 0.025$, and $0.167$, respectively*

| $\phi_3$ | $\phi_2$ 0.10 | | $\phi_2$ 0.105 | | $\phi_2$ 0.11 | |
| --- | --- | --- | --- | --- | --- | --- |
| | $L_1$ | $L_2$ | $L_1$ | $L_2$ | $L_1$ | $L_2$ |
| 0.06 | −0.11 | −0.19 | −0.06 | −0.23 | −0.02 | −0.27 |
| 0.062 | −0.11 | −0.15 | −0.06 | −0.19 | −0.02 | −0.23 |
| 0.065 | −0.10 | −0.10 | −0.06 | −0.15 | −0.01 | −0.18 |

For those who might not agree with our argument, we also mention the numerical estimation of the cost coefficients using the conventional definition; they amount to $\kappa_1' = 0.009$, $\kappa_2' = 0.136$, and $\kappa_3' = 0.327$.

## 5. Numerical solution for $\phi_2$ and $\phi_3$

In this section two sets of figures will be shown. The first set (Table 1) refers to the solution neglecting education costs (i.e., taking $\kappa_i = 0$ for all $i$). Equations (III) and (IV) can now be written in numerical form:

$$L_1 = \lambda_1/\phi_1 - \lambda_2/\phi_2 = -0.05 \qquad \text{(III')}$$
$$L_2 = \lambda_2/\phi_2 - \lambda_3/\phi_3 = -0.05 \qquad \text{(IV')}$$

This is based on the results of two numerical orientations, which show that both $y$ and $\Sigma \kappa_i \phi_i$ are almost insensitive to the relevant variations in $\phi_i$ (i.e., the variations around the solution values).

The second set of figures (Table 2) is based on the values for $\kappa_1$ discussed in Section 4 leading to equations (III') and (IV'):

$$L_1 = \lambda_1/\phi_1 - \lambda_2/\phi_2 = -0.06 \qquad \text{(III'')}$$
$$L_2 = \lambda_2/\phi_2 - \lambda_3/\phi_3 = -0.19 \qquad \text{(IV'')}$$

As indicated by the values in italics, the optimum values for $\phi_2$ and $\phi_3$ are 0.105 and 0.072, or 10.5 and 7.2 percent of the labor force if education costs are neglected. Inclusion of education costs changes these values for $\phi_3$ only, not for $\phi_2$. The optimum level of third-level educated manpower now goes down by 1 percent.

Clearly, the results depend on the coefficients of the production function. As shown elsewhere (Tinbergen, 1975, chap. 6), technological development can be represented by changes in these coefficients and during the twentieth century $\lambda_3$, if a Cobb–Douglas production function is assumed to be valid, must have risen considerably. This will also change the results for the $\phi_i$ as calculated herein.

### Notes

1 In thermodynamics, such processes are called adiabatic.
2 The phrase is A. K. Sen's.

### References

Haveman, Robert H. "Tinbergen's Income Distribution: Analysis and Policies – A Review Article," *Journal of Human Resources* 12 (1977), 103–14. Also published in the Dutch journal *De Economist* 125 (1977), 161–73, and as Reprint 232 in the *Reprint Series of the Institute for Research on Poverty,* University of Wisconsin, Madison, Wis.

Pen, J., and J. Tinbergen. *Naar een rechtvaardiger inkomensverdeling.* Elsevier, Amsterdam, 1977.

Tinbergen, J. *Income Distribution: Analysis and Policies.* Elsevier, Amsterdam, 1975.

# 13 The welfare economics of product quality under socialism

*Martin Spechler*

Abram Bergson has devoted much of his life as a scholar to probing the efficiency of socialism. As he has taught us, such a complex matter must be analyzed at several levels – growth performance, "working arrangements" for allocating resources, and the theoretic consistency of idealized systems for operating an economy with social ownership of the means of production. Conclusions at one of these levels draw support from those on others. Moreover, Bergson has always insisted that systems be compared on like levels. Unlike other nonsocialists, he has never tendentiously held actual Soviet shortages and waste up to scorn against the purity of general equilibrium market models. Rather, the Lange, "computopia," or other models are to be tried by the same procedures as the Walrasian or other parables of how capitalist economies work.

This chapter attempts to follow Bergson's lead by examining the question of product quality under socialism at the theoretic level.[1] What should be the quality of goods under socialism? Can a mechanism be designed to secure those results efficiently?

The most trenchant critics of socialism have long asserted that only a free capitalist market can produce the right goods at the right time and place. Although one may concede Stalin's superiority in mobilizing resources and forcing through major structural changes, nearly all Western economists would agree that the delicate adjustment of product quality to the precise needs of producers and to changing demands of consumers constitutes a critical test of any developed socialist economy. Many would add: a test that cannot be passed.

In the famous "socialist debate" among Ludwig von Mises, Friedrich A. Hayek, Oskar Lange, and others over the theoretical and practical possibility of socialism, one of the major points at issue was whether one could frame an appropriate system of incentives and directives for the socialist enterprise.[2] As will be recalled, Lange's fundamental proposal

311

was that each commodity's price would be set centrally by trial and error in light of excess supply or demand. Although Lange gave no explicit attention to how new quality goods would be decided upon, a fair gloss would be this: Since managers set outputs so that prices cover marginal cost, any and every quality will be produced whenever demand is sufficient to cover incremental (social) costs. Given a world without economies of scale, either Lange's mechanism or perfect competition, once at equilibrium, will maximize consumer surplus in this respect. However, it is precisely the allowance for quality variation which virtually assures that economies of scale will still be in effect at socially efficient output levels.

In a searching critique, Hayek found that Lange had overlooked how goods produced to order might be priced.

Much machinery, most buildings and ships, and many parts of other products are hardly ever produced for a market but only on special contract. This does not mean that there may not be intense competition in the market for the products of these industries, although it may not be "perfect competition" in the sense of pure theory; the fact is simply that in those industries identical products are rarely produced twice in short intervals; and the circle of producers who will compete as alternative suppliers in each instance will be different in almost every identical case, just as the circle of potential customers who will compete for the services of a particular plant will differ from week to week. What basis is there in all these cases for fixing prices of the product so as to equalize "demand and supply"?[3]

For custom orders, Hayek continued, negotiated prices and specifications would be unavoidable. That might not be serious if negotiations could be guided by prices of analogous standard goods. But negotiations among only a few parties might fail to reach an equilibrium at all, let alone an optimal one.

What of situations in which elements of bilateral monopoly and nonconvexity do not intrude? After all, such environments bedevil all known competitive models, too. For instance, where different qualities produced by a Chamberlinian group enter the marketplace, neither the number of types nor the output of any one of them will be optimal in general.[4] Let a central planning board (CPB) set clearing prices, Hayek warned, and "there will be less differentiation between prices of commodities according to the differences of quality and circumstances of time and place" than if prices were set by buyers and sellers in the market. "Without some simplification, the number of different commodities for which separate prices would have to be fixed would be practically infinite."[5]

Like any organization, the CPB could hardly cope with its work load without delegation of authority, general policy directives, and a sense of priorities. Thus, the CPB could set a price for a certain minimum quality level and premia/discounts for variants agreed on by supplier and customer.[6] But an analytic way to prescribe *which* key prices and qualities must be set by central authorities and the rate of premium/discount for close substitutes still escapes our understanding. Lange allowed for a small-scale business sector but without elaborating its relationship to the dominant socialist sector.[7] Conceivably, the independent, private sector could produce adaptations of the main lines of products, as well as the endless variety of clothing and food items required by individual tastes.

Speaking theoretically, though, neither the Lange CPB nor the beneficent regulator nor the Walrasian auctioneer will guide us to fully efficient outcomes without "recontracting" for the full range of goods and factors before execution and production. There seems to be no analytically perfect solution to the decomposition problem in economic planning with an indefinitely large number of goods produced under conditions of decreasing average cost. The methods available for planning an economy with a *finite* number of *independent* goods with decreasing costs require considerable information transfer. At least one message must be exchanged at each iteration for each separate producer and consumer of every identifiable good.[8] But then in a free-market competitive process, the informational flows can hardly be less, although the exchange of data may be carried on informally entirely within multiproduct enterprises.

### Optimal quality

Let us imagine, together with Lange, a socialist planning board empowered to weigh the various political and ethical considerations for amending consumers' market choices. These choices, of course, will already reflect rectifications in the distribution of income. But under welfare socialism, the board may see fit to provide free health care and education, to limit conspicuous consumption in the interests of solidarity, or to raise saving and lower interest rates as a benefit to future generations.[9] The board will surely act to offset external costs, valued according to principles of equality.[10] These matters settled, the central or industry authority must calculate the quality of goods that should be afforded and at which prices.

Leaving aside for the moment the possibility of producing a range of quality types, each a close substitute in use by the typical consumer, we may speak of each quality level as a separate good or of the *average* quality level to be offered. What economic principles will guide the choice of that level? Certainly, the optimum quality level for any economy characterized by scarcity will not be the highest technical level feasible, just as the ideal output of any single good is definite and limited. Like any economic activity, raising quality has an opportunity cost and can be underdone or overdone. In many actual cases, undeniably, poor quality is a kind of absolute waste; but poor quality *can* be an efficient choice. A socialist utilitarian would define *optimal* quality as the standard to which no further improvements or deterioration could be made that would benefit some consumers without hurting others as much, social effects considered. Are the changes worthwhile in terms of the resources used up (or recovered) and after any changes in distribution have been taken into account?[11]

A first implication of basic economic logic is that it probably would not be optimal for one country to imitate, or try to match and surpass, the quality of goods *consumed* in another, unless resources are quite similar.[12] Unless national cultures and income structures are quite different, one would expect that a richer country will demand both more and better goods than would a poorer one.[13] Our expectation would be even firmer for a single country seen before and after major economic growth. Contrariwise, the less the country can devote to consumption, the sparer its quality level of consumption ought to be.[14] A postrevolutionary society that is seeking to increase its investment and communal sector should therefore lower the planned quality of private consumption. By this rule, some – but surely not all – of the decline in quality of Russian consumer goods during the First Five Year Plans may have been proper in view of the goal of industrializing even at the sacrifice of current civilian consumption.[15]

Second, modernization usually means some equalization of incomes eventually – and under socialist auspices sooner than under capitalist. The size of the salaried classes in cities usually rises. The effect of these phenomena upon the absolute quality of any particular good depends on whether it is a necessity or a luxury. With growth, the poorer classes will demand more luxuries, but probably of a relatively low quality. On the other hand, the better-off will demand better quality. With the size of the urban working classes sharply increased, optimal quality may fall. Even when more extensive variety is practical, the average quality purchased may decline because of increased popular consumption.

Western experience offers examples of this "mass-consumption" effect – the rise of the model T Ford, lower standards of service on airlines and in resorts, and the arguable deterioration of broadcasting programming and public universities. In each case, the producers correctly lowered the quality offered in response to the means and tastes of the clientele.[16] Insofar as a socialist board concerns itself with equality of consumption, it might go even further in this direction.

### Optimal variety

Generally speaking, because of certain fixed costs, an economy should offer only a discrete number of quality grades. The number may be quite small for four reasons. First, there might be only a small number of consumer groups, each with a distinct quality demanded. Second, certain characteristics may be indivisible. Either an article has a certain feature, or it does not. A power shaver, for example, may work on DC current or not; it may have a mustache trimmer or not. If a good could be available with $n$ such accessories or features, at most $2^n$ types exist potentially. Third, fixed costs of production or distribution can be so substantial that only a few varieties can be produced in amounts such that the total benefit to purchasers exceeds full costs. This will be all the more likely when high fixed costs and falling average costs are encountered together with high substitutability among quality types. In a situation where most consumers are nearly indifferent whether a proposed new type (of equal cost) comes onto the market, the additional contribution to welfare will be negligible, and even a small fixed cost incurred will be unjustified. That quality grades are substitutes in use is the natural thing to expect. As a probable offset to these four conditions, complementarity in production within a single establishment or branch could favor enlarging the variety offered.

Optimal variety can be seen as comprising the optimal *number* of quality types, with each one optimal in quality given the availability of the others. This implies that the available types must be neither too alike nor too different, considering costs, the density of the consumer map for product attributes demanded, and mutual substitutability.

Recent theoretical work has produced examples in which standard types of competition will produce the wrong variety.[17] Unless a seller can discriminate fully, he cannot collect the full benefits yielded by a new quality type. Quite possibly, given startup and overhead costs for a desirable new entry, no single price will produce any profit at all. This recalls a familiar problem in the public finance of social infrastructure. Moreover, even in the case where a potential supplier *could* recover average total costs of the new quality type, he may be deterred from offering it by the consideration that some further entrant, producing the correct model for the market then, would wipe out the former's profits, owing to the close substitutability between the two models. Since both cannot exist in the market together, neither has the incentive to enter. Either of these cases would yield too few qualities. As Edward Chamberlin always insisted, the market can also exhibit too *many* qualities. Chamberlin was thinking of the effects of restricted output on the number of symmetrical firms (and types) in the market. Pricing above marginal cost is not necessary for this result. Excessive variety can also come about when a new entrant can cover his costs but only by reducing greatly the consumer surplus provided by his existing (imperfect) competitors. Their supernormal profits also decline.

What is the significance of these findings for market socialism? In the first place, they show a kind of market failure under any imaginable capitalist market mechanism. As Spence has explained it, when quality is improved, the nondiscriminating seller collects only the increment in price offered by the *marginal* customer.[18] Inframarginal customers may rate the improvement higher than the marginal ones would; if so, the inframarginals become free riders. Any market structure without discrimination will offer too little quality at optimum output. *Per contra,* if inframarginals care less for the improvement, the quality sold in response to market signals may be too good! Curiously, this bias might be offset by the monopolist, because by restricting output, the monopolist's marginal customer turns out to be one of the inframarginal customers served by the zero-profits competitor. In very special cases – such as linear demand or perfect substitutability between greater durability and more units, other attributes held constant – the monopolist may offer the socially optimal quality exactly. But he will do so in suboptimal quantities.

The new work in industrial organization for capitalist environments leads us to understand how the Lange-type manager may not serve the public welfare even when he conforms to Lange's instructions faithfully. Recall that Lange requires the enterprise to minimize costs at every output, avoiding absolute waste at established prices for the current technology, and to set output by marginal cost pricing. Consider the case exhibited in Figure 1. Our first socialist manager can produce one quality type $(Q_1)$ with constant marginal costs $MC_1$. He expands to meet demand $DD_1$ at quantity $q_1$. Since average costs there $(AC_1)$ are still declining, he must obtain a subsidy sufficient to cover his fixed costs. The subsidy is warranted in this case because the average demand price for type $Q_1$ – that is, $p(\frac{1}{2}q_1)$ – exceeds the average cost of $q_1$.[19]

It now appears that another firm can introduce a close substitute for $Q_1$ at equal marginal cost but lower fixed costs, owing to the marketing costs already undertaken. $AC_2$ represents the average cost schedule for type $Q_2$. Let us assume for the sake of simplicity that with proper selection of $Q_2$, a new establishment can attract just half of the customers already purchasing $Q_1$, provided that both charge the same price $(= MC_1)$. No effects from the wider variety are anticipated on total unit sales of the good. Thus the second manager faces $DD_2$, which exactly warrants production with costs $AC_2$, by the previous argument. If the new establishment is a separate socialist enterprise, production of output $\frac{1}{2}q_1$ can be justified on the following reasoning. The lower output $q_2$ exactly covered its average cost, and the extra output up to $\frac{1}{2}q_1$ pays its incremental cost.[20] Alternatively, one might argue that as the first enterprise was justified in commencing production of $Q_1$, the second is even more so, for it serves the market equivalently and has lower fixed costs. If decisions about variety were to be taken on such grounds, both $Q_1$ and $Q_2$ would enter the marketplace.

Such a decentralized process of decision making could lead to excessive

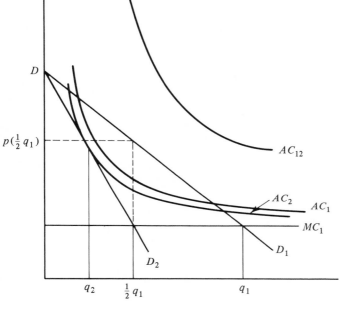

Figure 1. Production of two quality types under market socialism.

variety, as is easy to see in this example. The introduction of $Q_2$ at marginal cost reduces the demand for $Q_1$ to $DD_2$, and the two firms share the market equally. Since fixed costs have risen in the industry (as shown in $AC_{12}$ for both enterprises operating simultaneously), the total surplus of both could easily fall short of covering fixed costs for both types.[21] In retrospect, the decision to allow the first enterprise to produce seems wrong, but that is not necessarily so, because the second's superiority depended on the marketing efforts of the first. Although without experimentation we do not know in general which enterprise would have lower average costs working *alone,* the authorities should certainly have prevented one of them from entering and remaining in the industry, because the second quality type reduces the market and the surplus of customers for the existing type. Thus, sequential trial-and-error decentralized decisions about new qualities can lead to *excess* variety, even where each firm charges its marginal cost only. Furthermore, in the case in which the inferior enterprise is established in the industry first, it is not clear how Lange's CPB would know to replace it. We are therefore led to require that the industry authority make a *simultaneous* decision in light of nonmarket information about substitutability in use and an analysis of joint costs. How that might be done is the subject of the next sections.

### Deciding optimal quality

Let us consider first the simple, but often important case where each consumer buys at most one unit of a certain good per period. Because of high overhead costs, only one type is to be produced at present. What should its quality be?

Figure 2 represents the preferences of two typical households in the economy, here labeled upper class and lower class. In socialist society, class membership derives entirely from labor contribution; nevertheless, because of the need for material incentives and the inability to tax away the intramarginal rents in vital occupations, short-term incomes probably cannot be perfectly equal among all citizens.[22] As price to each purchaser will vary directly with marginal costs for the quality chosen, we can find the point of equality between the marginal rate of substitution of all other goods for greater quality of the given good and the budget line, provided that marginal costs do not rise too steeply. Here we assume they are constant with respect to increased quality, measured by some scalar characteristic index.[23] In the period just ahead only two choices will be open to households – a unit of a certain quality or none at all ($Q = 0$). We will suppose the good is an automobile.

In the upper panel (Figure 2a), society might make available price–quality alternatives no more favorable than those along $Y_1RQ$. As indicated by the tangent of indifference curve $U_2$ with the minimum price line, this lower-class household would prefer quality $Q_c$ over any other standard. Similarly, the upper-class household in Figure 2b prefers quality $Q_a$. Suppose that, as a result of compromise, only $Q_b$-type cars were to be made available, owing to cost considerations. The poorer household would settle at $R$ and attain no better than the utility level $U_1$, on the assumption that it pays $Y_1S$ for its auto and is left with $OS$ income for other goods. Even $Q_a$, had it been available to the poorer household at cost, would have been preferred to no auto at all. On the other hand, any quality and cost in excess of $Q_c$ imposes a welfare burden on the poorer household. If $U_o$ is the level of utility attained without purchasing a car at all, the board's selection of $Q_b$ would reduce this household's consumer surplus (as measured at $Q_b$) from $WV$ to $RV$. Here the consumer surplus measures the maximum payment that could be exacted from the auto buyer without reducing him below the utility level he had with no car.

Let us now define a compensating variation as the payment necessary to restore this household to the situation as it was under its *ideal* quality

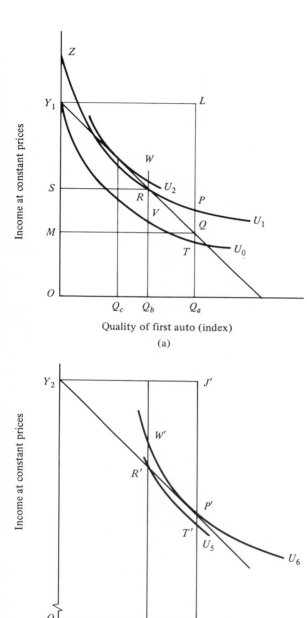

Figure 2. Consumer surplus for quality variation of a single luxury good: (a) lower-class household; (b) upper-class household.

choice. This compensating variation is one measure of its loss when any other arrangement is made.[24] By making $Q_b$ – which is better and more costly than its ideal choice, $Q_c$, in the upper panel – the lower-class household loses $RW$: If its household income were increased by $RW$ and a car purchased at price $Y_1S$, this household would be indifferent as between $Q_b$ and $Q_c$. Were quality to be improved to $Q_a$ and sold again at cost $Y_1'M$, the payment necessary to compensate the lower-class household for accommodating upper-class tastes would be larger by the amount $PQ$, because quality $Q_a$ is worth only slightly more to this household than quality $Q_b$. That is, $T$ is only slightly below $V$.

Now we turn to the upper-class household, which we said would want $Q_a$ best of all. If $Q_b$ is adopted over $Q_a$, the upper-class household's compensating variation is $R'W'$, assuming that it may buy cars at cost. It is as if that household has lost $R'W'$ in income.

Thus, for every improvement of quality above $Q_c$ to a point less than or equal to $Q_a$, there is a conflict of interest. Here, for a potential move from $Q_b$ to $Q_a$, $P'T'$ (weighted by the numbers in this class) must be offset by (minus) $PQ$, similarly weighted if the socialist government is committed to utilitarian equity. An optimal judgment would have to consider all households that would buy an auto of the least quality envisioned during the model year in question. Hence, the optimal quality must lie somewhere between $Q_c$ and $Q_a$, where gainers can just compensate the losers for the improved quality.

If classes were identical in size and tastes, Figure 3 shows how optimal quality might be determined on the basis of the distribution at $Q_c$. $Y_u$ and $Y_1$ are the incomes of the respective classes, and the parallel minimum price lines emanate from those points. At some $Q_b$, given continuous indifference functions, the positive compensating variation $PT$ offsets the negative one for $RQ$ (marked by a double-hatched line in Figure 3). Clearly, this optimum is relative to the base situation. The higher the base, the higher the optimum – which is a compromise.

Soviet conditions offer interesting opportunities for price discrimination because of queueing. This fact can yield us estimates of the needed preferences over qualities. Suppose that $Q_a$ cars were to be offered to the lower class at $LP$ (in Figure 2a), which is below cost $LQ$. This would just compensate them for an unwelcome improvement from $Q_b$ to $Q_a$. By offering the rest of the run at $J'T'$ (Figure 2b), which is above the cost $J'P'$, the government could recoup some or all of the subsidy to customers who have bought through regular channels. Queueing and discriminatory pricing may be a rough way to compensate the poor for consumer goods of excessively high quality. In the extreme case in which the lower class wants no more than a minimal quality, they might be charged the minimum price, with the upper class paying the rest of the bill as a kind of

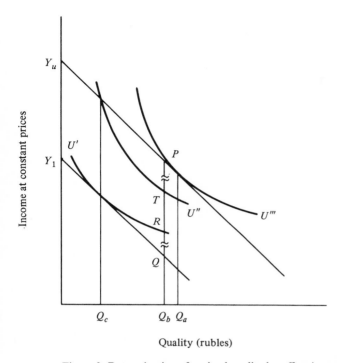

Figure 3. Determination of optimal quality by offsetting compensating variations.

quality tax paid for the privilege of determining the quality of automobiles sold to the public.

To accommodate many different consumers, instead of two identical ones as in Figure 3, consider the following procedure for deciding upon and pricing the new model autos to be made available. As this is a good in substantial excess demand in the Soviet Union and in other socialist countries, we can rightly suppose that the number of potential buyers ready to register before the car is designed will exceed the number of units to be produced. Each potential buyer is to be asked about a range of possible models and instructed to bid how much he would be willing to pay for each, were it to be sold to him during the ensuing model year. Each registrant is told that the available autos will be sold to the highest bidders – but at a price between the marginal cost and his own bid, if higher than cost.[25] Any individual has an interest in bidding high enough to assure himself an auto at a tolerable price, but being one among many, he has negligible strategic interest in hiding his true feelings about alternative qualities. The social choice of quality hardly depends upon him; neither does the marginal cost. Under assumptions of minimum regret, each po-

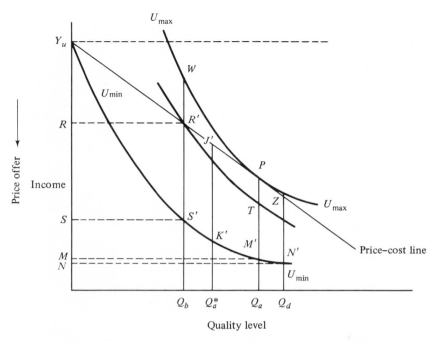

Figure 4. Social surplus for a single household for various quality levels.

tential buyer will be drawn to provide just the *ex ante* information needed by the CPB for its decisions. To see this, examine Figure 4, drawn on familiar principles to represent one kind of consumer, an upper-class one.

Our household responds to proposal $Q_b$ with a price offer $Y_u S$, because they absolutely refuse to miss out on an opportunity to improve their welfare over the carless condition ($U_{min}$). For their choice of quality ($Q_a$), they bid $Y_u M$, and for $Q_d$ a somewhat higher $Y_u N$. Under the stated assumptions, this household is drawn to trace out their indifference curve $U_{min}$. Of course, they have no definite idea of costs yet, nor of the eventual price to them. In order to estimate the best quality choice, unknown to this point to anyone, the board simply maximizes the difference between the true marginal cost of each proposal and the household's bid. By construction, this occurs at $Q_a^*$, near but probably below $Q_a$ because of the income effect on quality demanded for this significant item. The estimated consumer surplus would be $J'K'$. Since the extent of the income effect for changes of welfare in terms of income of magnitude $J'K'$ can be approximated from cross-section data, an upward adjustment of $Q_a^*$ might be made to come closer to $Q_a$. But with *ex ante* information alone and diverse tastes, any one household's ideal cannot be known exactly.

The suggested procedure avoids all but a small incentive to falsification and indicates the best choice for the household without revealing the projected cost to them. Since cost depends also on the quantity to be produced, the procedure will allow one round of information collection to serve several iterations of computation.[26]

Now let the CPB consider each alternative quality level for a range of different households. In Figure 4 we see that $Q_b$ yields a social surplus to the household in question of $R'S'$, positive but still less than $J'K'$. For other households in the registrant sample, of course, $Q_b$ will be more suitable and their social surplus will rise as we move down the quality spectrum from $Q_a$ toward $Q_b$. Recalling that the surplus is defined as the maximum willingness to pay minus marginal estimated cost, it can be interpreted as measuring the welfare one would sacrifice to improve the quality of the auto to be purchased. As the CPB can regard the money measures of welfare for each citizen as commensurate, it must choose the quality variant that maximizes their total.

Which price should be charged? If a single price were considered the fairest procedure, the CPB should choose the highest one that clears the market of the autos planned to be built. Clearly, the household shown can have no complaint if a price less than its bid is settled on, and continuity of the underlying functions assures us that a clearing price can be found.

To sum up, we have a registration procedure that determines the optimal quality to produce (given the amount) of any good subject to decreasing costs. The registrants' bids can be used to determine who gets automobiles during the ensuing model year, for systematic underbidding as a strategy makes no difference once it is decided to produce a new type of auto. The bids for quality served only to judge the correct type to build and possibly who might buy them if there is excess demand at marginal cost. The procedure cannot be used to determine the magnitude of willingness to pay – say, for evaluating a close substitute in light of fixed costs – unless we are prepared to believe that each registrant reveals his *true maximum* bid. Such truth in bidding for actual purchases under easily imaginable price rules, it must be admitted, would run counter to self-interest.[27]

Up to this point, we have held the number of *actual* buyers fixed for the model year ahead. When income expands and more people would buy a car of minimum quality, then quality should usually decline. The larger compensating variation to the upper class – income effect minus a substitution effect for lower purchase price – easily might fall short of the "votes" of those new potential buyers demanding minimum quality. The mass-consumption effect on optimal quality will be stronger the larger the pool of these new customers and the less of its higher income the upper class wishes to spend on the commodity. Furthermore, if a second unit is a near-substitute for upper-class people who have previously purchased, the mass-consumption effect would be strengthened greatly. However, we shall have to leave the consideration of intertemporal substitutability with other model years aside for now.

The mass-consumption effect appears to have obtained for many consumer durable items in recent economic history. David Landes has remarked on the changes in consumption when wealth became more diffused during the first decades of Western industrialization: "Production functions are more capital intensive, while the rich consumer caters less to whim and satisfies himself with a greater abundance of those goods that are available on a smaller scale and in low quality to his poorer fellows."[28] S. M. Lipset believes that in the less wealthy of today's developed countries, consumption patterns of adjacent social classes are more dissimilar than in North America.[29] To the extent that the new socialist man's consumption choices will be similar to those now being made in Western Europe, the range of income classes buying any particular consumer durable might broaden. If Lipset is right, the mass-consumption effect dictates a lower level of quality for those consumer durables now being bought for the first time by the working classes. Interestingly, the Soviet Union has chosen in recent years to emphasize smaller, more affordable passenger cars over the bulky chariots of the past.

### Deciding to introduce a new quality good

We have been discussing how to choose the quality of a good if only a limited number of types can be produced. An allied question is how socialist planners must decide whether to introduce a new type at all. Answers to these two questions will yield the optimal variety, because further widening of the numbers of types would not be worthwhile. Of course, each new type will be introduced at the optimal quantity.

In some circumstances, the index number test may provide guidance on whether introduction of a new type in the correct amount is justified. Where $p_1$ is the price of the new type (called $x$) *after* introduction and $y_0$ and $y_1$ are the levels of income remaining for other goods before and after $x$ is introduced onto the market, respectively, we have the condition that introduction is justified if

$$p_1 x_1 + y_1 > y_0$$

and any distributional changes are not unfavorable.[30] This means that any new type which covers its costs from sales revenue, once possible price reductions for substitute types have been deducted, should be produced, at least as long as equity considerations do not rule it out.

This simple test would be valid for independent goods sold at clearing prices but could give perverse results when prices are generally below market-clearing levels, as in the Soviet Union. More to the point, if $x$ is a closely substitutable quality, its introduction might well reduce the *intramarginal* surplus to customers of existing types more than their prices.

Conversely, the market test can give the wrong result when *ex post* prices do *not* show revenues exceeding costs, even though *ex ante* prices show that

$$p_0 x > \sum_{i=1}^{n} p_0^i (x_0^i - x_1^i)$$

where the right-hand term is the difference in national product evaluated at base-period prices. Such a curious result can happen when tastes or incomes differ before and after the introduction of the new good, or where declining average costs prevail.[31] A case like this demands appraisal of consumers' surplus.[32] Market or profitability tests underestimate this surplus and also neglect possible loss of consumer or producer surplus elsewhere.

Alfred Marshall's analysis in terms of market demand curves is a more incisive one than is the market test, but it involves well-known assumptions. The income effect must be negligibly small; in effect, the new good must be a minor item in consumers' budgets after introduction. Marginal costs in industries from which resources are drawn must be constant. Otherwise, the marginal cost of the new good after introduction will overstate (understate) the social cost to the extent that marginal costs are rising (falling) elsewhere.[33] If costs are rising in the industry producing the new good, a producer's surplus will be generated in that industry. Finally, if price exceeds marginal cost elsewhere, there may be a loss in the removal of resources that is not fully reflected in their price.

When the income effect is not small, the Marshallian concept and measurement become somewhat more tenuous.[34] The maximum amount that could be paid for the new type may be much less than the minimum acceptable to forgo it. In such cases a decisive determination can be made only by evaluating the welfare gains and losses of individual households or groups thereof. As developed to evaluate large changes in quantities, Bergson's suggested method posits known indifference curves of subgroups.[35] For a reasonably accurate result in the case of a new good one requires demand data for several income groups and a considerable range of prices.

Referring now to Figure 5, we find that the typical consumer of a certain income and taste group faced with price $PB/QS$ will buy $QS$ of the new good, now of definite quality. His compensating variation is $OV$. Finding $A$

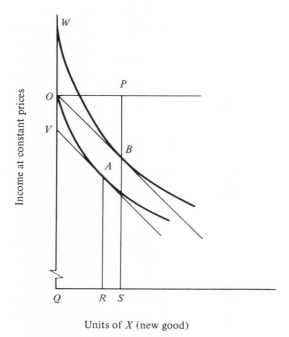

Units of $X$ (new good)

Figure 5. Quantity of a new good.

permits us to calculate $OV$, which is this person's maximum willingness to pay for the good sold at cost. We are to use the formulas[36]

$$\bar{E}_{xp} = E_{xp} + \frac{px}{I} E_{xI} \tag{1}$$

$$\bar{E}_{yp} = - \frac{px}{y} \bar{E}_{xp} \tag{2}$$

Once we are supplied with demand data for some prices up to the point where none of the good will be bought at all, estimation proceeds by iteration. One adds the income effect to the gross substitution effect for successive reductions of $p$ until the given price is reached. A socialist society might use interview data, experiments in different areas, or advance order material to estimate $\bar{E}_{yp}$ by means of equations (1) and (2). $\bar{E}_{yp}$ gives us an idea of the maximum amount households would pay for units for $x$, and from this we obtain the ideal number to offer. The excess of willingness to pay over marginal costs may be compared with any fixed costs in determining whether to produce. If the compensating variation (consumer surplus) does not cover average fixed costs, it is deleted from the selection offered in the market. But suppose that it exceeds average fixed costs? As we have seen, the new type might still be undesirable if consumer's surplus elsewhere is reduced. From our previous discussion, we know that all substitute types must be checked to see if their consumer surpluses still exceed average fixed costs. If not, either $x$ or its substitute must be eliminated. Which one depends on where the surplus is higher relative to average total costs, computed without the substitute in the market.

We have presented the determination of optimal variety as two processes, once socialist amendments to individual choices have been settled by the board. Generally, however, the two processes are interrelated, for the results of the quantity determination – including whether to produce at all – should feed back into the decision about quality for that and substitute types. Quality may be complementary with quantity on occasion, as well as a substitute for it, as Sheshinski has reminded us.[37] Accordingly, were the socialist board to decide on additional types than supposed in the prior determination of quality for a *given* type, then that prior choice would have to be reconsidered for each such existing type. For example, at high enough quantity or quality of the first type, a second type might be justified for different consumers. Once a second, lower, quality is introduced, adjusting the quality *and* quantity of the first is in order. That would be so even when imports are called on to satisfy particular domestic consumers.

From all this, we would have to admit that a fully general solution to quality policy would be extremely complicated and that a theoretic analysis of all the possibilities is probably beyond our grasp.

### Conclusion

Abram Bergson is fond of citing the adage that socialist economics, meaning Marxism, is the economics of capitalism, whereas "bourgeois" welfare economics is the economics of socialism. This is so when and if welfare socialism can claim to have solved the quality problem to the point where price calculations have welfare meaning. And only a democracy can make the kind of collective decisions needed when externalities occur. Since socialism in the European sense always meant the expression of democracy in the economy and the implementation of fraternity and equality by public agencies, at least the second half of that Bergsonian paradox seems well founded.

The determination and execution of quality policy seems no less crucial for the intellectual appeal of socialism today than its promised remedy for instability and unemployment did to Oskar Lange in the mid-1930s. This is because the quality of contemporary life depends more and more on what kind of goods and services are used. For the case of private goods produced with nondecreasing costs – that is, the classic environment – the Lange procedure is not less plausible than the parables told to support free competition under private ownership. In the harder cases of decreasing costs, potential monopoly distortions, substitutability, and potential market failure in providing the proper quality and variety, the procedures examined seem to offer advantages over private determination. These procedures owe much to the inspiration and writings of Abram Bergson, who has done so much to elucidate the market socialism alternative. Perhaps Lange would agree that Ludwig von Mises should not be the only liberal to be commemorated in a future socialist Hall of Fame.

### Notes

1 On the empirical side, see Abram Bergson, *The Economics of Soviet Planning* (New Haven: Yale University Press, 1964), pp. 289–99, and the present author's "The Pattern of Technological Achievement in the Soviet Enterprise," *The Association for Comparative Economics Studies Bulletin,* 17 (Summer 1975), 63–88.
2 See Oskar Lange and Fred M. Taylor, *On the Economic Theory of Socialism* (New York, 1964; originally, University of Minnesota Press, 1938); and F. A. Hayek, *Collectivist Economic Planning* (London: Routledge and Sons, 1935) and *Individualism and Economic Order* (Chicago: University of Chicago Press, 1948), chaps. 7–9. The debate has been reviewed by Abram Bergson, "Socialist Economics," in *Essays in Normative Economics* (Cambridge, Mass.: Harvard University Press, 1966), pp. 193–236, and originally presented in Howard S. Ellis, ed, *A Survey of Contemporary Economics* (Homewood, Ill.: Richard D. Irwin, 1952).
3 Hayek, *Individualism,* p. 189.
4 Michael Spence, "Product Differentiation and Welfare," *American Economic Review,* 66 (May 1976), 407–14. A Chamberlinian group produces a range of goods or services closely and equally substitutable for each other.
5 Hayek, *Individualism,* pp. 192–3.
6 Such a procedure could lead to a second best in a regulated industry [A. Michael Spence, "Monopoly, Quality, and Regulation," *Bell Journal of Economics,* 6 (August 1975), 417–29].
7 Bergson, "Socialist Economics," p. 223, and his "Market Socialism Revisted," *Journal of Political Economy,* 75 (October 1967), 662; Lange and Taylor, *Economic Theory of Socialism,* p. 107.
8 In the so-called Lange–Arrow–Hurwicz procedure, consumers are replaced by "distributors," whose job it is to report the marginal social utility of each good at every round of the tâtonnement. Just how these welfare guardians are to do their job is left open [G. Heal, *The Theory of Economic Planning* (Amsterdam: North-Holland, 1973), chap. 4]. As surveyed by Heal, most theoretic effort has been devoted to overcoming the deficiency in the Lange mechanism when nonconvexities occur (e.g., short-run economies of scale). In such cases, the Lange procedure will not necessarily converge to an equilibrium; even if achieved, the equilibrium of managers, distributors, and the CPB need not be optimal. The deficiencies identified by Bergson –

assuring proper incentives for managers, nonegalitarian rents to occupations in short supply, and resistance of the private sector – have so far defied analytic treatment at the same level as the problems of informational efficiency and nonconvex technical environments, which have been addressed by Malinvaud, Hurwicz, and Aoki, in ibid., pp. 220ff.

9 "The case for standardization or a smaller range of commodities . . . must rest on an overriding of consumers' choice, on the ground that people are irrational; or the ground must be that consumers never have the choice between the small range of cheaper goods and the large range of more expensive ones . . ." [I. M. D. Little, *A Critique of Welfare Economics*, 2nd ed. (London: Oxford University Press, 1960), p. 269]. Soviet preference for standardized goods is related to their unbounded confidence in serial production methods and specialization [A. C. Pigou, *Economics of Welfare*, 4th ed. (London: Macmillan, 1962), pp. 28–30; S. A. Marglin, "The Social Rate of Discount and the Optimal Rate of Investment," *Quarterly Journal of Economics,* 77 (February 1963), 95–111; Joseph Schumpeter, *Capitalism, Socialism and Democracy,* 3rd ed. (New York: Harper, 1962), chap. 14].

10 Lange conceived of an industry authority to deal with externalities internal to the industrial branch; he did not explicitly consider other external effects.

The valuation of externalities depends on income distribution and upon the income effect of the externality. Mishan points out that one measure of the value of a nuisance is the maximum a person would pay to avoid it. This amount clearly depends on his income. Alternatively, the minimum a person would accept in compensation for the nuisance, even if he is telling the truth, might be quite large because alternatives had become scarce [E. J. Mishan, *The Costs of Economic Growth* (London, 1967), pp. 57ff]. Even where income effects are negligible, there is a further question of whether sensitive people ought to count more than the thick-skinned and thus collect damages for what they consider nuisances. Private and public agencies commonly need not by law take individual sensitivity into account without some limit; there *is* reasonable compensation for most harm or expropriation. Perhaps the reason for this is that to compensate for harm is to encourage sensitivity to it.

When externalities occur, people quite generally have an interest in exaggerating their losses from it (or minimizing their actual benefit). The search for a mechanism to induce true revelations of willingness to pay has so far been large fruitless, because suggested mechanisms work only in highly restricted environments [Jerry Green and Jean-Jacques Laffont, "Characterization of Satisfactory Mechanisms for the Revelation of Preferences for Public Goods," *Econometrica,* 45 (March 1977), 427–38, referring to work by T. Groves and M. Loeb].

11 Theoretically, the size of the benefit would have to be evaluated at prices corresponding to the optimal distribution or at least to the *ex ante* and *ex post* distribution. If redistribution had already occurred, it might be enough to use preexisting prices – which alone are available – if foreseeable losses due to price changes are rectified. Because of expected income effects, this would give a lower estimate of the benefit–cost ratio than using later prices. See J. L. Nicholson, "The Measurement of Quality Change," *Economic Journal,* 77 (September 1967), 512–30.

12 This would not deny that backward countries may find that borrowing technology may save innovational costs, if the end products and factor costs are not too dissimilar. When the final good is for war or export, of course, imitation can make good sense.

13 Unless offset by lowered domestic prices for lower-quality goods. Economies of scale and industrialization may create a greater advantage to large-scale production of homogeneous goods, while destroying the small craftsmen who "maintained standards." In that case consumption could be diverted into some lower-quality goods than formerly. A further possibility is that a poor country will specialize in some hand-made luxuries for *export* while importing capital-intensive necessities and obsolescent investment goods. The quality consumed need not be identical to the quality produced, although there are pressures to make them so in welfare democracies.

14 According to one source, American watches and radios may have declined in quality during the Great Depression. Lower consumer incomes may have prompted such deterioration [Richard E. Low, *Modern Economic Organization* (Homewood, Ill.: Richard D. Irwin, 1970), p. 235].

15 G. Warren Nutter, *Growth of Industrial Production in the Soviet Union* (Princeton, N.J.: National Bureau of Economic Research, 1962).

16 Admittedly, factor costs and competing goods were accompanying features of these deteriorations. Lower prices were often the result, and not the cause, of mass consumption. Among the deteriorations listed by Nicholson ("Quality Change," note 11) which occurred in Great Britain, most seem to have been caused by the entry of large numbers of households into the comfortable range of income, as well as decreases in the numbers of poor. I include here more crowded holiday resorts and less frequent public transport; the difficulty in finding antiques, premium-quality foods, and hand-made goods.

17 J. E. Meade, "The Optimal Balance between Economies of Scale and Variety of Products: An Illustrative Model," *Economica*, 41 (November 1974), 359–67; Spence, "Product Differentiation and Welfare."

18 The identity of the marginal consumer is unambiguous when only one unit is purchased by each buyer.

19 That is, consumer surplus measured as the area under the Marshallian demand curve offsets the fixed costs, even allowing for any income effect. Ignoring the latter effect, it is sufficient here that the demand curve touch or pass above the average cost curve somewhere to the left of $q_1$. Any additional output adds to consumer surplus without increasing fixed costs.

20 As required by Lange, in Lange and Taylor, *Economic Theory of Socialism,* p. 79.

21 Meade has produced a proof for two substitute goods with identical cost structures but different demand conditions ("Optimal Balance," pp. 365–7).

22 Bergson, "Principles of Socialist Wages," in *Normative Economics,* pp. 175–91.

23 Average cost for any quality will exceed marginal cost, but if only the former is falling, the exact price will depend also on the quantity demanded. In the case of fixed costs and given output, average costs exceed marginal costs by a certain amount. If fixed costs and marginal costs rise proportionally with quality and each buyer is to be charged full costs, the budget line could be interpreted as reflecting *average* costs.

24 We might have defined an equivalent variation, based on the new situation, on the reasoning introduced by J. R. Hicks, *A Revision of Demand Theory* (London: Oxford University Press, 1956), chap. 8.

25 A fraction of the difference to be determined, so that all available cars are sold at maximum proceeds to society.

26 For now, we leave aside the matter of convergence to equilibrium. We have also assumed that the government has arbitrarily fixed the number of cars to

be provided, but clearly one could decide this in light of quality chosen and the number of registrants indicating a willingness to pay the cost involved. See below.

27 Discrimination is possible in price charged but tends to encourage underbidding. This consideration also might bar the actual payment of compensation for the fact that most households are provided the "wrong" quality. The "quality tax" described earlier, like any specific tax, tends to distort behavior away from the full optimal allocation.

28 David S. Landes, *The Unbound Prometheus* (Cambridge: Cambridge University Press, 1969), pp. 49–50. Here factor price changes, and demand shifts are operating on what the market demands. For the goods Landes probably had in mind, however, greater variety was possible. Since manufacturing processes allow closer tolerances, finer differentiation of quality became feasible with industrialization.

29 S. M. Lipset, *Political Man* (Garden City, N.Y.: Doubleday, 1963), p. 50. When Lipset wrote, North America was still believed to be the richest part of the developed world.

30 Bergson, "On the Appraisal of Indivisibilities," in *Normative Economics*, pp. 157–71.

31 Hicks, *Revision of Demand Theory*, pp. 54–8.

32 Indeed, to satisfy the market test with passable distribution effects, some investigation of this sort would be necessary to discover those distribution effects.

33 One application of this rule is to a new good introduced at the top of the price category for its class. Assuming a Social Welfare Function that evaluates inequality of real income negatively, the profitable new good is unambiguously good if the marginal cost of substitutes is constant or rising. If they are falling, there will be some loss to presumably lower income consumers.

34 Hicks, *Revision of Demand Theory*, p. 177; but see Robert D. Willig, "Consumer's Surplus without Apology," *American Economic Review*, 66 (September 1976), pp. 589–97.

35 Bergson, "On the Appraisal of Indivisibilities," p. 157.

36 Ibid., pp. 158–60. $X$ is the amount of the new good and $p$ is its price. Household money income is $I$. $E_{xp}$ and $E_{xI}$ are the elasticities with respect to price and income. $\bar{E}_{yp}$ is the elasticity of consumption of all other goods, $y$, with respect to the price of $X$. $\bar{E}_{xp}$ and $\bar{E}_{yp}$ are the elasticities of compensated demand – where income is allowed to vary so that the household remains on the same indifference curve as before.

37 Eytan Sheshinski, "Price, Quality and Quantity Regulation in Monopoly Situations," *Economica*, 43 (May 1976), pp. 127–37.

# Abram Bergson: Biographical sketch and bibliography

Abram Bergson was born April 21, 1914, in Baltimore, Maryland. He attended Johns Hopkins University, where he received an A.B. degree in 1933; and then studied at Harvard, obtaining his A.M. in 1935 and Ph.D. in 1940. From 1940 to 1942 he was an Assistant Professor of Economics at the University of Texas.

During World War II, Bergson worked at the U.S. Office of Strategic Services and became Chief of the Russian Economic Subdivision. This experience gave him a firm base for his subsequent research on Soviet national income. After the war Bergson served briefly as a member of the American Reparations Delegation in Moscow and then was appointed to the economics faculty at Columbia, where he remained until 1956. From 1956 to the present he has held the post of George F. Baker Professor of Economics at Harvard. During this period he also served as the Director of the Harvard Russian Regional Studies Program (1961–4) and the Harvard Russian Research Center (1964–8, 1969–70). Bergson has been a consultant to the Rand Corporation since 1948, a member of the Social Science Advisory Board of the U.S. Arms Control and Disarmament Agency (1966–73), its Chairman (1971–3), a consultant to various federal agencies, and is presently President of the Association for Comparative Economic Systems.

In recognition of his distinguished scholarship, Professor Bergson delivered the Benjamin F. Fairless Memorial Lecture at Carnegie-Mellon University (1967), the John and Dora Haynes Foundation Short Lecture at the University of Santa Barbara (May 1970), the Moskowitz Lecture at New York University (1972) and the Knut Wicksell Lecture, Stockholm (1974). He was accorded the Distinguished Contribution to Soviet Studies award by the American Association for the Advancement of Slavic Studies in 1975, and in 1980 became a fellow at the National Academy of Sciences.

333

## Publications and research papers of Abram Bergson, 1936–80

### Books

*The Structure of Soviet Wages: A Study in Socialist Economics,* Harvard University Press, Cambridge, Mass., 1944; Japanese translation, 1950.

*Soviet National Income and Product in 1937,* Columbia University Press, New York, 1953.

(Editor and contributor) *Soviet Economic Growth: Conditions and Perspectives,* Row, Peterson, Evanston, Ill., 1953. Japanese translation, 1955.

(with Hans Heymann, Jr.) *Soviet National Income and Product, 1940–1948,* Columbia University Press, New York, 1954.

*The Real National Income of Soviet Russia since 1928,* Harvard University Press, Cambridge, Mass., 1961; Japanese translation, 1965.

(Coeditor with Simon Kuznets and contributor), *Economic Trends in the Soviet Union,* Harvard University Press, Cambridge, Mass., 1963.

*The Economics of Soviet Planning,* Yale University Press, New Haven, Conn., 1964.

*Essays in Normative Economics,* Harvard University Press (Belknap Press), Cambridge, Mass., 1966.

*Planning and Productivity under Soviet Socialism,* Columbia University Press New York, 1968.

*Soviet Postwar Economic Development,* Almqvist & Wiksell, Stockholm, 1974.

*Productivity and the Social System – The USSR and the West,* Harvard University Press, Cambridge, Mass., 1978.

### Journal and other articles

"Real Income, Expenditure Proportionality and Frisch's New Methods . . . ," *Review of Economic Studies,* October 1936.

"A Reformation of Certain Aspects of Welfare Economics," *Quarterly Journal of Economics,* vol. 52, no. 1 (February 1938), pp. 310–34.

"Incidence of an Income Tax on Savings," *Quarterly Journal of Economics,* vol. 56, no. 1 (February 1942), pp. 337–41.

"Distribution of the Earnings Bill among Industrial Workers in the Soviet Union," *Journal of Political Economy,* vol. 50, no. 1 (April 1942), pp. 227–49.

"Prices, Wages and Income Theory," *Econometrica,* vol. 10, no. 3 (July–October 1942), pp. 275–89.

"Price Flexibility and the Level of Income," *Review of Economic Statistics,* vol. 25, no. 1 (February 1943), pp. 2–5.

"The Fourth Five Year Plan: Heavy versus Consumers' Goods Industries," *Political Science Quarterly,* vol. 62, no. 2 (June 1947), pp. 195–227.

"A Problem in Soviet Statistics," *Review of Economic Statistics,* vol. 29, no. 4 (November 1947), pp. 234–42.

"Soviet Defense Expenditures," *Foreign Affairs,* vol. 26, no. 2 (January 1948), pp. 373–6.

"Socialist Economics," in H. Ellis (ed.), *A Survey of Contemporary Economics,* Richard D. Irwin, Homewood, Ill., 1948, pp. 412–48.

(with J. Blackman and A. Erlich) "Russian Postwar Reconstruction and Development," *Annals,* May 1949.

"Soviet National Income and Product in 1937," parts I and II, *Quarterly Journal of Economics*, vol. 64, nos. 2, 3 (May/August 1950), pp. 208–41, 408–41.

"On Inequality of Income in the U.S.S.R.," *American Slavic and East European Review*, vol. 10, no. 1 (April 1951), pp. 95–9.

"Reliability and Usability of Soviet Statistics: A Summary Appraisal," *American Statistician*, vol. 7, no. 3 (June–July 1953), pp. 13–16.

"The Concept of Social Welfare," *Quarterly Journal of Economics*, vol. 68, no. 2 (May 1954), pp. 233–52.

"The Russian Economy since Stalin," *Foreign Affairs*, vol. 34, no. 2 (January 1956), pp. 212–26.

(with R. Bernaut and L. Turgeon) "Basic Industrial Prices in the U.S.S.R., 1928–1950," *Journal of Political Economy*, vol. 64, no. 4 (August 1956), pp. 303–28.

"Russia Turns to Economic Competition," *Challenge Magazine*, vol. 6, no. 5 (February 1958), pp. 50–4.

"The Great Economic Race," *Challenge Magazine*, vol. 11, no. 6 (March 1963), pp. 4–6.

"The Current Soviet Planning Reforms," in Alexander Balinky (ed.), *Planning and the Market in the USSR: 1960's*, Rutgers University Press, New Brunswick, N.J., 1967, pp. 43–64.

"Market Socialism Revisited," *Journal of Political Economy*, vol. 75, no. 4 (October 1967), pp. 655–73.

"The Economic Organization of Communism," *International Encyclopedia of the Social Sciences*, vol. 3, Macmillan and the Free Press, New York, 1968, pp. 132–9.

"On Prospects for Communist Foreign Trade," in A. A. Brown and Egon Neuberger (eds.), *International Trade and Central Planning*, University of California Press, Berkeley, Calif., 1968, pp. 384–92.

"Development under Two Systems: Comparative Productivity Growth since 1950," *World Politics*, vol. 23, no. 4 (July 1971), pp. 579–617.

"Soviet Economic Prospects," In Y. Laulon (ed.), *Soviet Economic Growth, 1970–1980*, Brussels, 1971.

"Comparative Productivity and Efficiency in the Soviet Union and the United States," in A. Eckstein (ed.), *Comparison of Economic Systems*, University of California Press, Berkeley, Calif., 1971.

"East–West Comparisons and Comparative Economic Systems: A Reply," *Soviet Studies*, vol. 23, no. 2 (October 1971), pp. 282–95.

"Comparative National Income in the USSR and the United States," in J. D. Daly (ed.), *International Comparisons of Prices and Output, Studies in Income and Wealth*, vol. 37, National Bureau of Economic Research, New York, 1972, pp. 145–85; Reply, pp. 216–24.

"Soviet National Income Statistics," V. Treml and J. Hardt (eds.), *Soviet Economic Statistics*, Duke University Press, Durham, N.C., 1972, pp. 148–52.

"Optimal Pricing for a Public Enterprise," *Quarterly Journal of Economics*, vol. 86, no. 4 (November 1972), pp. 519–44.

"Productivity under Two Systems: USSR versus the West," in Jan Tinbergen, Abram Bergson, Fritz Machlup and Oskar Morgenstern (eds.), *Optimal Social Welfare and Productivity: A Comparative View*, Barnes & Noble, New York, 1972.

"Soviet Economic Perspectives: Toward a New Growth Model," *Problems of Communism*, vol. 32, no. 2 (March–April 1973), pp. 1–10; condensed version in *Challenge Magazine*, vol. 17, no. 2 (May/June 1974), pp. 23–36.

"On Monopoly Welfare Losses," *American Economic Review*, vol. 63, no. 5 (December 1973), pp. 853–70.

"Note on Consumers' Surplus," *Journal of Economic Literature*, vol. 13, no. 1 (March 1975), pp. 38–44.

"Index Numbers and the Computation of Factor Productivity," *Review of Income and Wealth*, vol. 4, no. 3 (September 1975), pp. 259–78.

"On Monopoly Welfare Losses: Reply," *American Economic Review*, vol. 65, no. 5 (December 1975), pp. 1024–31.

"Social Choice and Welfare Economics under Representative Government," *Journal of Public Economics*, vol. 6, no. 3 (October 1976), pp. 171–90.

"The Impact of Education on Income Distribution: Comment," in M. Pfaff (ed.), *Grants and Exchanges*, North-Holland, Amsterdam, 1976.

"Welfare Economics: Comment," *American Economic Review*, vol. 67, no. 1 (February 1977), pp. 240–4.

"The Soviet Economic Slowdown," *Challenge Magazine*, vol. 20, no. 6 (January–February 1978), pp. 22–33.

"Taste Differences and Optimal Income Distribution," in *Pioneering Economics: International Essays in Honour of Giovanni Demaria*, Cedam-Padua.

"Managerial Risks and Rewards in Public Enterprise," *Journal of Comparative Economics*, vol. 2, no. 3 (September 1978), pp. 211–25.

"Conclusions," in NATO, "The USSR in the Eighties," NATO, Brussels, 1978.

"Profits and Capital Formation in Other Economic Systems: Commentary," in B. M. Friedman (ed.), *New Challenges to the Role of Profit*, Lexington Books, Lexington, Mass., 1978, pp. 93–8.

"Consumer's and Producer's Surplus and General Equilibrium," in H. I. Greenfield et al. (eds.), *Theory for Economic Efficiency: Essays in Honor of Abba P. Lerner*, MIT Press, Cambridge, Mass., 1979.

"Notes on the Production Function in Soviet Post-war Industrial Growth," *Journal of Comparative Economics*, vol. 3, no. 2 (June 1979), pp. 116–26.

"Consumer's Surplus and Income Distribution," *Journal of Public Economics*, vol. 14 (1980), pp. 31–47.

"The Geometry of Comecon Trade," *European Economic Review*, vol. 14 (1980), pp. 291–306.

**Discussions and comments on papers contributed to published proceedings of conferences and conventions; congressional testimony**

"The Economy of the USSR," *American Economic Review*, vol. 37, no. 2 (May 1947), pp. 643–6.

"The International Comparison of Real National Income," Conference on Income and Wealth, *Studies in Income and Wealth*, National Bureau of Economic Research, New York, 1949, pp. 252–9.

"Capitalism and Equation of Incomes," *American Economic Review*, vol. 40, no. 2 (May 1950), pp. 369–70.

"Business Cycles in a Planned Economy: Comment," *Conference on Business Cycles*, Special Conference Series, vol. 2, National Bureau of Economic Research, New York, 1951.

"Current Trends in Soviet Capital Formation," Conference of Universities – National Bureau Committee for Economic Research, *Capital Formation and Economic Growth*, Princeton, N.J., 1955.

Testimony, in *Foreign Policy and Mutual Security*, Hearings of Foreign Affairs Committee, U.S. House of Representatives, December 1956.

"The Soviet Debate on the Law of Value," in G. Grossman (eds.), *Value and Plan,* University of California Press, Berkeley, Calif., 1960, pp. 36–46.

"Decision-making in Taxation and Expenditures," Conference of Universities National Bureau Committee for Economic Research, *Public Finance,* Princeton, N.J., 1961.

"Study of the Soviet Economy," in N. Spulber (ed.), *Study of the Soviet Economy,* Indiana University Press, Bloomington, Ind., 1962.

"Consumer's Sovereignty," *American Economic Review,* vol. 52, no. 2 (May 1962), p. 284.

"East–West Trade," in Committee on Foreign Relations, *East–West Trade Views of Businessmen, Bankers and Academic Experts,* November 1964.

"Development Strategy and Planning: The Soviet Experience," Conference of Universities, National Bureau Committee for Economic Research, *National Economic Planning,* New York, 1967.

"Economic Reforms in Eastern Europe and the USSR," *American Economic Review,* vol. 58, no. 2 (May 1968), pp. 580–2.

"Centralization and Decentralization in Economic Systems," *American Economic Review),* vol. 59, no. 2 (May 1969), p. 537.

Testimony, in *The Military Budget and National Economic Priorities,* Hearings, Subcommittee on Economy in Government of the Joint Economic Committee, June, 1969.

"Soviet Defense Expenditures," Testimony before Joint Economic Committee, U.S. Congress, 1971.

"R and D Economic Growth," Testimony before Committee on Science and Astronautics, U.S. House of Representatives, 1972.

"The Soviet Economy in the Seventies," Testimony before Joint Economic Committee, U.S. Congress, 1973.

"U.S.–Soviet Economic Relations," Testimony before Committee on Foreign Relations, U.S. Senate, 1974.

# Index